The Creator's Game

Allan Downey

The Creator's Game

Lacrosse, Identity, and Indigenous Nationhood

UBCPress · Vancouver · Toronto

25 24 23 22 21 20   8 7

Printed in Canada on FSC-certified ancient-forest-free paper
(100% post-consumer recycled) that is processed chlorine- and acid-free.

Library and Archives Canada Cataloguing in Publication

Downey, Allan, author
   The Creator's game : lacrosse, identity, and Indigenous nationhood /
Allan Downey.

Includes bibliographical references and index.
Issued in print and electronic formats.
ISBN 978-0-7748-3602-9 (hardcover). – ISBN 978-0-7748-3603-6 (softcover). –
ISBN 978-0-7748-3604-3 (PDF). – ISBN 978-0-7748-3605-0 (EPUB). –
ISBN 978-0-7748-3606-7 (Kindle)

   1. Lacrosse – Canada – History.   2. Native peoples – Sports – Canada.   3. Lacrosse – Social aspects – Canada.   4. Native peoples – Canada – Ethnic identity.   I. Title.

E98.G2D69 2018   796.36'208997071   C2017-906869-5
                                                   C2017-906870-9

Canadä

UBC Press gratefully acknowledges the financial support for our publishing program of the Government of Canada (through the Canada Book Fund), the Canada Council for the Arts, and the British Columbia Arts Council.

This book has been published with the help of a grant from the Canadian Federation for the Humanities and Social Sciences, through the Awards to Scholarly Publications Program, using funds provided by the Social Sciences and Humanities Research Council of Canada.

Every effort has been made to identify, credit appropriately, and obtain publication rights from copyright holders of the material reproduced in this book. Notice of any errors or omissions in this regard will be gratefully received and correction made in subsequent editions.

The author will donate proceeds of the sale of this book to the Nak'azdli Whut'en Youth Centre.

UBC Press
The University of British Columbia
2029 West Mall
Vancouver, BC V6T 1Z2
www.ubcpress.ca

Dedicated to the youth of Nak'azdli Whut'en
who inspired me to see this book through to the end

Contents

Illustrations

Acknowledgments

NUMEROUS INDIVIDUALS AND organizations have made the completion of this book possible. First and foremost, my loving and supportive family, including my brothers Jon, Sam, Shane, and their families, my parents, David and Darlene, my grandparents John and Marjory, my cousins Melissa Isaac and Gina Isaac and their families, as well as everyone in the Downey, Isaac, and Malyk families. Also, a special acknowledgment must go to the person who has witnessed and experienced both the highs and lows of writing this book and who has supported me throughout, my partner, Aimee Malyk. Thank you for all your love, patience, and encouragement.

This project would not have been possible without my mentors and project partners, to whom I am forever indebted, including Cam Bomberry, Victor Bonspille, Onawario (John Cree), Teiowí:sonte (Thomas Deer), Joe Delaronde, Karen Etienne, Angus Goodleaf, Rick Hill, Greg Horn, Sla'wiya (Andrea Jacobs), Paitsmauk (Dave Jacobs), Dao Jao Dre (Delmor Jacobs), Jonathan Kane and family, Martin Loft, Kaheranoron (Ernie Mitchell), Kerry Mitchell, Gaylene Powless and the entire Powless family, Kevin Sandy, Billy Two Rivers, and David White. Thank you to these individuals and to the communities for investing their time in me to help tell this story.

I am grateful to several people and organizations who provided help while I conducted the research for this book and who invited me to present early drafts of it, including the Ontario Graduate Scholarship program, Ansley Jemison and the Iroquois Nationals, Sue Ellen Herne and the Akwesasne Cultural Center, Reaghan Tarbell and the Kanien'kehá:ka

Onkwawén:na Raotitióhkwa Language and Cultural Center, the Kahnawake Survival School and Haggersville Secondary School, the Iroquois Lacrosse Program, Virve Wiland and the Woodland Cultural Centre, Deyohahá:ge: Indigenous Knowledge Centre at Six Nations Polytechnic, the North Vancouver Museum and Archives, the City of Vancouver Archives, the Waterloo Region Museum, the Tri-University Graduate Program in History, the Department of History at Wilfrid Laurier University, the Department of History and Classical Studies at McGill University, Jean Becker and Wilfrid Laurier University's Office of Indigenous Initiatives, Melissa Ireland and the Indigenous Student Centre at Laurier, Paige Isaac and the staff at the First Peoples' House at McGill University, the Yale Group for the Study of Native America, the Carrier Sekani Tribal Council, Dennis Cumberland, Angel Ransom, Fred Sam, Winnie Sam, the Nak'azdli Education team and especially Mark Prince, Priscilla Sagalon, and Corinna Coutorielle, the Nak'azdli Whut'en Chief and Council, and the entire Nak'azdli Whut'en community.

I cannot express my gratitude enough to my supervisor at Laurier, Susan Neylan. Susan is the embodiment of a role model and a mentor, and if there is anything insightful in the following pages, it is largely due to her intuition, support, and dedication. I am also profoundly grateful to my PhD committee, Ken Coates, Adam Crerar, John Lutz, and Susan Roy, for their time and thoughtful feedback. I would also like to thank Susan Roy for the opportunity to serve as a research fellow at the University of Waterloo, Will Straw, Suzanne Morton, and the McGill Institute for the Study of Canada, where I served as an academic associate, and Keith Carlson and Dana Lepofsky for the opportunity to participate in the Sliammon Ethnohistory Fieldschool.

No acknowledgment would be complete without recognizing the support of my friends as well as my colleagues in the Tri-University Graduate Program in History, including Lorene Bridgen, Jill Campbell-Miller, Amy Clive, Cynthia Comacchio, Jonathan Crossen, Andrea East, Colleen Ginn, Kristin Hall, Matthew Hall, Ryan Kirkby, Jeannie Martin, Tim Merlis, David Miller, Jan Raska, Kathryn Rose, Matt Roth, Mark Sweeney, Jane Thomas, Dana Weiner, Cindi Wieg, and Suzanne Zeller. I am also appreciative of those who offered comments, feedback, and support throughout the various stages of this project, including Kim Anderson, Ned Blackhawk, Shanon Fitzpatrick, Katsi'tsakwas Ellen Gabriel, Susan Hill, George Kennedy, Lianne Leddy, Erica Violet Lee, Louise McDonald, David Meren, Audra

Simpson, Leanne Betasamosake Simpson, the anonymous reviewers, and the editorial team at UBC Press. A special thank you goes to Angela Tozer, who was vital in helping me prepare the manuscript in the final stages. Finally, I owe a significant debt of gratitude to my editor, Darcy Cullen, who guided me through the publishing process, making it enjoyable throughout.

To all those who have helped me during this journey, *snachailya* (I thank you all for the deeds that you have done).

The Creator's Game

Dewa'áọ':gajíhgwa'e'

Prologue:
The Creator's Game

THE FOLLOWING STORY, "The Creator's Game," was told to me in 2011 by
Ga·yo·go·ho:nǫ' (Cayuga) Faithkeeper Dao Jao Dre, Delmor Jacobs, on a
hot and humid summer's day in Six Nations of the Grand River. It forms
the centre of this book's web of stories and weaves itself throughout this history of lacrosse. It is one version of the creation story of lacrosse, told from
a Hodinöhsö:ni' Longhouse perspective, but it does not stand alone. Rather,
it sits within several interconnected histories, some of which are introduced
here – the creation of Turtle Island, Sky Woman, Hadoui, the False Face
Society, and the Seven Thunderbeings – and demonstrates the centrality of
lacrosse in Hodinöhsö:ni' culture and the Longhouse epistemology.[1] It
further helps to indicate the web that oral history weaves, but it is important
to remember that it is not intended to be the definitive account, rather just
one of multiple versions that vary by storyteller, community, and nation.

∼

The Creator's Game
Delmor Jacobs is my English name and I got it through my father's friend,
who was a co-worker of his in Burlington, Ontario. My parents were told

---

Dewa'áọ':gajíhgwa'e' is the Ga·yo·go·go·ho:nǫ' (Cayuga) Nation's word for lacrosse. It has multiple
meanings, including "they play with webbed sticks," "to throw or pass the ball," and "hitting
their hips." Correspondence, Sue Ellen Herne, April 4, 2011, Akwesasne Culture Centre,
Ogdensville, New York.

3

that we as Indigenous people had to have English names to deal with Canada. My father told his work friend, who was of German descent, about this dilemma and he told my father, "You call him Delmor, and he'll be a good man." I hope it's so. Dao Jao Dre is my Qgwehǫweh Hodinöhsö:ni' name, which I received in the customary naming ceremony. The majority of the stories come from my family and nation's leaders, such as fellow Faithkeepers and traditional chiefs. I will begin by saying that, and this is where it began:

It began in a land just above the clouds, we are told. Just above the clouds is where we came from originally. Above the clouds there was a community, a land, a reality that looked very much like the lands here. There are longhouses, fields, plants, trees, etc. In this land, there are beings, among them is a male leader, referred to as the Sky Chief. He is designated to look after this special tree, which grows in the centre of this land. This tree is referred to in two different ways; one way is the Tree of Light or the other is the Tree of Life. I heard it more prominently called the Tree of Light, so even though when I am educating people, I point these things out, but it was a Tree of Light. *The Sky Chief and his wife, the Sky Woman, were expecting a child ...*

Now, being pregnant, like many women, she developed cravings and through a dream, she was told that if she made a tea from the bark of this Tree of Light it would alleviate these strong cravings. So she went to her husband, told him about the dream, and asked him to take her to the tree so she could gather bark to make the tea. Then, as it is now, dreams are a very strong cultural element, which is taken very seriously. The dream world is very much a part of this world. *The Sky Chief's duty was to let no harm come to this special tree. So when the Sky Woman came to him, he was flabbergasted that she even asked him to do that.* I also point out, nobody but the husband and wife knows how they interact together, she was very, very persistent and he was saying, "No, no, no I can't do that," but the wife is saying, "Yes you can, yes you can." I'm talking about disagreement because it has significance within the story. It begins the Good and Bad Mind and how it weaves itself within individuals and lives.

And so he gives in and they get to the tree, and when there, she notices something under the roots of the tree. Through a space by the roots she could see something under the tree. She looked and asked, "What is that under there," and he didn't say anything about it, but she was so curious. She wanted him to lift up the tree this time so she could see, curious, and again that argument, "I can't do that," kept going. And eventually after much argument, he gave in. I am also pointing out love is so much in the story, because between husband and wife if it is not there, they are not going to be together, period. Even giving in, it is because you care – because he loved her, he broke the rules to do this, *he lifted up the tree and thereby making a hole. When she looked into the hole, we are told, it was all dark with the exception of a little blue ball, and again, she was so curious, she looked and she looked, so curious, she got down on her knees getting closer to the edge and looked right into that hole.*

At this point I have two ways of telling this part because this is what came to me. One is that she got so very close and she fell in. And the other one is what I demonstrate, is this, you have the Sky Chief husband, he is standing just behind her kneeling on the edge of the hole, he is kind of like [Delmor bumps his hip], and he pushes her. So, I usually get a laugh at that, but I am saying, again, she fell into the hole, but she is falling. We are told she fell for a while, and we are told that what she heard was the wind, wwwhhhoooossshhhh, this was the sound that she heard. Eventually this blue ball was getting bigger and bigger, and what she noticed was that it was all water. We are told it was the birds, the geese specifically, that saw her and they knew that if she hit the water she would perish. So they flew under her to save her and they carried her for a while, but they knew they couldn't carry her indefinitely.

It was the great sea turtle that rose up and said, "Put her on my back," so they landed her safely on his back, and over time she asked all the creatures if there was any earth, any dirt in this world. If so, she could create a world like she had. They said, "Yes there is, but it was way under the water." We are told three different aquatic animals went after earth beneath the waters. It was the Beaver, the Otter, and the Muskrat. They all tried and they all died, the Muskrat, which was last to try also came up dead, but in his paw Muskrat had some earth. When she got it, she put it on the turtle's back, spread it around [Delmor demonstrates by shuffling his feet in a circular motion], and it's that dance we still have, it is a women's shuffle dance, she spread it around like this, going around and around in a circle moving to her right and each time the earth spread further and further apart. Eventually, she created Turtle Island. That is why we call North America Turtle Island.

Sky Woman had a female child, and when her daughter grew to child-bearing age, she became pregnant! Now, how does that happen when there are no males around? Her mother asked, "How did this happen?" When she told her mother, she said that through a dream, the spirit of the West Wind came to her and placed two arrows crossed like this [Delmor demonstrates], across her belly like an "X." One arrow was sharp and the other was blunt. She was pregnant with twins. We are told that even in her womb the twins fought. When it came time for them to be born, our Creator, the good twin – also referred to as Sapling,

Deliverance of Sky Woman painting by
Arnold Jacobs. | *Courtesy of Arnold Jacobs and
the Two Turtle Art Gallery.*

Holder of the Heavens. Sapling, it is like if you look at a young tree, it's supple, it's young, it's got a lot of promise. He is the "Good Minded Twin."

So Sapling was born the normal way that we are born into this world. Now our uncle, who came second. Now our uncle, who came second, came out of his mother's side, out of her armpit, we are told, and killed his mother, he is evil. He is totally evil, he is born that way, and that is all he knows. We are told he was so grotesque he was even hard to look at. He was referred to as Flint, we are told his skin was like flakes of flint. He is the "Bad Minded Twin." Good and evil were born. Other cultures refer to them as "God and Satan." In our culture they are brothers as the universe is all related.

Now because Flint killed their mother, she was buried into the earth, and from then on this planet is called Mother Earth. Now Sky Woman was left to raise the twins. Remember, she was a young maiden already educated in the workings of the Sky World. She knew that the Creator's game [lacrosse] and the great peach bowl game were played in the Sky World as a method to peacefully resolve disputes. So this she taught her grandchildren, the twins.

We are told our Creator was going to create people here, and his younger brother apparently never had that kind of power, but he wanted it. He wanted the people of this world to follow his evil ways. To argue, hurt, and kill each other. Our Creator wanted the people he was going to create here to be good, love each other, help each other, be kind to each other, etc. <u>This was the dispute!</u> Now our uncle, being evil, all he wanted to do was kill. It was our Creator that reminded him how disputes were settled in the Sky World. "So instead of simply trying to kill, we settle it through games." Whoever won the game would win the dispute and would win the world. This is a very important point because they both agreed. "Ok, let's try it."

So they both agreed, that's what we do even today, so within your agreements no matter what it is, the words are important and how you keep to those words, whether it be written or whatever ... *So even here, they decided the first game was going to be the great peach bowl game ... We are told that at first chickadees' heads were used to be the pits for the game, but today it is peach pits which are used in the great peach bowl game in Longhouse ceremonies.*

Now the twins played this game with the world at stake. We, the Qgwehǫweh Hodinöhsö:ni', play this today and we play clan versus clan. This is a very fun game! Now, because the Hodinöhsö:ni' are matrilineal, I am Wolf Clan, my children are Turtle Clan, they follow their mother's clan. We begin the rivalry at home, saying, "This time you're gonna lose" or "Why even bother showing up, we usually take it anyway!" [laughs] Then it gets even more intense when we go head-to-head at the game. The game is usually played on the last day of our midwinter and midsummer ceremonies. We announce the four male Faithkeepers who are going to gather the bets, be referees, and pick the players. On the day of the game two female Faithkeepers are chosen and announced who keep track of the counters. There are around 250 beans used as counters. We play until one side wins all the counters. These ceremonies are played at the longhouses of each nation. Cayuga Nation has two longhouses on Six Nations; also there are Onondaga, Seneca, and Mohawk longhouses.

So if you've been asked to collect the bets, you collect them from your family, your relatives. In the early morning, you head out but not too early, otherwise you are waking people up who aren't going to wake up [laughs]. So you go to the house, knock on the door, collect their bet, and tell them, "Now get ready, come and play the game now."

Bets are: Wampum, which is the highest item one can bet. Wampum can only be bet with wampum, but the other bets can be lacrosse sticks, all naturally made lacrosse sticks, snapping turtle or horn gourd rattles, your Native clothing, moccasins, your headdress, eagle feathers, a number of different things of that nature. Bets have to be made of all-natural materials. For instance, rattles with cherry pits, stones, or dried seeds. We are told to bet the most precious items we have. With bets collected, the male Faithkeepers match them. For instance, a lacrosse stick is bet by both clan sides, they are bound together, that is a bet. All the bets are placed off to one side but right in the middle of the two clan sides. Fairness is ultimate and no member of either clan shall go to the other clan's side of the longhouse.

Prior to all ceremonies, everything regarding the ceremony is explained. Three whoops begin the game, players are selected to start the game, and the clans surround the game and vigorously cheer for their clan/family. The game goes back and forth, it's amazing, it could come down to one bean on one side ... And they come right back and this goes back and forth, it is amazing how it goes. We are told, it is for the Creator's entertainment too, as is lacrosse, because the entertainment factor is a very high factor of the game. Not only that, but it is also a medicine game too, again as is lacrosse. There are a few games in our society which are viewed as medicine games. The great peach bowl game is an awful lot of fun ... To me it alleviates the tenseness of the week, because [in] the week, you have your ceremonies, you have the dances and number of different things to mentally ensure are performed correctly.

I have seen the game go as much as five days. I have seen it go really quick too, before even lunch it's like, "Oh wow, really." So when the game is decided, three whoops announce the end. Now the winning side collect their bets.

Now I point this out regarding the great peach bowl game, betting players don't really win, nor do they really lose. Now, the lacrosse stick that was bet, here in this world, you would lose that to the other person whom it was tied to, but we are told "our bet is being sent ahead." This means when I get to our Creator's land, the lacrosse stick will be there waiting for me, and we play again with our ancestors. So that is what we strive [for], to go back to our Creator's land. We are going back there. This is an overview of the great peach bowl game, and each nation play it a little differently, and I should point out that the player who finished the game is required to begin the next one. That is to say, if it was midwinter's game, then they have to begin the midsummer one. Therefore, the game is an unbroken continuous game rooted right from the very beginning.

So that is what they played for six days, nobody won, they put that to the side and the next one was the stick-ball game. The ultimate rule, you can't touch the ball with your hand, that is where everything evolved from ... A ball was agreed upon along with something between the ball and your hand, a stick. All other rules were also agreed upon. The goals, playing area, etc. There were rules right from the beginning of the game.

So when I talk about this and I am talking with, especially young people, I remind them that *"you are playing the Creator's game"* [emphasis added by Delmor] – other cultures have God and a Devil and what have you – and saying, *"You are playing the Creator's game"* [emphasis added by Delmor], so when you go out there to play, you are actually being looked upon, how would you talk to your Creator if you were going to see him? How would you act in this situation with our Creator? And we are also told that people took it to the extreme of where they actually passed away and died in this game ... And when they passed away like that, there was no animosity against who did what or whatever, the very respect for the game they knew that our Creator wanted that person to play for him. So he is gone to play in the Creator's land. So even with that, that is just one avenue to get to the Sky World. The other is if you pass away at the time of the ceremonies, in those times, we are told that the pathway is direct and clear from there to our Creator's land, you are on that path, it's clear so there is nothing keeping you here. That is just some of the things on how you are told how to get from this world to the other world.

The twins played for six days, nobody won, a stalemate. Our uncle being our uncle, a real bad dude, it is almost like you've got bad things in your mind, even today when I talk to people about it, those bad things can actually make your mind sick, and then your mind can make your body sick and onto the rest of your holistic being. It starts in your mind. It can bring ailments on you can't source – you don't know where it came from. It can make you do anything out there, your mind. It can also heal if you go in the other direction. *I say this about our uncle, his bad mind kept building up, building up, even in these games, he just wanted to win to get it over with, even that is a bad part – building up and building up, then he says, "We aren't getting anywhere," so he just flew into a rage. He threw his stick away, he would have just gone [Delmor demonstrates throwing a stick away], then when he did that, our Creator wouldn't do that. He would set it down ...*

And then he [our uncle] grabbed the nearest thing – a sharp stick, a spear! He lunged at our Creator, to kill him, because he is the evil bad-minded twin, destruction is foremost in his mind, our Creator eluded him and grabbed a deer's antler and subdued our uncle. This is why the leaders, chiefs, of the Qgwehqweh Hodinöhsö:ni' have deer antlers in their feathered bonnets. They have to have "Good Mind" thinking and actions to their leadership and are recognized as leaders.

And so that is where it began and as I bring things forward, when we look at the stick, the stick-ball game. When you accept and agree to play the Creator's game you begin to place things in your mind. This is to understand the power of your mind in how it controls all else. Then you must get your body ready. Taking medicines to clean and influence your body for the rigours of the game. Next is emotional control. We must control our emotions to ensure we use it for good and not to allow it to become so intense that we forget it is a game after all, the way our Creator designed it to be. Otherwise we would just try to kill each other like our uncle originally wanted to. Next is the spiritual aspects, offering tobacco inspiring the medicinal, spiritual, and ancestral worlds to play in a peaceful way but at the highest level.

So you are all ready to play the game and you go out there and you give it your best, because again you are performing for our Creator, along with playing for your family, your clan, there are a lot of connections. If it so happens that you won the game, that is another aspect, the endorphins that connect and make the experience into a better, healthier, happier event. If you take the game to its ultimate highest achievement, you got a one-one tie, it's the fourth overtime, and somebody so happens to score, even in that environment, I've been there, I say you just feel so good, you just feel so good, whether you won or lost, because you gave it all you got, and it just feels great. It is hard to describe until you do it.

So this is where the Creator's game originated. Sometimes other people and nations have said, "It sounds like you guys invented lacrosse." I say, "No we never invented it, our Creator established it here on Earth, as a way to settle disputes," as he was taught by the Sky Woman. We play it because we honour the medicine and entertainment the game offers all of us.

Now another aspect to the Creator's game. When our Creator was looking over his creation, he ran across Hadoui. Hadoui is a very prominent being then and today. He was described as sitting on a rock. He was described as being older looking with long windblown hair, disheveled. He had with him a hickory tree he used as a cane and a snapping turtle rattle. When our Creator saw him, he didn't know where he came from, so he asked, "Where did you come from and what are you doing here?" He said he was born out of the West Wind and he come to look over this world. If it pleased him, he would stay and rule it. Upon hearing this our Creator said, "No, I created it and it is my world." This became their dispute.

This was a challenge of power. Hadoui said, very arrogantly, that he possessed more power than our Creator and he could prove it! The challenge was which of them could move a mountain that was some distance away, closest to them, would win the contest. Our Creator accepted the challenge. Hadoui began, he started hitting his cane on the earth, hitting his rattle on things and began chanting. He was moving all around and after a time the mountain started to shake and move, it moved about halfway to them and stopped. Right away he was so excited about what he had done, he turned to the Creator and spoke right in our Creator's face and said, "There is my power! I'm more powerful than you! Let me see yours!" So our Creator said gently, "Turn around." So Hadoui was so anxious to see what happened, he turned around, his face led, and the mountain was right there, right behind him. So close that he broke his nose on the mountain ... Dejected Hadoui said, "Yes, you are more powerful than me, I will leave here and never return."

Our Creator said to him, "I recognize that you have power" and he said that he is going to be creating people here and if he accepts the job, would he stay, to use his power to help the people look after disease and weather in this world. Hadoui said, "I'll agree, if the people that ask for help will give me tobacco and feed me." So that is two offerings we give to our Grandfather when we ask for his help. We refer to the Hadoui as our Grandfather, as we are all related. An official sanctioned Hadoui [False Face] will have little white tobacco pouches in its hair. The Seven Thunderbeings are connected to the weather and Hadoui is their leader. The Creator's game is a medicine game and comes under the Seven Thunders as their game also. Now the Cayuga Nation honour them by having a lacrosse game every April for thanking and entertaining these beings and our Creator. When we have this, we bring the wooden sticks out ... Tobacco is burned, we are telling them again we thank them for doing their job. It is usually about the middle of April – that is, when the first thunderstorms come back, even last night there was a pretty good thunderstorm. So we thank them. This game played with no helmets, no gloves, back to the way it was and is. This specific game is to seven, one goal score for each of the Thunders, whenever the seventh goal is scored the game is over.

This is the Qgwehqweh Hodinöhsö:ni' origin of the Creator's game – lacrosse. It is weaved into a lot of areas of our culture. It remains highly ingrained that every family has at least one member who plays or has played. I know that everyone has had a stick in their hands at one time or another.[2]

Baaga'adowewin

Introduction:
A Trickster History of Lacrosse

>>> *Nak'azdli Whut'en, Dakelh Keyoh (central British Columbia), June 2011*
Nak'albun (Stewart Lake) lies still, the tree-covered mountains mirror
off the surface of the lake in tranquility, and the steel blue sky is inter-
rupted by only a few wispy clouds. It's a hot and dry early summer
afternoon, and everything is quiet in town. The tourists at Fort St. James
National Historic Site have come and gone, the band office has closed
for the weekend, and Our Lady of Good Hope Catholic Church stands
empty, peering over the Dakelh Keyoh community as it has done since
1873. In the shadow of the mountains and at the outdoor hockey rink,
only a small group of young people, lacrosse sticks in hand, disturb
the peace. Wrapping up the Nak'azdli Lacrosse Camp, Allan thanks
them for attending: "It's amazing where something as simple as a
lacrosse stick and following your passion can take you. It can lead
you to places you never thought possible. There is power in this game,
there is power in this stick. I've often been taught that it has the power
to heal, whether you want to recognize it or not. If I didn't believe it
before, there is no question, I do now. I really appreciate everyone
coming out this weekend, and it was an honour to meet all of you."

Baaga'adowewin, "the game of lacrosse" or "playing lacrosse," is one of the Anishinaabeg Nation's (specifically Ojibway) words for lacrosse. Alternatively, *baaga'adowe*
means "she or he plays lacrosse." *The Ojibwe People's Dictionary* (Minneapolis: Department of American Indian Studies at the University of Minnesota), http://ojibwe.
lib.umn.edu/main-entry/baaga-adowewin-ni.

Leaving the rink, Allan walks along Highway 27 as it courses through the middle of the reserve, making his way back to the street where his family has lived for generations. Tired from the day but inspired by it, he gazes off in the distance as he turns down the dirt Spruce Road, reflecting on his experience and being back in Nak'azdli. Suddenly, a spiralling wind violently blows in off the lake, causing the trees to sway on either side. The dirt seemingly begins to lift up to mountain-top heights, with the dust swirling all around. *Crack!* A tree limb snaps clean from its body and crashes to the ground, and the usually calm waters of Nak'albun rage with fury and shatter the sky's portrait.

All hell seems to be breaking loose, so Allan's pace quickens, as does his breathing. Leaves and spruce needles rain down like a mid-winter snowstorm, covering the potholes that scar the old dirt road. As quickly as it started – it is over. A few leaves and small branches continue to rattle down as calm is restored. Allan relaxes and stares into the sky, wondering where the blow-up came from and where it all went. Behind him, a small spruce needle floats down from the treetops, un-characteristically weightless, and lands in one of the few puddles left from last night's rain. And suddenly, the peace is shattered by a voice from behind.

"Hey, you!"

Stunned by the voice, Allan stumbles over his stick and turns to see who is behind him.

"'Usdas!" he says.[1] "You scared the hell out of me, what are you doing here? Nothing like making an entrance. I heard you were gone for good, left on the island to never return."[2]

"I heard you needed help, that someone has been trying to replace me with their trickery."

"I knew I'd find the answer back here, 'Usdas, I knew I could find you. Well, the frustration that I'm running into is where to start this story – there are so many layers, twists, and turns?"

"You could start with telling everyone how I met Queen Victoria," 'Usdas chimes in, "how I created all the lakes and rivers in Dakelh Keyoh, or even how I brought the game of lacrosse to the West Coast. What about residential schools? Canadians don't know much about that. Tell them how I invented hockey and used Turtle as a puck at school." 'Usdas laughs at the memory. "Or better yet, you should introduce me! That's a great idea, tell them who I am!"

Laughing at these overzealous suggestions, Allan says, "I don't think they're ready for your tricks – not yet at least."

"Okay, how about you introduce yourself and how you ended up back home. I'm not sure I even know that story."

"Well, you know that I'm Dakelh from Nak'azdli Whut'en and of the Lusilyoo Clan, but in many ways, it was the lacrosse stick that brought me back."[3]

'Usdas turns to Allan with a puzzled look. "You rode your lacrosse stick from Waterloo to Nak'azdli Whut'en?"

Laughing at 'Usdas' confusion, Allan replies, "No, you fool, I took WestJet! But in many ways, it was the lacrosse stick that brought me back here."

"You know I'm the one that plays tricks, right?"

"I'm not playing tricks. I'll explain. I was born and raised in Waterloo, Ontario – about an hour and small change outside of Toronto – and I started playing lacrosse when I was ten. It was a summertime alternative to hockey, and some of my friends had already played a year or two before I started playing for the Kitchener-Waterloo Braves." 'Usdas chuckles at the name. "Yes, I know, yet another racist depiction of Indigenous peoples as static and 'uncivilized.'[4] Mascots and team names are just *one* of the accepted forms of racialization of Indigenous peoples.[5] Don't think so? Name another minority or racialized group that serves as a caricature of a professional sports team in North America. I'm not saying that Indigenous peoples are alone in this – hell, we still see blackface, redface, and other more horrific forms of racialization and racialized violence. Fact is, whether the 'Indian' portrayals are 'positive' or 'negative,' they have adverse psychological consequences for Indigenous youth and for relations between Indigenous and non-Indigenous people.[6] Sports leagues are full of what are often labelled 'honorary names' – especially in lacrosse, where teams are called the Redmen, Mohawks, Tomahawks, Braves, and Chiefs, and hyper-masculine-warrior caricatures and Indian-head mascots remain commonplace.

"But hey! I was an Indigenous youth playing for the Braves and donned feathered logos and hyper-masculine Indian-heads, so it couldn't be that bad, right?" Allan's sarcasm spikes. "I used to think I was reclaiming those images, and it felt empowering to do so. 'I'm taking this back and redefining it for my own purposes,' I would say."

Allan laughs wryly at the tragic thought. "However, as I became aware of the racialization that this was imparting, I began to understand that my individual reclamation didn't negate the larger socital impact that these images had. The intent didn't negate the effects.[7] They were and remain racist.

"Growing up in Waterloo with a mother from the Dakelh Nation and a non-Indigenous father, I also typically failed the authenticity test of my teammates, the one that Thomas King talks about: 'Did you grow up on a reserve, do you powwow dance, do you know your language? How's that free ride on taxes?' 'No,' I would say, 'didn't grow up on a reserve – just visited a lot. My mom was looking for a fresh start before I was born and moved east. I don't dance either, and thanks to my grand-mother's residential school experience I don't know my language.' See, after her horrific years at the Lejac Residential School, she refused to teach her children the language because she didn't want them to go through the same experience. She wanted to protect them. That time in residential school, that horrifically violent state-sanctioned act of attempted extermination, left a devastating legacy in our family, and we'll struggle with it for generations, but my grandmother always made sure her children were proud of who they were, something that was instilled in me from the beginning. So, sorry, no – I'm two generations removed from a fluent speaker, and I don't know my language, but I'm acutely aware of it every day. As for the free ride, I've yet to see any signs of it. I can tell you about the ticket that my family, community, and nation got toward legislative and state-sanctioned genocide, though. Do you want to hear about that?

"Part of my struggle with my identity as a young teenager was that I wasn't from an Indigenous community, I was travelling back to one. I'd been going back on my own annually since I was twelve, but my community was on the other side of the contient, and what I knew of Indigenous culture and ceremonies was mostly fragmented bits that I picked up selling crafts with my mom on the summer powwow circuit in Ontario. A little of Hodinöhsö:ni' here, a little Anishinaabeg there, and the odd Nêhiyawak."

"A real renaissance Indian," 'Usdas jokes.

Laughing at the poke, Allan says, "Yeah, I guess so, but a lot of urban Indigenous peoples have similar experiences. I was always vocally proud to be an Indigenous person, whether it was taking pride in playing an Indigenous sport or in the face of teachers who were convinced that 'Indians' were just a bunch of drunks, ahistorical, or 'uncivilized.' Anyway, as I metioned, I took tremendous pride in the fact that I was playing an Indigenous game. From the day I picked up a stick, it was never lost on me that this was 'our game.' In the lacrosse circle, it's common knowledge that lacrosse originated with Indigenous peoples, and I often heard stories of Indigenous role models and great players like Ross and Gaylord Powless.

"'Usdas, you like tricks – listen to this one. When I was a kid, I was always told that field lacrosse – that is, the outdoor kind – was a 'gentleman's game,' and we as players would be penalized if we swore. Later, I learned that this dated from an 1860s effort to construct lacrosse as a gendered white middle-class sport for Canadians who were naturalized as gentlemen. I also remember the persistent racism. My teammates 'jokingly' called me Chief Little Burnt Face, Chief Running Water, Feather, and so on or would ask me if I felt 'wronged by the Canadian government,' insinuating that I wasn't all that Indigenous, so what could I complain about? As I uncomfortably laughed it off, I too would jokingly call myself names as to not seem too bothered by it.

"At other times, when parents and coaches said they were afraid to go to the reserve because it was a 'savage and lawless place,' I again pretended that it didn't bother me, but I was eternally conscious of it. I can still remember my physical reaction to their comments as if it were yesterday. For this reason, I feared nothing more than going to play in the Hodinöhsö:ni' community of Six Nations, an anxiety still at the forefront of my memory. Anticipating what my teammates and coaches would say made my skin crawl, and they rarely let me down. 'We can beat these fucking Indians,' one coach said during a pre-game speech. 'They're fucking lazy and undisciplined – oh, sorry, Downey.' 'Downey is a good Indian,' one teammate piped up. I didn't know it at the time, but these were all part of stereotypical myths created in the eighteenth and nineteenth centuries about the 'lazy and savage Indian.'[8] For my teammates and coaches, who knew that I was vocally proud to be an Indigenous person, I was 'their Indian.' As Philip Deloria explains it, I was unwittingly participating in a theatrical performance where they cast me in the role of the noble savage, whereas our opponents were given the part of the bloodthirsty savage. Over time, these experiences, spurred by my interest in history and lacrosse, led me to seek out avenues in which I could combine my passions and investigate this entrenched colonialism."

"I love the story, Allan, but it isn't very historian-like of you. What does it have to do with your history of Indigenous lacrosse?"

"Patience, 'Usdas, patience! My point is that I don't pretend to separate myself from the story I'm telling, as I centre myself in it. And in the end, it is a story. Now, don't get me wrong; I had a lot of fun playing lacrosse and made a number of lifelong friends, both Indigenous and non-Indigenous. Today, I also understand that their remarks were as much a reflection of the structure of settler-colonialism as they were offensive personal views. As I continued to play lacrosse in Kitchener-Waterloo, I eventually got the chance to go to the United States on an athletic scholarship. That decision was a turning point in the flourishing of my identity and political consciousness of being Dakelh. Identity" – Allan pauses in thought – "it's what this book is all about, such a simple but laden word. Such a –."

"A damn Trickster," 'Usdas interrupts.

Allan laughs in agreement. "You got that right. I always had to wrestle with the insecurity of being a proud Indigenous person but not necessarily knowing what it meant to be Dakelh. Though I'd been travelling to Nak'azdli Whut'en since I was twelve and relied on my kinship networks to know who I was and where I came from, I never felt that I completely belonged. I saw myself as an outsider – I was from that place but not 'of' that place. My identity as an urban Indigenous person was something I struggled with. After completing my athletic eligibility at school and earning my undergraduate degree, I continued to play lacrosse at the Senior 'A' level. Later, I was drafted professionally, and from that series of events I received an e-mail asking me to swing by the council office during my annual trip to Nak'azdli Whut'en. When I showed up, I was shocked that the entire council, Elders from the community, and my extended family – many of whom I'd never met – welcomed me back home with a luncheon. They had been watching me all along, proud that I was 'one of them.' Though the process of re-empowering my identity had begun earlier, I continued to travel back each year, not as an outsider, in my mind, but as a member of the nation. I attempted to recover my culture, stories, ceremonies, language, and more importantly my identity as Dakelh from Nak'azdli Whut'en and of the Lusilyoo

Clan – a process that is ongoing. This book is certainly part of that process. My identity is everything that I am, a part of everything I do, and everything I produce as a historian."

"So what does this have to do with your historical study of lacrosse?" 'Usdas asks.

"That's easy, 'Usdas; you are me. You and the Trickster-Transformer stories at the beginning of each chapter are me reflecting on my understanding of the questions at hand throughout the history of lacrosse while pointing out the often hysterical" – Allan utters in the most sarcastic of tones – "contradictions within settler-colonialism and Canada's colonial history. And yet, I'm not interested in stopping there; I'm not interested in simply centring Indigenous history on colonialism or claiming that Indigenous history is 'Canadian history.' I want to contribute, in some small way if I can, toward 'resurgent' histories of 'intellectual sovereignty' that can be used in the re-empowerment of Indigenous communities.[9] You remain the Trickster-Transformer that you are, but at times your stories are my Indigenous-self, my non-Indigenous-self, my colonized-self, and my decolonized-self speaking to the audience."

∿

A GIFT FROM THE CREATOR, that's where it all began. In Hodinöhsö:ni' culture, as demonstrated in the Prologue of this book, the game is understood as a gift from the Creator. Although I follow the Hodinöhsö:ni' in describing the stick-and-ball game as "the Creator's Game," my intent is not to insinuate that all Indigenous nations shared the same creation story, epistemological links, and/or qualities of the game. Prior to, and during, European colonization, lacrosse existed from the northeastern shores of the continent in present-day New Brunswick, Nova Scotia, and Maine among the Mi'kmaq, Peskotomuhkati (Passamaquoddy), and Panawahpskek (Penobscot); in the southeast among the Aniyvwiya (Cherokee), Mvskoke (Muscogee/Creek), Choctaw, and Seminole Nations; down into Mexico following the Kiikaapoi (Kickapoo) displacement and subsequent migration in the 1830s; west to California with the Pomo and Yokuts; up to Washington State and British Columbia among the Coast and Interior Salish nations; and throughout the interior of the continent.[10] A French word, "lacrosse" initially appeared in missionary records during the first half of the seventeenth century, which also included non-Indigenous descriptions of the game.[11] Popular folklore erroneously states that the game was named after a bishop's crosier but as Thomas Vennum points out, the name actually stems from the expression "jouer à la cross," which was a common descriptor for games with a curved stick used in France a century before the term "la crosse" appeared in North America.[12]

Throughout the continent, Indigenous nations had their own names for the game. For non-Indigenous enthusiasts, the most common Indigenous names are the Anishinaabemowin (specifically, Omàmiwininìwak or Algonquin) Pàgàdowe, the Ojibway-specific Baaga'adowewin or Baaga'a-dowe (commonly appears as Baggataway), and/or the Kanien'kéha word Tewaá:rathon.[13] Furthermore, there existed various versions, styles of play, and stick types that were grounded in the regional and cultural specificities of Indigenous nations and in relation to their spiritual, medicinal, and social lives. Despite the variations of the stick-and-ball game, there were numerous similarities, including oral traditions that were shared between distant nations. For example, Vennum notes that the oral story "Animals as Star Players" has crossed linguistic and cultural boundaries among Indigenous nations.[14] Although there were numerous forms of the stick-and-ball game and associated epistemologies, the Hodinöhsö:ni' game and stick became the dominant form in Canadian settler communities.[15]

This book is a history of lacrosse in Indigenous communities from about 1860 – the time at which Canada took over "Indian policy" and lacrosse was appropriated by non-Indigenous enthusiasts – to 1990, with the participation of the Iroquois Nationals in official international competition as representatives of a sovereign nation. Using lacrosse as a lens, *The Creator's Game* reveals how the construction, articulation, and activation of nationhood and cultural identities fundamentally informed Indigenous experiences during Canada's Colonial Age. That is, this book examines the process through which identity is created and articulated – the process by which both Indigenous and non-Indigenous people constructed their shared histories and imagined how they belonged within a larger group, whether that be a community, nation, or confederacy. Focusing largely on Indigenous communities within the colonial borders of Canada, it also evaluates the transformation that occurred in them as they continued to play lacrosse and maintain it as an Indigenous game while responding to external forces as well as internal challenges and conflicts (such as intercommunity tensions and differing views on Indigenous identities and gender roles). Extending well beyond simply documenting a specific sport, this history of lacrosse shows that the game mirrors larger issues in Indigenous identity formation during Canada's Colonial Age and in relations between Indigenous and non-Indigenous people. To better reflect the relationship between Canada and Indigenous nations, I use the term "Canada's Colonial Age" to identify the period in which the Dominion of Canada, later Canada, took over control of Indian policy from the British Crown and adopted the role of colonizer of Indigenous nations.[16]

Although this book begins with mention of lacrosse in the 1840s, it focuses mainly on developments during Canada's Colonial Age (1860 to 1990). Of course, the colonial period did not end in 1990, the year with which this book concludes. In many ways, it persists today through shape-shifting forms of colonialism and, as Glen Coulthard reminds us, in the neoliberal politics of "recognition."[17] Canada has yet to reach what academics term a "post-colonial" period. In and of itself, as Linda Tuhiwai Smith argues, "post-colonial" insinuates that imperialism and its agent, colonialism, are things of the past, despite evidence to the contrary such as the continuation of the paternalistic Indian Act.[18] It obscures the reality that colonialism and colonial legacies persist at the expense of Indigenous self-determination. Education scholar Margaret Kovach makes the point: "Within a Canadian Aboriginal context, this is problematic because the non-Indigenous majority are adept at forgetting this country's colonial history, thus maintaining its reproduction. While the colonial visage of our ancestors' time has shifted, the relationship continues."[19] A significant process of decolonization is, first, to acknowledge the reality that Canada had, and still has, a history as an imperial nation that employed settler-colonialism as a structure of dominance and land-dispossession.

The Creator's Game is one of the first full-length studies of any Indigenous sport in Canadian historiography. It contributes to a growing field of Indigenous and Canadian sport studies and is one of the few academic lacrosse studies in North America. Consequently, it is also the first full-length study to examine lacrosse as it relates to Canadian history, relations between Indigenous and non-Indigenous people, and Indigenous identity formation. Building on recent trends in Indigenous and Canadian historiography, *The Creator's Game* also attempts to articulate the history of lacrosse within Indigenous epistemologies by using oral history, interviews, and Indigenous perspectives and epistemologies from Elders, Knowledge Holders, writers, activists, and academics. Although this work is certainly informed by the important field of post-colonial studies, lacrosse from an

Indigenous perspective is theory, and I place that at the forefront. The oral histories and knowledge, with which the game is in reciprocal relation, are theories built, developed, and articulated – in some cases – since time immemorial by generations of theorists, both human and non-human. I turn to these Knowledge Holders, thinkers, and this game as my theoretical approach. Lacrosse embodies, and fits within, a series of layers of sophistication and complexity that predate and extend beyond the comparatively new field of post-colonial studies.

However, it must be made clear that this work deals with competitive lacrosse, not with lacrosse played for Indigenous ceremonies, in the areas in which the game has consistently remained part of the sporting landscape, including Montreal, Toronto, and Vancouver. A major fear of the Indigenous communities that I visited was that I would expose the private and hereditary knowledge of the Longhouse or Potlatch ceremonies and treat it as anthropological data. This was never my intent, and I have tried to follow the oral history and "paper trail" of competitive lacrosse to reveal the intersection of Indigenous identities, the game, and relations between Indigenous and non-Indigenous people. Where I included information about the Longhouse – for instance, to explain how lacrosse fits within Hodinöhsö:ni' identities and epistemologies – I leaned on my project partners and mentors to determine whether the information presented was appropriate. And yet, this book does not limit itself to the history of a sport, because it uses lacrosse to demonstrate how Indigenous peoples formed and reformed their identities. In many ways, it is not a sport history at all.

From the non-Indigenous appropriation of the game during the 1860s, to the barring of Indigenous players from lacrosse in the second half of the nineteenth century, to the use of the game in residential schools, and to the continued institutionalized racism against Indigenous athletes in the 1970s, the history of the game is emblematic of both Canada's relationship with Indigenous peoples and the structure of settler-colonialism. Lacrosse in itself has historically been a prime example of a "contact zone," a term coined by Mary Louise Pratt.[20] That is, it has been a social space "where disparate cultures meet, clash, and grapple with each other."[21] Much like Mary-Ellen Kelm's significant work *A Wilder West,* this book uses sport to present the complexity and multiplicity of relations between Indigenous and non-Indigenous people.[22] And yet, beyond offering a historical investigation, *The Creator's Game* seeks to capture the cultural relativity of lacrosse to Indigenous peoples through a combination of Western academic research,

Indigenous worldviews, and traditional teachings. What makes the game such an intriguing case study is that non-Indigenous people appropriated it as their own and used it to express their national identity even as it remained an integral part of Indigenous societies, cultures, and epistemologies – including their gender relations and spirituality. The story of lacrosse is a potent illustration of how identity is formed and reformed, and of how competing interest groups can claim a source of identity as their own. Furthermore, Indigenous players and communities continued to maintain their historical practices of lacrosse and to assert their self-determination even as they disseminated and embraced the changes that non-Indigenous Canadians introduced into the game. In turn, Indigenous teams played an integral part in the international growth of lacrosse.

The Creator's Game unfolds through five chapters, each one headed with an introductory story featuring the Dakelh cultural hero and Trickster-Transformer 'Usdas. Sometimes, 'Usdas is accompanied by Raven, a prominent figure in Dakelh oral history. The use of the Trickster-Transformer, borrowed from several oral histories based on Indigenous, and specifically Dakelh, epistemologies and recent literary works, is an attempt to better frame Indigenous perspectives and the history of Indigenous athletes' continued participation in the game. As is typically the case in Indigenous oral history, I cannot separate my study of lacrosse from my own experiences as a lacrosse player, as a storyteller, and most importantly as an Indigenous person. I draw on those reflections quite explicitly throughout, introducing every chapter with a short Trickster-Transformer anecdote.[23] In her seminal *Indigenous Storywork*, Stó:lō Nation member Jo-ann Archibald may have defined the Trickster best. The Stó:lō are south of the Dakelh, and one of their Trickster figures is Coyote:

> Among many First Nations, Coyote and her/his/its many manifestations is considered a Trickster character who has lots to learn and teach while travelling the world. The English word "trickster" is a poor one because it cannot portray the diverse range of ideas that First Nations associate with the Trickster, who sometimes is like a magician, an enchanter, an absurd prankster, or a Shaman, who sometimes is a shape shifter, and who often takes on human characteristics. Trickster is a transformer figure, one whose transformations often use humour, satire, self-mocking, and absurdity to carry good lessons. Other well-known Trickster characters include Raven, Wesakejac, Nanabozo, and

Glooscap. Trickster often gets into trouble by ignoring cultural rules and practices or by giving sway to the negative aspects of "humanness," such as vanity, greed, selfishness, and foolishness. Trickster seems to learn lessons the hard way and sometimes not at all. At the same time, Trickster has the ability to do good things for others and is sometimes like a powerful spiritual being and given much respect.[24]

Since the chapters in *The Creator's Game* constantly overlap temporally and thematically, the 'Usdas stories assist in maintaining a fluid narrative and help introduce several issues while navigating the ambiguities, contradictions, and uncertainties in the historical record. They also undermine the colonial history of the game.

This is not the first time that Trickster-Transformers have appeared in relation to lacrosse. In fact, Coyote, Nanabush (Nanaboozho), Hare, and Glooscap, to name a few, play the game.[25] Although 'Usdas was not historically known to be a fan or a participant in Dakelh territory, as I worked my way through this project, there was absolutely no question in my mind that the Trickster-Transformer was ever-present and at play in this history. 'Usdas, like other Trickster-Transformers, is known for their travels, curiosity, and for frequently operating in mischievous ways while serving as a cultural hero, cautionary tale, and teacher. If I could travel to play lacrosse and write a history of the game, why couldn't 'Usdas? 'Usdas has allowed me to understand and make sense of the colonial history of lacrosse and of the nation-state's history. Lacrosse has also allowed me to further empower my identity as Dakelh by reconnecting me with our nation's knowledge systems, stories, and ultimately 'Usdas while I learned from the epistemologies of other Indigenous nations.

Finally, using the Trickster-Transformer figure also enables me to draw on humour and humility to discuss otherwise difficult topics and issues, such as sports in residential schools. In an attempt to move toward an Indigenous-centred approach, *The Creator's Game* is not limited to strictly defined academic sources. Without question, the greatest influences on its methodology and storytelling, beyond the oral histories, are Thomas King's *The Truth about Stories* and *Green Grass, Running Water,* as well as his children's book *A Coyote Columbus Story;* Leanne Simpson's *Islands of Decolonial Love* and *Dancing on Our Turtle's Back;* Richard Wagamese's *Indian Horse;* and Lee Maracle's *Celia's Song.*[26] These authors are particularly good at merging the practices of oral storytelling and Indigenous epistemologies in their literary works. In this book, I have tried to emulate their example to create a more Indigenous-centred historical methodology.

I have also attempted to put into practice Dale Turner's concept of "word warriors" – that is, the notion of Indigenous scholars listening "to their 'indigenous philosophers' while engaging the intellectual and political practices of the dominant culture."[27] Again, as I told 'Usdas in the beginning, I don't pretend to separate myself or my identity from the history that I am writing, but I must emphasize that I speak for myself and not my community, nation, or those with whom I worked, and that any mistakes are my own. This is my take on the story. But as Chris Andersen reminds us, history is "a crucial resource in Indigenous claims to peoplehood, as it is for all Indigenous claims, because it challenges dominant colonial national/historical narratives that marginalize or attempt to altogether erase our prior presence."[28] By making use of Indigenous methodologies, philosophies, and worldviews in a Western academic pursuit, I offer blunt sarcastic quips and critiques in demonstrating Canada's relationship with Indigenous peoples during its Colonial Age, while also attempting to move this history toward a more Indigenous-centred approach. In this endeavour, I have used the original self-identifications of the Indigenous nations as well as Indigenous terminology for lacrosse in my chapter titles. Like the writing of Indigenous history, terminology also needs to be reclaimed.[29]

The opening chapter of the book examines the use of lacrosse from about 1844 to 1904 as a form of cultural exhibition in which Indigenous athletes performed for non-Indigenous audiences. After the Kanien'kehá:ka (Mohawk) of Kahnawà:ke and Ahkwesáhsne introduced non-Indigenous Montrealers to the game and began competing aginst them in 1844, non-Indigenous lacrosse enthusiasts quickly appropriated it as their own.[30] They used it as an expression of a gendered Canadian nationalism and banned Indigenous players from championship competitions, following the "logic of elimination" that is foundational to settler-colonialism.[31] In recent years, several authors have published important examinations of lacrosse and early Canadian nationalism, including Gillian Poulter, Michael A. Robidoux, and Nancy Bouchier. Although these works are a valuable contribution and focus on Canadian nation-building studies, the historiography has yet to focus on the response of Indigenous peoples to these nation-building activities.[32] In the very cultural history they helped form, Indigenous peoples and their voices have typically not been heard. The present study will demonstrate the importance of Indigenous peoples, the

"Other," in this period, while at the same time detailing how they maintained and reformed expressions of their nationhood.

Setting the foundation for Chapter 1 are a number of seminal works that examine Indigenous authenticity, including *Authentic Indians* by Paige Raibmon and Thomas King's *The Truth about Stories*. A unique and critical examination, Raibmon's work sets out to define what Indigenous peoples and non-Natives saw as authentic Indigenous culture and identities.[33] Most non-Natives in the late nineteenth and early twentieth centuries associated such authenticity with a static former way of life. Anything otherwise was seen as inauthentic. King adds, "In the end, there is no reason for the Indian to be real. The Indian simply has to exist in our imaginations. For to be seen as 'real,' for people to 'imagine' us as Indians, we must be 'authentic.'"[34] This perception helped fuel the myth of the disappearing Indian, but it also drew thousands of non-Indigenous spectators to lacrosse games in the nineteenth century, and it focused media attention on the matches. As established practices of Indigenous peoples shifted, or were reimagined, to more contemporary ones, as they incorporated newer technologies, expressions, and politics, they themselves became increasingly invisible to settler society. As this chapter demonstrates, such innovations included "playing Indian" while participating in the wage-labour economy and observing the rules introduced by non-Indigenous lacrosse organizations. The notion of what constituted authenticity was not limited to non-Natives; Indigenous communities themselves developed their own ideas of the authentic and selectively played Indian for non-Indigenous audiences.

Philip Deloria's *Playing Indian* and *Indians in Unexpected Places,* which offer critical examinations of both imposed and self-imposed Indigenous identities, lie at the heart of the chapter's analysis.[35] In *Playing Indian,* Deloria documents the connection between the "authentic Indian" and American identity while also examining the reactions of Indigenous peoples to non-Natives who assumed the role of stereotypical Indians. Through these works, *The Creator's Game* examines differing understandings of authenticity in the relations between Indigenous and non-Indigenous people, and documents the "powerful and shifting set of ideas" concerning racialized and cultural identities.[36]

Throughout its history, lacrosse was reflective of the racialized and colonial spaces established in Canadian society. At times, Indigenous athletes were excluded from domestic and international competition because of their "race," and yet they formed all-Indigenous games, leagues, championships, and international – referring to Indigenous nations – competitions. By the late nineteenth century, the game was deemed "civilized enough" and an appropriate performance of whiteness for use in the assimilation programs of residential schools. Elsewhere, Indigenous players and teams competed, representing their clans, communities, nations, with and against non-Indigenous teams while continuing to face discrimination. Chapter 2 explores how lacrosse, and sport more generally, was employed in residential schools between 1880 and 1930, and explains why an Indigenous game was seen as a useful instrument for assimilation. By 1889, lacrosse was so firmly associated with Canadian nationalism that residential schools from Ontario to British Columbia – with the exception of Alberta – used it as part of their efforts to destabilize and eliminate Indigenous cultures and identities. And yet, though Indigenous communities adopted the game after experiencing it at residential schools, its introduction goes well beyond the adaptation and accommodation paradigm that, sport scholar Michael Robidoux points out, so often appears in contemporary Indigenous history.[37]

The story of lacrosse demonstrates that throughout Canadian colonialism not everything Indigenous peoples did existed within the framework of that colonialism. Indigenous peoples continued to exist, act, and reform their identities on their own terms and outside the classifications of adaptation or rejection. For example, as discussed in Chapter 3, members of the Coast Salish Sḵwx̱wú7mesh Nation (Squamish) in present-day North Vancouver, who were introduced to the game in residential schools, re-appropriated it as a Sḵwx̱wú7mesh and Indigenous form, and used it to help restructure their own Indigenous identities.[38] This is a prime example of a Trickster tale: rather than assimilating Indigenous peoples into the dominant society, lacrosse helped Indigenous nations such as the Sḵwx̱wú7mesh to reform their cultural identities.

Throughout, this particular story provides an understanding of Indigenous history within local Indigenous frameworks – using Indigenous epistemologies – and demonstrates how Indigenous understandings of sport do not slot into secularized Western perceptions.[39] In Indigenous worldviews, sport spills over into all spaces and embodies the concept of Indigenous holism. In other words, it is part of the interconnectedness of the spiritual, physical, intellectual, and emotional, informed by the specificities of each nation's language, culture, ceremonies, and socio-political relations. Although this theme recurs throughout the book, its relation to the Hodinöhsö:ni' Confederacy and communities is most evident in

Chapters 4 and 5. These demonstrate how, why, and under what conditions Hodinöhsö:ni' communities and teams re-entered championship lacrosse, asserted their unique identities, and helped competitive lacrosse survive in Canada with the creation of box lacrosse while continuing to face institutional racism.[40]

For example, Chapter 4 shows how lacrosse organizations contributed toward helping dissolve rivalries among Hodinöhsö:ni' nations and served as an additional source of Hodinöhsö:ni' nationhood. It also reveals the complexity and multiplicity of Hodinöhsö:ni' identities, which transcend the perceived Longhouse and Christian divide. Chapter 5 demonstrates how the Hodinöhsö:ni' attempted to reclaim the game as an expression of Hodinöhsö:ni', and more generally Indigenous, nationhood and as an activation of their sovereignty during the 1980s by founding the Iroquois Nationals. The chapter also explores how the Nationals – a team representing the Hodinöhsö:ni' as a soverieng nation in international competition – constituted a resurgence of Hodinöhsö:ni' traditionalism in communities that were attempting to counter the continued onslaught of settler-colonialism and how the team attempted to reinfuse the Longhouse epistemology of lacrosse back into Hodinöhsö:ni' communities and the game itself.

A number of recent works lie at the core of these chapters. For example, this book builds on a definition of nationalism as provided by the Kanien'kehá:ka political scientist Gerald Taiaiake Alfred in *Heeding the Voices of Our Ancestors:* he describes nationalism as having a stable core with more mobile and fluid peripheral elements that can adapt to changing circumstances.[41] This model also led me to incorporate Audra Simpson's *Mohawk Interruptus,* John Borrows's *Recovering Canada,* Lina Sunseri's *Being Again of One Mind,* and the work of John Mohawk, scholarship that comprises just a few of the Indigenous epistemologies, in addition to the partnered Elders and Knowledge Holders, that I have used in my attempt to frame the independence of Indigenous identities and philosophies.[42] By incorporating these works, I hope to understand how specific Indigenous communities see their history in relation to non-Indigenous perspectives and to help demonstrate Indigenous understandings of nationhood.

Through its case study approach, this work is methodologically an ethnohistory – combining documentary and oral records – of lacrosse. However, its dominant source base consists of interviews, Indigenous community-produced texts, archived oral histories, and autobiographies that have been complemented by records in Library and Archives Canada, the Archives of Ontario, the British Columbia Archives, the Canadian Lacrosse Hall of Fame, the Ontario Lacrosse Hall of Fame, local cultural centres, and city archives. I have also referred to the annual reports of the Canadian Department of Indian Affairs. My intent was to triangulate community stories and oral history, personal stories, and the archival documents, not for validation, but rather to understand how the various forms of evidence spoke to each other.

The use of oral history and community-produced works in various forms is critical to avoid what Onyotaʔa·ká· (Oneida) Nation member Lina Sunseri explains as a colonized trap of Western research: "To recognize only these historical texts [written works and archives] as valid sources of knowledge is to adhere to a Eurocentric bias within Western academia. The view that only the written text is a 'good' source subtly shows the sense of superiority the West has felt over those peoples considered to be Others."[43] This book also refers to a number of works and websites from amateur lacrosse historians, autobiographies, Indigenous cultural centres, and major newspapers. Without question, these sources have their limitations. For example, newspaper articles and the annual reports written by non-Natives at the Department of Indian Affairs are fraught with colonial and racist discourse. Nonetheless, they do offer an alternative way of accessing Indigenous voices. And like the amateur lacrosse histories and websites, they aid in tracking teams, players, and promoters, and they provide statistical information regarding league standings and proficient players.

Throughout Canadian history, the popularity of lacrosse has fluctuated dramatically, especially in rural regions. Although the same pattern occurs in Canada's largest urban centres, consistency has been greater there, and thus the historical record is more complete. As historian David Sampson reminds us, organized sport in its institutionalized form initially developed in urban centres.[44] Because Hodinöhsö:ni' communities within the borders of Canada lie relatively close to Toronto and Montreal (the traditional hotbeds of lacrosse, along with Vancouver), this book tends to concentrate on them, though it discusses other Indigenous nations wherever possible. As mentioned above, non-Natives appropriated the Hodinöhsö:ni'-specific stick-and-ball game, and the Hodinöhsö:ni' remained consistent actors in the game's history.

Interviews constitute the main source material for this book. I conducted twenty-one formal interviews with twelve mentors, over several years, all of whom had a particular expertise in lacrosse history and Indigenous culture.

They included Elders, Hodinöhsö:ni' Faithkeepers, members of the Lacrosse Hall of Fame, sports broadcasters, and the families of proficient players and founders. Their input was invaluable. Of course, the formal interviews were greatly amplified by other meetings, correspondence, and informal interviews with community members, which were extremely helpful in tracking down important issues, sources, and themes.[45] My focus has not been on profiling individual athletes, accomplishments, statistics, rules, equipment, or the "evolution" of the game – topics that may be interesting to historians of lacrosse. Rather, I examine particular themes of race, identity formation, and nationalism to demonstrate how the game has a unique history in Indigenous and Canadian societies, and has never been far from the issues and confrontations in Indigenous-non-Indigenous relations.

From my experience, Indigenous oral tradition is best described by the analogy of a web, which Jo-ann Archibald introduces in *Indigenous Storywork*. In oral history, there are numerous points in the web – stories – that seemingly lead in different directions and rarely follow an immediate path to a central teaching; however, they are fundamental to the structure of the web, serving as its strength, and they stem from a central teaching or a subject that needs further consideration.[46] Even beginning to understand the teachings in these powerful oratories requires concentration, patience, and humility. Oral traditions are alive; consisting of a stable core, they are a living, breathing combination of thoughts, experiences, teachings, and traditions that can be personally, regionally, or nationally distinctive and ever changing, being influenced by the elements surrounding them – the storyteller, the listener(s), the environment, current events, history, time, and space.

Within this process, you as a listener, reader, or viewer are an active participant, even if you are not aware of it. This doesn't mean that you have acquired rightful ownership of this knowledge – it too must be acknowledged and "cited," and consent to share this knowledge must be given – but it does mean that you have an influence on the way in which the story is being told.[47] A story that has nothing to do with you or your life experiences often becomes a source of introspection; we internalize oral history, as I hope you will internalize this story of lacrosse and Indigenous relations in Canada. To avoid detaching the oral history from its web and to provide as much context as possible, I have chosen to let it speak for itself, with little interpretative intrusion; I also use the terms "oral history" and "oral tradition" interchangeably.[48] In this book, the oral history and memories of lacrosse often appear in lengthy block quotes to invite readers into my discussions with the experts and mentors. The purpose of this is not to criticize the perspective but to engage readers in our conversations and to step into the participants' viewpoints, memories, or teachings of lacrosse history.

Like oral history, Canadian and American sport histories also inform this book. A key source is Joseph Oxendine's *American Indian Sports Heritage* ([1988] 1995), which contributed the first comprehensive study of Indigenous peoples in sport while providing a rarely seen Indigenous perspective in the field.[49] Not until 2013 did UBC Press publish the first book on Indigenous sport in Canada, a multidisciplinary collection of essays titled *Aboriginal Peoples and Sport in Canada*.[50] The time lapse between the two works demonstrates the gap between American and Canadian Indigenous sport studies. However, a number of proficient Canadian studies have appeared as journal articles. For more than two decades, Victoria Paraschak has been a leader in the field, and her studies have dealt with a number of significant issues that had not been raised in the literature, such as the importance of sport in the lives of Indigenous women, the development of all-Indigenous teams and leagues, and comparisons between female participation in all-Indigenous and non-Native sport systems.[51] Furthermore, Paraschak's work shows that Indigenous peoples have used sport as a form of resistance, as a source of continued tradition, and as a manifestation of identity. Similarly, Christine O'Bonsawin, Michael Heine, Janice Forsyth, and Audrey R. Giles have recently contributed a number of critical studies relating to Indigenous sport and recreation.[52] Like these scholars, *The Creator's Game* demonstrates the complexity of multiple intersecting Indigenous identities and gender constructions, and more importantly, how sport has come into conflict with those identifications and constructions, but it does so through a historical lens rather than a sociological one.

This book would not have been possible without the few full-length studies that deal specifically with lacrosse, including Alexander M. Weyand and Milton R. Roberts's *The Lacrosse Story; Tewaarathon (Lacrosse);* Michael Zogry's *Anetso;* Thomas Vennum's *American Indian Lacrosse;* and Donald M. Fisher's *Lacrosse: A History of the Game;* the latter three focus predominantly on Indigenous peoples within the United States and are academic studies of the topic. Produced by the North American Indian Traveling College in 1978, *Tewaarathon (Lacrosse)* is a popular history from Ahkwesáhsne and one of the few Indigenous lacrosse histories from a Kanien'kehá:ka perspective that makes use of Indigenous oral history. This was followed by an updated version in 2010, retitled *Teiontsikwaeks (day yoon chee gwa ecks): Lacrosse, the Creator's Game*. Using a religious studies lens, Michael Zogry's *Anetso* examines the Aniyvwiya game as the performance of Aniyvwiya identity. Fisher's *Lacrosse* is a nuanced history that examines both Indigenous and non-Indigenous developments of the game, beginning in 1844, and introduces the themes of race, gender, class, and culture through the sport. Dealing solely with Indigenous lacrosse, Thomas Vennum's important work starts with the game before "contact" and ends at the turn of the twentieth century, and would later be complemented by his *Lacrosse Legends of the First Americans*, which explores oral lacrosse traditions.[53] In using these important studies as well as Indigenous oral history and community-produced texts, *The Creator's Game* examines lacrosse in Canadian and Indigenous history to showcase its importance in Indigenous lives, identity formation, and expressions of nationhood.

Tewaá:rathon

1

The Canadian Appropriation of Lacrosse and "Indian" Performances

>>> **Windsor Castle East Terrace, England, June 26, 1876**
A reporter, who had watched from the sidelines, recalled the previous day's exhibition game between the Canadian and Kahnawà:ke lacrosse teams played before Queen Victoria.

> Yesterday was one of the most charming days we have had this
> year; the sun shone brightly; the heat was tempered by the
> refreshing breeze; the recent rains had effectually laid the dust,
> and the great masses of foliage which stretched away in all
> directions ware [sic] resplendent in their summer beauty ...
> The ground prepared for the game was a lovely break of turf
> immediately under the walls of the Italian Garden which lies
> beneath the windows of Her Majesty's private apartments ...
> Each side, animated, no doubt by the presence of Her Majesty
> and the Royal party, played with great *verve* and spirit and dis-
> played an amount of skill and dexterity which called forth the
> admiration of her Majesty ... As the game grew exciting the
> Indiarubber ball was thrown from end to end of the ground with

---

Tewaá:rathon – sometimes written as *tewa'á:rathon* – is the Kanien'kehá:ka Nation's word for lacrosse in Kanien'kéha; it refers to the netting of the stick. Correspondence, Sue Ellen Herne, April 4, 2011, Akwesasne Culture Centre, Ogdensville, New York; Michael Kanentakeron Mitchell, *Teiontsikwaeks (day yoon chee gwa ecks): Lacrosse, the Creator's Game* (Akwesasne: Ronathahon:ni Cultural Centre, 2010), 19.

marvellous rapidity, sometimes bounding under the wheels of the royal carriage ... The game lasted a considerable amount of time, and it was just six o'clock when the Canadians succeeded in forcing the ball through their opponents' goal. Directly after the game was over, it was intimated that the Queen would now leave the ground to take her usual drive in the park [after the troupe of dancers performed]. [Afterward,] the Iroquois Chief advanced to Her Majesty's carriage, carrying in his hands a basket beautifully and deftly constructed of Indian grass, which he begged the Queen to receive as a present. Her Majesty was graciously pleased to take this proof of Indian skill from the hands of Big John, and handed it to the Lord in Waiting, to be conveyed to her drawing room. Big John then made a little speech in English. He said – "Mamselle, Madam, Queen, I thank God we have played before you today." Her Majesty bowed in response to this spontaneous expression of Iroquois loyalty and devotion to her person.[1]

As the royal carriage heads off into the park and the crowd disperses, Dr. W.G. Beers approaches Big John and the Kanien'kehá:ka team, congratulating them on the grand performance. Not far behind, 'Usdas runs to catch up and joins the conversation.

"Well done, Big John," Beers says. "I think the Queen was thoroughly impressed, and this certainly helped to demonstrate the loyalty of her Indians and the progress of young Canada and its culture."

Laughing at Beers' ignorance and the implied Canadian possessiveness, 'Usdas gives an eye-roll and thinks, "They just made it up and played you for a fool – how authentic." "Well," 'Usdas replies, "we 'Indians' get a real kick out of it, and besides, the Kanien'kehá:ka honour the game, Beersie."

"It's played for the enjoyment of the Creator," Big John adds, "so it should be promoted. The money, trip, and fame aren't bad either. The Canadians looked much improved out there today, but that's pretty easy when you keep making all the rules."

"We had to tame the pursuits of the redmen," Beers replies. "The civility of our young dominion couldn't be tainted by the disorder and violence of the old game. It's a much more civilized and scientific venture now."

'Usdas turns in puzzlement. "Scientific? Civilized? Violent? Your ahistorical, 'blood-thirsty savage' take on the history of this game is profoundly ignorant."

"Our modification of the game —"

Beers is cutoff by 'Usdas. "You mean *colonization* of the game ..."

"Our modification of the game," Beers continues, "has made it a civilized pursuit. Gone is the savage violence that only the redmen could deem acceptable."

'Usdas snorts in disbelief. "The colonial lens through which you are interpreting the place you call Canada and this game is beyond comprehension. The medicine game, the original game of peaceful conflict resolution from the Sky World, and land which gave rise to and sustained Indigenous nations, confederacies, and peoples since time immemorial as violent and primitive?"

Big John continues, "You should take a closer look at the Hodinöhsö:ni history of this game. You'd see there are strong warnings against playing outside of the expectations of accepted physicality. I'll share a Ga·yo·go·ho:nǫ' story of the Thunderers and maybe you'll be enlightened." 'Usdas chuckles at the word play and listens attentively:

> An old man and his nephew (once) went hunting and made a rather lengthy journey into the bush, as game was very scarce. They put up a good shanty at their stopping-place, and the old man told the younger to remain at home, as he was too young to go out by himself and would be sure to meet with bad luck, especially as they had gone towards the west, a direction which the older people had always warned them to avoid.
>
> The old man, however, had decided to find out why this was, so he kept on travelling west, but got only a little meat from time to time.
>
> He came, after a while, to the neighbourhood of some Indians who spoke the same language, but he cautioned the boy not to go near them. The fact was that he had begun to give most of his meat to a woman there, which he did not wish his nephew to know.
>
> The woman had a boy who noticed that the man always went in the same direction and decided to follow him.

Next time the old man came, the boy followed at some distance, saw the shanty and crept up behind it to listen. He heard the old man scolding his nephew and warning him again not to go towards the west. The strange boy lay down, thinking he would wait and play with the other boy, as there were only grown-up people at his place. When the old man had gone, he came around and called to the other boy to open the door. He also told him that he was a cousin and that the old man was his uncle, too.

After he had got inside the shanty, he told the first boy that there was to be a lacrosse match presently, and coaxed him to come, to which the first boy agreed. "I know where our uncle is," he said, "and we shall not go there." He had two lacrosse sticks hidden away and proposed that they should get these when they arrived at the place.

When they reached the field, they saw some men getting ready to play. The second boy got the sticks, handed one to his friend and they sat down beside the others and not far from a grove of trees. While they sat there another boy about the same size came out of the bush and asked for a stick, too, saying that he would help.

When the players were ready to start they said there was room for another, but they thought that none of the boys was big enough.

After the boys had watched the men play for a while, the first boy said, "I think I shall join them"; so he started into the next game. The other two boys saw that their friend was being used rather roughly; so the boy who had come out of the bush sprang up and began to make all sorts of plays, just like [a] man. He was strong, too. At least, one of the players butted him, but fell dead with his neck broken. The boy picked up the man's head and threw it at a tree trunk, making a lump on it like those used for war-clubs or wooden bowls. He was really one of the Thunderers.

The players all quit then, and the third boy handed back the stick, first telling the other boys that he was going to where some more games of lacrosse were to be played and that he would do the same there. Before going, he gave the two boys power, touching both shoulders of each and saying, "Now you will have as much power as I for the ball game, or for anything else, such as lifting; so don't be afraid." He also told the first boy to go and stay with his uncle, as it was not safe for him to stay in the shanty alone.

When the latter arrived at the woman's place he was made welcome. The two boys now became the best hunters and excelled at running, lacrosse, wrestling and jumping, though they were only little fellows.

After a while, when they found that they could get no more game where they lived, they journied [sic] on until they found some other people. Presently they were invited to play lacrosse. The people here were accustomed to play roughly and the opposing team thought they would have it easy this time, as there were two little boys on the other side. They were beaten badly however, and started to fight, but the two boys were good at that, too, and picked the players up and threw them wherever they wished, and also threw some of their opponent's heads into trees, as their friend had done.[2]

Big John continues. "Although these histories and sophisticated philosophies are retold throughout our lifetime, kids get a real kick out of that story, but funny how they understand the premise of it – play rough and there are consequences! I like to remind them that their heads will be thrown into the trees if they get out of hand." 'Usdas laughs at the thought of wide-eyed children listening to the story.

"Do you understand, Beersie?" 'Usdas asks. "Indians had rules too, you know. Lumps – tree knots – are reminders of the consequences of breaking those rules. This is our game."

Annoyed, Beers snaps back, "It's Canada's game; it's 'Our Country and Our Game'!"[3]

"Nice premise, but 'Stolen Land and Stolen Game' has a better ring to it. And though it may be enshrined in folklore, we both know that lacrosse isn't Canada's national game. Parliament won't be meeting on that issue until 1994.[4] But I like tricks, Beersie, so let's call it Canada's national sport. No one will know the truth, at least not for a while. What's the worst that could happen? It's not like Canadians are going to ban Indigenous athletes, appropriate their lacrosse identity, or use it to assimilate them."

~

GIVEN AS A GIFT from the Creator in the Hodinöhsö:ni' epistemology, lacrosse has been a central element of Indigenous cultures and worldviews for centuries. The records of early missionaries, anthropologists, and oral histories show that various forms of the stick-and-ball game were widespread throughout the continent before and during European colonization. Hodinöhsö:ni' and Wendat (Huron) players carried a large stick, whereas the Anishinaabeg on the northern shore of Lake Superior used a smaller one,[5] and in the present-day southeastern United States, competitors might carry two small sticks, speaking to the variety of forms across the continent.[6] All these sticks were fitted with pockets – some taut, others loose – to help control and cradle the ball, but the Nêhiyawak (Plains Cree) had a game known as We Pitisowewepahikan (known as "double ball" in English), in which a slightly curved stick was used to pass two balls that were strung together by a length of sinew. Similarly, the Coast Salish in present-day British Columbia and Washington also speak to a history of the game in their communities.[7] As exemplified in "The Creator's Game" told by Dao Jao Dre, Delmor Jacobs, in the Prologue, the basic premise of the game remained the same – with a few exceptions – regardless of where it was played: competitors could not touch the ball(s) with their hands, so they needed a stick to manipulate it.[8]

From a Hodinöhsö:ni' Longhouse perspective, the lacrosse stick was, and continues to be, more than just a piece of sports equipment; rather, it is alive and is a form of medicine that allows the game to heal, whether an individual, a community, or a nation.[9] Again as exemplified by Dao Jao Dre's story, Indigenous peoples across North America, including the Choctaw, Aniyvwiya (Cherokee), Hodinöhsö:ni', and Anishinaabeg, understood that the healing powers of the game went beyond the physical realm; it played a significant role in their epistemology.[10] Furthermore, games in the Hodinöhsö:ni' tradition were, and are, held to honour holistic entities and to be a means of dispute resolution. For example, using traditional wooden sticks and playing to a score of seven, the Ga·yo·go·ho:nǫ' Nation has a game every mid-April to honour the Seven Thunderers (also called Thunderbeings).[11] If lacrosse is to be used for healing, a game can be requested by an individual, clan, nation, or even an entire confederacy. Once the game ends, the ball remains with the person who made the request or the one who needed the curative powers of the match.[12] As the Jesuits observed in the first half of the seventeenth century, the Anishinaabeg also understood lacrosse as filled with healing power. In 1636, Jean de Brébeuf wrote,

Of three kinds of games especially in use among these peoples [Ihona-tiria or St. Joseph near Thunder Bay, Ontario] – namely, the games of [la]crosse, dish, and straw, the first two are, they say, most healing. Is not this worthy of compassion? There is a poor sick man, fevered of body and almost dying, and a miserable sorcerer will order for him, as a cooling remedy, a game of [la]crosse. Or the sick man himself, sometimes, will have dreamed that he must die unless the whole country shall play [la]crosse for his health; and no matter how little may be his credit, you will see then in a beautiful field, village contending against village as to who will play [la]crosse the better, and betting against one another beaver robes and porcelain collars, so as to excite greater interest. Sometimes, also, one of these jugglers will say that the whole country is sick, and he asks a game of [la]crosse to heal it; no more needs to be said, it is published immediately everywhere; and all the captains of each village give orders that all young men do their duty in this respect, otherwise some great misfortune would befall the whole country.[13]

According to the Hodinöhsö:ni' Longhouse perspective, the stick also has power: it is imbued with *orenda,* or *orenta,* a life-giving force.[14] William Fenton notes that this force "adheres to inanimate and animate things, to aspects of the environment, and to sequences of behaviour."[15] William Engelbrecht explains that natural elements such as False Face masks have orenda, which they retain from their original state:

The Seneca [Onöndowa'ga:'] believe that all natural entities have spirits, and hence inherent power or orenda ... Iroquois false face masks [or lacrosse sticks] provide a contemporary example of human-made objects charged with great spiritual power. A block of wood that is to become the mask is removed from a living tree, so that the power inherent in the tree becomes part of the mask. Once the image is formed, it gains power as a representation or icon of the spirit forces it portrays. Ritual use of tobacco adds to this power, as does the mask's use in ceremonies such as Midwinter, or in curing the sick.[16]

In the Hodinöhsö:ni' Longhouse epistemology, lacrosse remains a critical holistic element – the interconnectedness of the physical (i.e., land, humans, animals, environment) and spiritual worlds (i.e., creation, medicine, afterlife).

Thus, it is a significant aspect of Hodinöhsö:ni' identity, culture, ceremony, spirituality, and as the Code of Handsome Lake states, the afterlife.[17] From the beginning, it played an important role in Hodinöhsö:ni' traditions, and the "People of the Longhouse" have historically turned to it during times of need.

This is demonstrated by the story of Sganyadai:yo' (Handsome Lake), an Onöndowa'ga:' prophet.[18] He was born in 1735 at the village of Conawagas on the Genesee River near present-day Avon, New York, during a turbulent period in the history of the Hodinöhsö:ni' Confederacy.[19] After moving to the Allegany, he suffered from a "wasting disease" and alcoholism, with the result that he became bedridden and was cared for by his daughter.[20] During the next four years, he reflected on the condition of the nation and the devastation surrounding him (such as the population destruction, alcoholism, capitalistic greed, political breakdown, and the loss of land, wealth, and traditional ways).[21] Dao Jao Dre, Delmor Jacobs, explains that Sganyadai:yo' began to invoke a state of the Good Mind and positive and thankful thought, "but he had a relapse when he let bad thoughts enter his mind. The bad thoughts flung him back to illness. He found he needed to rekindle his relationship with our Creator and his people. This was the only way he could help his people survive. So he did."[22] According to Edward Cornplanter's (So-Son-Do-Wa) 1912 rendition of the Code of Handsome Lake, the Creator felt sorry for the destruction brought to Turtle Island, so he sent out four messengers to deliver the Gai'wiio (Good Word or Good Message) of Shongwayàdíhs:on (the Creator's highest code of ethics) on earth.[23] The messengers attempted to deliver the Gai'wiio several times, but no one would listen until finally they found Sganyadai:yo'. Cornplanter continues the story:

> Now at this time the daughter of the sick man and her husband are sitting outside the house in the shed and the sick man is within alone. The door is ajar. Now the daughter and her husband are cleaning beans for the planting. Suddenly they hear the sick man exclaim, "Niio'!" [So be it!] Then they hear him rising in his bed and they think how he is but yellow skin and dried bones from four years of sickness in bed. Now they hear him walking over the floor toward the door. Then the daughter looks up and sees her father coming out of doors [sic]. He totters and she rises quickly to catch him but he falls dying. Now

they lift him up and carry him back within the house and dress him for burial. Now he is dead.[24]

After hearing of his death on June 15, 1799, a number of community members gather.[25] Among them is his nephew, Tää'wŏnyăs, who touches his body, discovers a warm spot in the middle of his chest, and proclaims that there is still hope.[26] Later the brother of Sganyadai:yo', Gaiānt'wakă, also feels the warm spot. Checking Sganyadai:yo' once again, Tää'wŏnyăs finds that the warm spot has spread. Suddenly, Sganyadai:yo' begins to breathe and he opens his eyes.[27] Upon waking, he proclaims that he is well and states, "Never have I seen such wondrous visions!"[28] As he explains, at the time of his death the messengers showed him "the past, present and the future of Native peoples of the world. They showed him how men spoiled the ways the Creator made for all life to live in harmony with each other. They showed him good and evil, the rewards and punishments of both."[29] Through his journey and later sharing his visions, Sganyadai:yo' recounts the teachings given to him by the messengers during the Skyroad journey on which they had taken him.[30] Dao Jao Dre, Delmor Jacobs – as recorded by Calder and Fletcher – continues the story of Sganyadai:yo', who sees a number of visions on the Skyroad:

> When he neared the Creator's land, he came upon a grassy clearing with small trees and bushes. Here, he heard a voice. The voice said there would be a lacrosse game the next morning and that Awenhen: seh ("New Flower") would take the face-off. Handsome Lake knew the voice was that of his friend Johahi:seh. Johahi:seh had been dutiful in his earthly life and had carried on his leadership ways in the Creator's land. Handsome Lake also knew Awenhen: seh, but at the time of his collapse, Awenhen: seh was still among the living. Only upon his earthly revival did Handsome Lake learn that Awenhen: seh had passed away the previous day. Awenhen: seh was now in the Creator's land, where he took the face-off as predicted.[31]

When Sganyadai:yo' asks the messengers how long he will be delivering the message, he is told, "When the people gather to uphold your spirits and have a lacrosse game for you, very soon you are going to come home."[32] He spends years spreading the Gai'wiio. Just before his death, he visits the

Onöñda'gega' (Onondaga), and the residents hold a lacrosse game to comfort and possibly heal him.[33] As Cornplanter recites,

> Now it happened that they all wished to comfort him. So for his pleasure they started a game of lacrosse[34] and played the game well. It was a bright and beautiful day and they brought him out so that he might see the play. Soon he desired to be taken back into the house ... Now shortly after he said a few words. To the numbers gathered about him to hear his message he said, "I will soon go to my new home. Soon I will step into the new world for there is a plain pathway before me leading there. Whoever follows my teachings will follow in my footsteps and I will look back upon him with outstretched arms inviting him into the new world of our Creator."[35]

Together, "The Creator's Game" and the founding of the Gai'wiio provide a glimpse into the cultural philosophies and the epistemological importance of lacrosse in the Hodinöhsö:ni' Longhouse worldview. Both stories will be referred to throughout the book to explain how this understanding of lacrosse relates to Indigenous identity formation – specifically in Hodinöhsö:ni' communities – as well as to continuation, gender roles, and the stick as a medicinal element.

As various imperial nations fought to establish themselves in North America during the eighteenth and nineteenth centuries, lacrosse remained important among Indigenous nations, much to the disdain of Christian missionaries. For example, as Michael J. Zogry documents in his history of Anetso, because of its connection to spiritual practices – many Indigenous nations saw the game as a form of ceremony – missionaries perceived it as "heathen" and lobbied against it. However, because Western perceptions separate games from religious activities, colonial agents, including missionaries, tended to focus on more "objectionable" non-Christian practices.[36] Zogry writes, "Though it [Anetso] was actively suppressed during certain times in Cherokee history, it escaped sustained overt suppression because many government agents, missionaries, and observers separated the activity itself from other accompanying activities, in their own minds choosing to focus on those as ills rather than on the 'thing' itself."[37] In the mid-nineteenth century, when settlers were in the process of formulating a Canadian identity, the relationship between Indigenous nations and lacrosse began to shift dramatically as non-Natives increasingly participated in the game and eventually appropriated it as their own.

From 1844 to 1867, a span of slightly more than twenty years, British immigrants and English-speaking enthusiasts in Montreal took up the game through the 1856 formation of the Montreal Lacrosse Club (MLC) and introduced a code of rules and non-Indigenous governing bodies; at the time of Confederation, they unofficially proclaimed it Canada's national sport. Although francophone Montrealers also played lacrosse, British immigrants and anglophone Montrealers at the MLC, and later the Montreal Amateur Athletic Association (MAAA), facilitated and controlled this new identification. As this chapter demonstrates, they achieved this dominance by casting the game in classic colonial dichotomies: it was allegedly the uncivilized pursuit of a disappearing people, but it could be salvaged if it were infused with Western ideas about sportsmanship, athleticism, and scientific regulation. Attempting to establish a cultural hegemony through lacrosse and instituting the game as a main pillar of Canadian identity formation in major urban centres, Canadian organizations limited the participation of Indigenous players in 1867 and barred them outright in 1880. Throughout the 1860s, lacrosse was one of the earliest visual representations of the transformation of a British North American colonialist identity to a distinctly Canadian one.[38] The game became a source of identity on which Canadians could build what they imagined to be their own distinctiveness, connected to the land they now occupied. As Michael A. Robidoux argues, "the task of defining a national identity is a creative process that requires constructing a shared history and mythology(ies) that best suit the identity *imagined* by those few people responsible for responding to this task."[39] By 1885, British colonialists and anglophone Canadians, those in control of the organized development of lacrosse, used the game to form what they described as a legitimate Canadian identity but one that, as Gillian Poulter reminds us, "further solidified the emerging Canadian identity as anglophone, white, male, and middle-class."[40]

Ever-present during this appropriation were the Hodinöhsö:ni' communities near Montreal and Toronto. Even as Canadians used lacrosse in their efforts to define "Canadianess," Indigenous peoples continued to play the game, embracing the changes introduced by non-Natives.[41] Furthermore, as anglophone settlers increasingly employed the game in nation-building activities such as at holiday celebrations, and encouraged immigration through overseas lacrosse tours, Indigenous peoples used their cultural identities, both "authentic" and "fabricated," to secure additional income, fame, and the opportunity to travel. Often, they "played Indian" to satisfy their audiences' notions of authenticity while becoming highly successful negotiators for their "performances."[42] In this, they carved out a form of control, however limited, by mirroring back the colonial gaze cast upon them and manipulating non-Indigenous perceptions for their own purposes.[43] In the second half of the nineteenth century, lacrosse demonstrates how both Canadians and Indigenous peoples, mainly the Hodinöhsö:ni', competed to frame and perform national identities through a sport that both claimed as their own.

Colonizing the Creator's Game

The first recorded lacrosse game between Kanien'kehá:ka and non-Indigenous athletes took place on August 29, 1844, a significant day in the history of the sport.[44] It also marks the dramatic refashioning of lacrosse and the beginning of the non-Native seizure of the game.[45] In 1856, a group of young, influential Montrealers created the MLC after being introduced to the game by the Kanien'kehá:ka of Kahnawà:ke and Ahkwesáhsne.[46] Exhibition games put on by the Kanien'kehá:ka of Kanehsatá:ke and Onöñda'gega' from Onondaga, New York, further influenced these lacrosse enthusiasts.[47] The establishment of the MLC bolstered support for lacrosse throughout the city, and Montreal dentist Dr. William George Beers was central to the club's early years. Although he did not act alone, Beers was the primary architect of the colonization of the game. He and the MLC were largely responsible for its systematic reorganization, regulation, and control during the 1860s. In 1860, Beers published a small pamphlet that supplied a general set of rules, regulations, and instructions; in 1867, he expanded this to create the first uniform code of written rules informed by his class, religion, gender, and race disposition.[48] Before this point, the rules governing field lengths, the number of players, and the duration of games were negotiated before each contest and abided by Indigenous expectations of acceptable physicality.[49] By standardizing the rules, Beers helped to colonize a particular version of the game, that of the Kanien'kehá:ka, transforming it into the "authentic" variant. Field sizes were significantly shortened, and strict rules were implemented to counter Indigenous expectations of physicality and to curb the supposedly violent racialized aspects of the Indigenous game to make it more widely appealing to Canadians.

William George Beers, 1868. |
I-30326, McCord Museum.

Although the rules and regulations would change over time, the Hodinöhsö:ni' stick and the game that was played in and around the Montreal area became the cornerstone of "modern lacrosse" globally, a development that delegitimized forms of the game as played by other Indigenous nations. In many ways, the codification of sport per Western values served as an act of cultural imperialism and colonialism.[50] All told, Beers's systematic restructuring of the game marked a change in practice. As he later wrote, this produced a "new era" of lacrosse: "When civilization tamed the manners and habits of the Indian, it reflected its modifying influence upon his amusements, and thus was Lacrosse gradually divested of its radical rudeness and brought-to a more sober sport. Only a savage people could, would or should play the old game; only such constitutions, such wind and endurance could stand its violence."[51] Through this racialization and colonization of the game, Beers was an architect of the structures of settler-colonialism in Canada.

As lacrosse developed in urban and smalltown Canada, middle-class men used it to establish cultural hegemony.[52] Throughout the mid- and late nineteenth century, prominent anglophone Montrealers appropriated certain Indigenous activities to forge a Canadian identity by way of various organizations such as the Montreal Snowshoe Club and the MLC, which later partially comprised the influential Montreal Amateur Athletic Association (formed in 1881).[53] Through visual images, celebrations, compiled histories, and popular media reports, the MLC and later the MAAA established and praised a specific type of Canadian nationalism that served as a prototype for other Canadian organizations to emulate.[54] In British colonialist ideology, according to Poulter, "the belief in the value of independence, industry, self-discipline, and moral behaviour was part and parcel of middle-class Victorian respectability, while order and progress were essential ingredients of British rule throughout the empire. These were all qualities Victorians believed to be inculcated by sport."[55] Beers and others took these understandings of sport and applied them to a game that was "native" to the land – legitimizing their claim to a distinctive identity connected to place. In doing so, they differentiated the game as Canadian and maintained the Victorian perception of sport as respectable competition. Poulter notes, "This new 'Canadian' identity was a very particular creation in the ways that it was identified, imagined, and manifested. Even though it claimed to be 'national,' it was the identity envisioned by a particular class at a particular time and place."[56] Following the lead of the MLC and later the MAAA, "local moral entrepreneurs" founded amateur athletic associations elsewhere in the dominion, which often included lacrosse clubs, connecting them with the larger urban reform movements initiated by the Montreal organizations.[57]

Specifically, promoters attempted to control the image that lacrosse conveyed to Canadians by monopolizing the game through a series of non-Indigenous organizations such as the MLC and the National Lacrosse Association of Canada (NLA), and through publications such as Beers's 1869 *Lacrosse: The National Game of Canada.*[58] In doing so, they wanted to express that the game was now civilized, an appropriate national symbol, and that it reflected prevailing Muscular Christian attitudes regarding progress.[59] For example, an 1860 exhibition match staged for the visiting Prince of

Wales pitted the Montreal and Beaver lacrosse clubs against Kanien'kehá:ka teams from Kahnawà:ke and Ahkwesáhsne; the latter also played a game against an Omàmiwininìwak team.[60] The event was one of the earliest public performances in which Canadian enthusiasts attempted to showcase their claim to the game as a source of Canadian identity and to use it as an articulation of Canadian distinctiveness before a royal audience.[61]

By 1860, sport was generally seen as a vehicle for moral training and a means to address the social ills of society.[62] Once the Indigenous "savageness" of lacrosse was corrected, it could be used to instill Western notions of masculinity. It "ultimately turned boys into men" by enabling male Canadians to engage in aggressive physical competition, as tempered by the Victorian perceptions of gentlemanly accord.[63] Between 1870 and 1890, this gendered notion, Nancy Bouchier points out, was adopted in other parts of the dominion and reproduced in smalltown settings.[64] Robidoux further explains that lacrosse enabled a merger of Canadian nationalism with a distinctively Canadian form of masculinity: "One of the primary reasons lacrosse served as a viable alternative to imported British sports such as cricket was its emphasis on physical aggression, volatility, and danger. The game appealed to males who identified with a more physically aggressive notion of masculinity rather than the reserved and civil expressions of masculinity exemplified in cricket."[65]

In an era of assimilative federal government policies that founded residential schools, created the Indian Act, and perpetuated the myth of the vanishing Indian, lacrosse, snowshoeing, and tobogganing were unusual in that they were incorporated into the dominant society for the purposes of generating a national identity.[66] Furthermore, non-Native lacrosse enthusiasts and popular media outlets zealously celebrated the Indigenous roots of the game and often emphasized that, like the "Indians" themselves, it was *of* this land. However, these sporting colonialists believed that the pursuits of Indigenous peoples needed to be "tamed" and that the game must be imbued with the notions of British Canadian "progress," modernity, and scientific regulation.[67] With this in mind, Beers and several of his associates led an initiative to organize the game nationally, forming the NLA in 1867 to administer rules, regulations, and player eligibility. They coined "Our Game and Our Country" as their slogan.[68]

Thus, the first standardized rules were put in place, and the direct colonization of the Creator's game was set in motion. One of the new NLA rules stated that "no Indian must play in a match for a white club, unless previously agreed upon."[69] Ironically, this race-based discrimination stemmed from beliefs about the natural physical prowess of Indigenous males, as enshrined in the noble savage myth. Donald Fisher notes that lacrosse organizers of the time often regarded Indigenous players as far superior to themselves, and many felt that the rule could level the playing field.[70] And yet, Indigenous clubs were still permitted to hold NLA memberships and compete in NLA championships, but no Indigenous individual could play on non-Native teams without consent.[71] As Thomas Vennum argues, "the rule was a blatant, segregationist 'separate but equal' clause."[72] Although lacrosse retained its larger cultural significance in Indigenous communities, the game as played in the dominant society was shorn of its epistemological grounding and distanced from the Creator. As the Kanien'kehá:ka from Ahkwesáhsne later reflected, non-Indigenous organizations and promoters had a significant impact on their traditional game: "The fact that the game was arranged and promoted by some of the businessmen around Montreal provides a good indication of the extent to which the relation between Tewaarathon/lacrosse and the Creator had deteriorated."[73] This deterioration did not come about by accident, as Patrick Wolfe reminds us – it was part and parcel of settler-colonialism's "logic of elimination" in its effort to create a new society on an expropriated land base. The systematic organization and appropriation of lacrosse, as represented by the new rules, clubs, and bans on Indigenous participation, was a manifestation of that logic. With its assertion of ownership and exclusion, the NLA motto "Our Country and Our Game" sums it up perfectly. These "organized developments" were just one example of the formation of settler-colonialism, not as a temporal act but as a structure that sought to fashion something "anew" while using the Indigenous connection to the game to make place-based claims about identity.[74]

The Continued Indigenous Presence

Regardless of how much control Beers and others thought they had, sport in the nineteenth century also played a critical role in the establishment of reformed Indigenous identities. Discussing the American context, historian Philip Deloria observes that sport as a performative exercise of collective identities worked both ways for Indigenous peoples and non-Natives:

> If sports were an important part of a new Indian world, they were instrumental to transforming and reshaping modern American culture

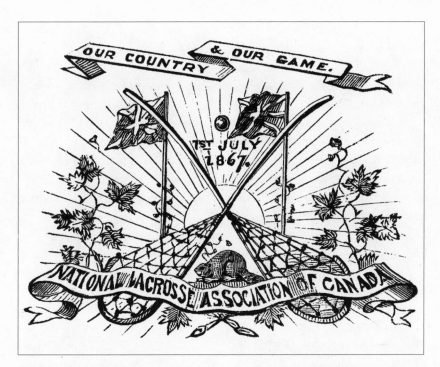

Emblem of National Lacrosse Association of Canada, c. 1867. The emblem and motto of the NLA, "Our Country & Our Game," highlights the connection between the appropriation of Indigenous territories and the game in the attempt to reform both as "Canadian." Since Indigenous peoples and their game were *of* the territory, in the eyes of sporting colonialists, the game's appropriation gave legitimacy to a unique Canadian identity. | *M930.50.1.742, McCord Museum.*

at the turn of the century. As with Wild West shows and movies, the meaning built around sports helped the contemporary world make sense ... As compelling and meaningful performances, then, sporting events rapidly came to function as powerful commodities, offering meanings, collective identity and sense of self, and entertainment, all for the price of a bleacher ticket.[75]

In many ways, despite its specific class and gender limitations, sport in the second half of the nineteenth century was an important vehicle driving the formation of a national unity. Although the *act* of Confederation "united" the upstart dominion regionally and politically for non-Natives – of course, not without considerable tension or holdouts – the social constructions of sport identified and gave meaning to being Canadian, even for those who did not play sports. However, as Audra Simpson reminds us, the formation of the nation-state generated not the elimination of Indigenous sovereignties and nationhood, but rather "nested sovereignties," in which sovereignty existed within sovereignty.[76] For Indigenous nations such as the Hodinöhsö:ni', and later the Sḵwx̱wú7mesh of southern coastal British Columbia, sports were used for their own purposes and to articulate and redefine their nationhood during Canada's Colonial Age. While non-Natives were devising an identity through the appropriated sport and lands, Indigenous peoples themselves negotiated, adapted, and performed their own identities as individuals, nations, and eventually as a pan-Indigenous community through lacrosse. As they began to define what it meant to be "Indian," they never relinquished their ownership of the game, and as we will see in Chapter 3, that sense of ownership expanded to other Indigenous communities and nations, such as the Sḵwx̱wú7mesh.

Just as the Hodinöhsö:ni' from Kahnawà:ke and Ahkwesáhsne were instrumental in introducing the game to non-Natives in the Montreal area, the Hodinöhsö:ni' from Six Nations of the Grand River (hereafter Six Nations) in Ontario also played a key role in establishing lacrosse in Toronto and elsewhere during the late nineteenth century. For example, on September 25, 1867, more than three thousand spectators witnessed a game between a group of Torontonians and a Hodinöhsö:ni' team from Six Nations – the community had a number of teams that were often based in the various nations (the Kanien'kehá:ka had a team, as did the Onöñda'gega' and Ga·yo·gǫ·ho:nǫ').[77] Lacrosse games that featured Indigenous teams were a tremendous draw for Canadians and were often financial successes for promoters. Indigenous athletes were a source of curiosity and spectacle for Canadian enthusiasts, as the *Toronto Globe* coverage of the game reveals:

> Interesting, most interesting, was the great Lacrosse Match which came off yesterday afternoon, on the Toronto Cricket ground. Over three thousand of our citizens were present, and all seemed to enjoy the sport to the utmost. So intense was the eagerness of the vast crowd to have a good view, that the line of demarcation for spectators was utterly disregarded despite the unceasing efforts of Sergeant-Major Hastings and his assistants to keep them at bay ... The match was between 12 Indians and 12 Torontonians. The former had been invited some time ago by the Toronto Lacrosse Club to this friendly contest, with the

Lacrosse players from Six Nations of the Grand River, c. 1892. | *Daniel Wilson Album, 892.4 91ETH14, Royal Ontario Museum.*

view of observing how the red men played, and testing the metal [sic] and skill of the veterans of the Six Nations.[78]

The Toronto game would be credited as the catalyst for lacrosse in the city. Within a year, Toronto would have thirteen lacrosse clubs with more than six hundred members, including the first collegiate team, at Upper Canada College.[79]

For spectators, one of the more exciting moments occurred after the game, when the Indigenous athletes performed a dance exhibition. Throughout the nineteenth century and into the early twentieth century, travelling Indigenous lacrosse teams often held exhibitions before and after the game.[80] This also reveals the spectators' curiosity about Indigenous peoples and their fascination with observing Indigenous customs – which were deemed culturally inferior – performed by "real Indians" before they disappeared as predicted by the disappearing Indian myth. From a settler perspective, Poulter notes, Canadians hypocritically wrestled with the concept of portraying Indigenous peoples as primitive while claiming a civilized national identity for themselves through the appropriation of Indigenous culture where lacrosse was a validation of their supposed distinctiveness.[81] Portraying Indigenous peoples as primitive while simultaneously using aspects of their culture to construct a civilized identity was inconsistent at best and hypo-critical at worst; Canadians deemed Indians to be inferior and on the verge of extinction at the same time they appropriated aspects of Indigenous culture to be employed in the construction of a civilized national identity.

For Indigenous peoples, the game was an opportunity to share their culture with a paying audience while earning a portion of the gate receipts. The demonstrations enabled the Hodinöhsö:ni' to produce revenue for their communities and "helped maintain a spirit of material independence from both the British and Canadian governments."[82] Men, women, and children commonly participated in the ceremonies and sold and exhibited the baskets and lacrosse sticks that they had made.[83] In addition, for the Hodinöhsö:ni', lacrosse games had always been part of larger events, social gatherings, and Longhouse ceremonies.[84] For example, after the September 1867 exhibition game in Toronto, the Six Nations team gave a demonstration of the War Dance, which the *Globe* recorded:

> Then came the famous war dance. The "braves" gave a good idea of this pre-historic, quaint performance, once of terrible significance, but now interesting only as a national characteristic. The sight was novel to most, new to many, amusing and interesting to all; and when it was over the vast assemblage quietly dispersed, expressing satisfaction at the treat provided for them by the Toronto Lacrosse Club.[85]

Seen as non-threatening amusements, these exhibitions for paying customers symbolized a taming of Indigenous peoples while reminding settlers of the "'Indianness' of the game and the country," and, consequently, of their perceived control over both.[86] Ironically, Indigenous peoples could symbolically evade the cultural subjugation that performing in "non-Indigenous" controlled spaces entailed by sometimes offering "show" dances that they had created or adapted specifically for these events. In a way, they were suspending their own modernity to mirror back a precieved "authentic" cultural performance – that is, to meet the expectations of non-Indigenous audiences regarding themselves and their customs.[87]

Indigenous peoples acquired an income by selling both real and fabricated adaptations of their culture to non-Native consumers. This is similar to what Paige Raibmon found in her examination of the Vancouver Island Kwakwaka'wakw, who performed a Hamatsa Dance at the Chicago World's Fair in 1893. Indigenous peoples commonly participated in these types of

A Skarù·ręʔ lacrosse
team, c. 1892. | *Daniel
Wilson Album, 892.4 91ETH13,
Royal Ontario Museum.*

An Onöñda'gega' and Ga·yo·gǫ·ho:nǫ'
lacrosse team, c. 1892. | *Daniel Wilson Album,
892.4 91ETH15, Royal Ontario Museum.*

ethnographic showcases as a form of wage labour, using adaptations and the commodification of their traditions to secure an income while bolstering their own governing structures and economies.[88] Although they certainly performed in the expectation of financial reward, historian Susan Roy refers to the Xʷməθkʷəy̓əm (Musqueam) performances at the 1966 BC Centennial celebrations to argue that they often autonomously redefined the meaning of such events.[89] What was intended to portray the stoic and savage Indian actually allowed Indigenous peoples to "speak" to their audiences. Roy adds that "participation in state-organized celebrations offered Aboriginal people the opportunity to appropriate and to reshape representations of dominant history for their own purposes, enabling them to 'upgrade' their Aboriginal identity in the public's eye."[90]

Throughout the late nineteenth and early twentieth centuries, lacrosse teams from Kahnawà:ke, Ahkwesáhsne, and Six Nations travelled internationally, playing exhibition games in the United States, France, England, Ireland, and Scotland.[91] For example, as a result of the exposure from the 1867 match in Toronto, a Hodinöhsö:ni' team from Six Nations was invited to Troy, New York, in October of that year to hold a lacrosse exhibition in conjunction with a baseball tournament.[92] Accompanying them was Onwanonsyshon (Chief G.H.M. Johnson), who had also attended the Toronto match.[93] After he addressed a large crowd of onlookers and explained the basic principles of lacrosse – demonstrating that the Hodinöhsö:ni' had adopted the recent rule changes to their original game – the Six Nations team played a match among themselves, reportedly dressed in brightly coloured tights and extravagant feathered headdresses.[94] Next day, the Hodinöhsö:ni' convinced a group of non-Indigenous baseball players to exchange their bats for sticks and to compete in a friendly bout of lacrosse, which the Six Nations team won easily.[95] The *Troy Daily Times* later reflected that thousands had attended and that the team had been paid in silver for its efforts.[96] Troy subsequently formed the Mohawk Lacrosse Club, forging the modern game in the United States for non-Indigenous players.[97]

Canadian Cultural Imperialism

By the end of 1867, there were eighty lacrosse clubs in Canada, and few other sports were as popular throughout the second half of the nineteenth century.[98] However, the perception that lacrosse was representative of Canadian national identity did not limit itself to domestic circles. For instance, the *Chicago Daily Tribune* stated the following in 1887:

The lacrosse champions of 1869, from Kahnawà:ke. While individual Indigenous athletes were barred from playing in lacrosse games for non-Native teams in 1867, Indigenous teams could still participate in lacrosse championships. However, this changed in 1880, when Indigenous teams and players were barred outright. | *Photographer James Inglis, C-001959, Library and Archives Canada.*

St. Regis Lacrosse Club (Ahkwesáhsne), 1867. | *I-29104.1, McCord Museum.*

Lacrosse is to the Canadian what base-ball is to the Yankee and cricket to the Englishmen. It is his national game, and he is devoted to it with an enthusiastic pride and affection unequaled by the devices of any other sport. A thoroughbred Canadian's version of the national anthem is "God Save Lacrosse," and he is always ready to make any sacrifice of personal convenience for the sake of what he affectionately calls "the game." Wherever he goes he carries his crosse and does missionary work among the athletes, and if he succeeds in organizing a lacrosse club in a country previously unenlightened he dies happy.[99]

On those "missionizing" efforts beyond the United States, Canadian promoters toured a number of lacrosse exhibitions to the British Isles between 1867 and 1883; featuring Kanien'kehá:ka athletes, these exhibitions helped establish the game overseas.[100] One of the first tours, led by Kahnawà:ke community member "Big" John Rice (Jean-Baptiste Taiaiake Rice), took place in 1867, when Rice formed an all-Indigenous team from Kahnawà:ke. W.B. Johnson organized the tour, which visited England and France, resulting in the establishment of the first lacrosse clubs in England and the formation of the English Lacrosse Association.[101]

However, the most significant tour occurred in 1876, when the MLC and a Kahnawà:ke team played a series of games, including an exhibition for Queen Victoria.[102] Appealing to spectator curiosity and improving the take at the gate were significant reasons for including Indigenous athletes in the tours. Historian Donald Fisher states that promoters zealously pushed the stereotypes of Indigenous savagery and simplicity to encourage attendance. "By making Aboriginals a tour focal point," Fisher argues, "the promoters hoped to cement cultural ties between England and Canada. Watching white and Indian athletes battle one another in lacrosse allowed English spectators to see a symbolic representation of Britain's New World conquests."[103]

Despite a partial ban on Indigenous participation at home, the Hodinöhsö:ni' were a critical part of the diffusion of lacrosse among non-Natives and remained so for the coming decades. Though Beers and other promoters believed that Indigenous peoples were of inferior intelligence and culture, and that they were on the verge of extinction, they also believed that exhibiting the originators of the game and the "primitive red men" whom audiences expected to see would help to sell lacrosse at home and abroad. Audiences were presented with spectacles of skill that reportedly pitted the savage against the civilized. In his examination of American football games, Deloria cites a parallel theme: Indigenous athletes echoed what audiences expected to see and "were part of the long tradition of Indians playing Indians, a tradition with a certain bicultural sophistication and an array of meanings clustered around labor, adventure, and conviviality."[104] Deloria's point can certainly be applied to lacrosse. As more lacrosse exhibitions were held throughout the late nineteenth century, promoters became as concerned with satisfying audience notions of Indigenous authenticity as with the entertainment value of the games themselves.[105] An article from a Vermont newspaper, written in about 1879 and titled "Lacrosse: The National Game of the Indians," provides a valuable insight into the attraction of Indigenous athletes for non-Native spectators:

> Anything connected with the earlier history of the Indians never fails to excite an interest in the breasts of the old as well as the young, when read from history ... *If the reading of their daring prowess excites our wonder and admiration be excited by standing face to face with the Indians themselves, and witnessing in life what we have considered so marvelous in the shadows.* Ever from the imperfect history of the different tribes of our country has the game of *Lacrosse* been their great national amusement ... Bethel Fair for the first time in Vermont since the settlement of the State by the whites, the Society having been to the trouble and expense to bring two of the celebrated native Indian Lacrosse teams, from the Indian tribes near Montreal to play there. The Indians will have their bows and arrows with them, and will give some of their "wonderful feats" of "Indian archery."[106]

As this revealing passage indicates, inducing "Indian shows" to perform at local celebrations, gatherings, and sporting events was costly, but the very fact that non-Natives did so confirms the settler demand for such entertainment. As sport historian Christine O'Bonsawin documents, the appearance of Indigenous peoples at the Vermont fair was part of a significant nineteenth-century trend in which Indigenous peoples and artifacts were major fixtures at exhibitions, World's Fairs, and events involving royalty.[107]

Kanien'kehá:ka Lacrosse Performances and "Indian" Commodification

Although non-Native promoters did use Indigenous athletes as "objectified signifiers of Canada," Indigenous promoters and athletes were not sitting

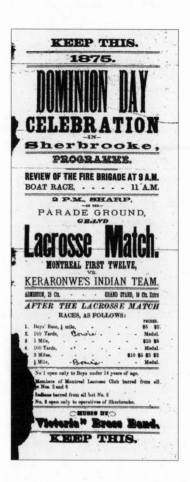

1875 Dominion Day poster advertising the appearance of "Keraronewe's Indian Team" from Kahnawà:ke. | *General Scrapbook No. 1, Montreal Amateur Athletic Association Fonds, MG 28, I 351, vol. 15, Library and Archives Canada.*

idly by while Canadians created an identity through their appropriated sport.[108] Instead, they were exploiting the dominant society's desire for this consumption of savagery and negotiating deals to perform and play Indian. They were aware of the way in which they were being depicted, but for a variety of reasons, they engaged in such portrayals.[109] Just as Canadian lacrosse promoters exploited Indigenous peoples, culture, and activities to captivate the public, Indigenous promoters also participated in this commodified exchange of "authenticity" and Indian consumption. As early as 1866, Indigenous promoters such as Jean-Baptiste Taiaiake Rice understood the value of engaging in lacrosse exhibitions.

In the late 1870s, Kahnawà:ke fielded two major teams that competed against the premiere Indigenous and non-Native senior clubs (whose players were approximately age twenty-one or older), under the direction of two local Indigenous promoters. Both vied for the title of best Indian team in the world and marketed themselves for the purpose of competition with non-Indigenous teams. They also reaped the financial rewards that accompanied playing against non-Native teams. The Iroquois Lacrosse Club, under the captaincy of White Eagle, and the Caughnawaga – sometimes Indian – Lacrosse Club, under Kararonwe (Peter Dellebault), quickly developed a rivalry.[110] Competing against other clubs during holiday celebrations and in exhibitions, both teams attempted to position themselves as the one to beat and as the epitome of lacrosse excellence. Describing themselves as "champions" and being officially recognized as such by the NLA had its financial rewards for both the teams and their promoters, as an 1880 letter to *Town and Country* suggests:

> No one ever heard of an Indian team traveling 300 or even 50 miles to play a match just for the fun of it to see which were the better man. They themselves are honest enough never to pretend to be influenced by any such motives, and they have no hesitation in saying as much. Even when they have risked some little time and even money for the sake of winning "championship honors," it has been with the idea of making an honest penny out of the title after they had it in their possession.[111]

Further to the point, an 1879 newspaper article demonstrates that White Eagle and Kararonwe were competing against each other for the remuneration offered by lacrosse exhibitions. Kanien'kehá:ka teams, and the Hodinöhsö:ni' more generally, were not merely passive participants being rewarded for their presence; rather, they were actively negotiating their value to get the best financial result possible. The newspaper stated,

> The Montrealers endeavored to arrange a match with White Eagle's team, and with this object in view Mr. Featherstonhaugh visited Caughnawaga a few days ago, but owing to the poor inducements offered, and a previous understanding between the Shamrocks and the Indians, a match could not be arranged. The Montrealers only offered $45 to White Eagle for his expenses, but the offer was indignantly refused, on the ground that the figure was too low, and for more cogent reasons. A match was then arranged with Keraronawe's team, which will take place tomorrow. The secretary stated that he

expected that three or four of White Eagle's men would be on the team, but the statement, according to the captain of the Shamrocks, is very improbable, as there is some trouble between Keraronawe and White Eagle. It is also thought unlikely that the former will play. Mr. Featherstonhaugh states that the Indians were not offered $40, but a share in the gate money, equal to $45.[112]

As the 1887 minutes of the Montreal Lacrosse Club reveal, the Kanien'kehá:ka teams were well versed in negotiating for fair pay:

April 20, 1887: Moved by Mr. Cleghorn that Mr. Bruce be written to and see what arrangements could be made to have a team of Indians for 24th May.

April 27, 1887: A letter from secy [the secretary of the] Caughnawaga team was read agreeing to play a match on 24th May here.

May 4, 1887: A letter was read from the secy of the Caughnawaga asking for sixty dollars for the match on 24th May. The secretary was instructed to answer in reply that we had their acceptance for fifty dollars, and to say that we would see the [rail?] by G.T.R. [Grand Trunk Railway] would not be higher than formerly and to wire us reply.

May 11, 1887: A letter from the secy of the Caughnawaga's was read stating that they would not accept less than 60 for the 24th May match. The secretary was instructed to write him stating that as they refused to accept our offer of 50 that we declare the match off.

May 18, 1887: Letter was read from Indians affirming to accept $50.00 to play on 24th. Secy instructed to write that other arrangements had been made.[113]

Indigenous lacrosse players themselves were also instrumental in this process of selling and playing Indian. Such was the case for Jean-Baptiste Raiontonnis – later shortened to Aiontonnis, "He works with wood" (Big John Canadian, or Canadien).[114] Born in 1840 at Kahnawà:ke, Aiontonnis was a famous voyageur and guide on the St. Lawrence River, where he learned his trade from Jean-Baptiste Taiaiake Rice and was often contracted by shipping companies to provide safe passage for steamships running the Lachine rapids throughout the 1860s and 1870s.[115] Sought after for his expertise, Aiontonnis was among the voyageurs whom British officers retained to lead Colonel Garnet Joseph Wolseley to the Red River settlement in Manitoba during the first Métis struggle for recognition of their nationhood. Later, he joined the Canadian crew that led an expedition down the Nile River in 1884, attempting to free Major-General Charles George Gordon in the Sudan.[116]

Aiontonnis, Kararonwe, and White Eagle were among the most important Indigenous lacrosse players, promoters, and showmen of the nineteenth century. Even before Aiontonnis (Big John) travelled to Windsor Castle in 1876, there is evidence that he fully recognized the opportunity of playing Indian for financial gain. As Johnny Beauvais explains, "When assigned to a boat going downstream, Big John, who was never accused of being an introvert, would come on board dressed in colorful Indian regalia. Those thrill seeking tourists of the Victorian era were apparently as taken with the spectacle as they were with the memorable headlong ride down the wild and treacherous waters."[117] This financial opportunism, which by 1876 was well understood by the Kanien'kehá:ka of Kahnawà:ke, and their athletic competiveness led them to become a headliner in an 1876 lacrosse tour of Britain. The tour was initiated by Beers, Charles Rose, the MLC, and the English Thames Hare and Hounds Club, the latter requesting the presence of Indigenous players to ensure the success of the tour.[118] The 1876 series followed in the wake of earlier lacrosse tours, but it was also part of a larger trend of Indigenous athletes and teams travelling to Britain as, in the eyes of the spectators, anthropological curiosities from around the empire. For example, from 1861 to 1863 Onöndowa'ga:' distance runner Ha-ga-sa-do-ni (also known as Louis Bennett and Deerfoot, his pseudonym) shattered records in Britain and captivated audiences.[119] In 1868, thirteen Indigenous cricketers from the Jardwadjali, Gunditjmara, and Wotjabaluk Nations in Australia also toured Britain, competing in matches and performing for audiences.[120] Historian David Sampson argues that the cricket "tour was part of settler and colonial power over Aborigines ... It was consistent with, not an exception to, the accompanying British prejudices, ideology, and science [social Darwinism that bolstered the disappearing Indian myth] that perceived Australian Aborigines as racially distinctive, fascinating, primitive and inferior."[121] This held true for the Canadian lacrosse tours but with one significant difference: whereas the Australian cricket tour did not express a distinctive Indigenous identity, the lacrosse tours were visual signifiers of an important piece of Hodinöhsö:ni' and Kanien'kehá:ka identity and nationhood.[122]

The Kanien'kehá:ka on Tour

A not-for-profit series, the 1876 tour was intended to function as a national promotional piece and to help export the game overseas.[123] In a letter to the *Montreal Gazette,* "Canada Forever" made the connection:

> Dear Sir – It seems to me that the gentlemen conducting the national enterprize have not been public enough in their appeal for support. Here in Montreal we rush into the mouth of every foreign subscription list, back up any and every enterprize for every object – all of which speaks well for our generosity. But let us do handsomely for our own Canadian national game, and encourage this spirited venture, which really will draw a great deal more attention to Canada than all the emigration agents put together. Let us make it a' credit to the country, as I am sure our players are able ... and show England the stuff of which "Young Canada" is made.[124]

Despite the rhetoric, when one considers the tour from an Indigenous perspective, it becomes clear that much more was involved than national promotion. As the MLC recruited players from Toronto, Montreal, and Saint John to form its own team, it approached Kahnawà:ke to join the tour with a team of its own, offering to cover its travel costs, to pay each player $20 a month, and to provide him with a new "suit of clothes."[125] Kararonwe took up the task of organizing the Kahnawà:ke team.[126] Beyond the financial incentive, the tour enabled players to travel internationally and to become celebrity performers while also renewing a long-standing relationship between England and the Hodinöhsö:ni'.[127] As Kararonwe selected his players, controversy arose both internally and externally regarding his choices. Many Kahnawà:ke community members were greatly interested in joining the tour, largely because of its various incentives, but spaces were limited and thus many proficient players would inevitably be passed over. Some community members felt slighted by the MLC decision to invite Kararonwe as team captain.[128] Kararonwe's rival White Eagle, whom the MLC had not asked to form the team, used the Montreal press to criticize the selection of players and to question their competiveness.[129] In a letter to the editor, Kararonwe defended his choices and attempted to quell fears about the quality of the team:

> The Montreal Club authorised me to select [whoever?] I wished, only restricting me to pick good moral ... *full-blooded Indians,* and at the same time good players. I did the best I could in selecting and grooming men whom I knew would do their duty. Some were not chosen who call themselves first twelve men, but I question if they are better than those picked, or anything extra. I deny that my team cannot play, and it is absurd to state they cannot handle a stick, because you cannot find in all Caughnawaga a youth or man over the age of ten years who never handled a stick.[130]

As Kararonwe's reference to "full-blooded Indians" suggests, the team was to emphasize the "authenticity" of its members. He refused the selection of one of Kahnawà:ke's strongest players, White Eagle, on the basis that White Eagle had made it known that his participation was predicated on the inclusion of his cousin, Lefaivre.[131] But Lefaivre was not asked to join the team; the reason given for his exclusion was that he was non-Indigenous, or at least not "full-blooded." Despite the controversy, the MLC supported Kararonwe's selections, and the team headed overseas in April 1876. Both it and Aiontonnis were an instant hit in Britain, and the tour was covered extensively by the Canadian and British press. Reporters were quick to note the differences between what they referred to as the "Caughnawaga Indian team of professionals" and the "Canadian amateur gentlemen," focusing on the dress and racialized "styles of play" that differentiated primitive Indigenous lacrosse from its scientific and methodical non-Indigenous counterpart: "They were attired in Indian playing costume – viz., red and white striped guernseys, and knickers, and white hose. They displayed a variety of ornaments; their faces were streaked with several colours, and on their headdresses they all show to a greater or less extent brilliant fluttering feathers."[132] Poulter points out that "the primitive 'Indianness' of the Native players was emphasized by exotic and colourful costumes."[133] As in Toronto and Montreal, the players staged cultural performances such as the "war dance" and "green corn dance" – reimagined as show dances for the entertainment of non-Indigenous spectators – further portraying the "authenticity" that audiences expected to see.[134]

A poster from the 1876 Royal Tour. Lacrosse was frequently advertised as "Canada's National Game" to construct and present the game as a piece of the nation-state's "unique identity" to audiences at home and abroad. Further helping to promote this idea was the participation of the original peoples from which the game originated, who "played Indian" and provided demonstrations. | *General Scrapbook No. 1, Montreal Amateur Athletic Association Fonds, MG 28, I 351, vol. 15, Library and Archives Canada.*

The dress that the Kahnawà:ke team wore, its performance dances, and the decision to exclude Lefaivre – citing his apparent lack of "full-bloodedness" – were all displays of Indianess. Adding to this perception, team captain Kararonwe used language to manipulate audiences. His letter to the editor shows that he knew English well and had an articulate, responsive, and poetic grasp of the language. But one reporter suggested that he also used English to help himself play Indian:

> I asked him [Kararonwe] at his hotel, after his return from the game, what had excited him so during the day – whether it was the desire for success or not?
>
> "No," he said, with a peculiar smile, "Canadians more goods as my boys. They (his players) young, weak, no breath. What make me happy, much people – much money I see our good father, Dr. Beers, have."

Reality

To dispel the romance of this speech before it takes deep root in the minds of any of my young readers, fresh from the pastures of green of the "hair-raising literature" of the weekly journals, I may say that the worthy captain of the Iroquois talks English quite well when he chooses, and that the slowness with which he speaks to strangers and those outside the line (as I was) is ascribable to the difficulty with which he finds in talking the Indian-English of [dime novelist] "Ned Buntline." It is, of course, quite essential that he should talk badly, but he evidently finds it a bore.[135]

On several levels, the Kahnawà:ke team performed as Indians, reworking their culture, language, and dress to please their audiences. They were putting on a show that sold well, and they knew it.

As part of the tour and at the request of the royal family, the Kahnawà:ke and Canadian teams played a private game for Queen Victoria and her family at Windsor Castle on June 26, 1876.[136] In attendance were the queen, Princess Beatrice, Prince Leopold, Prince Christian, Dominion of Canada agent Mr. Dore, and the attorney general of Quebec, among others.[137] The historical record identifies thirteen players for Kahnawà:ke, including – using the original spellings and translations printed in the newspaper coverage – Aiontonnis (Sakatis Aientonni); Tier Karoniare – Blue Spotted (Peter Dellebault); Antiomua Taronkowa (Atonsatekanennaosiheu) – Hickory Wood Split (Thomas Jacob); Sawatis Anosotako – Pick the Feather (John Dionne); Wishe Tasemontie – Flying Name (Michael Dellebault); Atiomua (Atonla) Taronkowa – The Loon (Thomas Jacob); Wishe Ononsanoron – Deer House (Michael Deerhouse); Saksarrii Tontariiakon (Saon-

Aiontonnis "Big John Canadian" (middle, standing, with headdress) and an 1876 Kahnawà:ke lacrosse team. | *II-41679, McCord Museum.*

Aiontonnis "Big John Canadian" in 1876. | *II-41672.1, McCord Museum.*

tariiakon) – Crossing the River (Francois Skye); Tier Skanensati – Outside the Multitude (Peter Laforce); Legare (Rasar) Kanentakeron – Scattered Branches (Legare Suchana); Kor Kanentakeion – Spruce Branches (Paul Delarimier); Sasaarii Shakosennakete – Great Arm (Francois Snehe...)[138]; and Alonsa (Alonwa) Sekanennowhen – Wild Wind (Thomas Ross).[139]

In anticipation of the game, one newspaper published an edited version of the speech the Kahnawà:ke team had written for the occasion. It focused on the historic Hodinöhsö:ni' connection with the Crown, recounting their relationship with the royal family and reminding the queen of their shared history. Written on birch bark in both Kanien'kéha and English, the speech was apparently composed well before the game and was sent to the queen in advance. After General Ponsonby introduced the team to the queen, "Chief" Aiontonnis read the speech to her:

To our great and good mother Queen Victoria across the big water, we, the Iroquois Indians of Caughnawaga, near the city of Montreal, at the head of the mighty rapids of Lachine, send you our true love and loyalty. We hope to see you some day in this great land which once belonged only to the Indians; but we hope you will come and look upon us playing *our own great game* of La Crosse in England against the pale-faced young men of Canada, who now play *our game* like us, and sometimes beat us in fair play. But the English were always a brave people, and the Indians love and trust them. When the English soldier dies, he dies firm, like an Indian. He makes no cry. Good Queen, our forefathers were once one people, and became the six nations. They were first in war, first in eloquences, first in loyal love to the English. Our warriors carried victory in the war-path from Quebec to the Carolinas, and from the prairies of the West to the forests of Maine. They feared no foe – they loved the war path as a bird loves the air. The war-whoop was ... a sweet sound. They fought every enemy and exterminated many tribes, and made the foes of their people scatter like leaves in the wood before the wind. At the council-fire, at the chase, on the war-path, in the playing-field, the Iroquois were the first. Great Queen, our young men used to play La Crosse on the prairies and at the forts before your brave soldiers. When other tribes were against the English the Iroquois always were true. When death with torture came the Iroquois still kept true. When Pontiac, the great head chief, planned to kill your brave soldiers and asked the Iroquois to join, our forefathers kicked the war-belt of wampum and would not go because they and the English were friends. On the 4th of June, 1763, the birthday of our great father King George, at fort Michillimacheinac, your brave soldiers ... were killed by the Indians. A great game of La Crosse was played to put them off their guard ...[140] Will you, great and good Queen, hear the petition of your Indian children? God save the Queen![141]

Beyond the reflections of the historic relationship between the Crown and the Hodinöhsö:ni', a reminder of the Covenant Chain, it is clear that the Kanien'kehá:ka of Kahnawà:ke recognized lacrosse as their game despite Canadian claims to ownership.[142] As Mary-Ellen Kelm explains through her examination of rodeos, "Aboriginal people, like other disenfranchised or marginalized people, used such events to claim a public presence, to intervene in dialogue about nation-building, and to put forward their own interests upon a highly visible stage."[143] Although settlers proclaimed the game as distinctly Canadian in a way that was emblematic of Victorian Euro-Canadian middle-class principles, that assertion hinged on it being rooted in a particular place – lands now known as Canada. Hence, as both Indigenous peoples and non-Natives claimed lacrosse as the source of their identities, *our game* had multiple and co-existing meanings.

Though Indigenous peoples participated in the tours and the exhibition matches against non-Natives for the purpose of financial gain, it is important to understand that the events were also sources of tremendous pride for Hodinöhsö:ni' communities. The lacrosse tours of the nineteenth century stand firm as historical moments and identity markers for Kahnawà:ke, but few are remembered as fondly as the 1876 example. Even today, it is celebrated as a great moment in Kahnawà:ke's history. As community member Johnny Beauvais states, this international recognition gave the community the opportunity to confront the sterotypes being cast on Indigenous peoples:

The royal spectators were fascinated by their aboriginal guests. Rather than the primitive and crude natives they had read about, they met a group of naturally cultivated, and most importantly, interesting people. Queen Victoria's imagination had been captured by Big John. In him she saw a mammoth of a man, with a demeanor remarkably similar to her own fabled Robin Hood.[144]

Stories of the 1876 tour have permeated Kahnawà:ke's collective memory, as successive generations have grown up hearing about the famous team and "Big John Canadian."[145] Joe Delaronde explains that the 1876 tour had a profound impact on the community and specifically his family. His grandmother's grandfather, Frank Cross the River, was part of the tour:

> He was the first Cross the River ... The story I always heard from her [Joe's grandmother] was that when the team went over, there were so many people named Jacobs and there were so few first names back then, there were probably three John Jacobs on the team. So she always told me the story that the queen said, when she met Frank, "You're Jacobs too?" He goes, "Yeah."
>
> [QUEEN:] "Well, what is your Mohawk name?"
> [FRANK:] "Saontariiakon."
> [QUEEN:] "What does that mean?"
> [FRANK:] "Cross the river."
>
> "Well," she said, "from now on you are Frank Cross the River." And so for him, it was a matter of pride, he took his Mohawk name as his family name, a name that still lives on today. Usually they just called them Cross, my grandmother was always Cross. Many times I heard that story about her grandfather. It really was – she really did talk about that a lot ... [That tour] was a matter of great pride! ... They were proud to be there and they figured if they are invited by the queen, we must be doing something right. It is recognition. Because back in the 1880s, what more recognition could you have had in the world than the most powerful empire on earth! And the head of that empire saying, "I want to watch you guys play lacrosse." So it was acknowledgment at the highest level. So they had to be proud of that.[146]

The Indigenous Ban

As they continued to compete against non-Native teams for the Canadian lacrosse championship and in exhibition play at home, Hodinöhsö:ni' teams found themselves increasingly becoming the focus of organizational mismanagement by the NLA. As members of the working class who were subject to race-based discrimination, Indigenous athletes and teams were on the bottom rung of the Canadian lacrosse hierarchy. So, when amateurism became a requirement in the sport, they were easy targets. On the whole, though non-Native organizers and team representatives denounced professionalism in lacrosse, this had not applied to Indigenous teams before June 1880.[147] Until that date, it was widely accepted that Indigenous teams, mostly made up of manual labourers, would receive a portion of the gate receipts as pay and to cover their travel costs.[148] This changed dramatically in 1880, when the NLA became the National Amateur Lacrosse Association (NALA) and barred Indigenous teams from competition.[149] Yet in numerous respects, the ban had been building for some time, which becomes clear when one examines the expansion of lacrosse regulations. As mentioned previously, a founding rule of the NLA segregated Indigenous athletes to all-Indigenous teams in league competiton.[150] However, in 1876 the NLA revised its rules, introducing two new ones that directly affected Indigenous organizations.[151] Essentially, according to the new rules, any Indigenous team that competed in NLA championships would subsequently be "debarred from the privilege of playing for money."[152] Indigenous teams could continue to earn financial compensation for "challenge games" against non-Indigenous NLA teams, but when it came to championship play, any and all exceptions were removed.

As the years went on, this rule remained in place and even expanded to the Pacific Coast Lacrosse Association, founded in 1879 and based in San Francisco, which copied the NLA rule set.[153] The amended NLA rules embodied an attempt by non-Native clubs – mainly the MLC – to denounce lacrosse professionalism. The MLC withdrew from the NLA in protest after it accused the Shamrock Lacrosse Club and others of continuing to use professional players.[154] During the early years of team formation, non-Native clubs were often grounded in class and religious affiliation, further exacerbating rivalries. For example, the MLC consisted largely of middle-class Protestants, whereas its crosstown rival, the Montreal Shamrocks, was made up of working-class Irish Catholics.[155] This created a number of class and religious conflicts, not to mention a vicious competitive environment that endured well into the early twentieth century, as the MLC, the Montreal Shamrocks, and the Toronto Lacrosse Club fought for control of the NLA.[156] Despite the proclamation by the non-Indigenous clubs that lacrosse should be an amateur sport, the paying of proficient individuals – secretly – was widespread at the highest levels of Canadian lacrosse.[157]

On June 4, 1880, the reformed NLA – now the National Amateur Lacrosse Association (NALA) – adopted a series of amendments to its official rules at its Toronto convention and banned Indigenous teams:

"Clubs in this Association shall be allowed to employ Indians, who shall hereafter rank as professionals, either as trainers or for the purpose of playing exhibition matches."[158] In short, Indigenous athletes were now barred from official league competition in Canada. As Fisher reminds us, the Indigenous teams were used as scapegoats for larger problems that were hampering the NALA, such as the struggle over professionalism, class conflicts, and inefficiencies within the league itself.[159] With league operations no longer needing the participation of Indigenous teams and the solidification of the game as an "idealized white middle-class sport," the racialized Indigenous athletes – marked further by their class and professionalism – no longer fit.[160]

Leading the charge in favour of amateurism was the MLC, which was the most influential association of organized lacrosse and a main source of middle-class rhetoric regarding the game. It insisted that the sport must remain amateur. During the late 1870s, the professionalism debates initially pitted the middle-class Protestants against the working-class Irish Catholics; specifically, the MLC accused the Shamrocks team of paying its players and of competing in an "ungentlemanly manner."[161] However, whereas the Catholic team was targeted due to its class and religious identity, Indigenous teams were positioned even lower in the social and racial hierarchy. The oral history documents that the MLC had a two-fold reason for advocating a ban on professionalization: the "purification" of the game based on class and race, and possibly for more self-serving reasons in pursuit of Canadian championships. Within the span of fourteen years (1866–80), from the first recorded championship match, the MLC won ten of the twenty-one championship games in which it competed. The Montreal Shamrocks competed in thirty-five and won twenty-six, including seven in a row in 1879, the year that the MLC pushed for the banning of professionalism.[162] For its part, Kahnawà:ke played sixteen championship matches and won four, whereas Ahkwesáhsne (identified as St. Regis) competed in four and won two.[163] Although at the time of the ban in 1880, numerous non-Native lacrosse enthusiasts were calling for the classification of Indigenous athletes as professionals, some questioned the wisdom of this measure. Following the announcement that the MLC had left the association and was now considering forming its own amateur organization, a letter to the *Montreal Evening Post* expressed concern over the classification of Indigenous athletes as professionals:

Sir – The Montreal Lacrosse Club is agitating for the formation of a new lacrosse association, open only to amateur clubs, thereby implying that *professional* clubs belong to the existing associations. Now Mr. Editor, the Indians alone, in my opinion, can be objected to on this score, and even they can scarcely be termed professionals in the strict sense of the word, as they are neither *salaried* to teach the game nor play it, like regular American baseball players. But admitting them to be professional, yet would it be more ungracious on the part of the white men, and most damaging to the best understood interest of lacrosse itself, to debar our [dusky or darky] athletes from future championship matches. The sport is essentially an Indian one, and to the redskins consequently are we indebted for all the sterling enjoyment and amusement at all times derivable from this manly exhibition. For no lacrosse contest excites more feverish interest in true lovers of the game, or is more anxiously looked forward to, than that in which White Eagle's team, for instance, are announced to compete for championship honors. Is it the desire then, of the "Montrealers" to ostracise clubs like this? The moment that sees that accomplishment of so mean a desire must chronicle "the beginning of the end" of genuine lacrosse in Canada.[164]

Although barring Indigenous players was presented as a solution to the problem of professionalism, which nonetheless continued to plague organizations thereafter, Hodinöhsö:ni' oral history does not concur. It points to race- and class-based discrimination but also insists that Indigenous athletes fell victim to the competitiveness of non-Native organizations in their quest to be crowned champions. As Kanehsatá:ke Elder and former lacrosse player Onawario, John Cree, explains in reference to the ban, "I think it was because Native teams were too strong. They were too strong, so what they did was they banned them. They couldn't play."[165] With similar reasoning, Dao Jao Dre, Delmor Jacobs, suspects that the ban arose from a non-Indigenous desire for control.[166] Joe Delaronde emphasizes this point as he remembers what he was told as a youth:

I think more than anything, they [non-Natives] wanted to win. More than anything, for some it was "we can't have these heathens beating our athletes." For others, it was just "we want to win" at all costs, "let's tweak the rules." For others, it was maybe more innocent but certainly it was – I am sure our ancestors were pretty sad when it happened and upset and what have you, but it is something we dealt with because even growing up immersed in the lacrosse culture they didn't talk too much about the ban. What I heard growing up was still the matter of pride when they met the queen. That was a matter of great pride.[167]

Although the oral history suggests that the MLC encouraged the professionalism debate in hopes of faring better at championships, the 1880 ban is somewhat surprisingly not as significant in the oral history and collective memory as one might expect. Although the ban remains present in recollections, it is not depicted as a defining moment in the Indigenous history of lacrosse, despite it having had an impact on Indigenous participation for several decades. With respect to international competition, the consequences of that ban would be felt for over a century. Indigenous athletes were never solely defined by their ability to play against non-Indigenous organizations or in Canadian championships. Prior to the formation of the NLA and the first standardized set of rules, Indigenous teams held lacrosse games under mutual understanding and agreed upon the rules at the time. Following the formation of the NLA, Hodinöhsö:ni' teams continued to play against each other, using the new set of rules. For example, in a 1922 match between the Allegany Indians, an Onöndowa'ga:' team from New York, and the Onondaga Royal Reds from Six Nations, the teams held two games, one played under the Ontario Amateur Lacrosse Association rules and the second under American rules.[168] In addition, Hodinöhsö:ni' players continued to practise medicinal games as part of their Longhouse ceremonies.

Nonetheless, the ban had resounding consequences for Indigenous peoples, and it developed into a historical injustice that would not be fully corrected for over a century. The motivations behind it should be questioned: although it excluded Indigenous teams from NALA competitions on the grounds that they were professionals, it failed to solve the problem of professionalism in Canadian lacrosse.[169] Hodinöhsö:ni' teams from Kahnawà:ke, Ahkwesáhsne, and Six Nations travelled throughout North America and Europe to play exhibition matches, but they did not participate in national championship competitions held by the NALA, the National Lacrosse Union (NLU), or the Canadian Lacrosse Association until box lacrosse was created in 1931, and they did not compete internationally until 1990.[170] Although Indigenous teams did not participate in Canadian competitions, Indigenous athletes continued to play the game and used it as a means of obtaining an income. By 1880, Indigenous peoples who resided in Canada, especially those from Kahnawà:ke, Kanehsatá:ke, Ahkwesáhsne, and Six Nations, had created an economic niche for themselves through the game. They used their sport and culture to acquire additional income and complemented it via farming and manufacturing pursuits – including the production of baskets, beadwork, and lacrosse sticks – and working as Canadian Pacific Railway labourers, loggers, river guides, and berry pickers.[171]

The Indigenous Presence after the Ban

The manufacturing of lacrosse sticks became an important industry for Indigenous craftsmen, who attempted to satisfy the demands of both Indigenous and non-Indigenous players. Throughout the late nineteenth century, stick production was a primary industry in Kahnawà:ke and Ahkwesáhsne, as the game grew in popularity across North America. By the turn of the century, lacrosse had become one of Canada's most popular sports, especially in large cities – although baseball was increasingly challenging it for top spot – and organizations had been founded from Nova Scotia to British Columbia.[172] As Ahkwesáhsne Indian agent George Long reported in 1891, the production of lacrosse sticks, baskets, and beadwork earned their fabricators $8,000 to $10,000 a year in total.[173] The Kanien'kehá:ka at Wáhta – who originated in Kanehsatá:ke and settled in the Muskoka region of central Ontario in 1881 – continued to produce lacrosse sticks and earned approximately $1,700 per year.[174] Stick making would remain an important source of income throughout this time, especially in Kahnawà:ke, Kanehsatá:ke, and Ahkwesáhsne. During the 1880s, non-Indigenous entrepreneur Frank Lally founded the Lally Lacrosse Company.[175] Later, to help satisfy the increasing demand for sticks, he built one of the earliest and largest stick-making factories in the world, hiring an Indigenous workforce from Ahkwesáhsne to staff its production line.[176]

Barring Indigenous individuals from non-Native teams also created the phenomenon known as the "Native ringer." A proficient Indigenous player who could pass as non-Indigenous, a ringer, was paid to compete for a non-Native team.[177] This exacerbated the issue of professionalism, which was further complicated by the introduction of the now coveted Minto Cup in 1901 and the Mann Cup in 1910.[178] Both trophies intensified the rivalry among Canadian clubs and encouraged the practice of paying players for their talents, some of whom were Native ringers.[179]

Despite the absence of Indigenous teams in Canadian lacrosse competitions, Indigenous athletes created their own Indian World Championship, and both Indigenous and non-Indigenous promoters used their Indian appeal to attract audiences to local exhibition games and national, continental, and international tours.[180] Indigenous teams remained in high demand and were still paid to play against non-Native organizations. In the late nineteenth century, the Canadian government even got into the act by using the game for its own political purposes. During its overseas immigration campaigns, the Department of Agriculture capitalized on the popularity of the lacrosse tours and of Indians in hopes of attracting British immigrants to Canada.[181] In 1883, it sponsored one of the largest lacrosse trips in history, using the Hodinöhsö:ni' players, led by Aiontonnis, as an attraction to help entice Europeans to immigrate to Canada.[182] A *New York Times* article titled "Lacrosse as an Advertisement" reflected on the tour as a selling point for Canada:

> From a lacrosse point of view, the tour will be of great importance. From a totally different stand-point it promises to be of great importance to the most vital interests of Canada, and as such demands attention. With lacrosse as its nominal object, the tour will have practically as its object the diffusion in the mother country of information regarding Canada as a home for immigrants and a field for capital, and the promoters of the enterprise have laid their plans with the aim and end of advertising Canada in Great Britain and Ireland.[183]

Once again, the ever-vocal nationalist W.G. Beers was involved with the tour, as an April 1883 letter to the Department of Agriculture noted: "Dr. Beers will undertake to afford a systematic distribution, at the gatherings which it is proposed to attract, of pamphlets and other information in reference to Canada, in relation to its advantages as a field for immigration."[184] A total of 150,000 leaflets were distributed among spectators at the games.[185] Don Morrow and Kevin Wamsley argue that the presence of Indigenous athletes constructed an image of Canada as a conquered, "tamed and civilized," land.[186] The strategy seems to have worked, despite the reality that Indigenous peoples were far from "conquered" or silent in challenging the dominion at home. Watching what they perceived as a contest between the civilized and the savage, non-Native audiences may have accepted this idea;

▲ The Canadian and Kahnawà:ke lacrosse teams during their 1883 tour. | *M2000.21.7.17, McCord Museum.*

▼ The Kahnawà:ke lacrosse team (dark shirts) in action against the Canadian team in 1883 in Clifton, England. | *M2000.21.7.23, McCord Museum.*

all the while Indigenous peoples – including the Hodinöhsö:ni' – continued to assert their self-determination in their territories through the rejection of Indian policies and maintained a long tradition of travelling to England to protest the dispossession of their lands and the interference of colonial authorities.[187] As Susan Hill has documented, the Hodinöhsö:ni' had been protesting the Indian Act – and associated Indian policies – since its inception and consistently asserted Hodinöhsö:ni' sovereignty recognized in treaties. The community of Six Nations alone sent over a dozen appeals to the Department of Indian Affairs between 1887 and 1920.[188] However, the 1883 tour's publicity was in the hands of the non-Indigenous lacrosse enthusiasts and was influenced heavily by federal authorities from the Department of Agriculture. As such, what they hoped to portray fell in line with their attempt to create something new – in place of what already existed – and within the logics of Canadian settler-colonialism. The *New York Times* reported that lacrosse, and the attraction of Indigenous athletes, enabled Ottawa to portray Canada as a perfect destination for immigrants, emphasizing the supposed transition from an uncultivated landscape and people – represented by the Indigenous presence – to civilized modernity of lacrosse and public buildings:

> The novelty of the game, as well as the reputed skill of the players, has attracted immense crowds to view the matches played in various parts of England and Scotland during the last two months. An effort has been made by the managers of the tour to impress upon the inhabitants of the crowded manufacturing districts of the mother country the idea that the game of lacrosse represents in some sort the freedom and picturesqueness of life in the Western world. Moreover, at each of the exhibitions, some of which have been attended by as many as 7,000 persons, the advantage gained by the awakening of a temporary interest in Canada has been utilized by the distribution of illustrated newspapers devoted to the praises of the Dominion and filled with pictures of the Canadian scenery and public buildings.[189]

The 1883 tour was just one instance in which lacrosse enthusiasts used the game to promote the resettlement of Canada and form an evolutionary narrative of its history, helping to further dispossess Indigenous peoples of their land. In the summer of 1886, an amateur team from Ireland visited Canada – its formation was the by-product of the 1876 and 1883 lacrosse tours – where it played the MLC and nearby Ontario and Quebec teams such as the St. Catharines Athletic Club.[190] Kahnawà:ke was quick to inform the MLC of its enthusiasm to play the Irish team.[191] For their part, Beers and government representatives used the opportunity to sell the Irish team copies of a guidebook that promoted immigration to Canada.[192]

At the turn of the century, the Hodinöhsö:ni' continued to travel throughout North America, earning compensation for their exibitions, but they were not the only Indigenous nation that continued to play the game, and they were also not alone in staging lacrosse performances for the consumption of non-Indigenous audiences. The *Chicago Daily Tribune* reported in 1885 that the Anishinaabeg (noted as Chippewa) of Bad River and Red Cliff, Wisconsin, drew a Chicago crowd of 1,200 as they demonstrated their variant of lacrosse.[193] In 1893, Chicago hosted a second game between two nations that used differing forms of the lacrosse stick. Playing before ten thousand spectators, a Hodinöhsö:ni' team from Six Nations took on a team of Bodéwadmik (Potawatomi), with each nation using its own stick type.[194]

Racialized Styles of Play

For the Hodinöhsö:ni', one of the more widely publicized exhibitions during this time occurred in the summer of 1900 between a team from Six Nations and a number of American university and club teams. Travelling from upstate New York to New York City, the Six Nations team played Hobart College, Stevens Institute, and the Staten Island Lacrosse Club, and it challenged Cornwell University and the Rochester Rangers during its return trip to Ontario.[195] These exhibitions were a small piece of a longstanding relationship established between the Hodinöhsö:ni', mainly the Onönda'gega', and American universities such as Hobart College and Syracuse University.[196]

Aside from the attraction of Indigenous athletes as a curiosity, Indigenous teams were recognized as unparalleled lacrosse players by club and collegiate teams throughout the world. In part, the appeal of playing against Indigenous teams was due to their high level of skill, but such matches also enabled comparisons between "white and civilized" and "Indian and savage" racialized styles of play. This is clearly stated in the *New York Times* coverage of the 1900 tour. Describing an upcoming game between Stevens Institute and the Hodinöhsö:ni' team, the paper looked forward to the clash between two alleged styles: "Lacrosse was originally an Indian game, and the Brantford Indians are considered the best players of the Six Nations, so that their meeting with a representative college team will offer an opportunity for an interesting comparison of the *aboriginal and the civilized playing of the game.*[197] Remarks concerning "white" and "Indian" play are common in Beers's *Lacrosse: The National Game of Canada* (1869) and certainly predated that work in the overstated accounts of violence in lacrosse games, as written by early missionaries. The style of play developed by non-Indigenous athletes was explicitly associated with being "scientific," as a *New York Times* article reflected in 1886:

> In 1867, Lacrosse in those days was not the pretty, scientific game it has now become. It was a grand knock-down and drag-out, rough-and-tumble fighting affair, played with many casualties by the Canadian Indians. When the whites began the game and faced the Indians their more civilized souls revolted against cold-blooded attempts to maim and hurt. Consequently they were at a disadvantage with their red rivals.[198]

The new style of play was also in harmony with the pursuit of Victorian athleticism and masculinity. An 1875 letter to the editor stated that "lacrosse is *not* a rough and tumble game when *properly* played. It is essentially graceful and scientific and calls into play all a man's faculties, including those of his brain."[199] Although Indigenous peoples were racialized as superior athletic specimens with extraordinary strength and endurance, they were also seen as simple-minded. Thus, they could never master the non-Native version of lacrosse, with its sophistication and efficiency. As Beers explained,

> We may wish for the hereditary sagacity of the Indian, who plays mainly by instinct ... but the Indian never can play as scientifically as the best white players, and it is a lamentable fact, that Lacrosse, and the wind for running, which comes as natural to the red-skin as his dialect, has to be gained on the part of the pale-face, by a gradual course of practice and training.[200]

These race-based fantasies, which were not grounded in Indigenous cultural or historical practice, say far more about perceptions of whiteness than about the realities of Indigenous participation in the game. In portraying Indigenous peoples as uncivilized and bloodthirsty, Beers and other enthusiasts produced a skewed interpretation of Indigenous lacrosse, linking it with violence, lawlessness, and warfare[201] – this in spite of the fact that one of the game's central teachings, specifically from a Hodinöhsö:ni' understanding, is about dispute resolution.

As Robidoux explains, lacrosse was positioned at, and beyond, the "frontier" of acceptable physicality in European sporting practices such as cricket and curling – and their perceptions of acceptable masculinity – that was especially attractive to early French settlers.[202] For Anglo-Canadians, the physical nature of the game, when controlled by non-Native rules and institutions, was thought to reflect the qualities of settler Canadians and to re-create British Victorian values, complete with their socially constructed perceptions of acceptable physicality.[203] Indigenous games that predated Beers's standardized rules were not without regulations and certainly had a socio-political complexity that fit within Indigenous ideas of physicality. Although oral tradition does mention rough play, and popular news accounts of both Indigenous and non-Indigenous games report episodes of violence (such as illegal stick swinging, body checks, and fighting), the oral traditions of the Hodinöhsö:ni' and other Indigenous nations warn against overly rough play and the results of engaging in it.[204] Stories such as "Power Received from Thunderer," "The Creator's Game," and "The Great Ball Game" (told in Chapter 5) provide an understanding of lacrosse that is removed from the bloodthirsty savage portrayals. Although "Power Received from Thunderer" contains episodes of violence, it demonstrates that the game was meant to be physical within acceptable limits (such as body checking). More importantly, it is a reminder – at least in my interpretation – that crossing those limits and playing in a disrespectful manner has consequences. Knots in trees are tokens of that.

By 1900, despite mismanagement and the debates about professionalism, lacrosse had seemingly become a permanent and popular fixture in Canadian culture. In 1904, it made its first appearance at the Olympic Games, as part of the World's Fair in St. Louis, Missouri.[205] Three teams participated, including the Shamrock Lacrosse Club of Winnipeg, the St. Louis Amateur Athletic Association, and a team – probably Kanien'kehá:ka – from Six Nations. This was one of the few times in over a century that an Indigenous team was included in an official international championship competition. Prior to travelling to St. Louis, the Six Nations team paraded through the streets of Chicago, meeting spectators. The team then played a game before a crowd of over a thousand, ultimately going down to defeat.[206]

At the World's Fair, the lacrosse matches drew a small crowd and saw the Shamrock Lacrosse Club defeat the St. Louis club to take the gold medal.[207] The Six Nations team won the bronze medal, but little coverage of the event appeared in the media.[208] At the fair, the team also drew the curious, as described by Tom Hill, retired director at the Woodland Cultural Centre Museum in Brantford, Ontario, in the film *Lacrosse: The Creator's Game,* "My grandfather played and he played lacrosse with the team from Six Nations that ended up going to the World's Fair in St. Louis at the turn of the century. When they arrived there, many of the people arriving at the fair were more fascinated with the fact that these were Iroquoian Indians or Iroquoian savages."[209] Despite the original written record stating that there was only one team from Six Nations, a second Six Nations team is documented in a series of photographs from the competition – possibly an exhibition team that did not compete officially. While the official team from Six Nations represented Canada in the competition and wore the Canadian jersey, the second team is pictured with the Iroquois jersey.

Within the span of twenty years, since the popular practice of lacrosse had been infused into Canadian communities during the 1860s, Canadians had come to perceive the game as part of their own identity, part of the "ideal" characteristics with which they wanted to replace Indigenous cultures. The game was now deemed a manly pursuit of white middle-class Canadians. The issues of professionalism and the barring of Indigenous peoples, who were relegated as Others, were ignored. The new form of the game, organizations, and rules were all signifiers, at least to Canadians, that lacrosse had been tamed and that it embodied the triumph of civilization over savagery, Christianity over heathenism, and the colonizer over the colonized. Beers, among others, helped frame and define the original game within Western frameworks of sport that he precieved as having no spiritual or holistic significance. A prime example of this appears in Beers's description of the original Indigenous game:

> It was not played as a superstitious rite in honor of the Great Spirit; it had none of the religious element of the Grecian games. It was instituted as a pure amusement, and as one of the means of quickening and strengthening the body, and accustoming the young warriors to close combat. It was emphatically a sport, and brought out the very finest physical attributes of the finest made men in the world, – the impetuosity and vigor of a wild nature let loose.[210]

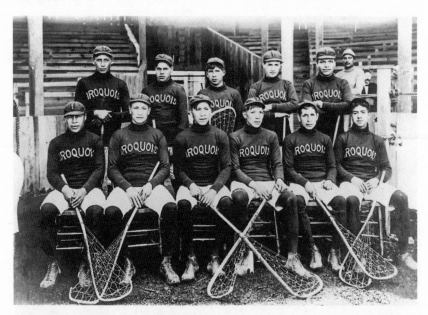

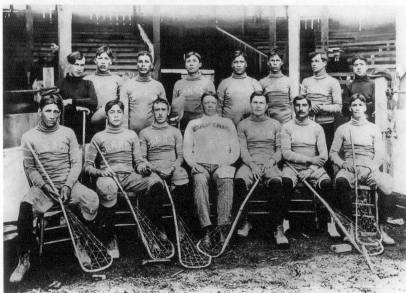

"St. Louis, Missouri – Six Nations team." Both photographs are undated but are almost certainly photos of the 1904 Hodinöhsö:ni' Olympic team(s). While the written record states that there was only one Hodinöhsö:ni' team, it is possible that there were enough players to make up two separate teams, one being an "exhibition" team that did not appear in the record. Also, note that one team is wearing Iroquois jerseys, while the other team is representing Canada as noted in the media coverage. | *Woodland Cultural Centre.*

Whereas Western culture perceived the practice of sport as a secular activity – while still using it as a vehicle to promote Muscular Christianity, as discussed in the following chapter – the Hodinöhsö:ni' saw their game within the realms of their epistemology and as a gift from the Creator.[211] To Canadians, Indigenous peoples were seen as static, and thus their participation in the modern game was participation in a *Canadian game*. What Canadian enthusiasts failed to realize was that while the implementation of rules and creation of Canadian lacrosse organizations might have signified a claim to lacrosse as a Canadian pursuit in their eyes, Indigenous communities adopted those same organizational developments as their own without relinquishing their ownership to the game. The fact that Beers and others helped to popularize lacrosse and introduced a new code of rules did not mean that Indigenous peoples released their ownership of the game or saw it as a non-Indigenous form – quite the contrary.[212]

∾

By the early twentieth century, lacrosse had become one of Canada's principal sports and its national, though unofficial, game. Its popularity spoke volumes regarding how far the Indigenous game had come from the first contest between Indigenous and non-Indigenous athletes in 1844 to the creation of national organizations in the name of representing a Canadian identity at home and abroad. Although influential Montrealers appropriated the game and associated it with the virtues of Victorian sport and society, it was plagued by organizational dysfunction, debates concerning professionalism, and the rise of other sports, such as baseball, that challenged its popularity. Paying the price for this were the originators of the game and the Indigenous peoples who introduced and celebrated it among non-Natives.

Despite this, Indigenous peoples cleverly found a way of capitalizing on the situation by using, adapting, and manipulating their own cultural identities and claim to the game. Moreover, though they adopted the new standardized rules, their participation in the sport was never defined by their ability to play within the non-Native systems of organization, and lacrosse retained its central significance in their epistemologies, as we will see. Following the 1880 ban of Indigenous players, the Hodinöhsö:ni' continued to play the game among themselves while engaging in exhibition matches against non-Natives. To claim that it had now crossed a threshold and was a purely Canadian game was to believe that Indigenous peoples were noninfluential in its systematic reorganization. Lacrosse was still played "in" the

Longhouse, and Indigenous peoples adopted the new rules and organizations – while they could – as a development of their original sport. To Canadians, the introduction of the new rules equated with civilizing the game, and though Indigenous peoples did adopt the rules and did not resist incorporating the changes introduced by non-Natives, Indigenous athletes did not see lacrosse as a Canadian game. Nor did they relinquish ownership. They saw the changes as a renewal of their original game, just one of many that had occurred over the centuries. Organized sport, rules, and organizations made practical sense, created uniformity that both Indigenous and non-Indigenous athletes could abide by, and helped grow the game as a combined effort between both Indigenous and settler societies – whether Canadian enthusiasts saw it that way or not.[213] The Canadian appropriation of lacrosse would continue at the turn of the century. The idea that lacrosse was a Canadian game and that it represented national distinctiveness had significant consequences for Indigenous peoples. It became so ingrained, so powerful, in the dominant society that it was soon used as a means of assimilating Indigenous children at residential schools.

2

Colonizing the Creator's Game in Residential Schools

>>> *Kâ-têpwêt, or Kâ-têpwêt-Sîpiy (Qu'Appelle River Valley,*
Saskatchewan) February 1889[1]

"There's no one to play with," 'Usdas complains. Unable to find any children, 'Usdas walks down to the frozen pond, running into an old friend, Turtle.

"Hey 'Usdas, what are you up to?" Turtle asks.

"I was hoping to find some other kids down here to play with, but I can't find anyone. Have you seen them?"

"Oh, you're always looking to play games, but they aren't here. They're at the school in Lebret."

"All of them?"

"Almost all of them. They're all gone – at least, the ones who aren't in hiding. They went to the big white school to learn how to read and write. Well, the trick is on the teacher, they already know how to write – you know that written language the Nêhiyawak have had for centuries.[2] The teachers told everyone that the school would help Indians survive in the new world, but I'm not so sure."

Metawewin is the Nêhiyawak Nation's word for a game of any kind of sport, including lacrosse. Thomas Vennum notes that lacrosse can also be referred to as *pakahatowan*, meaning "a ball for games." *Online Cree Dictionary, Miyo Wahkohtowin Community Education Authority*, http://www.creedictionary.com/search/index.php?q=metawewin &scope=1&cwr=54115; Thomas Vennum, *Lacrosse Legends of the First Americans* (Baltimore: Johns Hopkins University Press, 2007), 3.

"Sounds like fun, sounds like there are probably a lot of tricks being played. I bet they have a ton of games there too!"

"Haven't you been listening? It's not that kind of school! It's a place where the adults are playing tricks, horrible tricks!"

"Well, it must be better than being here alone. Will you play a game with me?" 'Usdas' face lights with delight at the thought of having someone to play with. "I have a great idea, follow me."

Following 'Usdas onto the ice, Turtle begins to get the feeling that something is up. Just then, 'Usdas flips Turtle on their back and begins swatting them around the ice.

Laughing hysterically, 'Usdas yells, "See Turtle, Indian hockey!³ 'Usdas fakes left, fakes right, winds up!" Turtle spins uncontrollably, bracing for the hit. *Whack!* "'Usdas scores and the crowd goes wild!" 'Usdas yells as Turtle scoots across the ice like a spinning top.

"'Usdas! Get over here, now!" Principal Hugonnard hollers from the road.⁴

Stunned by the voice on the shoreline, 'Usdas sprints over, wide-eyed. Reaching the towering figure and sliding to a halt, 'Usdas murmurs, "Yes, sir?"

"I've been looking for you. What are you doing down here? All the children are supposed to be at the school. Get in the wagon, I'll take you there."

"You mean I get to go to school with all the other kids?" 'Usdas asks in excitement. Before the principal can agree, 'Usdas jumps into the front and grabs the reins. "Come on, let's go, let's go!"

As the wagon rolls up the drive, 'Usdas quickly realizes that the school isn't what they expected; it isn't what 'Usdas thought. It was a trick. The trees along the drive sway and creak in the wind as they approach the grey building. The violence radiating from this place is unmistakable, and yet it is undercut by a beautiful Nêhiyawak resistance at all levels. In the distance, 'Usdas can see the children, their hair cut off and all wearing the same dull uniform. 'Usdas knows that something isn't right, something is amiss. The children aren't doing anything except working and praying, and many of them are sick. But this sparks an idea.

"Maybe if I show them my new game, they will let us play it," 'Usdas thinks. Jumping up and down, 'Usdas yells out, "Come quick, follow me!"

Gathering in anticipation, the students follow 'Usdas and rush down to the frozen river. Principal Hugonnard trails behind them. At the riverbank, 'Usdas comes across a familiar sight, a relative of Turtle's.

"Hey Turtle, can you come over here for a second? I want to show you a game." 'Usdas chuckles sadistically.

The students burst into laughter as they watch 'Usdas swat Turtle back and forth across the ice. They quickly join in and play their first game of Indian hockey.

Out of breath and giggling uncontrollably, one of the children says, "'Usdas! 'Usdas! This is so much fun. Maybe they will let us play some more games, and we won't have to work and pray so much!"

Watching from a distance and waiting for the game to conclude, Principal Hugonnard is contemplating the future.

"'Usdas," he says, "what a great idea. We can use sports to help teach these children the proper ways of civilized conduct. But I wonder, what will we do when the ice melts?"

"Well, lucky for you, I packed my lacrosse stick."

THE DEPARTMENT OF AGRICULTURE'S sponsorship of the 1883 tour of Britain initiated the Canadian government's use of lacrosse to promote its policies. It also marked one of the first times the state used its manipulating influence on the game and ushered in a new era in which the sport became a tool for the governing of Indigenous nations. By the 1890s, sport, including lacrosse, had increasingly become an assimilation tool in Canada's Indian residential schools, but this story is not well known. Even historian J.R. Miller's otherwise thorough *Shingwauk's Vision* overlooks the game: "In spite of the fact that equipment for it was inexpensive, that fields on which to play it were easily laid out, and that it held the potential to provide physical activity for large numbers of students, lacrosse apparently was not played in residential schools. The omission spoke volumes."[5] In fact, lacrosse was played in residential schools, and thus its *inclusion* speaks volumes. The claim to a national sport and the notion that lacrosse represented a civilized Canadian identity became so pervasive that it was used to further cultural genocide at residential schools.

Examining the methodical control of lacrosse by Canadian agencies between 1880 and 1930, including by residential schools and the Department of Indian Affairs, this chapter argues that the perception of lacrosse as a symbol of Canadian identity had critical implications for Indigenous peoples.[6] Here an Indigenous game, an important cultural and spiritual element, was reworked and deemed Euro-Canadian enough for use in the assimilation of Indigenous children. Despite this, however, lacrosse was often a high point in an otherwise dismal school experience, and it created a long-term mechanism for Indigenous communities to redefine their time at the schools. It also enabled nations such as the Sḵwx̱wú7mesh to reform their identities and nationhood, both locally and in a pan-Indigenous context. The story of lacrosse at residential schools is a powerful illustration of how competing groups can claim a source of identity as their own.

The development of residential schools began with the crusade of religious organizations to convert and "civilize" Indigenous peoples in Canada.[7] As early as 1879, the Department of Indian Affairs adopted the policy of systematically funding residential schools in the pursuit of "civilizing" Indigenous peoples and assimilating them into Canadian society. In *A National Crime*, historian John S. Milloy observes,

> The school system grew almost without planning or restraint and was, as a whole, constantly underfunded ... This rapid growth [1879–1923] was not evidence of the energetic application by the Department of a developmental strategy based upon careful forethought. There was ... no master plan. In fact, it was not until 1911 that the Department exercised significant leadership in setting out, by means of contracts with the churches, a comprehensive management of structure for the system.[8]

Similarly, the implementation of sport in residential schools got off to an inauspicious start. Throughout the 1880s and 1890s, as indicated in the Department of Indian Affairs annual reports, sport was steadily incorporated in residential schools across the country. Often, the initiatives of local school administrators, rather than any concrete government strategy, determined what recreational activities were offered.[9] Although the use of sport as an assimilation device did not become universal policy until 1949, as Janice Forsyth points out, sport nonetheless became a significant element in numerous residential school programs.[10]

Motivating Factors

Sports and recreational activities were offered at residential schools for numerous reasons. They were a fun way to break up the monotony of school life, they provided a physical outlet for students, and they also developed into a cost-effective means – even if unsuccessful – of improving student health.[11] However, a key motivation for their introduction, as reflected in Department of Indian Affairs reports, was the desire to introduce Indigenous youth to Western Muscular Christian ideas about progress, civility, morality, gender, language, and, of course, nationalism. In her study of Native American federal boarding schools, K. Tsianina Lomawaima observes,

> Using a curriculum that emphasized piety, obedience, and manual labor, these schools aimed to transform the Indian child. The essential transformation would be internal, a matter of Christian belief, non-tribal identification, mental discipline, and moral elevation. For female students, that meant training for domesticity; for male students, it meant instruction in semiskilled trades and agriculture. The regimentation of the external body was the essential sign of a new life, of a successful transformation.[12]

The attempts to reform the minds of students could, and did, have a devastating and lingering impact. As Kamloops Indian Residential School survivor "E.L." recalled in Agnes Jack's book *Behind Close Doors*:

> They stripped us of everything. Gave us brown uniforms and a number. And they put what they wanted in us, made us ashamed of who we are. Even right to this day, it still affects me. Like I really want to get into Indian things and I just can't because of them telling us it was of the devil ... Everything was of the devil. Stick games [Indigenous gambling games played with small sticks] were of the devil and even used to scare me when I used to watch them. And it still affects me, right to today.[13]

At the residential schools, occupational training was divided according to the Euro-Canadian gender binary where boys undertook vocational training in farming, a trade, or industrial work, whereas girls were instructed in the domestic role. But administrators also pushed for a complete eradication of their Indigenous epistemologies with the intention of instilling Western understandings of morality and of civilized life.[14] Principal Joseph Hugonnard of the Qu'Appelle Industrial School remarked in 1892,

> Much attention is paid to moral training, which must have a prominent part in the civilizing of Indian children to make it effective. To teach them only to read, write and speak English, would otherwise be productive of very little good, if it did not tend to make them worse. This moral training must be imported to the pupils continuously, from morning to night; and requires a considerable amount of self-denial and restraint.[15]

Sport and recreation loaned themselves to this endeavour in a way that reached beyond religious and vocational training. Historian Colin Howell explains that sport in the nineteenth century was seen as a vehicle for the integration of Indigenous peoples and new Canadians into the dominant society and the "new national order."[16] Superintendent General of Indian Affairs E. Dewdney reported in 1890 that recreation furnished an additional source of control at residential schools:

> In this respect the boarding school or Industrial institution has a great advantage over the day school, as the children, kept at a school of either of the former classes, are constantly under the control of those in charge of the institution; even the recreation allowed them being turned into a method of instruction to them at some specially well ordered establishments.[17]

To school administrators, sports such as cricket, football (soccer), and boxing were ideal introductions to Euro-Canadian culture and whiteness. As the inspector of Protestant industrial schools reported in 1888 concerning the Battleford Industrial School:

> A noticeable feature of this school is its games. They are all thoroughly and distinctly "white." The boys use the boxing gloves with notable science, and excellent temper, and play good games of cricket and football, with great interest and truly Anglo-Saxon vigor. The girls

The cricket team from Battleford Indian
Industrial School, c. 1895. | *PA-182265, Library
and Archives Canada.*

dress, make fancy articles of dress, and play such games as white children do. From all their recreations Indianism is excluded.[18]

Shortly afterward, this inspector would also implement lacrosse into school
programs as a further example of "whiteness" and Canadian nationalism.

The use of sport and recreation at boarding schools in the United States,
Lomawaima argues, emphasized the complete reformation of Indigenous
children and "reflected racist conceptions of the intrinsic link between
uncivilized minds and undeveloped bodies."[19] The same is true of Canadian residential schools. Although the use of recreation was not an official
state policy, the link between organized sport, recreation, and civility quickly
found a place, as Inspector T.P. Wadsworth reflected in 1889 at Battleford,
Saskatchewan:

> I cannot express myself in terms too praiseworthy of Mr. and Mrs.
> Ashby, the assistant Principal and governess; they are not only as
> siduous and indefatigable in instilling into the children's untutored
> minds the rudiments of education, but they gain their confidence by
> entering into their little lives, engaging with them during the hours
> of recreation, in sports and pastimes, such as cricket, baseball, boxing,
> swings, lawn tennis, croquet. Their object is to make the children

Carcross School boys playing football (soccer) against the crew of the streamer *Tutshi*, c. 1920s, Carcross, Yukon. |
P7538–604, General Synod Archives, Anglican Church of Canada.

feel that they are not different from white children; and, by interesting them in these games, to wean them from their wild habits and traditions.[20]

Across the country, institution after institution rejoiced at the prospects of using recreation to expose Indigenous children to non-Native youth, the dominant society, and the virtues of civilization.[21] By the early to mid-1890s, administrators had begun to permit their teams to participate in outside competitions and were inviting non-Indigenous athletes to visit the schools, thereby increasing the contact between Indigenous children and Canadian youth. One institution, the Wikwemikong Indian Residential School, even accepted non-Indigenous students to further this effort: "Besides Indians, some white children have been admitted; as they speak English their intercourse with the others will help very much in introducing more and more among all the use of that language."[22] If Indigenous students had increased opportunities to associate with Canadian youth, who sometimes attended as day-school students, through activities such as sports, the schools would be more effective in their assimilation scheme. Calgary Industrial School principal George H. Hogbin reported in 1897,

```
School routine is as follows :—
    Pupils rise.............................................  5.30
    Chapel.....................................................  6.00
    Bedmaking, washing, milking and pumping.........  6.30 to  7.15
    Inspection of pupils in the school rooms to see if
        they are clean and properly dressed, their con-
        dition, health &c., a note being taken of those
        requiring attention, if of clothes, this is done by
        the sister directly after dinner.....................  7.15 to  7.30
    Breakfast................................................  7.30
    Fatigue for small boys.......................  8.60 to  9.00
    Trade boys go to work........................  8.00
    School with 15 minutes recess..............  9.00 to 12.00
    Prepare for dinner.............................  12.00 to 12.10
    Dinner...................................................  12.10 to 12.40
    Recreation..............................................  12.40 to  2.00
    School and Trades .................................  2.00 to  4.00
    Fatigue, such as milking, carrying coal, ashes, filling
        tanks, wood boxes, pumping, sweeping.........  4.45 to  6.00
    Prepare for supper.................................  6.00 to  6.10
    Supper....................................................  6.10 to  6.40
    Recreation .............................................  6.40 to  8.00
    Prayer and retire .....................................  8.00
```

Sunday.

After breakfast the usual fatigues and dressing and preparing for church parade, and march to parish church; dinner at the usual hour, immediately after dinner a parade of the whole school for the doctor's inspection—then

```
    Recreation until .......................................  2.30
    Vespers ...................................................  2.30
```

The children form the choir of the church; after vespers the pupils change their clothes and do the necessary fatigues. From 5 to 6 every Sunday evening the prin-

An 1893 sample student schedule from the Qu'Appelle Industrial School. | Dominion of Canada, T.P. Wadsworth, Annual Report of the Department of Indian Affairs for the Year Ended 31st December 1893 *(Ottawa: Department of Indian Affairs, 1894),* 173, Library and Archives Canada.

I must record here the thanks which are due to the various football teams in this district who have taken the trouble and expense to come here and play with the boys from time to time. The effect is most marked; the boys take a pride in thinking they are treated like human beings, and the indirect education they acquire from mixing and contact with white people is incalculable.[23]

The Calgary Industrial School (Alberta), Qu'Appelle Industrial School (Saskatchewan), Elkhorn Industrial School (Manitoba), St. Boniface Industrial School (Manitoba), and Shingwauk Home (Ontario) were just a few of the schools that competed in outside matches and leagues in sports such as cricket, soccer, and hockey at the turn of the twentieth century.[24] Not only were such teams competing in outside venues, they were winning local championships as well. For example, the Elkhorn Industrial School won the soccer championship of western Manitoba in 1895.[25] By 1899, students had won three successive district soccer championships against non-Native teams and once again competed for the championship of Manitoba.[26] Being good at sports often had a number of benefits for students. It enabled them to escape the daily grind of vocational training and religious education, to travel to nearby towns and larger urban centres for games, and sometimes to receive special treatment such as outside dinners or activities.[27]

Throughout the 1880s and 1890s, recreation becomes increasingly visible in the reports of school administrators, as does the fact that each school's recreational program was tied to local initiatives. Activities varied from institution to institution and were often subject to local circumstance (such as the existence of ponds, rivers, or fields for skating rinks), as well as fields for cricket, baseball, soccer, and lacrosse, and facilities for indoor games, calisthenics, and gymnastics. On weekdays, the Qu'Appelle Industrial School had twice-daily recreation periods along with a fifteen-minute recess, a total of three hours a day, as well as after church and religious education on Sundays.[28] Similarly, the Shingwauk Home in Sault Ste. Marie, Ontario, had three hours of recreation each weekday and six hours on Saturdays.[29] Given that students attended school for approximately five hours a day, recreation formed a significant part of their lives. However, some school administrators saw it as an obstacle in the civilizing process, substantiating the point that recreation had more to do with provisional implementation by local administrations than with national policy. This point is further supported by Braden Paora Te Hiwi's analysis of the Pelican Lake Indian Residential School, in which he found that this ad-hoc policy continued well into the first half of the twentieth century.[30] For instance, as Elizabeth Graham recounts in her book *The Mush Hole,* the principal of the Mount Elgin Institute in Ontario took an active stance against recreation in 1920:

> We never seek to lead a child away from the church of its parents into the Methodist Church, but we do most earnestly seek to teach them to be true Christians and good Canadians. Many of them are both ... Amusements do not receive so large a place in the life of this, as some other schools, largely because we are seeking to develop a balanced life. Perhaps the Indian's greatest handicap is his readiness to drop his work and seek amusement. Everyone knows that a job that is worth holding must be held continuously. Here the Indian fails, and we are earnestly seeking by precept and example to break him of this habit. Yet each of the pupils is given several hours of recreation each day; skating and tobogganing in the winter, baseball and basketball in the summer, are their favorite pastimes.[31]

A major undertaking was getting the children to speak English during recreation and moving them away from their own languages. Principal T. Clarke despairingly reported, "During work and school hours, they can be induced to converse in English to a certain extent, but, at recreation, they invariably speak their native language."[32] At Wikwemikong (Ontario), Principal D. Duronquet also acknowledged the difficulty of getting the children to discard their language during recreation hours: "Neither did we make any progress in bringing the boys to speak English in recreation, nevertheless we do not abandon the undertaking and hope eventually to succeed."[33]

Administrators also stressed the importance of Western gender roles for Indigenous youth and used sport to introduce them.[34] Historian J.R. Miller notes,

> However deeply embedded and no matter how taken for granted, the ways in which people perceived the aptitudes, roles, and destinies of females and males profoundly influenced the operation of these institutions. And, eventually, both the Native people who were the objects of the schools' program and many of the members of the missionary staffs came to appreciate the presence and power of gender.[35]

Like the curriculum at residential schools, which slotted boys and girls into a Euro-Canadian gender binary, recreational activities were also infused with "idyllic" Victorian gender constructions, and each sex was assigned what were seen as appropriate games.[36] Discussing the Navajo Nation's residential school experience, Eric D. Anderson observes that sport played a key role in masculinizing boys: "With these schools came the structure and culture of colonial sports. Sports such as football, basketball, baseball and boxing were thought to produce qualities desirable to the colonizers, in that they represent masculinized territorialization through struggle and triumph against others."[37] Although some schools encouraged both sexes to play sports such as baseball and later basketball, administrators often limited their attention to boys and the "masculinizing project" – using sport to transform them into men.[38] Nancy Bouchier explains that sport, and specifically lacrosse, was used in Canada at the time to expose children to "respectable versions of masculinity while teaching them the importance of physical activity for their physical and spiritual health in an increasingly sedentary world."[39] This was something that administrators hoped to replicate in the

Alert Bay School Junior Soccer Team,
1933. | *P7538–109, General Synod Archives,*
Anglican Church of Canada.

residential schools. Principal John B. Ashby of Rupert's Land Industrial School in Manitoba argued that not only did recreation help instill the English language into students but it also facilitated their performance of gender identities, especially in the inculcation of Western notions of masculinity.[40] Principal Ashby reflected, "In the summer the boys' chief recreations are cricket and football; these they play in an effective and gentlemanly manner ... I believe their games have been a great factor in making them manly, in teaching them to speak out, and in civilizing them."[41] Western gender roles were embedded at every level in these institutions, including sport.

Whereas boys could engage in lacrosse, soccer, cricket, military drill, and hockey, girls were often reported as playing croquet, skating, skipping, going for walks, and dancing – all approved feminine pursuits.[42] They were often confined to activities that were seen as genteel and lady-like. Here, too, gender segregation in sports and recreation depended on local circumstance rather than official policy. At some schools, the sexes pursued separate athletic and recreational activities, whereas at others, girls could play soccer, baseball, and hockey.[43] At the turn of the twentieth century, basketball became increasingly popular among female students.[44] In one instance at the Mohawk Institute in Ontario, students resisted gender segregation policies,

▲▲ Sports Day thread the needle race at St. Peter's Indian Residential School (Hay River, Northwest Territories), June 23, 1936. | *P2008-01-0158, General Synod Archives, Anglican Church of Canada.*

▲ Girls participate in Sports Day at St. Peter's Indian Residential School in Lesser Slave Lake, Alberta, May 24, 1930. | *M2006-08-P782, General Synod Archives, Anglican Church of Canada.*

sometimes by passing notes in class, which prompted the school to desegregate its recreational activities. One of the Mohawk Institute's quarterly reports for 1923, as compiled by Graham in *The Mush Hole*, stated,

> We have been able to give more attention to sports this summer and many games have been played between the different divisions in the

school. The best ball games have been those between the boys and girls teams. The boys have the stronger team but our girls have been playing a very sporting game. This scheme of mixing the boys and girls on the playing field has had a very desirable influence on the school and such things as the passing of notes from boy to girl or girl to boy has not been heard of for some time. We find that by making the whole school play to-gether that they soon divide and the boys begin to play alone and the girls play their games, forgetful entirely of the boys.[45]

Lacrosse as an Assimilative Device

By the turn of the twentieth century, sports and recreation were playing a significant role in residential schools across Canada and the United States. Evidence suggests that the Canadian schools were years ahead of their American counterparts in implementing lacrosse as an assimilative device. One of the first references to the use of lacrosse at a Canadian residential school appears in an 1889 Department of Indian Affairs summary of school expenditures, which recorded that the Qu'Appelle Industrial School spent $11.66 on sticks and balls.[46] Following suit, the Battleford Industrial School, also in Saskatchewan, had put lacrosse in place by at least 1890.[47] Although the use of middle-class sports in the residential school agenda is significant, lacrosse is a particularly important case and an anomaly because of its Indigenous roots.

From Ontario to British Columbia – with the exception of Alberta – administrators had begun to introduce lacrosse into residential schools by the late nineteenth century and were referring to it in their annual reports. In Ontario, the reports of the Mohawk Institute, the Shingwauk Home, the Kenora Boarding School, and the Fort Frances Boarding School all mention lacrosse.[48] In Manitoba, the Elkhorn and Brandon Industrial Schools also incorporated lacrosse in their programs, as did the Regina Industrial School and the Battleford Industrial School in Saskatchewan.[49] Qu'Appelle Industrial School's principal, Joseph Hugonnard, regretfully reported in 1894 that the school grounds were too small for a lacrosse field, but the school did have lacrosse sticks.[50] In British Columbia, lacrosse was played at St. Mary's Mission Boarding School (also known as St. Mary's or Mission Indian Residential School) in Mission, the Squamish Indian Residential School (also known as St. Paul's Indian Residential School) in North Vancouver, the Sechelt Boarding School, and the Kootenay Industrial School (also known as St. Eugene's) in Cranbrook.[51] Although this list is not exhaustive and draws primarily from the annual reports of residential schools rather than reports for day schools, it shows that lacrosse was a significant feature of residential school recreation. The United States also used the game for assimilation.[52] In short, the introduction of lacrosse in residential schools was seen as a measure and an implementation of civilization. As the Report of the Royal Commission on Aboriginal Peoples later reflected, sport, and by extension lacrosse, was a means of reformation:

> In school, in chapel, at work and even at play the children were to learn the Canadian way. Recreation was re-creation. Games and activities would not be the "boisterous and unorganized game" of "savage" youth. Rather they were to have brass bands, football, cricket, baseball and above all hockey "with the well regulated and ... strict rules that govern our modern games," prompting "obedience to discipline" and thus contributing to the process of moving the children along the path to civilization.[53]

In appropriating an Indigenous element in the name of nation building, Canadians simultaneously denied that its refashioning – after the introduction of standardized rules – was the result of Indigenous influence; their game was seen as a thing of the past, and subsequently witnessed an "evolution." Modern lacrosse was not perceived as arising from the shared history or experiences between Indigenous peoples and settlers. Canadians deemed it an authentic aspect of Euro-Canadian identity rather than an infusion of two cultural identities.

For their part, the Department of Indian Affairs and residential school administrators used the Indigenous game to help eliminate the very cultures from which it had been appropriated. If Canadians could civilize a savage game and transform it into a beacon of their national identity, in turn "saving it from extinction," why couldn't they do the same with Indigenous children? Within the span of thirty years, the game – according to lacrosse enthusiasts and residential school administrators – had been stripped of its "Indianness" and was considered safe enough, in other words westernized enough, to service the assimilation of Indigenous youth. As Beers noted in 1869,

> The present game, improved and reduced to rule by the whites, employs the greatest combination of physical and mental activity white men can sustain in recreation and is as much superior to the original

as civilization is to barbarism, base ball to its old English parent of rounders, or a pretty Canadian girl to any uncultivated squaw ... It has no elaborate nomenclature to make it puzzling; its science and beauty need but eyes for discovery.[54]

Beers propagated this idea as early as 1869, but the Canadian government's 1883 immigration scheme (advanced by the Department of Agriculture through the lacrosse tour of Britain) and the residential school administrators' use of lacrosse demonstrate just how powerful this notion of a national identity had become. Further to the point, one of the first significant reflections on lacrosse in residential schools was written in 1893 by the principal of the Regina Industrial School, A.J. McLeod, who explained the perceived Canadian ownership of the game:

> The most popular game in which the boys indulge is the *"national game of lacrosse,"* for which their fleetness of foot and keenness of eye soon make them most formidable opponents. Two things helped popularize the game with our pupils; first, the complete suits that from one source and another we were able to give members of the first twelve, and secondly, a brilliant victory they gained over a strong team of boys and young men from Regina. This match took place on the occasion of our annual picnic, in which we joined forces with the members of Knox Church Sabbath School, and spent a most enjoyable day in the Qu'Appelle Valley, twenty-five miles away.[55]

Clearly, the idea of lacrosse as Canadian had become so deeply ingrained in the dominant society that school administrators adopted the game as a quintessential example of Canadian nationality. Similarly, at the turn of the century, the Regina Industrial School placed a significant emphasis on sport. Principal J.A. Sinclair noted in 1901 that

> football continues to be the most popular game among the boys, although lacrosse had its turn this season. Good success has attended them in their various matches, and what was better, they won the reputation of playing a notably clean game. Not only for the sake of the outdoor exercise involved, but because of the moral value of manly games as educators, we give such sports all possible encouragements.[56]

Students playing field hockey or lacrosse, Cariboo Indian Residential School, Williams Lake, British Columbia, 1949. | *Canada, Department of Indian and Northern Affairs, e011080297_s2, Library and Archives Canada.*

Like many others, Sinclair saw the value of using recreation, specifically lacrosse, for the assimilation of Indigenous youth.

Lacrosse was not the only Indigenous cultural element that was used in the residential school system. A number of schools and administrators across Canada encouraged the use of Indigenous elements, language, traditions, and culture in the "education" of Indigenous youth and sometimes portrayed these traditions in a positive light.[57] The difference here, however, was that administrators were claiming lacrosse as their own and as an aspect of Canadian identity. Even for the Nêhiyawak children who attended Qu'Appelle in Saskatchewan, forms of lacrosse were not unfamiliar to their nation.[58] Nêhiyawak women played We Pitisowewepahikan, or double ball.[59] As in lacrosse, players were not allowed to touch the ball with their hands and used sticks to toss it between them as they struggled to score a goal at the opposing team's end of the field. We Pitisowewepahikan differs from lacrosse in its use of two balls that were attached by a string or thong – hence the name double ball. The sticks were slightly curved at the end and were not fitted with a pocket. Unlike lacrosse, which was predominately a male game in Indigenous nations, double ball was overwhelmingly, but not exclusively, played by women. For instance, J.A. Mitchell recorded, in a quote compiled by Culin, that the game was exclusive to women in the Muscowpetung Saulteaux community located in the Qu'Appelle Valley:

> The game [here] is played by women only, any number, but not by the old women, as great powers of endurance are required. It is in many respects similar to lacrosse. The players are given various stations in the field and carry sticks. The goals are usually 1 mile or thereabout apart.
>
> Players gather in a circle at the beginning and the double ball is thrown aloft from the stick of one of the leaders, when the scrimmage commences and is kept up until one side passes the ball through its opponent's goal.
>
> The game is a very interesting one and develops much skill. It is, from a hygienic point of view, highly beneficial, as it develops a fine, robust class of women. As with all other Indian games, this is invariably played for stakes of some kind.[60]

Like the Nêhiyawak, the Coast Salish nations of southern British Columbia played variants of lacrosse long before it was introduced into St. Mary's Mission Boarding School in 1904 and the Squamish Indian Residential School in 1905.[61] In the 1930s, anthropologist Homer Barnett relayed a story that described an 1820s Xʷməθkʷəy̓əm village on the Fraser River that consisted of seventy-six housing segments centred on a lacrosse field.[62] In 1855, Paul Kane described the Chinook and SqWuqWu'b3sh (Skokomish) of present-day Washington as taking great pleasure in a stick-and-ball game that was closely related to those of the Nêhiyawak, Anishinaabeg, and the Dakhóta/Lakhóta (Dakota/Lakota).[63] In an interview for the Sliammon Treaty Society's Traditional Use study, Ernie Harry remembers that Coast Salish nations gathered at Sechelt to compete in lacrosse: "That's where Sechelt used to gather, all the people from Qoqomish, Point Gray, Nanaimo, everybody goes there to plays, called 'qwak'lotl' that's the lacrosse, do a lot of wrestling, everything."[64] Similarly, Kwantlen Elder Lekeyten recalled in a CBC interview the history of a lacrosse field located between Chehalis and Harrison Hot Springs in southwestern British Columbia.[65]

The Squamish Indian Residential School Experience

The introduction of residential schools in the Lower Mainland of British Columbia was due in large part to the work of the Oblates of Mary

**Squamish Indian Residential School
(St. Paul's), undated.** | *Photograph 4838,
North Vancouver Museum and Archives.*

Immaculate, who were centred in New Westminster. They established
St. Mary's Mission in 1861, which, due to the efforts of the Sisters of Saint
Ann, expanded in 1868 to incorporate a boarding school.[66] Further ex-
acerbating the rise of Canada's Colonial Age, the missionary work of the
Oblates took on an even more structured and controlled approach to assimilation during the late 1860s, thanks in large part to Oblate bishop Paul
Durieu. Recalled to New Westminster in 1867 after an initial year's stint
there in 1864, Durieu was the bishop's assistant and director of St. Mary's
Mission.[67] In 1890, after several years of rising through the ecclesiastical
ranks, he became the bishop of the New Westminster diocese and vicar
apostolic of British Columbia.[68] Although not created solely by Durieu
himself, the "Durieu system" that bore his name came to dominate the
lower Fraser Valley by the time the Squamish Indian Residential School
was established in North Vancouver in 1898.[69] As J.R. Miller explains it,

> This regime, named after Oblate Paul Durieu, employed methods
> of total control over mission Indians for the purpose of effecting a
> permanent conversion to Christian religious values and practices. The
> Durieu system aimed at eradicating all unchristian behaviour by

means of strict rules, stern punishments for transgressors, and use of Indian informers and watchmen or proctors to ensure conformity and inflict punishments as necessary. The second, more positive, phase emphasized symbolism and spectacle, and treated the celebrations of Catholicism as marks of community and acceptance.[70]

The Skwxwú7mesh Nation, described by anthropologists as Coast Salish located in North Vancouver, Howe Sound, and the Squamish River watershed, were always quick to respond to changing circumstances, informed by their centuries of historical knowledge and memory of regeneration and renewal.[71] Following the Fraser River gold rush of 1858, the Skwxwú7mesh residents in and around New Westminster experienced difficulties due to the rapid influx of various imperial projects, resource extraction, and settler-colonialism. Of particular concern for church representatives was the sharp increase in the presence of alcohol and violence in the communities brought upon by the wave of prospectors and related industries.[72] In response to the external pressures and significant change in the area, a number of Skwxwú7mesh Nation members, including Chief James Sraouten Snat, helped establish the permanent community of Slha7an' (Ustlawn); located on the north shore of Burrard Inlet, it was later known as the Mission Reserve No. 1. The community implemented the Durieu system and in 1898, the Indigenous residents of the reserve co-operated with the Oblates in establishing the Squamish Indian Residential School.[73] More complex than merely acquiescing to colonial forms, the community's adoption of the system and establishment of the residential school can be seen as an attempt to use available resources to respond to the rapidly changing circumstances brought on by the settler presence.

The school was the embodiment of differing objectives held by the Oblates and the Skwxwú7mesh.[74] The Oblates saw it as an opportunity to further their Christianization and civilization efforts, whereas the Skwxwú7mesh saw it as enabling their youth to respond to and participate in the rapidly changing socio-political relations and economy.[75] Just as St. Paul's Church on the Mission Reserve was built by Skwxwú7mesh people, so too was the residential school.[76] Like other Indigenous nations across North America, the Skwxwú7mesh initiated and capitalized on opportunities for their own purposes.[77] As Chief Louis Miranda reflected in a 1979 interview with Reuben Ware, Skwxwú7mesh Nation member Joe Thomas anticipated that education could afford youth with new opportunities but witnessed how quickly the school deviated from the Skwxwú7mesh vision: "Well he was glad that the children could speak English, but Joe Thomas was very very disappointed that they had to lose their culture with it. He had no objection about the education, but his strong objection was with the pride of the children and community spirit."[78] Why the Skwxwú7mesh would participate in this process must be clearly understood. Although they played an active role in founding their school in the attempt to respond to the rapidly changing surroundings, as did numerous other Indigenous nations, they did not, and could not, foresee that it would be used in the methodical application of cultural genocide and settler-colonialism, or the devastating legacy it would leave in its wake.[79]

Contributing to this process at some level was sport, including lacrosse. Although lacrosse was popular in the Vancouver area by the 1890s, and the Skwxwú7mesh would undoubtedly have been aware of it by that time, the written and oral records indicate that it was introduced to them at St. Mary's Mission Boarding School in 1904, the Squamish Indian Residential School in 1905, and the Sechelt Boarding School in 1906.[80] However, though the appropriated form of the game was a component of Canada's civilizing project, it simultaneously aided in resisting it. More than any other Skwxwú7mesh pupil, Andy Paull (Te Qoitechetahl or Xwechtáal)[81] experienced this first-hand and learned the power of the lacrosse stick.

Born in 1892 while his parents were visiting Potlatch Creek, Paull grew up on the Mission Reserve in North Vancouver, within the vigorous social control of the Durieu system – his father, Dan Paull, was a "watchman" under this regime.[82] Paull was the descendent of the hero Xwechtáal (Te Qoitechetahl), a famous serpent slayer in Skwxwú7mesh oral history.[83] Chief Louis Miranda stated in an interview with Reuben Ware that Paull's lineage would follow him throughout his life and would play a significant role in a number of his defining moments as an Indigenous rights activist, leader, and sports promoter.[84] In 1927, he appeared before the Skwxwú7mesh chiefs to ask permission to appeal directly to Ottawa to advocate for Indigenous land title, where he would also be representing the Allied Tribes of British Columbia, an organization he helped form. While standing before the Skwxwú7mesh leadership, he was reportedly reminded of the strength and duty that his lineage carried:

You are the direct descendent of Te Qoitechetahl. Te Qoitechetahl was a young man who had a wife. The serpent went by and he thought,

Andrew (Andy) Paull. |
Photograph 2191, North Vancouver
Museum and Archives.

you go and follow him. So he went. He was four years away. And then at the end of the four years, this serpent in Te Qoitechetahl's vision, this serpent comes to him and she was a young lady and she says "you have earned your reward for all the work you have done," she says "I am the two headed serpent. I am giving myself to you. You are going to kill that animal, that serpent down there, but my soul will enter you. Therefore you'll have the strength, my strength. You go down by where the body decays, you go down and you'll find a bow and that will be your reward for all your hardship ... If you see an animal coming all you have to do is wave this bow, and they'll all die. If you go out hunting ... all you have to do is take the bow and wave, and they will all die. You'll feed your people with this bow, and you'll protect the lives of the people with this bow."[85]

The name itself, Te Qoitechetahl, carried with it intrinsic powers and was given to Paull by his grandmother during his youth.[86] From a young age, he had been recognized as a potential leader among the Skwxwú7mesh, which resulted in his attendance at the Squamish Indian Residential School. As Father Herbert Dunlop notes in his biography of Paull, he was called before the Skwxwú7mesh chiefs at age seven and chosen to be among the first class of pupils to attend the new school in 1899.[87] Overall, Paull spoke of his experience there in positive terms, often remarking that the skills he acquired such as reading, writing, and organizing served him well in later life.[88] "Andy went to school," Dunlop states,

> and his purpose in going was not to learn how to become a white man. He went there to learn how to use the tools of the white man, and with these tools to speak for and fight for the rights of his people. Andy was selected by the chiefs to go to school, in order to become the spokesman and voice of the native people.[89]

One critical tool that Paull acquired at the residential school would eventually help to kindle a reformation of Skwxwú7mesh identity and nationhood while further aiding the nation in resisting the onslaught of Canada's "civilizing" efforts, just as the bow of Paull's ancestor Te Qoitechetahl protected the lives of his people.[90] This time, though, it was in the form of a lacrosse stick.

In 1905, while Andy Paull was a student at the Squamish Indian Residential School, its administrators introduced lacrosse as part of their recreation program.[91] Like other Skwxwú7mesh students at the school, Paull developed an affinity for sports, especially baseball and lacrosse.[92] Sport and recreation offered students a break from the tedium of school life. Like their counterparts in residential and day schools across the country, the Skwxwú7mesh students played soccer, baseball, lacrosse, and later hockey. Skwxwú7mesh Elder Paitsmauk, Dave Jacobs, who also attended the school, recalled that its religious instruction was so pervasive that students often attempted to excel at sports to escape it, even if only temporarily.[93]

On a more long-term basis, the introduction of lacrosse offered Indigenous peoples such as Paull a mechanism to maintain and renew their cultural independence and identity by reappropriating an Indigenous element as their own. Upon leaving the school, Paull took with him a basic knowledge of Canadian law, literacy, and, of course, lacrosse, which would serve him

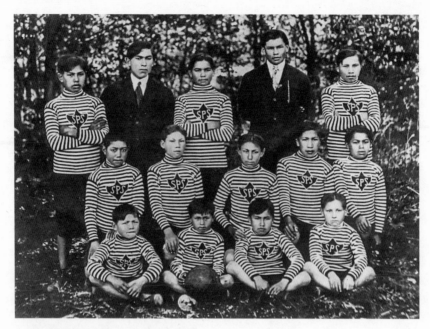

St. Paul's (Squamish) Indian Residential School soccer team, 1908. | *Photograph 4840, North Vancouver Museum and Archives.*

for the rest of his life.[94] However, he was not the only Indigenous rights spokesperson whom the residential school system and athletics unwittingly helped to nurture. In Herbert Francis Dunlop's book, *Andy Paull: As I Knew Him and Understood His Times,* former Sechelt Band chief Stan Dixon recounts, "I can vividly recall the days when, as a young man growing up in the Native Residential School system, I participated in school sports and individual athletic competitive recreational programs. That was where I was tuned up and prepared for what I do now. There I learned: Consistency! Control! Discipline! Anticipation! Habit! [Principles]!!!"[95] Through his attendance at residential school, his subsequent on-the-job legal training at the law office of Hugh St. Quentin Cayley, and his appointment as secretary of the Skwxwú7mesh Council in 1911, Paull developed a working knowledge of Skwxwú7mesh political affairs and land claims at an early age.[96] As he later reflected, he felt chosen to be the successor of Chief Joe Capilano as the voice of the Skwxwú7mesh people.[97] Simultaneously, he and other Skwxwú7mesh leaders helped establish a new cultural element, using it to help reinvigorate Skwxwú7mesh identities and nationhood, and create a racialized identity through sport, as will be covered in Chapter 3. For Paull, the game of lacrosse that he learned in residential school was the perfect tool to revitalize Sḵwx̱wú7mesh pride, identity, and nationhood, effectively countering its assimilative use in residential schools, and later to build links between Indigenous and non-Native communities.

As played in the residential schools of western Canada, this new version of lacrosse was essentially a foreign game for students. It had been fully transformed, distanced from its Indigenous brilliance and knowledge, and was now reflective of a specific set of Canadian values. Any fear that it would re-empower Indigenous identities due to its Indigenous connection was absent. It was one thing for administrators to use the game in the Prairie provinces or on the West Coast, where Indigenous peoples had little influence on its systematic reorganization, but it was clearly another for them to have the audacity to use lacrosse in residential schools in locations that included Hodinöhsö:ni' children, where the game and stick retained central significance. Yet, that is exactly what they did. Lacrosse had become so strongly associated with Canadian nationalism that residential schools such as the Mohawk Institute, which lay just outside the Hodinöhsö:ni' community of Six Nations, comfortably implemented it as part of the children's recreational activities.[98] In the heart of the Indigenous territories where non-Natives appropriated the game, the game's transformation, in the minds of Canadians, into a "national sport" was determined and without doubt.

Forming Residential School Recreation Policies

In Canada, the popularity of lacrosse fluctuated, as was the case for other sports, but numerous residential school principals reported the pleasure that their students took in the game. Principal A.J. McLeod of the Regina Industrial School wrote that students greatly enjoyed participating in athletic championships with outside teams. More importantly, at a time when student health at residential schools was in a deplorable state, he commented on the associated health benefits: "Good health has prevailed in the institution, caused in no small degree by good ventilation, good diet, outdoor exercise, and the watchful care by the various members of the staff. Our lacrosse team entered into competition for the championship of the Northwest Territories. Many of the boys are good athletes, and enjoy the manner of manly sports."[99] In residential schools, sport and recreation were a multifaceted tool: as the schools became breeding grounds for deadly diseases, they could be used to improve student health, as Janice Forsyth notes.[100]

Like the recreational activities themselves, health conditions at many residential schools were highly dependent on local administrators during the late nineteenth and early twentieth centuries.[101] This began to change in 1911, when the ad hoc approach was replaced with a more standardized policy. During that year, the Department of Indian Affairs finalized new contract policies with the churches in which it took greater responsibility for the education of Indigenous children and the management of the schools.[102] According to historian John Milloy, these contracts detailed the duties of both church and state: the two bodies would work together, but the schools would now operate under Indian Affairs regulations and would continue "to provide training in the moral and civic codes of civilized life."[103] While it marked a shift in policy, it did not mark an improvement in health conditions, owing to a criminal disregard by authorities for the health and lives of Indigenous children who continued to suffer and die at egregious rates.[104]

At about the same time – in 1910 – Indian Affairs published a booklet titled *Calisthenics and Games Prescribed for Use in All Indian Schools*.[105] The booklet, and the restructuring of residential school policies more generally, was the result of a series of damning reports from the Indian Affairs chief medical officer, Dr. Peter Henderson Bryce, who called upon the department to address the intolerable rates of tuberculosis in residential schools.[106] In 1907, Bryce reported that 24 percent of Indigenous children who attended Prairie residential schools had died of tuberculosis, an outcome that he recongized as the direct result of federal policy.[107] This number has since been raised to over 40 percent, with estimates as high as 50 percent at specific schools.[108] Chronically underfunded, the schools were neglected and inadequately built, which resulted in the egregious sanitary conditions and death rates.[109] Bryce would later term the conditions a "national crime."[110] Among the various other identified causes for poor student health, Bryce noted that lack of physical education played a key role.[111] Most of Bryce's recommendations between 1907 and 1910 fell on deaf ears, but the Department of Indian Affairs began to selectively amend its policies and take greater control of the schools. This included the publication of the calisthenics booklet in 1910.

Across the country, teachers were issued with copies of *Calisthenics and Games* and asked to familiarize themselves with its text so as "to carry out faithfully the Department's desire that the pupils be given daily a short period of instruction in those movements herein described that are best suited to conditions."[112] Although they failed to credit Bryce, the booklet's unnamed authors were clearly familiar with his report and stressed language closely related to Bryce's recommendations, focusing on combating pulmonary disease and encouraging the need for open-air or well-ventilated areas in the schools.[113] The booklet stated, "As Indian children show a tendency towards pulmonary disease, special attention to the several deep breathing movements should be given. It is most important that they be put through such exercises as serve to fill the lung space and expand the walls of the chest. Teachers should always keep this end in view."[114] Detailing twenty-five exercises to "improve circulation and breathing power," the booklet also included nine games that were suitable for both indoor and outdoor spaces. It instructed teachers to

> make themselves familiar with suitable games and sports to give their pupils as a means of recreation. *Running, jumping, ball games and similar sports are vitally important as a means of moulding the child's character and for general exercise.* During the open months of spring, summer and autumn, many regulation sports, such as football, baseball, basketball, &c., can be played in the field; but during the inclement weather of the winter suitable games for indoors must be chosen.[115]

One of the earliest manifestations of the new national policy that sports and recreation would be used in residential schools throughout the country, the booklet was unquestionably precipitated by their dreadful health records, which would not improve for decades.

The limited policy change would not be the department's last attempt to imply that it was taking an active stance by using physical education in hopes of preventing tuberculosis and improving student health. Fifteen years later, in 1925, a department memo detailing the condition of Indian education revealed that the problem had not yet been resolved: "The health of Indian children, particularly those in residential schools, has been the subject for considerable thought and activity. A special effort is now being made in the matter of physical education and the Department has arranged for fairly comprehensive medical and dental supervision and treatment."[116] From an administrative perspective, recreation offered a means to improve health, and though it did not achieve this goal, it was a valuable tool in the assimilation of both mind and body. And, as Forsyth reminds us, the associated cash outlay was small.[117]

Redefining the Residential School Experience

Although sport and recreation were intended to facilitate assimilation, they took on an entirely different meaning for the students themselves, which resulted in a number of outcomes that school administrators had not expected. Lomawaima writes that "boarding schools were not, however, perfect laboratories in which to fulfill federal intentions. Students adapted to regimentation and resisted authority in creative ways."[118] Whereas administrators such as J.P. O'Neill, principal of St. Mary's Mission Boarding School, praised student recreation as "a conducive agent both in their mental and physical development," the students themselves viewed it in a much different light.[119] In his study of US boarding schools, John Bloom argues that though Indigenous students were relentlessly pressured in the attempt to restructure both mind and body, they used sport and recreation as an escape and to refashion their identities:

> Yet even at their most oppressive, when student time was almost entirely occupied by chores, classes, marching, and discipline, the demands that boarding schools made upon students were never complete. Students found spaces, moments in time, and recreational activities in which to form their own alliances and communities, either through mischief, subversion of rules, or creation of their own identities and subcultures.[120]

Lacrosse and other sports offered students an escape from their heavily regimented and institutionalized lives.[121] In Elizabeth Graham's *The Mush Hole,* survivor Jennie Blackbird remembered that her "favourite sport was baseball. Both girls and boys played this sport. And this did break the monotony."[122] Time and again, residential school survivors have reflected on sport and recreation as a welcome relief from school life. For example, Sḵwx̱wú7mesh Elder Paitsmauk, Dave Jacobs, who attended the Squamish Residential School, recalls that sport became a source of positive resistance and a welcome relief during his time there:

> We never actually picked up a [lacrosse] stick ourselves and played until residential school. *Then we saw an opportunity to get out of the residential school and get on these teams that were off-reserve, they were white teams. So we said, "Gee, if they are playing Saturdays, whenever,*

or evenings, we'll get out of the residential school for a few hours." We all started that way. Guys that are older than me, they did the same thing, they got introduced to it and then they went out and started playing ... It [religion] was imposed on us so much, because when I got to residential school at six years old, I was punished so much because I spoke my language, I was always in the corner and I didn't understand why until one of the older boys told me don't speak the language, so I refused then. It was religion, religion, constantly religion ... So anything we could find to get away from that, and it was always sports, you would go to gymnastics, you go to boxing, you would go to this and go to that, that got you away from the school. A whole group of boys and girls would get away from the school and that's why we worked at it so hard and practised to be good, to win, so you kept away from the school ... So if we could find a way out, the best way to get out of it was athletics, sports. It was good.[123]

Being good at sports enabled students to travel and escape the institutions, at least temporarily, offering them special privileges that were not available to other classmates. By excelling in sports and later competitive travelling dance teams, or by participating in brass bands, students formed paths of resistance to the constant onslaught of the residential school experience.[124] As recounted in Agnes Jack's *Behind Closed Doors,* student Andrew Amos remembered,

I expressed myself through sports where the rewards [for winning in the school's name] were through special privileges and meals. The opportunity to travel to sporting events was always exciting and to see the many different places, such as Vancouver, Vernon, Lumby, Mission City or just across town. These were privileges many of the school children never did see or realize ... It was through competitive sports, and the girls with their dancing and travel, that we were able to cope and survive the daily routine of life at the residential school.[125]

For students across the country, sport and recreation were often high points of their otherwise dismal time at school. Although not every experience was necessarily negative, students with varied school backgrounds overwhelmingly found recreation an exception in their repetitive lives, filled as they were with rules, punishments, and horrific conditions. Sports offered moments of pleasure in which youthfulness could briefly be recaptured. This was true for many survivors, such as Martha Hill, who attended the Mohawk Institute from 1912 to 1918. In Graham's *The Mush Hole,* she remembers: "We had lots of fun. We had swings and teeter-totters, and baseball. We even played hockey – but the girls were a little clumsy at playing hockey. We couldn't get it to go right!!! We played ball – we had a basketball team."[126] Similarly, Bernice (George) Jackson, a Mount Elgin Institute survivor, may have expressed it best:

> We lost all our Indian language and culture for being there. We weren't allowed to speak our own language. If they heard us talking our language to someone they wouldn't like it and they'd tell us not to talk like that. I used to speak it and understand it. I knew English and our own language when I went there, but we used to like talking in our own language, but we were never allowed to do that. And if we done anything that wasn't suitable to the staff we would get strapped ... But there were fun times too. The teachers used to take us on little hikes, and we used to have baseball games. We used to get to slide down that great big hill. We used to go down into the river behind the barns. They used to let us go down there and slide.[127]

Furthermore, the pleasure of sport and recreation was not necessarily limited to the players themselves. For example, in the spring of 1922, when a group of Mohawk Institute boys participated in a community lacrosse league, they were a source of school pride and spirit, like other travelling teams.[128] "The boys joined the local School Lacrosse league and gave a very good account of themselves," Principal Alice Boyce wrote. "We were lucky enough to secure an old pupil, Mr. J Doxdator, as a coach. On May 24th all the pupils went to Mohawk Park to attend the opening game of the league."[129] Any trip from the residential school, as Paitsmauk states, was welcome, especially to watch classmates compete in an athletic event.[130] Despite the fact that teams were limited to a few students, sports seem to have inspired school spirit, and administrators often mentioned that students enjoyed their recreation hours. For Melva George, trips to see local teams play remained a lifelong highlight: "We used to have good times ... We used to go down and cheer for our local teams in the sports – the ball teams for all the area. Even in wintertime they'd have a team to come be near the river there. We'd go down and cheer for them."[131] Elizabeth Graham noted that recreational activities at the Mohawk Institute were generally positive and could furnish opportunities that were sometimes not available to students at home:

> Conditions on the Reserve were bad at that time and many parents could not afford to have their children home. The buildings were extensively renovated in 1922–3, and management went on much as before, with the introduction of team sports like lacrosse, a Cadet company, Girl Guides, a boys' band and much success in track and field competitions. These activities brought the school into the Brantford community and according to the principal, inspired some school spirit.[132]

Additionally, scholars Donald Fisher and John Bloom observe that sports nurtured Indigenous pride at the Carlisle Indian Industrial School in Pennsylvania; Fisher notes that "because students turned out en masse to witness matches, the varsity team functioned as a vehicle for Native American pride ... Carlisle's purpose may have been to anglicize the native students, but one unintended consequence was the fostering of an ill-defined pan-Indian identity."[133] The sports teams at residential schools unintentionally created a new cohesive Indigenous identity; Indigenous athletes were not only connected via their uniforms and school, they also developed a common identity through their shared experiences at the institutions. As John Bloom explains, "This pride is important, for it can allow such groups to combat the invisibility that they often face in mainstream society by imagining a common source of inspiration."[134] The Truth and Reconciliation Commission of Canada also found that sport and recreation could be high points in the experience of residential school survivors.[135] Nevertheless, whether a survivor's time at school was positive or negative, it must be emphasized that it existed within a framework whose purpose was cultural genocide. Students' cultures, languages, identities, and sense of nationhood were all to be eliminated, and their perceptions of family life, kinship, and gender relations were to be reworked. The same must be said of sport. Sport in itself was not apolitical; it was a powerful agent of colonialism, employed as a form of "re-creation."[136]

Despite the rise in morale and the expansion of the program in the early 1920s, the popularity of lacrosse declined at the Mohawk Institute, as elsewhere. In the early twentieth century, the game was constantly being challenged by other sports. Its appeal deteriorated at the onset of the First World War due to the issues of professionalism and "continuing concerns about rowdyism and ungentlemanly play" among Canadian lacrosse organizations.[137] The war itself also played a role in the decline. Fortunately for Canada's military, though not for lacrosse itself, the game produced excellent athletes whose physical condition made them perfect candidates for military service.[138] Clubs such as the MLC withdrew from competitions, stating that during wartime, it was their patriotic duty not to participate in games that charged an entry fee.[139] As men went overseas to fight, the popularity of lacrosse diminished significantly, and as sport historian Alan Metcalfe concludes, only baseball and hockey were still played on a widespread basis in Canada by 1914.[140] The war did not extinguish lacrosse, but it did help rival sports displace it. By war's end, it was clear that baseball was now the dominant summertime team sport.[141] This decline also occurred in residential schools, where the game – as indicated in the Indian Affairs reports – waned noticeably during the 1920s. For example, a 1930 report by Superintendent of Indian Affairs Thomas Murphy states,

> The Mohawk Institute has always given prominence to student organizations and this has been responsible for the fine spirit among the older pupils ... The chief sports have been hockey, football, basket ball, baseball and track events. In the early days, lacrosse was popular. Peter White, of the St. Regis reserve, who graduated forty years ago, became one of the most famous lacrosse players in Canada.[142]

The decline persisted throughout the interwar period, and the game was hard pressed to recapture its prominence.[143] It needed rejuvenation, and if it were going to survive in organized form, it needed to reinvent itself. As will be detailed in the following chapters, this is exactly what occurred in 1931, with the creation of a new form of the game.

∾

From their earliest beginnings, residential schools offered recreational activities. Initially provided on a provisional basis, these had expanded to include dance teams, brass bands, and many types of sports competitions by the 1940s.[144] Eventually, as Forsyth notes, the Department of Indian Affairs introduced a supervisor of physical education in 1949.[145] At the height of its popularity during the late nineteenth and early twentieth centuries, lacrosse was perceived as such an authoritative manifestation of Canadian nationality that the schools employed it as part of their assimilation project. The game was perceived to be the ideal performance of whiteness and a cost-effective and efficient means of exposing students to the dominant society and of infusing Western gender constructions.[146] However, by introducing lacrosse, other sports, and recreation more generally, the schools unwittingly created a mechanism for students to manage their residential school experience. They afforded a temporary escape from the monotonous regime and the school itself. They were a source of entertainment, pride, and, at times, resistance as the students themselves reshaped their meaning. And they provided tools for future leaders such as Andy Paull to help ensure both the short- and long-term persistence of Indigenous identities and nationhood. As we will see, lacrosse provided a new avenue for Indigenous peoples to assert control over their communities, governance, sport, and, most importantly, their identities. Not only did it help Indigenous students survive residential school, it was also an important mechanism for community integration and pan-Indigenous political mobilization, and it enabled Indigenous nations such as the Sḵwx̱wú7mesh a new way to articulate their identities and nationhood.

3

Articulating Indigenous Nationhood on the West Coast

>>> *Tiohtià:ke/Mooniyaang (Montreal), June 28, 1886*[1]
Fweeeehtt! Fweeeehtt!

"En voiture!"

"Good evening, Raven. How are you? Excited about the trip?" Indian Agent 'Usdas asks.

"Hi 'Usdas. I'm well, always excited to return home to the West Coast. Say, what are you holding there?" Raven is gleaming with a Trickster smile, asking this question rhetorically.

"Oh – this is a very powerful document called the Indian Act. It's beginning to usher in a new age for the Indians and release them from the bonds of their savagery. No more Potlatches or Balhats, new schooling, things are really starting to become civilized. Isn't it great?"

"Civilized? You should be careful, 'Usdas. Paper can hold a very powerful and oppressive story, but no, that isn't what I'm talking about." Raven points. "What's that in your other hand?"

"Oh this? This is my lacrosse stick from St. Regis (Ahkwesáhsne), only the best Indian lacrosse stick in the world!"

Sk'éxwa7 is the Sḵwx̱wú7mesh Nation's word for "lacrosse match." K'éxwa7 is the Sḵwx̱wú7mesh phrase for "to play modern lacrosse." *"Lacrosse match" and "Play lacrosse [modern]," in Skwxwu7mesh Snichim-Xweliten Snichim Skexwts/Squamish-English Dictionary (Seattle: University of Washington Press, 2011).*

Raven interrupts, "Did you steal those? Remember the last time you did something like that?"[2]

Without skipping a beat, 'Usdas continues, "I'm taking several of them out west with me, you know, help spread the game. It's Canada's game. This is part of who 'we' are and has been since 1867!"

Trying not to laugh at 'Usdas's ignorance, Raven jumps in. "I thought it was the Creator's game, since time immemorial?" Raven smirks in a smart-ass way. "You know, the game of dispute resolution, ceremony, and to be played for the Creator's amusement."

'Usdas sighs in frustration and rolls their eyes. "Well, we borrowed it! Don't worry, it's in good hands. I'm going to show the little savages out west how to play it. It will make them better Canadians, it'll teach them our values and the proper ways of gentlemanly conduct in order to exist in the new, modern world."

"Better Canadians? You're practically a week old," Raven laughs. "Canadians are predated on these territories since – well, since the beginning of time. What's wrong with being Dakelh, Tsek'ehne, or Sḵwx̱wú7mesh? Sounds like you're playing some tricks."

"Yep, there'll be some big changes out there. Soon enough, there won't be any Dakelh, Tsek'ehne, or Sḵwx̱wú7mesh – just Canadians. It all starts with this paper here."

"Be careful. That's a very powerful –."

Nodding, 'Usdas cuts Raven off, "Yeah, yeah, yeah. I know, a very powerful piece of paper, I know, I know."

"I'm not talking about the paper. I'm talking about the stick, 'Usdas! The stick!" Without knowing it, 'Usdas the Trickster had now transformed into 'Usdas the tricked.

>>> *July 4, 1886*

Fweeeehtt! Fweeeehtt! The whistle blows as onlookers gather at Port Moody on the Pacific coast to celebrate the arrival of the first CPR train to traverse Canada. At a distance, Indigenous villagers watch in anticipation.

"Sínulhka, Sínulhka," one of them voices to the crowd. "Sínulhka, the Serpent, has returned!"[3]

Peering out the window amid the steam and commotion, attempting to overlook the onlookers at the station, 'Usdas turns to Raven and points to the Indigenous people on the shore. "What's all the commotion about?"

"They are comparing it to the return of Sínulhka, the feared serpent that leaves a path of destruction in its wake."

"That's ridiculous! Don't they know it's a train, a great moment of progress? They should be celebrating!"

"Progress for who, of what?"

"The great nation – spreading west, uniting the country, settling the untamed lands."

"You mean dispossession, confinement, and imposition? How about the Canadian policies of ethnic cleansing and starvation that allowed these rails to be built?[4] Certainly, Indigenous peoples' resistance, resilience, and flourishing in the face of this imperial expansion is extradionary but your excitement over these acts of violence is morbid. In a way, Sínulhka has returned, but this time their gift is the power within the lacrosse stick." Raven peers at 'Usdas with a sinister smirk. "Just know the story you're about to write, and remember that is a very powerful piece –."

Once again, 'Usdas stops Raven in midsentence. "I know, I know – a powerful piece of paper that can hold an oppressive story, right?"

"The stick, 'Usdas, the stick. It too can tell a story."

DURING CANADA'S COLONIAL AGE, which brought about a great number of physical and cultural changes for Indigenous nations, the Skwxwú7mesh used lacrosse to unify and strengthen their nation. Ultimately, they created a vibrant identity through sport, merging pre-existing articulations of Skwxwú7mesh nationhood and new forms of pan-Indigeneity. Like their eastern counterparts, Indigenous players in British Columbia were barred from competition. However, unlike Indigenous athletes in central Canada, who had to wait until box lacrosse was introduced during the 1930s, the Skwxwú7mesh began to compete against West Coast non-Native teams in the late 1910s. Introduced to the game in residential schools and by non-Native Vancouverites, they quickly embraced it, not uncritically as an instrument of Canadian nationalism, as was the intention, but as citizens of the Skwxwú7mesh Nation. This chapter examines how the Skwxwú7mesh articulated their nationhood through the game and characterized lacrosse as "our game." Throughout the twentieth century, they saw it as an instrument for community integration, both locally and nationally, during Indian Sports Days, via the recreational activities of union members, and eventually,

in lacrosse leagues after Skwxwú7mesh community members facilitated
the end of the ban on Indigenous athletes in British Columbia. The
Skwxwú7mesh became a significant and much-needed feature in Canadian
lacrosse at a time when the sport's popularity was dwindling, and they helped
establish a new form of the game, box lacrosse, that ensured its continued
practice in British Columbia. Furthermore, their appropriation and integration of lacrosse allows us to see the intersection of multiple identities in
terms of local nationalism (of the Skwxwú7mesh Nation per se) and more
broadly a pan-Indigenous identity and political mobilization that extended
far beyond the playing field. The introduction of the Hodinöhsö:ni' lacrosse
stick and the eastern game helped to augment the historic sporting culture
of the Skwxwú7mesh. Nowhere is all of this more apparent than in the efforts of Skwxwú7mesh leader and sports promoter Andy Paull during the
1920s and 1930s.

During the second half of the nineteenth century, faced with the increasing appropriation of lands in and around Coast Salish territory, the
encroachment of the city of Vancouver, and the "civilizing" efforts of
Canada's Colonial Age, the Skwxwú7mesh participated both willingly and
unwillingly in one of the most significant transitional eras in modern Indigenous history. British Columbia's Lower Mainland, including Skwxwú7-
mesh territory, was transformed from an Indigenous-controlled space into
one that was controlled by settler governments and colonial institutions,
which sought to reshape it as an extension of British – and later Canadian
– imperialism.[5] As historian Adele Perry contends, reformers in the colonial
project that was British Columbia attempted to reconstruct the territory
as a white settler colony, and the years following the 1858 Fraser River
gold rush saw a remarkable period of change for the Skwxwú7mesh and
hənq̓əminəm̓ (Halkomelem) speakers who lived there.[6] The identities of
the Skwxwú7mesh were challenged as they were obliged to redefine their
collective distinctiveness as both Skwxwú7mesh and Coast Salish. Moreover, they were increasingly forced to place themselves within their larger
imposed – and legal – racialized identity as "Indians." At times, when one
identity began to shift or be demphasized (such as the Coast Salish collective), others were reinforced, such as Skwxwú7mesh nationhood itself
or that of the village/reserve.[7] The point is not that the Skwxwú7mesh
were passive victims in a wave of non-Native imposition and transition.
Like other Indigenous peoples, they continued to practise their long-
established ceremonies, culture, and economies while also fighting for their

self-determination and participating in the growing non-Indigenous–controlled wage-labour economy and organized sport that arrived during the mid to late nineteenth century.[8] Within this fluid landscape of power, economic permutation, and cultural exchange, the Sḵwx̱wú7mesh adapted and absorbed elements of distant Indigenous nations and peoples and non-Native cultures, just as they had always done.[9] Lacrosse was one example of this process.

Lacrosse in Coast Salish Territory

The establishment and growth of the new form of lacrosse on the West Coast was due in large part to British Columbia's entrance into Confederation in 1871.[10] As new residents arrived from the east, they brought with them their lacrosse sticks and transplanted the game to the fledgling province.[11] For non-Natives, lacrosse had taken on a national presence by the early 1890s. Their form of the game had expanded east from Ontario and Quebec to New Brunswick and Nova Scotia by 1870.[12] It reached Winnipeg in 1871, with the creation of the Prince Rupert Lacrosse Club.[13] Prince Albert, Saskatchewan, had its own club by 1891 at the latest.[14] In Alberta, an Edmonton club was founded in 1883 and the Calgary Lacrosse Club in 1884.[15] Of course, these clubs were predated by the presence of the game among the Indigenous nations that called these territories home.

In British Columbia, the first publicized lacrosse game between non-Indigenous athletes took place on August 28, 1886, between Victoria and Vancouver.[16] Following this match, the new form of lacrosse truly became a "national game" geographically: in March 1890, the British Columbia Amateur Lacrosse Association (BCALA) was founded, consisting of teams from Vancouver, Victoria, and New Westminster, and cementing the game's presence on the West Coast.[17] According to its rule book, the organization's objective "shall be to improve, foster, and perpetuate the game of Lacrosse as the national game of Canada, and to promote the cultivation of kindly feeling among the members of lacrosse clubs."[18] This included barring Indigenous peoples and other people of colour from membership so as to not challenge the performance of whiteness and nationalism lacrosse came to represent. "No Indians or other person of color," the BCALA rules stated, "shall be eligible for membership in the clubs of this Association."[19] This racialized discrimination fit within the previous decades of reform movements that attempted to recast Indigenous territories as belonging to white settler society.[20] As elsewhere, lacrosse in British Columbia became a site for the performance of masculinity and whiteness, and ultimately a tool in the structure of settler-colonialism.

Like other Coast Salish nations and the Nłe?kepmx (Nlaka'pamux) in the interior of British Columbia, the Skwxwú7mesh were familiar with lacrosse before the Hodinöhsö:ni' stick made its appearance on the West Coast. In fact, the introduction of the Hodinöhsö:ni' game was a reintroduction to stick-and-ball games that already existed in Coast Salish and Skwxwú7mesh tradition, and it simply augmented its historic sporting culture. Various Coast Salish nations played double ball, and anthropologist Charles Hill-Tout notes that the SqWuqWu'b3sh (Skokomish) had a form of lacrosse called Kekequa.[21] By extension, as historian Alexandra Harmon reminds us, through diverse kinship and international relationships among the Coast Salish, ideas, technology, and identities were widely circulated, and it is safe to presume that the Skwxwú7mesh also played lacrosse before the Hodinöhsö:ni' stick arrived in their territory.[22]

Despite the marked popularity of the new form of lacrosse in British Columbia, Indigenous teams scarcely figured in West Coast competition until the turn of the twentieth century. Initially, and due to the early BC ban, the Skwxwú7mesh had little input regarding how the game entered their communities, unlike the Hodinöhsö:ni', who exercised significant influence over the introduction of lacrosse to non-Indigenous organizations. Although by 1900, lacrosse had attracted a large following in Vancouver, Victoria, and New Westminster, the Skwxwú7mesh who lived on the North Shore of Vancouver remained on the fringes of the sport. This, however, soon changed with the introduction of the game in 1904 and 1905 at the St. Mary's Mission Boarding School and the Squamish Residential School.

Colonialism at Play

By the end of the nineteenth century, as we have seen, sports and recreation played a significant role in the assimilative project of residential schools across Canada and the United States. Although the Indigenous origins of the game were celebrated and exploited, it was seen as a new creation, one grounded in Victorian principles of masculinity, sportsmanship, and morality. As such, it was perceived to be a suitable tool for use among Indigenous peoples. Janice Forsyth explains the process:

> One of the ways in which church and state extended their power over
> Aboriginal lives was through the regulation of traditional beliefs and

practices, a mode of control that has a far-reaching impact on how Aboriginal people came to participate in the developing structure of Euro-Canadian sports ... Armed with documents that were conceived in private, and which justified their actions, church and state attempted to replace traditional practices, like the Potlatch and Sundance ceremonies, with activities that were seemingly secular but were imbued with Christian religious ideals, and relied on Euro-Canadian sports and games to help them accomplish this task.[23]

Chief Louis Miranda (Sxaaltxw) explained in an interview with Reuben Ware that the Oblates of Mary Immaculate initially affirmed the Sḵwx̱wú7-mesh desire to maintain their pride and culture. However, as the missionaries' civilizing efforts intensified, as evidenced by the implementation of the Durieu system and residential schools, the Sḵwx̱wú7mesh were increasingly stripped of both:

> When religion first came here they were taught that also [to have pride], but it was a late departure. When they took the children away that is when the people started to lose their pride ... The old man Joe. Thomas, my wife's stepfather, he said before the whiteman came, our people were very close, and then when the whiteman came we changed, we changed a little bit, and then when the priest came we started to change all together ... We lost our Indian culture but we still had our language. *But it was when the school came, then he says, that is when we lost everything.*[24]

As we have also seen, the Sḵwx̱wú7mesh experience was by no means unique. However, it remains that during the opening decades of the twentieth century, Sḵwx̱wú7mesh identity – that is, their culture, epistemologies, and historic understanding of what it meant to be both Sḵwx̱wú7mesh and Coast Salish – had suffered a great deal. The implementation of the residential school system, the encroachments of Vancouver and North Vancouver, the ultimate failure of the Durieu system, and the ever tightening control of the Department of Indian Affairs (which banned dancing and the Potlatch) all had a tremendous impact on the Sḵwx̱wú7mesh. Historical geographer Cole Harris points out that the reserve system controlled almost every aspect of Indigenous lives and identity:

In various ways in different parts of the province, Native life came to be lived in, around, and well beyond these reserves, but wherever one went, if one were a Native person, the reserves bore on what one could and could not do. They were fixed geographical points of reference, surrounded by clusters of permissions and inhibitions that affected most Native opportunities and movements.[25]

Nonetheless, within these spaces Indigenous peoples created paths of resistance, control (however limited), and flourishing of new forms of identity that would help them maintain their self-determination and establish their voices in politics, law, and sport during the mid-twentieth century. Alexandra Harmon explains in *Indians in the Making* that Indigenous identity formation is best conceived as a "process" in which both Indigenous peoples and settlers have negotiated the definitions of "Indian."[26] In some cases, the definition was imposed from outside, as in the case of the Indian Act. In other instances, Indigenous communities themselves negotiated what "Indian" meant – although this was never entirely removed from the legal categorization imposed by the Indian Act.[27] There are few better examples of the latter than the "Indian" identity formed via the game of lacrosse in Sḵwx̱wú7mesh communities.

Spaces of Empowerment

While the burgeoning centre of Vancouver owed its existence to the dispossession of unceeded Indigenous lands, the urban space exposed the Sḵwx̱wú7mesh to opportunities and forms of organization, resistance, and identity building that at times endured, incorporated, or rejected the boundaries of the reserve and urban life derived from their historic understanding of what it meant to be Sḵwx̱wú7mesh. Although lacrosse had been introduced in the service of non-Native civilizing efforts, it actually helped to defeat them in favour of flourishing Indigenous nationhood. Among the Sḵwx̱wú7mesh, lacrosse developed into a defensive force. It gave children and adults an outlet, helped instill a sense of pan-Indigeneity, and contributed to a further articulation of pride, identity, and connectedness, all of which would foster a surge of Indigenous political activity and leadership in the early twentieth century. The game helped to facilitate the fluidity of the various Sḵwx̱wú7mesh identities, whether they were local (village or community), national (the Sḵwx̱wú7mesh Nation itself), collective (Coast

Salish), or pan-Indigenous. Historian Keith Carlson notes that the Stó:lō Nation had a similar experience:

> While many mid- to late nineteenth century colonial forces conspired to fix Indigenous people onto specific sites by fracturing the links between settlements and tribes, and in other ways strengthening localized collective identities nested around individual settlements, other colonial actions simultaneously gave rise to countervailing developments of the modern sense of supratribal lower Fraser watershed-wide Stó:lō collective identity.[28]

For the Sḵwx̱wú7mesh in particular, the reserve system, urbanization, and sport combined to create a contested space in which an Indigenous identity was forged. Under the growing shadow of Vancouver, the implementation of residential schools, and the Indian Act, lacrosse became a tool used for aspirations that reached beyond sporting excellence.

The onslaught of the colonial system imposed a series of significant traumas on Indigenous peoples, but it also generated new responses that were uniquely their own. As Kim Anderson explains, a common value held by Indigenous peoples is a "continuous process of change" in spite of, and in resistance to, settler-colonialism.[29] Lacrosse was one such example. Its acceptance is perhaps best understood in relation to an abridged Sḵwx̱wú7mesh creation story, which emphasizes the importance of adaptability in changing times:

> Now after the disaster the people started to multiply again but in the years [of] confusion that followed the flood, all their culture had disappeared ... although they were the descendants of the first people, the catastrophe had made them entirely different ... A man appeared out of the air to help them rehabilitate themselves. His [name was] T-hii-ss ... [and] this man was known as the transformer. He showed the people methods of cooking, of preserving, of hygiene and of morals and decency. Most of the people of the coast met him with great kindness and respect but occasionally a man would decide that he knew all he wanted to know and would take no advice ... Now, as T-hii-ss approached Vancouver he met a man who was standing in the sea scrubbing himself with a hemlock bough. T-hii-ss came to him in friendship and attempted to chat with him about the changing times.

The man was surly, however, and said that he was not interested but was going to go on licing [delousing?] as he had always done. T-hii-ss told him that no man or beast could continue to live in the world unless he changed with the times. At this man cried ... "go and mind your own business." This made T-hii-ss so angry that he waved his wand and changed the man and his hemlock bough into "Ss-kly-ulch" or "Standing Still", to be an example till judgement day of a man who would not adapt himself to the times, and to be known to the white people as Siwash Rock.[30]

In essence, sport was an adaptation by the Coast Salish and the Skwxwú7mesh Nation. This strategy, which sprang from their own sense of nationhood, enabled them to avoid becoming like "Standing Still," the static entity. Carlson reminds us that the narrative above and the Coast Salish story of the Great Flood follow in the tradition of Coast Salish adaptation.[31] "Such stories," Carlson writes,

> do much more than help contemporary Coast Salish generations come to appreciate what their ancestors experienced in the distant past. Equally important is the role they play in guiding successive generations in negotiating responses to new events and happenings ... Perceived through local Indigenous modes of history we catch glimpses of the continuity in change, as well as the causes of change in continuity.[32]

For the Skwxwú7mesh, lacrosse, and likewise baseball and soccer, was that continuity in change, a new means of identity reformation.

Indian Sports Days

The first recorded Skwxwú7mesh lacrosse team was founded in 1911 under the direction of Andy Paull, but evidence suggests that the Skwxwú7mesh were establishing teams as early as 1907, if not earlier, for holiday celebrations.[33] For Paull and the other early organizers of the Skwxwú7mesh teams, such as manager Chief Joe Capilano and coach John Baker, lacrosse presented an opportunity not only to (re)build community pride and identity but to generate positive relations with settlers.[34] One venue that enabled this was the Indian Sports Days, held each year by non-Indigenous sports promoter Con Jones.

▲ Thousands of spectators line the field and rooftops during a lacrosse match at Homer and Smythe in downtown Vancouver, c. 1911. | *AM54-S4: Pan P87, City of Vancouver Archives.*

▼ Vancouver versus New Westminster, August 19, 1911. | *Photographer William John Cairns, AM54-S-2: CVA 371-596, City of Vancouver Archives.*

▶ Crowd of boys with lacrosse sticks in Vancouver, c. 1912. | *Photographer Stuart Thomson, AM1535: CVA 99-1165, City of Vancouver Archives.*

◀ Standing room only! Thousands attempt to watch a game in Vancouver, c.1912, with some spectators having to turn to creative measures to watch the game. | *Photographer William John Cairns, AM54-S-2: CVA 371-575, City of Vancouver Archives.*

▶ Vancouver versus New Westminster at Recreation Park in downtown Vancouver, c. 1912. | *Photographer William John Cairns, AM54-S-2: CVA 371-579, City of Vancouver Archives.*

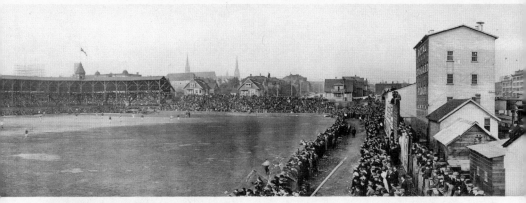

As Vancouver grew into the commercial centre of western Canada, spurred on by an influx of immigrants, developments in resource extraction, and, of course, the newly arrived railway system, authorities appropriated the unceded territory and removed Indigenous communities from within city limits – although not entirely – as they recast the area economically and socially as non-Indigenous.[35] Part of this social reformation included the establishment of organized sport. Enter Con Jones, who founded Vancouver's first professional lacrosse league in 1909, at the climax of the war against professionalism.[36] In early 1916, Jones was approached by the British Columbia Aero Club, which was seeking a way to raise funds for the training of military aviators.[37] Knowing the popularity of Indigenous athletes as performers and the demand for them among non-Indigenous audiences, Jones came up with the idea of hosting an inaugural Indian Sports Day in Vancouver to celebrate Queen Victoria's birthday.[38] Much like the entrepreneurs who developed cultural tours to the United States and overseas during the late nineteenth century, new lacrosse promoters such as Jones established Indian Sports Days as part of holiday celebrations and agricultural fairs. Here, Coast Salish communities engaged in all-Indigenous sports competitions such as lacrosse, soccer, and baseball – to which they had been introduced due to the encroachment of non-Indigenous society and residential schools. Confirming the link between Indigenous and non-Native people that sports offered, a *Vancouver Daily Sun* article of 1917 reported the view of several Indigenous participants:

> A number of leading Indians were yesterday in conference with Con Jones, the promoter of the sports, expressing their appreciation of the size the sports had already assumed and the growth they hoped it would assume in future years. They said they liked to show that they were men, not set apart to live on reserves, but able to enjoy themselves in a rational way and with as great an average of athletic ability as any class of the community.[39]

In fact, though the initiative was led by Jones, its success was secured by Sḵwx̱wú7mesh Nation members Andy Paull and Chief Mathias Joe, who were supported by Xʷməθkʷəy̓əm (Musqueam) and shíshálh (Sechelt) Nation members in convincing Coast Salish communities to attend.[40]

Indian Sports Days enabled Indigenous peoples to gather and compete against other local and distant Indigenous nations, to perform ceremonies

A Sḵwx̱wú7mesh championship lacrosse
team, possibly holding the Indian
Championship Cup, c. 1917. | *Photograph
4799, North Vancouver Museum and Archives.*

and dances that were banned by the Indian Act (such as the Potlatch, which
was made illegal from 1884 to 1951), and to acquire additional income. Indian
Sports Days also renewed a fierce sense of competition between the
Sḵwx̱wú7mesh and Xʷməθkʷəy̓əm Nations. For example, in 1916 and beyond, the two nations fielded teams to compete for the Indian Lacrosse
Championship, and their baseball, soccer, and canoe-racing teams faced off
against each other, exchanging the titles numerous times.[41] As Sḵwx̱wú7mesh
Elder Paitsmauk, Dave Jacobs, explains, "a lot of the canoe paddlers, there
would be a group of them, they went from sport to sport to sport. So
Xʷməθkʷəy̓əm, if they had a canoe team, soccer team, well then they picked
up sticks and went to play lacrosse."[42] The rivalry went beyond the
Xʷməθkʷəy̓əm Nation, as the Sḵwx̱wú7mesh often competed against those
within their kinship networks from Coast Salish nations on Vancouver
Island, helping them to maintain socio-political relations.[43]

At the same time, the championships offered financial rewards.[44] For
example, the tug-of-war match had a top prize of $50 for the winner, with
$20 going to the runner-up; the lacrosse contest offered a grand prize of
$60, with $24 going to second place. All told, cash prizes of $725 were handed
out at the Indian Sports Day in 1917.[45] As a pastor remarked concerning a

visiting Vancouver Island team, "The cash prizes are quite a boon to the boys ... It seems to me that nothing can stop them from going over and of course I shall be with them."[46] As mentioned previously, the use of performances to acquire income was not unlike what Raibmon found in her study of the Kwakwa̲ka̲'wakw, as the cash prizes were most certainly going to support the Potlatch, despite its ban.[47] Although the pay was attractive, there was a great deal more to Indian Sports Days than athletic competition and extra income. Mainly, many of these sporting and cultural performances, staged for the entertainment of non-Indigenous audiences, helped Indigenous peoples circumvent the restrictions and impositions of the Indian Act, especially in connection with dancing.

In 1884, the act had outlawed Indigenous ceremonies such as the Potlatch, and in 1914 it was amended to make off-reserve dancing punishable by incarceration and required Indigenous peoples in western Canada to obtain permission to appear in regalia.[48] As Sḵwx̱wú7mesh Elder Louis Miranda recounted in an interview with Reuben Ware, the new laws made it extremely difficult for the Sḵwx̱wú7mesh to assemble: "When they were strictly forbidden [and had] to give up Potlatch, they couldn't even invite a relative because they said you were giving a party [Potlatch]."[49]

It was at Indian Sports Days, similar to rodeo competitons, where the Indian Act met sport, and the two coverged. In 1916, Con Jones announced that the inaugural Indian Sports Day would feature "Indian dancing in Aboriginal costume," not realizing that this activity was restricted under the Indian Act.[50] He was quickly informed of the legal restrictions, and in response, presumably fearful of disappointing his non-Native audience, Jones, with the assistance of Member of Parliament H.H. Stevens, appealed to the Department of Indian Affairs to allow the dancing to go ahead.[51] He received permission from New Westminster Indian agent Peter Byrne and was told that "he might proceed with his plans, the only limitation imposed being that no objectionable features should be introduced and that the dancing should be under the supervision of Constable Grant."[52]

For the Indigenous participants, Sports Days provided an opportunity to circumvent the Indian Act. Whereas at other times and places, they could be jailed or fined for partaking in their own cultural practices, Sports Days were the exception to the rule. At these venues, Indigenous peoples were encouraged to engage in dance performances and to display their regalia; the "Indian Costume" competitions drew wide press attention. But competitors were not only publicly displaying "illegal" articles of their culture

– they were also continuing the Potlatch in covert form. While both church and state attempted to use sport and the Indian Act to eliminate the practices of Indigenous peoples, it was, ironically, an Indigenous game imposed in residential schools that would assist the Sḵwx̱wú7mesh in keeping their culture alive and witnessing a new articulation of their nationhood. The allure of "Indians" as an attraction, as well as potential gate receipts for promoters, often pushed Indigenous culture from the underground and brought it before a curious and paying public. Wayne Suttles observes that the participation of the Coast Salish in sporting, cultural, and holiday celebrations had "a picnic quality of the potlatch ... In fact the local group may emerge more clearly on this occasion because the principal participants are not individuals, for whom identity is only partly a matter of residence, but crews of canoes, which are more readily identifiable with a place."[53] Many nations sent teams to compete at Indian Sports Days: these included the Xʷməθkʷəy̓əm and the Sḵwx̱wú7mesh from the Vancouver area; the Quw'utsun' (Cowichan) and the W̱SÁNEĆ (Saanich) from Vancouver Island; the Lhaq'temish (Lummi) from present-day Washington State; and nations from northern and interior British Columbia.[54] According to a 1917 *Vancouver Daily Times* article, the Indigenous participants were "welcoming this opportunity of exchanging views with men of other tribes."[55] But Indian Sports Days were not simply an opportunity for "exchanging views" – rather, they served to maintain and renew Coast Salish kinship networks and socio-political relations, as Paitsmauk, Dave Jacobs, further explains:

If they could not have a Potlatch, if they couldn't have a feast or something, there was always that gathering [sport] that they could pass it on, talk about it. *Because you couldn't be jailed for gathering at a sport event but you could be jailed for gathering at a Potlatch. So they found a way to continue it by having these sport events, canoe paddling, lacrosse and those gatherings from different villages, together.* So that was a way to get the message out to families. They had to find a way – because they were jailing people at that time, there were many people that went to jail for Potlatch. My father, grandfather, got around that. He built a church and put a cross up on the gable ends, and so they just figured it was a church and not a Potlatch house [Paitsmauk and Sla'wiya laugh]. So they drove by on Marine Drive on the roads. "Aahhh it's a church, it's got the cross." They didn't [know] – no they didn't bother to come over and search.[56]

During a 1996 interview conducted by Karen Galligos, ɬaʔamin (Tla'amin) Nation member David George recalled that feasts, Potlatches, and Sports Days fused culture and tradition, particularly at Cape Mudge, at the northern end of Georgia Strait:

KAREN GALLIGOS: Do you know if our people used to have Potlatches down here? Where people would come from Squamish or Cape Mudge ...

DAVID GEORGE: Yeah, they called it No'hum. It's different from Potlatch ... With ours, I think if something came up, like a sports day or a wedding, we had a No'hum. Invite people from all over the place. It's something like a Potlatch, hand out some deer meat, smoked fish. Even when I was young, I remember mom and dad used to go to Cape Mudge, they had a big sports day, it was the same thing, everybody gets together, people from Alert Bay, Comox, Nanaimo, everyone would end up in Cape Mudge.[57]

While the paternalistic Department of Indian Affairs continued to attempt to eliminate the self-determination of Indigenous nations and, with it, their identities, these Indians Sports Days offered an outlet for Indigenous participants to circumvent the Indian Act and enabled them to maintain their kinship relations. In their study of Native brass bands, historians Susan Neylan and Melissa Meyer chronicle a resistance theme that parallels lacrosse and Sports Days: "The bands highlight the complexity of maintaining and adapting cultural practices in light of the rapid change and repression brought about by the Aboriginal-European encounter. These Aboriginal musical groups acted, in effect, as a connective institution that intertwined family, community, and culture."[58] Andy Paull also organized brass bands, as well as baseball teams and boxing tournaments, imports from colonial encounters that took on their own purpose within the Skwxwú7mesh cultural and epistemological context.[59] And Paull and the Skwxwú7mesh lacrosse contingent remained active each Victoria Day for several years after 1916.

Although the views of Indigenous peoples and colonial agents regarding the meaning and value of sport were not monolithic, Indian Sports Days demonstrate the stark contrast between them. As Susan Neylan and I have argued elsewhere, "From the perspective of Indian Affairs, sport days and other holiday events were not simply an apolitical exhibition of athleticism or Indigenous showmanship but a means to carry and instill a set of political objectives concurrently sought out through other forms (i.e., residential and day schools, laws, missionaries, etc.)."[60] A 1917 *Vancouver Daily Sun* article relayed the Department of Indian Affairs perspective:

> The Indian sports to be held on May 22, 23, and 24 are being promoted with the encouragement of the officials of the department of Indian affairs [sic] who wish to see competitions of strength and speed replacing the Potlatch of byegone days. The modern aim is to induce Indians to become members of the general community practising the same recreations as their paleface friends. They are being urged to devote themselves more to the cultivation of the soil – to become real producers – and it seems to be recognized that joining more fully in athletic sports is one of the steps towards slipping out of the old grooves.[61]

Conversely, as Elders Paitsmauk, Dave Jacobs, and Sla'wiya, Andrea Jacobs, reflect, using sports as a cultural marker and a community unifier had been with the Skwx̱wú7mesh well before the adaptation of lacrosse, but the implementation of the game had extra significance due to its Indigenous origins:

PAITSMAUK: Of course all the families and communities are involved, and it's been that way ever since, and that is how – in the tough times – they got all the communities together. Of course in those days there was a lot of marriages from different tribes, and families getting together, which was great. The competition started building and building and soccer [and lacrosse and baseball] came in, and was big and still is, on all the villages.

SLA'WIYA: It didn't matter what sport it was, we always, all the families, get involved, and then relatives of the family, and that is just the way it seems to work. It was the same people involved because it's their nephew or whatever, but it was always our family, then the relatives, then their friends and whatnot. That is how you get the people out. It kept our community close knit. It's been going on for years and years, doesn't matter what sport. *But when it comes to lacrosse, of course it's a different story we think, you know – because of the fact, it's our game!*[62]

Like the Hodinöhsö:ni', the Skwxwú7mesh know lacrosse as "our game." Thanks in large part to the zealous celebration of lacrosse as an Indigenous pastime, the Skwxwú7mesh, who had not traditionally known the Hodinöhsö:ni' game or stick, took ownership of lacrosse as something directly linked with pan-Indigenous nationhood. In his 1994 autobiography, Skwxwú7mesh chief Simon Baker, Khot-La-Cha, made this point as he reflected on playing in the 1930s: "I like most sports, but *lacrosse is our game. Lacrosse is a real Indian game.*"[63] The Skwxwú7mesh use of lacrosse is an example of what Neylan and Meyer refer to as "cultural collaboration," a way "in which Aboriginal culture adopted and adapted colonial forms to create new kinds of performative expressions."[64] In part, lacrosse became an identifier of what it meant to be "Indian" and Skwxwú7mesh. It helped connect Indigenous communities and nations, forming friendships, identities, kinship ties, and political relations that spanned the continent:

PAITSMAUK: It [being Skwxwú7mesh] is part of what we are ... You have definitions or words for [it], started out as Indian then you have First Nations, then you have Aboriginals and all of that. Those you can write down those you can see because you write them down but if you say what is inside of you ... it's there, it's part of your make up ... They say it's genetic, it's this, it's that. But we are the only people that have it, that's here [Paitsmauk points to his heart]. Mine comes from my father and grandfather, that's why it's here. That's the way our people are, all of our people are that way, it comes so far from in here [pointing to his heart]. You don't implant that, because it's there you are born with that, that's why our people are so proud.

ALLAN: So that just carries over to the sports?

PAITSMAUK: Oh yes, oh sports ... One canoe is from the village or two, there are literally thousands of people that gather because they have so much pride in their warriors that are out in the canoe. Soccer is the same way, lacrosse, all the sports are that way. It is the way they show their pride, they are able to holler and give them support, they are supporters. It is really good to see, and to carry on really.[65]

Whereas the Hodinöhsö:ni' recognize lacrosse as first and foremost a gift from the Creator, which they then distributed, the Skwxwú7mesh mark its creation by Indigenous peoples more generally and do not necessarily see it as the Creator's game. Although the Coast Salish nations may not have used lacrosse for the same spiritual purposes as the Hodinöhsö:ni', that is not to say that lacrosse or other sports were not infused into their own epistemologies. For example, community members in the ɬaʔamin Nation quickly embraced soccer after it was introduced by settler Canadians in Powell River, British Columbia, and used their traditional medicinal knowledge to enhance their health and athletic competitiveness, and to heal sports injuries.[66] Furthermore, Ts'msyen (Tsimshian) *swansx halaayts* (shamans) were known to use their power in an attempt to influence the outcome of games.[67.]

The development of lacrosse in the late 1910s and early 1920s not only fit within established epistemologies but also coincided with a new and significant political development among the Sḵwx̱wú7mesh, which saw Andy Paull take his political and sporting career in new directions. In 1913, the provincial government illegally appropriated the Kitsilano Reserve, which lay near downtown Vancouver.[68] Following this loss, the Sḵwx̱wú7mesh began to consider amalgamating their seventeen subgroups, so that the entire nation could speak with one political voice.[69] Instrumental in this process were Andy Paull and Chief Louis Miranda, both of whom pushed for integration.[70]

Although the amalgamation idea produced a great deal of apprehension, Palmer Patterson notes that "the existing kinship among the Squamish no doubt helped make the move less revolutionary than an inter-tribal amalgamation might have been."[71] United under a group of hereditary chiefs, the Sḵwx̱wú7mesh amalgamation was finalized on July 23, 1923, with the result that "all properties, interests, and trust accounts were treated as belonging to one band, and all Squamish Indians share equally in them."[72] Whereas the amalgamation created a unified political voice among the villages, lacrosse helped articulate this identity and "continuity in change, change in continuity" throughout the following decades.[73]

At the turn of the twentieth century, Vancouver enjoyed an economic and industrial boom, and the Sḵwx̱wú7mesh played a critical role in its development. Just as Hodinöhsö:ni' men left their communities to pursue ironworking opportunities, the Sḵwx̱wú7mesh had established themselves as accomplished longshoremen on the West Coast since the 1860s and were highly successful pan-Salish union organizers.[74] In 1913, they formed Local 38-57 of the International Longshoremen's Association (ILA), with Andy

Paull as a key member.[75] The labour organization of the Sḵwx̱wú7mesh, their unification movements, and the development of athletic teams all coincided with their growing concern for Indigenous rights. The relationship between the three is clearly demonstrated by the direct connection between Andy Paull, the ILA, and one of the first competitive Sḵwx̱wú7mesh lacrosse teams. Indian Sports Days and holiday celebrations had become critical reunification tools for the Coast Salish, as Suttles and Carlson point out, but they were limited engagements that enabled regionalized identities to be "showcased." Competitive sports, such as lacrosse, in themselves became elements of identity formation. Coaches, organizers, and players in the Sḵwx̱wú7mesh communities, who met regularly throughout the summer months, became "cultural producers," shifting modern sports for their own uses and naturalizing them within communities.

The Sḵwx̱wú7mesh Enter Canadian Competition

In 1919, the Squamish Indians, a team organized by Andy Paull, began to play in Vancouver's modest three-team City Senior Amateur Lacrosse League. It was one of the first regularly competitive Sḵwx̱wú7mesh lacrosse teams to engage in official league competition.[76] Unlike in central Canada, where Indigenous athletes remained barred from competition, the British Columbia Lacrosse Association (BCLA) changed its ban on Indigenous participation in 1919. An explanation as to why the league reversed or at least overlooked its ban – it remains unclear what exactly took place – has its origins in the connection between Con Jones, Andy Paull, and the efforts of the BCLA to increase ticket sales. In May 1919, the BCLA made a number of changes to its rules: it shortened field lengths, reduced intermission and period times, and curbed excessive rough play, all in an attempt "to give the spectators a big run for their money, without taking too much of their time."[77] Struggling to improve the diminishing popularity of lacrosse and to locate participants for the 1919 season, the BCLA hoped to find new ways of drawing fans back to the game. Days later, enter Andy Paull and the Squamish Indians.

During that year, the Indians had played against other Indigenous teams in exhibitions and "Indian Championships," as well as in exhibitions against non-Native teams, often organized by Con Jones, but they remained absent from official league competition. Nearing the June start date for the league competition, with only one team confirmed, the BCLA accepted the Squamish Indians and a third organization to play in the amateur league.

Beyond the shortage of teams, an additional factor helps to explain this development which effectively ended the Indigenous ban in British Columbia – the relationship between Andy Paull and Con Jones. The two had first met at Indian Sports Days, which Paull helped organize. During the 1919 season, Jones played a role in the league's organization, and he headed its operations during the following year.[78] Involved in the running of the league and attempting to repopularize lacrosse in Vancouver, he was fully aware of the drawing power of Indigenous athletes, and he had a three-year relationship with Andy Paull. Add to this Paull himself, a skilled Indigenous rights activist and organizer, who was able to convince the league to overturn or at least ignore the rule.[79] We can only speculate on why the BCLA ended its ban, but just as in times past and much to the relief of Con Jones and the BCLA, the Indigenous athletes boosted gate receipts. The link between Paull and Jones also points to the complexity of interactions in "contact zones" such as lacrosse. Although the legacy of Canada's Colonial Age as a co-ordinated structure of dispossession was never absent, relationships between Indigenous peoples and settler Canadians were not infinitely or automatically negative or destructive. Mary-Ellen Kelm explains, "Social relations in the contact zone can be surprising, atypical, carnivalesque, or they might be overdetermined by gendered, classed, sexualized, and racialized structures that emerge within them. Contact zones mark out territories within the grand narrative of nation-building and operate at the microhistorical level."[80] Sometimes the nation-building activities in contact zones were those of Indigenous nations rather than the nation-state of Canada.

This repositioning and articulation of Indigenous nationhood through lacrosse and its networks occurred in highly gendered ways, as both Indigenous understandings of the game and settler-colonial ideas about sports and masculinity sanctioned this particular contact zone as the virtually exclusive preserve of men. This of course had an important effect on shaping lacrosse's possibilities – and limitations – as a means of articulating Squamish nationhood, empowering Indigenous identities, or decolonizing intercultural encounters. This is also not to say that this particular articulation of nationhood was experienced by all or in the same way for every Skwxwú7mesh Nation member. However, what is significant is that the ways in which lacrosse built networks and shaped communities during the early twentieth century went beyond the actual players and individual games, resonating throughout Indigenous transnational networks, nations, communities, kinship, and identities.

Competing in the City Senior Amateur Lacrosse League for several seasons and consistently playing before 1,500 to 3,500 spectators, the Skwx̱wú7mesh team – renamed the ILA (International Longshoremen's Association) in 1920 – was highly successful and was often regarded as one of the most competitive and popular teams in the league.[81] Leading the league in wins throughout the 1921 season, it won its first championship that year, marking the beginning of lacrosse proficiency for the Skwx̱wú7mesh Nation that would last until the beginning of the Second World War.[82] As members of the team continued to work on the docks and became well known for their longshoring, the team itself was developing into one of the most accomplished in British Columbia. In 1923, it captured the local North Shore Senior "B" title – only one notch below the highest level of competition – and followed that up with five consecutive titles between 1925 and 1929, reaching the provincial finals three times during that period.[83] Furthermore, the union lacrosse teams of the early 1920s served as a catalyst for Skwx̱wú7mesh players to start joining non-Indigenous teams and for the establishment of the North Shore Indian teams of the 1930s that would see the reintroduction of Indigenous teams into Canada's top national competition. For instance, Skwx̱wú7mesh players Andrew Jack and Louie Lewis became the first Indigenous players to join the Senior "A" league when they played for the non-Indigenous Vancouver Terminals organized by Con Jones in the early 1920s.[84]

The Skwx̱wú7mesh were not the only Coast Salish nation that played lacrosse during the 1920s: Indigenous teams were scattered throughout the Fraser Valley. In fact, the Sts'ailes (Chehalis) community had been organizing teams since at least 1907, and Stó:lō Nation member Henry George Pennier noted that a number of Indigenous teams – mainly Stó:lō – played in the valley during the 1920s, including at Chilliwack Landing, Chilliwack Township, Sts'ailes, and Sardis, all of whom competed against each other.[85] Pennier vividly recalled a game against the famed Squamish Indians:

Worst game ever I was in was against the North Vancouver Indian club and we played at Brockton Point in Stanley Park, Vancouver. They were all older and more experienced and they sure showed us up. Their strategy was to sluff around until we followed suit and then all at once to break out of it and score. We got murdered. It was a bad day and after all these years I still shudder when I think of it.[86]

Sḵwx̱wú7mesh lacrosse team, 1917. |
*Photographer Stuart Thomson, AM1535: CVA 99-354, City
of Vancouver Archives.*

**Unidentified Indigenous lacrosse team in
Vancouver, c. 1920.** | *Photographer Stuart Thomson,
AM1535: CVA 99-1018, City of Vancouver Archives.*

In the 1920s, Andy Paull continued his involvement in athletics such as lacrosse, baseball, and canoe racing, and in organizing the local brass band, but the fight for Sḵwx̱wú7mesh rights, and Indigenous rights more broadly, remained his predominant focus. However, 1927 was a watershed for Paull, the Sḵwx̱wú7mesh Nation, and Indigenous peoples within the borders of colonial Canada. During that year, in response to a 1926 petition from the Allied Tribes of British Columbia, a Special Joint Committee of the Senate and House of Commons was appointed to investigate Indigenous land title in British Columbia. As secretary of both the Allied Tribes and the Sḵwx̱wú7mesh Band Council, Paull testified at the hearings. The parliamentary committee concluded that Indigenous title did not exist.[87] Furthermore, in 1927, Ottawa formally banned Indigenous land claims by making it illegal to expend funds or to fundraise for such purposes. Following these developments, Paull focused more intently on sports, but for some – mainly his friend and biographer Herbert Francis Dunlop – this equated with squandered talents:

> With his natural gifts he could have been in the political arena one of the foremost men of his time. His talents should not have been wasted in lacrosse arenas across the country playing games. His association with sports projected him as a wily and sometimes tricky coach, unpredictable and, of course, the darling of sports writers. He had much more to offer his people and his country. He could teach the young more than how to take their lumps or score a goal. He was capable of teaching them how to win a contest far more important than a lacrosse game.[88]

Dunlop did not perceive that Paull was offering the Sḵwx̱wú7mesh more than just a game. He helped organize one of the most important and unifying cultural elements of the twentieth century that would forever change the Sḵwx̱wú7mesh Nation. With a lacrosse stick in hand, he provided the nation with a means to escape, if only temporarily, the harsh realities of the Great Depression and left a legacy that continues to unite the nation to this day. No team that Paull organized better exemplifies this than the Squamish Indians lacrosse team – who had reverted back to their original name – of the 1930s.

Following the First World War and into the 1920s, and amid the growing popularity of rival sports such as baseball, promoters and enthusiasts attempted to re-establish lacrosse in Vancouver's sporting culture. As part of this endeavour, Skwxwú7mesh men increasingly played for non-Indigenous teams. By 1930, some of the greatest players ever to come out of the Skwxwú7mesh Nation were competing for the national senior championship of Canada, represented by the Mann Cup.[89] Although Indigenous athletes were joining non-Native teams in central Canada, mostly as ringers, they remained on the fringes of national competition due to the lingering effects of the 1880 ban. In contrast, Indigenous athletes in British Columbia were openly competing and identifying as Skwxwú7mesh. Although the war on professionalism that contributed to the eastern persecution of Indigenous athletes was alive and well on the West Coast in the early twentieth century, it predated the influx of Skwxwú7mesh teams and concerned itself with British Columbia's top teams and promoters such as the New Westminster Salmonbellies and Con Jones.[90] In eastern rule books, Indigenous players were originally barred because they were deemed professionals – although race and class were obvious factors – whereas in British Columbia the ban focused solely on their race, also targeting other people of colour.[91] As mentioned earlier, this followed the lengthy appropriation of Indigenous spaces; sport was just one of the many visible signs of the attempt to reform those spaces as a white settler colony and extend the reach of Canadian imperialism.[92] However, the ban in British Columbia did not have the lasting effect that it had in Ontario and Quebec; whereas Indigenous players continued to be barred in central and eastern Canada, the same was not true in western Canada.

In 1930, the Vancouver senior lacrosse team had a number of Skwxwú7mesh players on its roster, including members of the Baker family, one of the many famous lacrosse families from the nation. During a very successful 1930 season, Harry "Hawkeye" Baker, a goaltender, along with brothers Ray and Dominic, both "runners," played for Vancouver's predominately non-Indigenous senior team and lost to the New Westminster Salmonbellies in the Kilmarnock Cup – the provincial championship of British Columbia.[93] Although the Vancouver team lost the series and thus did not represent British Columbia in the national championship, the season helped establish the Skwxwú7mesh players among the lacrosse elite and sparked the idea that the Skwxwú7mesh should organize their own top-tier team. Not only did the Skwxwú7mesh have enough athletes to put a team together; they had some of the best players in the province, if not the country.

Throughout the 1920s and 1930s, Sḵwx̱wú7mesh players continued to work long hours on the docks and in associated industries, which sometimes limited the time they could devote to lacrosse. They also experienced difficulty in securing sponsorship funds to offset their travel costs.[94] In his autobiography, Chief Simon Baker, Khot-La-Cha, explained the problem:

> What made it very difficult for us, the North Shore Indians, was that everyone of us was playing lacrosse at the time we were longshoremen. We used to work ten-hour days. Imagine, in those days we used to work down the hole carrying lumber. It was heavy lumber, and after those ten-hour days we used to go play lacrosse the same night. We used to wonder how we ever did it, but I kept myself in good condition.[95]

As Louis Miranda elaborated, the Depression weighed heavily on the Sḵwx̱wú7mesh, as it did for most Indigenous communities:

> In the 30's, it hit us pretty hard here, that is when welfare came out. That is when I worked and get [sic] the welfare going. It did hit the people here hard. It seemed like the longshoring went poor at the same time, the beach died out, that made things so bad. It was pretty hard because everyone was on welfare.[96]

Further complicating the economic struggles of the Great Depression, Indian Agent F.J.C. Ball often refused to pay out the assistance to needy families in an attempt to accumulate funds and cut the cost to the government.[97] Responding to the economic hardships of the times, Andy Paull saw that lacrosse could provide both himself and the Sḵwx̱wú7mesh Nation with a source of income and social relief while also creating a positive public image of the Sḵwx̱wú7mesh.[98]

The Squamish Indians and the Indoor Revolution

Just as the Sḵwx̱wú7mesh were honing their skills as lacrosse players, the game in Canada was forever changed by the advent of box lacrosse. More importantly, this development dramatically altered Indigenous participation in the game. In February 1931, Montreal Canadiens owners Joe Cattarinich and Leo Dandurand began developing plans for a new form of lacrosse that would capitalize on the popularity of hockey, with which they saw numerous similarities, and fill empty rinks during the summer.[99] From the end of the First World War, the appeal of lacrosse had declined markedly, especially in Vancouver, so organizers looked for ways of rejuvenating the game. In April 1931, the first indoor lacrosse league was founded in central Canada and the United States, known as the International Professional Lacrosse League (IPLL), and the new form of the game reduced players from twelve to seven per side, a number that would later shrink to six.[100] In style of play and its rules, the game was reworked so that it resembled hockey: held in arenas from which the ice had been removed or in enclosed outdoor "box" facilities, games consisted of three twenty-minute periods, and hockey nets were used.[101]

Beginning competition in June 1931, the new league recruited players from Hodinöhsö:ni' communities, including Kahnawà:ke, Ahkwesáhsne, and Six Nations.[102] As in the past, promoters recognized that Indigenous peoples were skilled players but also hoped that they would attract the public and increase ticket sales.[103] As Donald Fisher notes, "Older lacrosse fans and veteran journalists recalled the big crowds that visiting Native teams used to draw in Toronto and Montreal decades earlier"; the Indigenous presence in the new sport rekindled that nostalgia.[104] The game of box lacrosse was followed closely on the West Coast, and promoters there, including Andy Paull, wasted no time in taking to the new form. The Sḵwx̱wú7mesh played an active role in establishing the game in Vancouver and the province, enriching Canadian, Sḵwx̱wú7mesh, and Indigenous culture on numerous levels.

Pondering the idea of joining the BCALA to compete for the provincial championship, Paull formed an all-Sḵwx̱wú7mesh team known as the Squamish Indians in the early summer of 1931, with himself as manager.[105] Simultaneously, the Vancouver media and western lacrosse promoters were following the developments in the east. Galvanized by the popularity of the professional box lacrosse league, amateur field lacrosse clubs in Ontario and British Columbia experimented with exhibition box lacrosse games throughout the summer.[106] Box lacrosse made its first appearance on the West Coast on July 14, 1931, and the Sḵwx̱wú7mesh played a critical role in its development, as the BCALA organized a series of games that included the team. Together, the BCALA and the Sḵwx̱wú7mesh reinvigorated lacrosse at a time when leagues were perilously close to folding.[107] As Cleve Dheensaw states in his history of BC lacrosse, "In many ways in the 1930s, they [the Squamish Indians] represented all that was best about the game – the links to the Indian past of the sport and the glowing promise of its future as represented in their exciting play in the box."[108]

Always a vocal and quick-witted opportunist, Andy Paull had a knack for drawing attention to his causes and the Skwxwú7mesh through his interviews and newspaper columns, in which he capitalized on large public events such as the box lacrosse demonstrations of 1931. He was such a well-known figure in political and sporting circles that the press often referred to the teams he coached as "Paullmen." Palmer Patterson captures the public image of Paull well, despite upholding the false dichotomy between "Indian" and "modernity":

> In the newspapers, for example, he appeared as a clever, enterprising, and Westernized individual who still retained a sense of his Indian heritage. With his willingness to make statements on a variety of subjects, his colorful character, and his role in promoting sports, he was "made to order" for reporters. In addition, his serious side as a defender of the Indians made him all the more newsworthy.[109]

Using what can be overlooked as self-effacing and ironic humour, Paull spoke to the Canadian public via local newspapers, attempting to break down barriers and attain public and political recognition for himself, the Skwxwú7mesh, and Indigenous peoples more generally. Herb Morden wrote in 1946 that "there's a wealth of story and legend behind Andy who is the eyes, ears and tongue for Canada's Indians in their fight for equal opportunity."[110] Herbert Dunlop notes that Paull could be relied upon to produce a sarcastic, humorous, and quotable comment: "The stories of Andy's antics multiplied, and the sportswriters loved him. He was always good for a quote, and so often through Andy they were able to inject a sense of humour in their column for people who in the Thirties needed so badly to laugh."[111] Never at a loss for words, Paull often poked fun at the Indian stereotype, turning it on its head to correct the errors of popular history and call attention to the ignorance of non-Natives. A *Vancouver Sun* article titled "No Tomahawk Tonight" is a case in point:

> Lacrosse featuring the aborigine against the white man is on tonight and a legend of history tells us that the wily red man once again took a fort from the whites by playing lacrosse for a period and then dropping sticks for the well known tomahawk and the ... bow string with

deadly arrow attached [this refers to the 1763 lacrosse game at Fort Michilimackinac]. Mr. Andy Paull, chief of the Redmen that will parade at Athletic Park tonight against the rejuvenated professionals, reports there will be no tomahawking but that the odd bit of impromptu scalping may occur. "You know how it is," said Mr. Paull, "my boys are all in first class condition and many of them can run with the speed of their forefathers who used to catch deer that way. Now the professionals, being a trifle stiffish on the getaway, may feel it essential to scalp one or two of my braves in order to slow them to their speed. I trust this will not take place because we all want to keep it very clean and nice. I think you will see the Pros take another beating," and Mr. Paull stepped briskly away upstreet to make another call.[112]

In 1932, following the 1931 Mann Cup championship, which continued to be played as field lacrosse, the Canadian Amateur Lacrosse Association voted that box lacrosse would replace the field variant as the official game for Canada's top championship series.[113] In the Vancouver area, the opening season for box lacrosse kicked off on July 2, 1932. Playing for the Squamish Indians were several Sḵwx̱wú7mesh baseball players, such as Simon Baker (Khot-La-Cha), who had been enticed by Paull to join the team.[114] Playing to crowds of greatly differing sizes, Paull's Sḵwx̱wú7mesh team led the three-team league – the other teams being the Vancouver Athletic Club and the New Westminster Salmonbellies – throughout the season. Interestingly, as Fisher points out, whereas Canadians made a near wholesale change to box lacrosse, practising field lacrosse on a much-reduced scale, the rest of the world did not follow suit.[115] The change would have a significant effect on Indigenous peoples: for the first time since 1880, Indigenous athletes across the country were encouraged to participate in non-Native leagues and championships. Box lacrosse, which quickly spread throughout Indigenous communities during the 1930s, revitalized the game in Canada and permitted Indigenous men to play in non-Indigenous competitions on a regular basis.[116]

International Competition

Just as Canadian and Indigenous clubs were making the transition to the new form of lacrosse, the Olympic committee decided that field lacrosse would be offered as a demonstration sport at the 1932 Los Angeles Olympics.[117] Despite the popularity of box lacrosse in Canada, and in the

United States to a lesser extent, field lacrosse persisted internationally.[118] As Fisher details, though lacrosse enthusiasts settled for participation as a demonstration sport, they pressured the American Olympic Lacrosse Committee to invite a Hodinöhsö:ni' team to participate in order to provide competition to the two participating nations, Canada and the United States. Because lacrosse was seen as a game of Indigenous origin, the organizers felt obliged to include a Native team, but they stopped short of simply giving it a berth in the games. Instead, it was decided that an all-star team would be created to represent the Hodinöhsö:ni' and that it would compete against some of the top American teams to win a spot at the Olympics.[119] The team was selected based on a Hodinöhsö:ni' lacrosse tournament between members of the Confederacy.[120] Following this selection tournament, the all-star team competed in early June for entry to the Olympics but was ultimately defeated by the Crescent-Athletic Hamilton Club.[121] Its elimination all but removed Indigenous representation from Olympic lacrosse.

However, there was at least one exception to this – Sḵwx̱wú7mesh goalkeeper and eventual Canadian Lacrosse Hall of Fame member Henry "Hawkeye" Baker. A veteran of non-Native teams, he was chosen as a member of the Canadian Olympic lacrosse team, which consisted mainly of players from the New Westminster Salmonbellies but also included men from Ontario and Manitoba.[122] Nicknamed "Hawkeye" for his hawk-like ability to spot the ball, Baker played for the Squamish Indians in 1932 and was recognized as one of the top goaltenders in the country.[123] His skill and ancestry quickly came to the fore in media coverage of the Olympic team. The *Vancouver Sun* articulated, "The question of a goalie, one of the weak points of the Salmonbellies last fall when they lost to Brampton (in the Mann Cup finals), appears to have been more than overcome by the selection of the Squamish Indian, Henry Baker. He will likely be the only full-blooded redskin to be found competing at the Olympics."[124] Despite their absence from the Olympic Games, Baker's Squamish Indian teammates were recognized as some of the best lacrosse players in British Columbia. In an exhibition match between the Olympic team and an all-star team from the province, at least three Sḵwx̱wú7mesh men played for the all-stars, including Gus Band, Stan Joseph, and Louie Lewis.[125]

Canadian enthusiasts hoped that the 1932 Olympic exhibition would help rejuvenate lacrosse in North America despite the differences between the old and new forms of the game.[126] At the opening game of the Olympic contest, over 75,000 people watched a match between the Canadian team and its US counterpart, from Johns Hopkins University, while waiting for the track and field events to begin.[127] Playing a three-game series, Canada lost to the United States by two games to one; due to a solid showing by Winnipeg goalie Frank Hawkins, Baker did not compete.[128] In winning the series, the Americans also obtained the Lally Cup, a trophy donated by Canadian Lacrosse Association president Joseph Lally in 1930 to the winner of an annual competition between Canada and the United States.[129] Notwithstanding Baker's backup role, it remains significant that an Indigenous player was recognized as a highly proficient athlete at a time when Canada's Colonial Age was arguably in one of its most openly oppressive stages. This would not be the last time that Baker would represent the Skwxwú7mesh and Canada in international competition. In 1935, he was once again selected to represent Canada at the Lally Cup, along with his teammate and brother Ray Baker, as well as Indians teammate and Hodinöhsö:ni' citizen Stu Bomberry. Two other Hodinöhsö:ni' players, Harry Smith and Jack Squires, would play in the Lally Cup in 1936.[130] Although equally deserving players could be found in Hodinöhsö:ni' communities, Baker's inclusion in the Olympics and the Lally Cup, along with the selection of Gus Band, Stan Joseph, and Louie Lewis for the BC all-stars team, signalled the arrival of a new dominant Indigenous presence in lacrosse and the introduction of all-Indigenous teams in Canadian box lacrosse.

The Squamish Indians in the Early 1930s

Returning from Los Angeles, Baker rejoined the league-leading Squamish Indians, which had continued their strong play in league competition despite his absence. During the Depression, the success of the team furnished both Andy Paull and the players with an alternative source of income. As Paull stated in 1932, "I do not see how we can be kept away from leading the parade to the playoffs and that gives us choice of grounds for the first playoff game as well as fifty percent of the receipts."[131] Work on the docks slowed and longshoring waned during the Depression, which meant that lacrosse became a new means for a select few Skwxwú7mesh to acquire an income.[132] Nonetheless, both Paull and his players felt the full effects of the Depression. Like members of other Coast Salish nations, the players continued to pursue subsistence fishing and hunting throughout the 1930s despite restrictions imposed by the colonial government.[133] Recounting a story that he heard from his uncle, Elder Paitsmauk, Dave Jacobs, reflects on the intersection of lacrosse, identity, employment, and ties between Coast Salish communities, including sexual relationships:

> The majority of the lacrosse players of the '36 team and that, they were fishermen. They would get on their fish boats and they would go up north [into Nuxalk Nation territory] to say Bella [Coola], Bella Bella, maybe Ocean Falls, and there were canneries. The Native women, they worked in these processing plants, anyway these guys would go up fishing and they would come back ... My uncle Dan Baker, he got involved in lacrosse later, but he said, "When we went back up there fishing again," because he was a fisherman, "We would carry a lacrosse stick up there, and we would throw the lacrosse stick on the dock, and if they [kids] picked it up they were Squamish." [laughs] ... He said, "Yeah those kids they picked up that stick, they are Squamish!" [laughs]. He was a character.[134]

Throughout the early 1930s, lacrosse audiences varied greatly in size from a few hundred to a few thousand on any given night. Weighing heavily on families and sport enthusiasts, the Great Depression diminished ticket sales, as those who could afford to attend athletic events usually waited for the hockey season to spend their limited incomes.[135] However, as the decade rolled on, lacrosse experienced a renewal in which the Squamish Indians would play a central role. In 1932, the team captured the BC provincial championship and secured the opportunity to compete to represent western Canada at the Mann Cup. The first Indigenous team to represent the province in pursuit of the national title, it headed east, stopping in Calgary for a two-game series in which it beat the Calgary Shamrocks, and later travelled to Winnipeg to take on the Winnipeg Argonauts for the western Canada box lacrosse championship.[136] Once again, the association of the "Indian" with the game came to the fore in press coverage, as a *Vancouver Sun* article demonstrates: "The Indians, the race which originated Canada's national game, were a treat to watch. They presented a team strong in every department of the game. From their brilliant goalkeeper [Henry Baker] out, there was not a flaw in their makeup."[137] Ultimately losing the Winnipeg series, the team returned to the North Shore, stopping en route to play an exhibition match in Lethbridge, Alberta, just short of returning an Indigenous team to the national lacrosse championship of Canada.[138]

Andy Paull (right) and the Squamish Indians
lacrosse team, c. late 1920s or early 1930s. |
Photograph 7119, North Vancouver Museum and Archives.

Following the 1932 season, the team disbanded for two years due to a lack of sponsorship funding, but some of its star players found a place on non-Indigenous teams, mainly the New Westminster Salmonbellies, helping take it to the Mann Cup finals in 1933 and 1934.[139] By 1934, games that had once attracted only a hundred or so were now drawing thousands and pushing the limits of local arenas.[140] In this development, the Sḵwx̱wú7mesh team would become a centrepiece of the league.

Restructuring as the North Shore Indians

After their short absence from the lacrosse scene, the Sḵwx̱wú7mesh re-entered the highest level of senior competition for the 1935 season. They bore a new name and boasted a new contingent of players. During that year, Andy Paull began recruiting Hodinöhsö:ni' athletes to play out west, and he dropped "Squamish" from the team's name, changing it to the North Shore Indians.[141] No longer would the North Vancouver team carry the Sḵwx̱wú7mesh identity alone; rather, it helped solidify a pan-Indigenous identity and international relationship for the players, their fans, the Sḵwx̱wú7mesh and Hodinöhsö:ni', and more generally the non-Indigenous public that followed the team.[142] As North Vancouver sports writer Len

Corben suggests, "Paull wanted an all-Native contender for the Mann Cup and sold the club's former players on the idea of returning to his team as a matter of Native pride and responsibility."[143] Perceiving that the Skwxwú7mesh men were too small to compete at the highest level, Paull decided to add more physical players while maintaining the all-Indigenous team, as Paitsmauk, Dave Jacobs, explains:

> Well he [Paull] was involved in a lot of the land transactions here early and he had a knack of putting things together. So then when, of course, lacrosse came along he was an organizer, he had that kind of skill and he could write. That was his kind of gift, of organizing and putting it all together, hence the lacrosse team. He followed it through ... I think him recognizing, although the North Shore Squamish players had skills, they didn't have size and of course playing against the white guys, who were great big guys, they were getting beat up and stuff. I guess he figured out a way to remedy that by bringing in – of course you're bringing in the Bomberrys, the Beef Smiths, Hughie Smiths ... and all those big skookum [strong] guys to help out this team, to balance it out. And once he got that going, they were unstoppable then.[144]

It did not take long for the North Shore Indians to penetrate the soul of the Skwxwú7mesh Nation and to serve as an intersection between a pan-Indigenous, national, and sporting identity. As the season progressed, the team's fan base and popularity grew immensely among both Indigenous supporters and non-Native Vancouverites, until by the end of the summer, its games were attended by three thousand to more than ten thousand people.[145] One game in September 1935 drew a full crowd of ten thousand, with the police reportedly turning away at least three hundred more.[146] The North Shore Indians arguably became the most popular sports team in British Columbia during the middle years of the Depression, with audiences paying twenty-five cents a head for admission.[147] Filling one of western North America's greatest sports facilities, downtown Vancouver's Denman Arena, the Indians became a hallmark of the city and its sporting culture.[148]

Often, the North Shore Indians found themselves playing before large and boisterous crowds, as fans from their own communities travelled to the games; cheering and the sound of drums became synonymous with the team.[149] Describing the cultural phenomenon that the Indians became for

**Denman Arena, at the corner of Georgia
and Denman Streets in Vancouver, c. 1929. |**
*Photographer Stuart Thomson, AM1535: CVA 99-2080, City
of Vancouver Archives.*

the Sḵwx̱wú7mesh and Indigenous peoples, Herbert Dunlop emphasizes
the importance of the team during the Depression:

> And for the men [referring to Sḵwx̱wú7mesh lacrosse fans] who had
> not won an encounter in months [they were down on their luck due
> to the Depression], sports offered a momentary substitute. Those who
> could find a few pennies headed for the arena and the forums and
> found relief in sharing vicariously victories of their favourite team.
> And when they lost, a responsive chord was sounded in the depths
> of their souls. Down on Denman and Georgia Street in Vancouver,
> the old forum opened its arms to this generation of men whose jackets
> were of yesteryear, whose pants were seedy and baggy, and whose
> shoes were tired and worn, and in most cases recalled from retirement
> by way of the half sole ... Down on Denman Street, in the old forum
> they forgot for a few hours that the corner around which prosperity
> lurked was still far beyond their reach. They forgot how poor the poor
> were and how maddeningly rich the rich were. They forgot these things

because before them were the darlings of the lacrosse world, the Squamish Indians! Smaller in stature than the white teams they played, how easy it was to identify with them as they moved with lightning speed and downed teams twice their size. They were always the underdogs, but underdogs that clawed their way to the top time and time again and many a man tasted with them a momentary sip of sweet triumph.[150]

Throughout the midyears of the Depression, the Hodinöhsö:ni' and Sḵwx̱wú7mesh united to become the dominant summertime fixture on one of North America's greatest metropolitan sporting stages. The North Shore Indians were playing for the pride of the nation. Every summer, villagers from Sḵwx̱wú7mesh communities in North Vancouver and Howe Sound went to Vancouver to support *their* team. As Sla'wiya, Andrea Jacobs, recalls about later teams, "From the time I remember, I was very young and I just remember the roar of our people when we scored."[151]

As the team entered what would be its most successful season in 1936, it brought with it the support of the Sḵwx̱wú7mesh Nation. Other sports such as baseball and soccer offered localized opportunities and were significant in their own right, but the North Shore Indians united the nation unlike any other team in Sḵwx̱wú7mesh history and embedded themselves as a significant cultural development in the twentieth century for the Sḵwx̱wú7mesh due to their national success. The team practised for hours on end in the field behind St. Paul's Catholic Church at the Mission Reserve, and members from Sḵwx̱wú7mesh communities gathered to watch, with the result that the field became their central assembly place, regardless of whether they followed the Longhouse tradition or Catholicism.[152] Although there were epistemological differences between Sḵwx̱wú7mesh communities, especially between the Capilano Reserve (Xwemelch'stn), which was a Longhouse stronghold, and the Mission Reserve, which was staunchly Catholic, these were not as rigid as Indian agents and missionaries portrayed or hoped. Although many Sḵwx̱wú7mesh were Catholic converts, several Sḵwx̱wú7mesh individuals continued to uphold the Longhouse tradition, often travelling to the Capilano Reserve to participate in Potlatches and other ceremonies at a Potlatch House that had been disguised as a church to conceal its true function.[153] Paitsmauk, Dave Jacobs, recalls the gatherings in the field behind St. Paul's:

▲ **North Shore Indians player Louis Lewis, November 1935.** | *Photographer Stuart Thomson, 16290, Vancouver Public Library.*

▶ **North Shore Indians player Harry Newman, c. 1936.** | *Photograph 3514a, North Vancouver Museum and Archives.*

There was a field just behind the church, Andrea's granny lived right next to this field. That field was so important to the community at Mission Reserve because all the athletes, they all played there, whether it was soccer, baseball, lacrosse. They all played there, they all gathered there, and from Capilano here, they would go down there as well and, you know they would participate in it. And as I said earlier, at Capilano here they weren't Catholic, but when they went to play that was all put aside; most of the Mission were Catholic, but not here [at Capilano]. But when they got to the sports [field], to play sports, it was all one [and] the community just got together to play. Even if they weren't participating in the games, there was always a relative or a cousin or somebody that was there, so they would always go and watch the games. It was a gathering place for the communities. As I said this morning, the Capilano bunch not being Catholic, yet they played right behind the church, the Catholic Church [laughs]. Yeah, that was all put aside.[154]

Paull convinced a number of other Hodinöhsö:ni' players from Six Nations to join the team in the summer of 1936, bringing their numbers to a half dozen.[155] Paitsmauk, Dave Jacobs, notes, "That was one of the great things and most important things about those Indian teams, it was East [Hodinöhsö:ni'] meets West [Sḵwx̱wú7mesh]."[156] Not only were the Sḵwx̱wú7mesh establishing an identity for themselves; they were also helping to create a pan-Indigenous identity through lacrosse, developing a relationship with the eastern Indigenous communities that would extend beyond sport to include inter-marriages. For the Hodinöhsö:ni' players, joining the North Shore Indians enabled them to travel and play for an all-Indigenous team at the highest level in Canadian lacrosse. Furthermore, they quickly found themselves learning a new Indigenous culture and language:

> There was one interesting thing with Andy Paull. Andy spoke fluent Sḵwx̱wú7mesh and all the players spoke fluent Sḵwx̱wú7mesh. When they would score a goal, they would line up and they would stop deliberately, Andy would say, "Stop and talk about your next play and what you are going to do." So they would get out to centre floor and they would stop and start talking Sḵwx̱wú7mesh. They would talk Sḵwx̱wú7mesh, the referee standing there waiting to put the ball down and they would all be talking Sḵwx̱wú7mesh and all these white guys are looking, "what the hell is going on?" [laughs] "Let's get the game on. They are talking Sḵwx̱wú7mesh!" [laughs] So what happened was when these eastern players came in, they started to learn Sḵwx̱wú7mesh, the Mohawk speakers. All of a sudden they were learning words here, here, and there [all over the place]. Because I remember one of the players, Oscar Bomberry, married my cousin, and spoke Sḵwx̱wú7mesh. That was coming from him – he said, "Yeah we were learning Sḵwx̱wú7mesh when we were over here," and they were Mohawk speakers. It was kind of interesting, it was Andy, he was the one. He's chivalry [canny] that guy [laughs]. "Stop the game and speak Sḵwx̱wú7mesh!" and get them wondering what are they up to, what are they going to do.[157]

For members of the North Shore Indians, playing at a high level and belonging to a team where they could speak their language in the face of their non-Native opponents, often tricking them, was a high point of their experience. Player Simon Baker, Khot-La-Cha, recalled,

> We were good stick handlers. That's how come we used to beat them guys, and the best part of it was that we all talked Indian and when we hollered in our language the white man would look, and when he looked the other way, we were gone. They used to really swear at us Indians talking our own language.[158]

The significance of using the Sḵwx̱wú7mesh language during games cannot be understated. In a sport dominated by anglophone non-Natives, it was a pronounced anomaly. A game appropriated by non-Natives, introduced to the Sḵwx̱wú7mesh as part of the attempt to eliminate their language, culture, and sense of nationhood, became a public assertion of defiance, unification, and cultural adaptation and collision.

The 1936 Mann Cup

In September 1936, having once again claimed the BC championship, the North Shore Indians made their way east in hopes of representing western Canada in the national championship. A large "crowd of supporters and well-wishers" gathered at the CPR station as the Indians departed for a brief stop in Kamloops, where they were assured of an enthusiastic welcome.[159] As Andy Paull summarized, upon reaching the city, the team was greeted by a boisterous crowd, the mayor, and the brass band from the Kamloops Indian Residential School.[160] Given "one of the greatest receptions ever tendered [to] a travelling lacrosse team," Paull was especially moved by a gift from the residential school students: "Two boys from the Indian school also presented two boxes of apples grown on the school farm to the players, which gift was very deeply appreciated."[161] In Calgary, the Indians defeated the home team and eliminated Winnipeg a few days later, thus securing the western championship. Their next engagement was a best of five-game series at Maple Leaf Gardens in Toronto against the Orillia Terriers, the reigning champions. The victor would claim the Mann Cup and the title of Canadian national champion.[162]

Despite their cultural differences, the Sḵwx̱wú7mesh and Hodinöhsö:ni' players were united by a common game, and they symbolized the pride of

How the Lacrosse Boys Looked to Cartoonist Les Callan

▲▲ **1936 North Shore Indians cartoon. Despite the well-worn stereotypes employed in this cartoon, the media often noted the** boisterous Sḵwx̱wú7mesh fan presence at games in the 1930s. | *Les Callan,* Vancouver Sun, *September 19, 1936.*

▲ **The 1936 North Shore Indians team.** | *Author's collection.*

all Indigenous peoples. As almost nowhere else in Canadian society, they enjoyed an equal footing with their opponents. Paull expressed what it meant for the Indians to vie for the championship and to have a public presence as an Indigenous team. During an interview with Canadian Press staff writer Allan Nickelson, he reminded Canadians about the origins of the game:

> The Indians played lacrosse first, Andy Paull of the Squamish tribe conceded in a swift survey of Mann Cup history, and after all these years the Indians are ready to win a Canadian championship. "Yes" said Paull ... "we have a strong team, perhaps the best all-Indian lacrosse team ever assembled. I'm confident we have the greatest Indian outfit, but you can't be sure. This series will tell us that. Occasionally a strong Indian team has cropped up – we used to have them on the coast, some were in Ontario. Yet the Mann Cup always eluded us – until now."[163]

As soon as the North Shore Indians arrived in Toronto, they became the talk of the town and were covered extensively in the press – which often used bloodthirsty or noble savage monikers and captions. A *Toronto Globe and Mail* article stated, "Still trying to reclaim lacrosse for the Redskins, the North Shore Indians from Vancouver will again attempt to shake off the all-too-pesky Terriers ... There's so much sports color to the Indians that they must be rated as fan-pleasers as well as expert lacrossists."[164] While in Toronto, the Hodinöhsö:ni' players returned home to visit for the first time since travelling to Vancouver, and they invited the entire team to attend a party in Six Nations.[165] Across Canada, newspapers picked up on the story of the North Shore Indians, who were hosted by Maple Leafs owner Conn Smythe.[166] In Vancouver, the *Province* and the *Sun* devoted columns to the series, as did the *Toronto Globe and Mail* and the *Toronto Star,* with many other papers following suit. Sports broadcaster and Canadian radio icon Foster Hewitt provided the play-by-play broadcast for the Toronto area, and Leo Nicholson gave his take on the games over the Vancouver airwaves.[167]

Before "a shrieking crowd of approximately 7500, largest gathering to witness a final in Toronto for several years," the Indians lost their first game against the Terriers.[168] Cheering on their fellow community members, fans from Six Nations came out to support their team, expressing a unified pan-Indigeneity rather than a sole identification with their own nation. The *Toronto Star* reported, "Six Nation Indians turned up in full panoply. A picturesque touch to the scene was added when two of these chiefs, feathered and richly dressed in tribal costume, took the floor and presented a big floral horseshoe to Skipper Van Every."[169] A number of the Sḵwx̱wú7mesh players had never been to Toronto before, and despite having played in front of crowds of ten thousand before, some were in awe of the size of the arena:

SLA'WIYA: The one thing I will never forget is, my uncle Joe [Johnston], when he said they had to go to Toronto to play that big game. When they all walked into that arena. They were in a different world, they have never seen something so huge.

ALLAN: They were at Maple Leaf Gardens?

SLA'WIYA: Yeah. He always said, "We lost the game because they were in awe of that arena"; they said it was just so big. The fans did a good job. You know how it is when you're playing and you're on one side, as the visitors team. You know how that is. He said that the fans and whatnot [the first game of the series had a largely pro-Orillia fan base in attendance].[170]

For Paull, the trip became particularly difficult when the Department of Indian Affairs notified him that his fourteen-month-old daughter, Evelyn Paull, had passed away following a ten-day illness.[171] The Indians would go on to win the second game, but sadly, though they put up a hard fight, they lost the best-of-five series in four games, and Orillia once again captured the Mann Cup. Despite losing the championship, the Indians were a major factor in one of the grandest exhibitions of lacrosse in the history of the game. Close to 31,000 spectators watched the four-game series, one of the largest audiences ever to attend the Mann Cup.[172] The match was a great financial success for its promoters, and the Indians received a portion of the gate revenue.

The 1936 Mann Cup series quickly developed into a source of pride for the Sḵwx̱wú7mesh, one that continues today. Stories of the summer of 1936 are still told in Sḵwx̱wú7mesh communities and beyond. The North Shore Indians were, and remain, more than a lacrosse team. They were the pride of a nation, a chance for Indigenous peoples, especially the Sḵwx̱wú7mesh, to meet their non-Indigenous counterparts on an equal footing. As Paitsmauk, Dave Jacobs, explains, they were a team of Indigenous athletes, representing Indigenous communities, and establishing an identity that all Indigenous nations across Canada could share:

> I think they were very proud of their achievements, for the first thing. They won the league, they got to represent the league, but they were also an Indian team. They're also an Indian team. So that to them is first and foremost. But you know we're playing the same game, of course our people are very very proud. That is a seed in all of our Native people, pride, there is always that pride. It survived. Our people have survived and so has our game. They go together, that will never change. As long as our people stand on this earth, it will be here. It will always be here because our people are here. As you say, it's our game![173]

As they entered the 1937 season, the North Shore Indians reportedly experienced divisions concerning Paull's management, and he did not return to coach them at the start of league play – exactly why remains unclear.[174] He was not one to shy away from either controversy or the pursuit of his own interests, and though he was a beloved figure in the lacrosse world and the media, he was also a contentious person, both in and out of his community.[175] After starting the 1937 season in unspectacular fashion, the

Indians met to debate the status of Paull as their coach.[176] By the next week, in late June, he had resumed his coaching duties, a development that was not supported by everyone on the team.[177] Once he was back on the bench, Paull again recruited Hodinöhsö:ni' players, such as Angus "Buckshot" Thomas and Angus Taiostarate George, both from Ahkwesáhsne. In this, he helped to cement a relationship with the Hodinöhsö:ni' communities that would persist for decades to come. Despite a series of losing streaks, the Indians regularly played to capacity crowds of over five thousand at the Forum in Vancouver and at Queen's Park in New Westminster, and the two Ahkwesáhsne players established themselves as fan favourites alongside their Six Nations and Sḵwx̱wú7mesh teammates. Although the team did not reach the playoffs in 1937, Paull was contacted by lacrosse promoter, sports writer, and hockey referee Bill Shaver concerning the possibility that the North Shore Indians would travel to Hollywood to promote box lacrosse.[178]

Although the Indians evidently received several offers to visit various North American locations, California quickly became the favourite destination, as the promoters "figure if the game is properly put over in the movie colony especially by the Indians, it will take like wildfire ... A complete Indian team would bring out the customers in carloads."[179] Much like the Hodinöhsö:ni' teams before them and the Sḵwx̱wú7mesh lacrosse teams that Paull had organized for Indian Sports Days, the North Shore Indians found themselves a marketable commodity for promoters who hoped to cash in on the new game of box lacrosse. Moreover, ever the opportunist and promoter, Paull also saw a chance to derive an income for himself and the team through playing an exhibition series in California. Plans to start the series in 1937 did not bear fruit, but they did serve as a catalyst for a future promotion.

Returning to the senior amateur series in 1938, the North Shore Indians continued to compete against the country's top lacrosse teams though not with their previous skill or success. Nonetheless, promoters saw the Indians as a valuable asset in their proposed California exhibition series, and plans had rematerialized by the fall of 1939 for the Indians to travel south. Former Indians player Simon Baker, Khot-La-Cha, explained,

Andy Paull was a great promoter ... I used to watch Andy. How that guy used to work. My god, he could manoeuvre people around. He knew how to talk to people, how to convince people ... He was like

Two Orillia Terriers *(left and right)* **defend against a North Shore Indians player during their 1939 trip to Los Angeles.** |

John Curran scrapbook, John Edward Gardiner Curran Fonds, MG30-C85, r2230-0-3-e, Library and Archives Canada.

a lawyer. He was why a lot of people had respect for the North Shore Indians ... He promoted a professional team and took a bunch of players down to Los Angeles.[180]

Formed as the Pacific Coast Lacrosse Association, four teams gathered in Los Angeles to create the new professional league. These were the Orillia Terriers (known as the Hollywood Terriers in Los Angeles), the New Westminster Adanacs (Canucks), a group of American all-stars and the New Westminster Salmonbellies (Los Angeles Yankees), and finally the North Shore Indians (Indians or Warriors).[181]

The league quickly attracted interest. On opening night, Bing Crosby was the ceremonial host and referee, and throughout the season the Indians games often drew crowds of four thousand or more.[182] In both Vancouver and Los Angeles, the press closely followed the team, frequently mentioning the Indigenous origin of lacrosse and portraying the players, in stereotypical terms, as being on the "war path."[183] Despite the high hopes of organizers, the league was short-lived, as relations between lead promoter Frank Sweeny and officials at the Olympic Auditorium broke down after less than a month of play.[184] However, this was not the last time the Indians played in California: in the spring of 1939, they competed against the New Westminster Adanacs in a three-game exhibition series at the Golden Gate International Exhibition at Treasure Island as part of the San Francisco World's Fair.[185]

Unfortunately for the North Shore Indians and the non-Native Canadians who had gone to the United States, the amateur Canadian Lacrosse Association (CLA) suspended them for playing in a professional league. As soon as it was announced that the four teams would form the US league, the CLA and the BCLA asserted that the players would be banned from senior amateur competition back in Canada.[186] As a result, the North Shore Indians were suspended for two years upon returning to Canada – a development that simply fuelled the amateur-professional debates that continued to cripple lacrosse organizations.[187] Only after vocal protests from the banned organizations, CLA president James A. McConaghy reversed the suspension by mid-June 1939, but the damage had been done.[188] For the North Shore Indians, the California tour marked the last hurrah of the great team in its original all-Indigenous form. As Simon Baker, Khot-La-Cha, recalled, the ban had a significant impact on the identity of the team: "After that we couldn't use many of our boys to play amateur, so the team became half Indian and half white."[189] As players aged and were not replaced by younger men, and as the Second World War drew away both players and audiences, the fate of the original Indians was sealed, leading the team to leave the senior amateur lacrosse league after 1941. Dunlop concludes,

> By the year '39, the team had lost its fire and its class. Later a few whites joined the club but its soul was dead and there was little hope of resurrection. It was best that this hollow shell of a once great team be respectfully laid away to rest. And so it was interred in the early Forties and a few there were on hand to see its passing. The team that saw the Forum fill to standing room only drew nary a tear or a sigh as it silently passed from the sports scene.[190]

The Second World War slowed box lacrosse participation in Canada, but its conclusion saw soldiers return home and renew an interest in the

**Stan "Bunny" Joseph makes the save,
May 19, 1948.** | *Photographer Artray, 84118E,
Vancouver Public Library.*

sport. Box lacrosse teams re-emerged throughout the country, including
a revised version of the North Shore Indians, who continued to be highly
competitive in provincial competition. The original players started to move
on, and a new generation of Sḵwx̱wú7mesh superstars who had been inspired by the 1930s teams began to make their names as dominant players.
One of these was Stan "Bunny" Joseph, Jr. – an eventual Canadian Lacrosse
Hall of Fame member and son of 1930s North Shore Indians player Stan
Joseph, Sr. In 1945, the North Shore Indians, renamed the Indian Arrows
(the team's name changed several times during this era; they were known
as the Indian Arrows, the PNE Indians, and again as the North Shore Indians between 1945 and 1955), re-entered Senior "A" competition. Among
them were Hodinöhsö:ni' players, most recognizably Ross Powless from
Six Nations.[191]

∾

Although the spirit of the once great team predictably waned over time, it
was never forgotten, and both the team and the sport of lacrosse remain a

critical identity marker for the Sḵwx̱wú7mesh Nation. In building a relationship with the Hodinöhsö:ni', the North Shore Indians sought to create the best all-Indigenous team in the country, but as time went on, an important sports rivalry arose between the two nations and would contribute to a growing reclamation of lacrosse by Indigenous communities that was initiated by the North Shore Indians in the 1930s.

Introduced to the game by the encroachment of the dominant society and in residential schools, the Sḵwx̱wú7mesh played a trick that 'Usdas and Raven might envy, taking an oppressive tool and refashioning it as a source of cultural and identity survival and regeneration. The Sḵwx̱wú7mesh embraced lacrosse as an instrument for community integration, both locally and nationally, throughout the twentieth century, and created a new articulation of their nationhood through sport. Lacrosse helped the Sḵwx̱wú7mesh to extend their "continuity in change" and to adapt to changing conditions, such as the Canadian government's genocidal assimilation scheme, the impacts of their land base being reduced to reserves, and the economic hardships of the Great Depression, while also helping to foster a pan-Indigenous identity.[192] The Sḵwx̱wú7mesh helped end the ban on Indigenous athletes and were at the centre of organized box lacrosse in British Columbia, but as we will see, other Indigenous athletes and teams also played a significant role in developing lacrosse in Canada more generally. Still to this day, the North Shore Indians can be seen playing on summer nights in the Vancouver area.

4

Box Lacrosse and Redefining Political Activism during the Mid-twentieth Century

>>> *'Usdas's Sporting Goods, June 26, 1978*

Cling, cling! Raven enters 'Usdas's Colonial Sporting Goods store.

'Usdas, who has transformed into human form, greets the new customer: "Good afternoon, I'm 'Usdas. How can I help you?"

"I'm in the market for a new lacrosse stick, and I'm wondering what you have," Raven replies.

"You're in luck, my friend. Follow me." 'Usdas leads Raven to the lacrosse section at the back of the store. "A new shipment of these Brine sticks has just come in. They've become extremely popular over the past few years." 'Usdas hands the plastic stick to Raven. "So, what do you think? It's light, it's easy to maintain, and it handles the ball better than the old wooden sticks."

"It looks like Tupperware and feels like it too! Cold. Lifeless. No character. What happened to your wooden sticks by Etienne, Martin, or Chisholm?"

"Well, when the Chisholm factory burned down in 1968, I had to find a replacement. The demand was increasing, and the other stick makers couldn't meet it. So I started to market the plastic stick here at the store. It's mass produced, it's progress!"[1]

Ga-lahs is the Onyota'a·ká· Nation's word for lacrosse. Correspondence, Sue Ellen Herne, April 4, 2011, Akwesasne Culture Centre, Ogdensville, New York.

"Oh, what have you done? What have you released into the world? Don't you know that there's power in the wooden stick?"

'Usdas ponders the thought. "I can't remember where, but I'm sure I've heard this before. What power?" 'Usdas asks.

"It's not just about competition, it's not just about celebrating zero-sum contests where there's a winner and a loser, that's an infiltration. It's more than that, and the stick represents that."

"Represents what? Deep conversation for a stupid piece of sports equipment."

"For one thing, it represents Hodinöhsö:ni' nationhood, the connection to the original game, and the medicinal qualities of the Creator's game. It's a part of that power, the game's connection to the land and its power. Don't you see – certain trees have the power to absorb negativity and sickness. They can filter it through their roots into the ground, and a stick carved from one of them retains that power. Your stick is alive, it has a memory of sorts, a power bank, and is a special piece. If you can imagine the power in this game, the power in this stick and ball, you really are surrounded by a spiritual place at all times while you're playing it.[2] This plastic stick is lifeless and has none of that! 'Usdas, the wooden stick is a powerful –."

"Yeah, yeah, I know, a powerful piece –." He pauses in a moment of déjà vu and thinks, wow, I know I've heard this before. "But the old 'woodie' is too difficult to play with."

"Well, maybe North American settlers should rethink the meaning of sport in their lives. That and practise a little more."

THE CREATION OF BOX lacrosse in the early 1930s marked a dramatic shift in the practice of the game in Canada and among Indigenous nations. Barred from field lacrosse since 1880, Indigenous athletes were not excluded from the new variant, which saw their return to national competition. During the early era of box lacrosse, from 1931 to about 1960, they once again solidified a new form of the game within Indigenous and Canadian sport culture, becoming highly visible in non-Native organizations. Their prominence, and box lacrosse more generally, played a significant role in rekindling the articulation of Hodinöhsö:ni' nationhood. Amid persistent institutional racism in the sport and the wider attempts at cultural genocide aimed at their sense of nationhood, Hodinöhsö:ni' athletes were engaged in a performance of "refusal," a phenomenon that Audra Simpson discusses in *Mohawk Interruptus*.[3] In their performance of refusal, Hodinöhsö:ni' players confronted colonial agendas and asserted that lacrosse was a signifier of the continuation of Hodinöhsö:ni' nationhood. In addition, the wooden stick remained an expression of Hodinöhsö:ni' identity and the Longhouse epistemological foundations of the game, including its practise in the Sky World. This identity even began to express itself among non-Longhouse Hodinöhsö:ni'. As new generations of players joined all-Indigenous teams during the second era of box lacrosse (c. 1960–80), teams were formed through, or at, ironworking sites and became spaces of dialogue between the various Hodinöhsö:ni' nations, which strengthened the Confederacy. This ultimately saw the formation of all-Indigenous lacrosse associations and governing bodies, and it challenged the institutional racism on an international scale.

Redesigning the Game

As Montreal Canadiens owners Leo Dandurand and Joe Cattarinich (a former lacrosse player with the Montreal Nationals) helped establish a box lacrosse league in early 1931, they presented a summertime alternative that would appeal to hockey fans.[4] Thus, the lacrosse teams were named after the hockey teams, and many of their rules were patterned on those for hockey.[5] Created by the owners of a professional team, box lacrosse was intended to be a professional sport from the start. The primary motive for its generation was the profit that franchise owners would reap from ticket sales. This marked a significant shift from the approach of late-nineteenth-century lacrosse organizations, which had insisted on the amateur status of their players and had championed the game as the performance of whiteness and Canadian nationalism. As historian Bruce Kidd explains, the Great Depression also played a key role in the move from amateurism to professionalism:

> The Depression irreparably damaged the material and ideological conditions on which amateurism was based, especially among athletes. Young men were the most heavily hit by the massive lay-offs resulting from the collapse of commodity prices and the downward spiral of investment, consumption, and production that followed the Great Crash of 1929 ... The situation forced many to find an income anywhere they could. Under these devastating conditions, the "honour" of abiding by the amateur code became a luxury many could not afford.

Few athletes in sports such as track and field, gymnastics, and swimming would ever have the chance to consider making money from their efforts. But in such team sports as hockey, baseball, football, and lacrosse, the desire of local and regional boosters to "maintain the community" in the face of economic and social adversity further elevated the importance of representational teams, giving the top athletes in those sports some bargaining power.[6]

The owners of professional box lacrosse teams also relied on a proven ticket seller: Indigenous athletes. By May 1931, organizers were seriously contemplating the inclusion of an all-Hodinöhsö:ni' team from Six Nations in the new International Professional Lacrosse League (IPLL). Adopted on June 4, 1931, the constitution and by-laws of the IPLL did not bar Indigenous players from competition and made no specific mention of them.[7] On May 8, the *Toronto Daily Star* reflected on the league proposal to incorporate an Indigenous team and on the former appeal of Indigenous athletes as "show Indians" in the Toronto area:

> The proposal of "Scotty" Martin of Brantford [Six Nations of the Grand River] that an Indian team be included in the seven-man style sounds like a reasonable proposition. As a drawing card the Indian braves should go over big. One of our earliest recollections was watching the Indian teams of years ago crossing Huntley St. bridge to the old Sherbourne St. lacrosse field to do battle with the Torontos. The red skins, bedecked in their feathers and war paint, made a fine spectacle, and drew many thousands of citizens to their local contests.[8]

Early Indigenous Box Lacrosse Teams

According to newspaper reports, the Six Nations community appears to have displayed little interest in Scotty Martin's proposal.[9] Thus, when play began in the summer of 1931, none of the teams that formed the first-ever professional box lacrosse league – the Montreal Canadiens, Montreal Maroons, Toronto Maple Leafs, and Cornwall Colts – were Indigenous.[10] Nevertheless, the four teams did include a number of athletes from Kahnawà:ke, Ahkwesáhsne, and Six Nations.[11] When the IPLL resumed play in the summer of 1932, ticket sales were so poor – owing to the impacts of the Depression – that the league folded by the halfway mark of the season. However, it was quickly replaced by a new professional league that consisted of the Toronto Maple Leafs, the Toronto Tecumsehs, and a new all-Indigenous team, the Buffalo Bowmans.[12]

Although the IPLL eventually failed, its formation would significantly change the Canadian lacrosse landscape and provide a much-needed boost during the interwar period. It did not take long for box lacrosse to begin to reign supreme in Canada. By the summer of 1931, its popularity had forced the Ontario Amateur Lacrosse Association (OALA) and the British Columbia Amateur Lacrosse Association (BCALA) to consider jettisoning the old version of the game. By the end of the season, the Canadian Amateur Lacrosse Association had voted that, beginning in 1932, the Mann Cup would be awarded for box lacrosse. Following suit, both the OALA and the BCALA adopted box lacrosse as their official sport in the spring of 1932.[13] It is safe to assume that these bodies were attempting to tap into the spectacular rise of professional hockey, where, as Bruce Kidd shows, "in just two decades [beginning in 1917], the NHL became the best-known sports organization in Canada, with its players household names and the term 'professional' synonymous with 'excellence.'"[14] Lacrosse enthusiasts had seen their sport supplanted by baseball and recreational activities such as camping and cottaging, and there is little doubt that by adopting the rules, styles of play, and facilities of hockey, they were attempting to reinvent the game and recapture the following it once had. Although the transition to box lacrosse in Canada was swift, it was far from smooth.[15]

Across the continent, Indigenous athletes and teams were instrumental in developing the new form of lacrosse and showcasing it to audiences. As discussed in the previous chapter, the Squamish Indians participated in British Columbia's inaugural box lacrosse league, playing against the New Westminster Salmonbellies and the Vancouver Athletic Club in 1932 and eventually drawing thousands of fans.[16] In Ontario, Quebec, and throughout the northeastern United States, Indigenous athletes played for non-Native teams in the short-lived IPLL and formed their own team in 1932, the Buffalo Bowmans (of Buffalo, New York).[17] Made up of athletes from Six Nations, the Bowmans competed for the professional league title throughout the 1932 season. That summer, they also travelled to Atlantic City, reformed as the Atlantic City Americans, and played a series of professional and all-star teams in an effort to expand box lacrosse.[18] One of the Six Nations' most famous players, Alexander Ross Powless, remembered hearing stories of the Atlantic City team from its goaltender, Judy "Punch" Garlow:

I was about six years old when my Uncle Cec [Cecil VanEvery] and Judy Punch and the Smith boys, Beef and Harry and Don and Sid [Smith], and the other Six Nations boys went down there to introduce box lacrosse.

See, quite a few of the boys had been working and playing lacrosse in Buffalo. In Atlantic City, it was sort of the World Championship of Lacrosse with the boys representing Atlantic City and playing off for six weeks against five other teams from Montreal and Toronto and Boston, the top teams in lacrosse in them days.

The first week went okay. Everything was new and the boys had never been to a place like Atlantic City before. But after that they started getting tired of the fancy hotel, tired of the beach and even tired of the movies they went to every afternoon to pass the time. The boys from Six Nations were used to working hard and always having something to do. So there they were, in the Playground of the World, bored to death. The only time they were happy was when they were out playing lacrosse. They never lost one game down at Atlantic City.[19]

Returning home in the late summer, the team continued to play as the Bowmans. Other Hodinöhsö:ni' professional teams would quickly establish themselves, such as the Rochester Red Hawks, which formed in 1933.[20] Non-professional teams, such as the Hornell Bears and the Rochester Iroquois, also followed suit, competing against each other for the amateur box lacrosse championship of New York in the mid-1930s.[21] From Vancouver to Montreal and places in between, such as Wallaceburg, Streetsville, and Hamilton, and from Los Angeles to Atlantic City in the United States, Indigenous athletes were participating in the various professional and amateur box lacrosse leagues during the 1930s. At times, they played for non-Native organizations; at other times, they registered their own teams, such as the Mohawk Stars from Six Nations – a team that had once played a critical role in raising money for Deskaheh Levi General and the Hodinöhsö:ni' sovereignty movements in the early 1920s – which engaged in amateur "Intermediate" inter-city OALA competition in 1932.[22] A further example occurred in late 1935, when Onöndowa'ga:' chief Nick Bailey from the Tonawanda Reservation in New York established an all-Indigenous team inspired by the success of the Hornell Bears and the Rochester Iroquois.[23]

▲ 1932 Atlantic City Americans team photo.
Back row (left to right): **Cecil VanEvery, Harry Smith, Wade Isaacs, Herman Miller (trainer), Bill Stevens (referee), James Lodwig (manager), Beef Smith, Dave Groat, Clinton Jacks.** *Front row (left to right):* **Les Martin, Boots Martins, Donald Smith, Punch Garlow, Henry Groat, Sid Smith, Scotty Martin, W.H. Stephens (assistant trainer).** | *Woodland Cultural Centre.*

▼ 1938 Rochester Iroquois. *Back row (left to right):* **Tremain General, Arleigh Hill, Harry Green, Mac Martin, Bill Isaacs.** *Middle row (left to right):* **Bob Jamieson, Jack Squire, Herman Jamieson, Nelson Martin, Alvie Martin.** *Front row (left to right):* **Sawdie Groat, Bruce Hill, Smiley Young.** | *Woodland Culture Centre.*

In Canada, the top senior teams recruited Indigenous athletes from local reserves to help bolster their rosters and provide a competitive edge toward a national championship. A number of men from Six Nations were excellent players and thus were sought-after by senior teams. For example, brothers Bill and Lance Isaacs were two early stars throughout the 1930s who often finished near the top of league scoring races. According to the *Toronto Daily Star,* they played as a tandem and were unparalleled anywhere in the world; they competed for Hamilton in the OALA Senior "A" league and later for the Toronto Marlboros in 1936 and 1937 at Maple Leaf Gardens.[24] Similarly, players such as Cecil VanEvery, Sidney Smith, Judy "Punch" Garlow, Oscar Bomberry, Stanley Bomberry, and Jack Squires, to name a few – all from Six Nations – travelled the continent, playing on various teams throughout the 1930s, including the Atlantic City Americans and the North Shore Indians.[25]

As Fisher points out, the relationships between Hodinöhsö:ni' communities, such as Six Nations, Cattaraugus (New York), and Onondaga (New York), hastened the transition to box lacrosse and contributed to the dissemination of the game within Hodinöhsö:ni' territory and on both sides of the imposed international border.[26] Although both Canadian and Indigenous organizations distanced themselves from the field game during the 1930s, the Hodinöhsö:ni' – specifically, the Kanien'kehá:ka of Ahkwesáhsne – reportedly found box lacrosse much more satisfying because it offered a fast-paced physical contest played in close quarters:

> The Indian players particularly enjoyed the increased body contact afforded by the reduction in space and more lenient rules regarding the use of the stick for purpose of checking than field lacrosse afforded. Having enjoyed a hearty brand of play throughout the history of their participation, it was a pleasure for these players to return to the increased contact which has been affected by the English and Irish who played a brand of field lacrosse which prohibited body checking.[27]

The new form of lacrosse quickly spread throughout Indigenous communities during the 1930s and revitalized the game in Canada as a whole – though lacrosse never again surpassed more popular sports such as baseball and hockey – and for the first time since 1880 Indigenous athletes were once again regularly and openly participating in championship competitions in central Canada.[28] Many, such as Ross Powless, rose to national prominence, and with their success in the game, lacrosse became an avenue for political activism in Indigenous communities.

The Political Connection

The members of the Powless family – notably Ross and his son Gaylord – have long been seen as a catalyst in the re-emergence of lacrosse, mainly because of their superior play and ability to impress audiences with their proficiency.[29] Nor did Ross Powless's contribution end with his retirement. Indeed, following his playing days, he became a pivotal member of the Six Nations lacrosse community as a volunteer, coach, and organizer. He won three national titles at three different levels as a coach, helped establish the Brantford Warriors Senior "B" and "A" lacrosse teams and the Six Nations Minor Lacrosse Association, and served on the Six Nations Band Council for over a decade.[30] After numerous championships as both a player and a coach, two Tom Longboat trophies – awarded annually to the top Indigenous athlete in Canada – and playing most of his career in Ontario, he had fond memories of his early days in Skwxwú7mesh territory.[31] Equally, he remembered the influence of Andy Paull, which helped him enter into politics and serve on the Six Nations Band Council:

> In 1945, when I was nineteen, Chubby and me were playing lacrosse out on the west coast with Andy Paull's North Shore team ... I had the chance to meet lots of interesting people out at the Coast. When Jimmy Martin and I got there, who should be standing at the train to meet us but Chief Mathias Joe of Capilano and his son. Both of them dressed in full Indian regalia. Boy, they had some good lacrosse players out there. The Baker boys, Stan Joseph Sr. and Stan Joseph Jr., Joe Johnson. The man I really learned a lot about life from was Andy Paull. He'd been recruiting players from Six Nations since the thirties. And he was a respected man all across Canada. I stayed with Andy and his family my first time out there. I remember he had poor eyesight and he used to like to smoke roll-your-owns. He'd be at the typewriter, cigarette hanging out of his mouth, nose pretty much touching the page, averaging about seven and a half words per minute. Maybe he couldn't type, but he really had a legal mind. An Indian person would get into some kind of trouble upcoast or downcoast and he'd be right there getting information and feeding it into the lawyers. He saved a lot of Indian people from prison. He cleared up misunderstandings

Ross Powless. | *Courtesy of Gaylene Powless.*

between Indian and non-Indian people. At one time he was the President of the North American Indian Brotherhood and it was Andy Paull who first got me interested in politics. Course in them days, my mind was mostly on lacrosse. After I met the Paulls, I visited them every time I got the chance to go to B.C.[32]

Andy Paull often facilitated connections between lacrosse and politics, sometimes combining his lacrosse trips with political activities. For example, when the Squamish Indians lost to the Winnipeg Argonauts in 1932, as Brendan Edwards found, Paull continued on to Ottawa for political purposes: "I was in Ottawa, last October, I went with our lacrosse team as manager, they returned from Winnipeg but I and another Squamish man Gus Band kept on going to Ottawa, so I am still in the fight."[33] Eleven years later, in 1943, he was still in the fight, as he attempted to form the North American Indian Brotherhood, a national Indigenous rights organization, using his sports contacts to help get it off the ground.[34] During that year, as the business manager of the Native Brotherhood of British Columbia

(NBBC), Paull travelled to Ottawa with Dan Assu from the Pacific Coast Native Fisherman's Association to attend a conference relating to fishing rights.[35] At that time, Paull and Assu were invited to a meeting in Montreal by a coalition of Indigenous activists who hoped to establish a national Indigenous rights organization. As a result of that meeting, the group formed the Brotherhood of Canadian Indians, which became the North American Indian Brotherhood (NAIB) in June 1944.[36] Its purpose was to move beyond Indigenous labour and resource rights and to call for amendments to the Indian Act, especially concerning taxation and enfranchisement.[37] In early 1944, Paull had a contentious split with the NBBC but was elected to a five-year term as NAIB president in September 1945.[38]

During his attempt to create the NAIB, Paull stayed with the Kanien'kehá:ka family of Billy Two Rivers. A young boy at the time, Two Rivers later became an internationally famed wrestler, film star, and political activist. He remembers,

> What happened is that he [Andy Paull] had organized across the country. He wasn't a rich man, he was living on donations, and people would collect money, and then he would move on ... He came from BC, and he worked his way east and all the way down. My father was a member [of the NAIB], and several people over here [Kahnawà:ke], I think it was four or five of them, that are listed as members of Kahnawà:ke [on the NAIB list] and my dad was one ... And I remember him as a young boy, this man came, and he stayed with my father because they put him up wherever he was going, and they would sort of make a collection or send him a ticket or pay his train fare to the next community, and he got all the way to Halifax ... The reason I am saying Andy Paull is that he played lacrosse before, and he organized the team. He's the one, or may have been the one, who was first involved in recruiting players from the east here. Bringing them to Squamish and incorporating them into the team and into the families [this refers to Kanien'kehá:ka players who started families while out west].[39]

In the 1950s, Paull's interest shifted to boxing, but as he moved on from organizing lacrosse teams, new Indigenous players rose to prominence on teams in non-Native organizations.[40] However, non-Natives continued to control the governing bodies and organizations in the premiere leagues of box lacrosse. In Ontario, Indigenous athletes who wished to play at the highest level and be compensated for their talents often had to leave their communities and join teams in larger centres. This was true for Ross Powless and Roger "Buck" Smith, two of the most accomplished lacrosse players produced by Six Nations.

In the early 1950s, both Powless and Smith travelled from Six Nations to Peterborough to play in Canada's top Senior "A" league and to compete for the senior national championship. At the time, there were very few Indigenous players in the league, and those who did play regularly suffered racism from both opponents and teammates.[41] At his first Peterborough tryout, Ross Powless quickly became a target, as he later recalled in a documentary:

> We got together afterwards, and they were telling me how mean they treated me when I first went to Peterborough. Right off the face-offs they would crack me in the legs and everything, and they wondered if I was yellow or not ... by hitting me and me not retaliating ... But I wanted to make the team, I didn't go up there to fight.[42]

During his first season with Peterborough, Powless helped lead the team to the Mann Cup in 1951 and was joined by Roger "Buck" Smith the following year to claim the national championship in 1952 and 1953.[43] For Smith, the 1952 season was the beginning of a historic career that would see him inducted into the Canadian Lacrosse Hall of Fame. For his part, Powless was awarded the Mike Kelly Memorial Medal as the 1953 Mann Cup's most valuable player.[44] Both the Powless and Smith family names are well known in Six Nations and across Hodinöhsö:ni' communities today as synonymous with lacrosse. Many enthusiasts see Ross Powless as one of the greatest lacrosse players of all time, and he and his eight sons, among them Gaylord Powless, established the most recognizable surname in the game's history.

However, Hodinöhsö:ni' athletes were not alone in establishing themselves as star players during the 1950s: the Snuneymuxw – whose territory is located on Vancouver Island in and around the city of Nanaimo – also became proficient at high-level lacrosse. The Snuneymuxw were not unfamiliar with lacrosse, and like other Coast Salish nations that played forms of lacrosse, they played before the Hodinöhsö:ni' lacrosse stick was transferred to their territory.[45] Ernie Harry, a ɬaʔamin Elder, remembers when the Indigenous communities from the Nanaimo area used to gather in Sechelt to engage in sports competitions, which included lacrosse.[46] Like

Indigenous athletes in Ontario and Quebec, the Snuneymuxw played an important role in promulgating box lacrosse when it struggled to maintain its meagre popularity following the Second World War. Although the game had survived the Depression and the war, in part because the Canadian army and navy established lacrosse teams, Canada's "national" sport was in a tenuous state by the 1950s. Vancouver CBC reporter Bill Good observed in 1957,

> According to the official books on sport, lacrosse is still listed as the national sport of Canada. That's official ['Usdas interrupts with a chuckle, might want to check that],[47] but to many thousands of Canadians it's just so much malarkey because they have never seen the game played. So how can it possibly be considered a national sport? This doesn't matter so much but right now lacrosse men right across the country are wondering just what can be done to stage a lacrosse revival to bring the sport back to what they consider its proper place in the Canadian sporting sun. In recent years crowds have practically disappeared in many parts of Canada, one time great lacrosse clubs have completely folded, and the only time there appears to be any interest what-so-ever is when the national final for the Mann Cup rolls around. This is particularly true in British Columbia.[48]

The state of Canadian lacrosse after the Second World War and into the 1950s was one of uncertainty. As Fisher reminds us, though some stability was provided by provincial organizations and the Canadian Lacrosse Association, which governed competitions and championships, "clubs formed, dissolved, and changed classifications with regularity."[49] Although Snuneymuxw players had been proficient in the game and an important part of Nanaimo box lacrosse history since at least 1939, one of their greatest achievements came in the 1950s, when they helped establish the Nanaimo Timbermen as the best team in Canada, ultimately winning the senior national championship in 1956.[50] A number of Snuneymuxw were instrumental in founding the Nanaimo Native Sons in 1951 – the name was later changed to Timbermen – including Don White, Doug White Sr., and Bill Seward, as well as Peter Good and Jimmy Rice-Wyse, each of whom played a partial season.[51] As former players recalled, the Nanaimo Native Sons built a strong rivalry against predominantly non-Native teams in Victoria, Vancouver, and New Westminster, and particularly with the re-established North Shore

Indians (known as the PNE Indians for a few years beginning in 1952), their greatest Mainland opponents.[52] One of the best Snuneymuxw players in the 1950s was Joe White, who helped Nanaimo capture the national championship in 1956, his first year with the team.[53] White and Mike Good played for Nanaimo throughout the 1950s and into the early 1960s, becoming lacrosse icons in their home communities and for future stars such as Doug White Jr., who would lead Nanaimo to the national championship finals in 1968 and was inducted into the Nanaimo Sports Hall of Fame in 2009.[54]

The prominence of early box lacrosse stars in Indigenous communities cannot be understated. The oral record across Indigenous communities features stories of the stars from the 1930s to the 1960s. "They were all of our heroes," remembers Ontario and Canadian Lacrosse Hall of Fame goalkeeper Ernie Mitchell, Kaheranoron.[55] As a young boy growing up in Ahkwesáhsne, he travelled to the lacrosse "box" in Hogansburg, New York – within Ahkwesáhsne territory – to watch the local legends play. These were "the Peter Burnses, Frank Benedicts, and they had a lot of influence in us playing lacrosse."[56] Furthermore, Joe Delaronde recalls that players from Kahnawà:ke and Ahkwesáhsne served as role models for him during his youth at a time when the imposition of Canadian colonialism threatened the Kanien'kéha language, cultural traditions, and identity:

Role models! Growing up, these guys were role models to me and for us and my generation. We are from the more modern era, we were losing our language, and my generation, we didn't learn Mohawk. We are familiar with a lot of it, but we didn't learn it [in school] and we liked everything else, we liked football, baseball, hockey, but I always remember having such a pride when it came to lacrosse – it meant something. [As kids] you would go to the games, and we [Kahnawà:ke] would play teams from Montreal, Ville Saint-Pierre, Sorel, Drummondville in this league that they had, and for us it was big league as kids. "Yes! Our guys!" ... We are so proud of that because that is our game! And really that is what it is, there is always a link for us too [lacrosse as a form of survival]. *At a time when we really seem to be losing some of the things that identified us, the language especially, lacrosse was our major league thing that was still us. We never really lost our identity, we always knew who we were, and we were always proud of it, but some of the things and the symbols were starting to fade away but lacrosse didn't.*[57]

Many Hodinöhsö:ni' families did not have access to a car, which limited their ability to attend games in communities other than their own. Nonetheless, players such as the Powlesses became legendary throughout the nations.[58] Whether they competed for all-Indigenous or predominantly non-Indigenous teams in either the amateur or the professional leagues, the early generation of Indigenous players infused communities with a sense of pride and accomplishment. According to Kanehsatá:ke Elder Onawario, John Cree,

> They left a sense of pride, that achievement, that you can achieve things. When I was young, I remember a lot of these old players, and they talked about lacrosse. It doesn't matter where we go, I don't know about other communities, but with us it is part of our ceremonies and is traditional. So when we play lacrosse, it is not about who is going to win or who is going to lose, it is about getting involved in the game and playing your heart out.[59]

Additionally, the early era of box lacrosse helped to break down regional isolation between Hodinöhsö:ni' communities and renew their pan-national identity. Joe Delaronde points out that Hodinöhsö:ni' individuals often did not have the means to travel regularly to other communities in the Confederacy, which reduced contact between them.[60] Of course, relations between the various Hodinöhsö:ni' nations persisted, both before and during this period, in Longhouse ceremonies, council meetings, and social events. However, among individuals, the continued and increasing importance of ironworking, trade work, and lacrosse helped form and renew relationships between the six nations of the Confederacy.[61] Lacrosse also encouraged community members to form Hodinöhsö:ni' teams (i.e., Kanien'kehá:ka, Onöñda'gega', Onyota'a·ká·).[62] Anthropologist Gerald Reid shows that Kahnawà:ke men increasingly joined the high-steel workforce from the mid-nineteenth century and that by the 1920s onward, ironworking was an important source of employment for Hodinöhsö:ni' men, who often travelled to jobs in New York City and elsewhere in the northeastern United States.[63] Here, they reconnected with members of other Hodinöhsö:ni' nations, but it would be lacrosse, especially early box lacrosse, that would help cement a resurgence of pan-Hodinöhsö:ni' identity.

In and of itself, early box lacrosse did not create the unified Hodinöhsö:ni' identity, which had clearly existed since the formation of the Confederacy in about the fourteenth century.[64] However, it did help to break down the regional isolation of Hodinöhsö:ni' communities, which was exacerbated by Canada's Colonial Age, and similarly by the imperial pursuits of the United States, such as the geographical restrictions of reserves, as Cole Harris reminds us.[65] And though the Hodinöhsö:ni' lacrosse teams of the late nineteenth and early twentieth centuries were able to travel – such as the Onöndowa'ga:' teams from New York who often went to Six Nations for Sunday matches during the 1920s – games were usually pre-planned events, occasions, and competitions rather than consistent meetings.

As Onawario, John Cree, explains, even the Kanien'kehá:ka communities of Kanehsatá:ke, Kahnawà:ke, Tyendinaga, and Ahkwesáhsne struggled with lack of contact, even though they lie a relatively short distance apart and played lacrosse against each other throughout the late nineteenth and early twentieth centuries:

> It [lacrosse] plays such a big part, even in communities. At one time, Kahnawà:ke and Kanehsatá:ke didn't really know each other or Ahkwesáhsne, we were so divided ... but it brought our families together, and we started playing and started talking to each other. I know when I played in Ahkwesáhsne, I didn't know I had relatives up there until I played and started whacking around one of them [laughs], but it brings [it] back [the community and family connections]. After the game, you got together and you laughed and you talked, you talked about different plays, and you talked about different methods, different tricks. Then we went to Onondaga [in the 1950s and 1960s], and you know Onondaga didn't like Mohawks [laughs] ... That would have been in the sixties, sixties and fifties, when we started to form teams and we started to [contact Ahkwesáhsne, Onondaga, Kahnawà:ke] ... We [the lacrosse teams of the 1950s and 1960s] started bringing the Confederacy, the nations, together. Then we played with Tyendinaga, we started playing with [and against] all different teams.[66]

Community estrangement was even more pronounced between the Kanien-'kehá:ka and the Onöñda'gega', where it continued to foster a historic international and cross-generational rivalry. Historian José António Brandão explains that tensions between the Kanien'kehá:ka and the Onöñda'gega' had ancient roots within the original five-nation Confederacy.[67] Not unexpectedly, the varying degrees of community isolation, the self-determination and autonomy of each nation within the Confederacy, and the differing views of traditionalism helped form a series of rivalries between the Six Nations.[68] Onawario, John Cree, discusses the historic rivalry between the Onöñda'gega' and the Kanien'kehá:ka, as well as its connection to the Kanien'kehá:ka as protectors of the Confederacy's eastern door:

ALLAN: Why [were the Onöñda'gega' rivals of the Kanien'kehá:ka]? Was it historic?

ONAWARIO: It was a rivalry; this goes back to the nationhood and stuff like that.

ALLAN: So it goes beyond lacrosse?

ONAWARIO: Yeah beyond lacrosse because you got to figure the Mohawks were the eastern doorkeepers. We were the biggest nation, and then there was the Senecas, who were in the west; they were the western doorkeepers. So we kept our little buddies safe, the Onondagas, the Cayugas, the Oneidas ... I remember going down there [Onondaga] and right away got into a fight with two Onondagas. They said, "You are Mohawk?" We started fighting you know [laughs]. I think after that and I joined the team [in Onondaga], we got to be more open. Now it isn't like it used to be, we got a better relationship with our brothers at Onondaga.[69]

The formation of box lacrosse teams was a significant factor in the reconnection and relationship building between the Kanien'kehá:ka and Onöñda'gega' Nations, very often facilitated by travelling ironworkers and tradesmen.[70] There are countless stories of Hodinöhsö:ni' ironworkers, and more generally other tradesmen, who played informal lacrosse games after the workday or on weekends, helping to encourage this reconnection between the nations at the community level. Kanien'kehá:ka lacrosse players from Kahnawà:ke, Ahkwesáhsne, and Kanehsatá:ke often worked with individuals from other Hodinöhsö:ni' nations, and during the 1950s and 1960s, they travelled to places such as Onondaga and nearby Syracuse in search of employment.[71] While there, they were asked to join teams such as the Onondaga Athletic Club, which consisted largely of Onöñda'gega' players but was not limited to that nation, and to compete against other Hodinöhsö:ni' communities such as Cattaraugus (Onöndowa'ga:' Nation),

Six Nations, and teams from other nations, including the Onyota'a·ká, the Skarù·rę' (Tuscarora), and the Onöndowa'ga:' at Tonawanda.[72]

The informal box lacrosse games of the 1960s eventually led to the establishment of the North American Lacrosse Association, an Indigenous-operated body among the Hodinöhsö:ni' communities.[73] Its foundation was significant for relationship building between the Hodinöhsö:ni' communities during the 1960s and 1970s, as teams advertised themselves as "All-Indian Team[s] playing in an All-Indian League."[74] It was an important factor in the creation of the Iroquois Nationals team during the 1980s.[75] As Joe Delaronde recalls, box lacrosse leagues and teams helped foster a renewed relationship between the Kanien'kehá:ka of Kahnawà:ke and Kanehsatá:ke and the Onöńda'gega', even as late as the early 1990s:

> Some people will tell you we are all Hodinöhsö:ni' and some people will have travelled and worked with people [from other Hodinöhsö:ni' nations], but generally speaking the rank-and-file Kahnawà:ke people couldn't name five rank-and-file people from Onondaga back in '93. In '93, that all changed [with the formation of the Iroquois Lacrosse Association Box Lacrosse League]. The same thing happened with Oneida and even to a lesser extent Ahkwesáhsne – all of sudden there was much more interaction, and until then I had never gone to Onondaga, I couldn't name one person from Onondaga other than Oren Lyons, and it was just a big mystery to, I would say, almost everyone in Kahnawà:ke.[76]

Thanks to the North American Lacrosse Association and the subsequent Can-Am lacrosse league, community teams playing at the Canadian Lacrosse Association's Senior "B" level became a source of pride for Indigenous peoples across Canada.[77] One instance of this occurred in Six Nations, with the 1964 founding of the Ohsweken Warriors. The team finished the regular season in first place and went on to defeat the Streetsville Derbys four games to two in the best of seven to win the President's Cup.[78] Teams from the Capilano and Mission Reserves in British Columbia and from Ahkwesáhsne, Tuscarora, Onondaga, and Cattaragus all won the Canadian championship, and the Kahnawà:ke team was a finalist several times, with the result that the President's Cup became emblematic of an Indigenous world championship. Although most of the Senior "B" teams were non-Native, it was at this level that Indigenous teams became most prevalent and where they competed against other Indigenous teams for national honours.[79]

Institutional Racism in Canadian Lacrosse Organizations

For Indigenous peoples, playing for Canadian lacrosse-governing bodies afforded no protection from the racism that pervaded the dominant society, and it certainly did not signify equality. As he explained in a CBC Radio interview, Ross Powless and other individual players often encountered discrimination:

> Oh there was a lot of discrimination when I first started, cause I think I was ... there was one or two of us playing at the time and they would have names all ready for you and hollering and when you would go to take the draw there was just netting along ... above the boards, and first thing you know they would take a drink of their, whatever they were drinking, and squirt it at ya through their straws [chuckle] while you're taking a face-off or waiting for a face-off ... Oh they would call you blanket ass, wagon burners, and every other quote that you have ever heard about Indians, you get use to it, it doesn't bother you, they wouldn't say that if they were beating you, because you're beating them that's why they are saying it. I was told by the great Bill Isaacs, he was one of the first players that really got to be good, and I guess he's as good as they ever came from off our reserve or in Canada, and he told me one time, "Ross" he says, "as long as they are booing you, you're alright you must be playing okay, but once they quit booing you then watch out they are starting to pity you, so don't wait until that day comes you make sure they keep booing you."[80]

Entire Indigenous teams could be the targets of bigotry. For example, throughout the 1965 season, the Ohsweken Warriors from Six Nations were subjected to racist taunts at a number of communities where they played, with incidents being overt enough to catch the attention of the mainstream press, such as the *Toronto Star*:

> Jim Naish, President of the Ontario Lacrosse Association said Friday that spectators at Ontario Senior B League Lacrosse games have been showing discrimination against members of the Ohsweken Warriors,

an all-Indian team. Naish said in a statement that he has received reports that spectators called the Indian players names and made defamatory remarks about their color and race. Naish said the discrimination charges apply to all centres where the team plays – Fergus, Wallaceburg, Orangeville, Streetsville, Sarnia and Windsor.[81]

In the oral history of lacrosse, evidence of exclusion, racism, discrimination, and injustice was, and is, widespread across the country. In every Indigenous community where a team or individuals competed against or for non-Indigenous teams, the topic of racism was never far below the surface in our discussions. Due to the prominence of the Indigenous teams, lacrosse exposed Indigenous and non-Indigenous communities to each other on a consistent basis, and issues of discrimination and racism in Canadian society often came to the fore. But this wasn't always the case: sometimes it had the opposite effect, building "bridges" between non-Native and Indigenous communities and individuals. However, sports teams are typically seen as representative of their communities, and given the stereotype of Indigenous peoples as inferior and naturally violent, it is hardly surprising that modern lacrosse – seen as a "civilized version of a savage game" – perpetuated rivalries and outbursts of racism targeted at Indigenous teams and their supporters.

Thanks in part to lacrosse, Indigenous groups were no longer out of the public limelight, isolated on rural or even urban reserves, but were competing on a regular basis. Since its appropriation by non-Natives, the game has been reflective of Canada's relationship with Indigenous nations, from Beers's lacrosse history and subsequent popular texts infused with romantic portrayals of noble or bloodthirsty savages, to the barring of Indigenous athletes and the constant exclusion and institutionalized discrimination. Sḵwx̱wú7mesh Elders Paitsmauk, Dave Jacobs, and Sla'wiya, Andrea Jacobs, experienced this first-hand on numerous occasions. As Paitsmauk explains,

> Player wise, most of them [non-Native individuals] are good. But as I say you get one, two, or three, they haven't changed. On all the teams you will see here, whether it's [New] Westminster, Coquitlam, Burnaby, or so, they have that stigma against Indians. We were at a game out in Surrey one time, and the North Shore were playing out there. It was a close game and it came down to the last minute or so. We scored the goal to win the game and a fight broke out because they

said it was a disallowed goal on the floor. And then the fans, one of them was swearing at us saying, "You f'n Indians, you guys aren't even good Canadians, you don't pay taxes." And I was just looking at this person there: "What does that have to do with the lacrosse game?" What does it have to do with Native people and them, nothing! But they come up and say something like that, I say why, what brings that on?[82]

In Quebec, Kahnawà:ke and Kanehsatá:ke community members remembered travelling to play in the provincial senior lacrosse league, where they too ran up against discrimination. Joe Delaronde recalls attending games during the 1960s:

I'll never forget as a kid going to the Verdun Auditorium and the Mohawks, the Kahnawake Indians at the time, would be playing a team from Drummondville – and Drummondville and Sorel seemed to have the most racist fans. Oh my god, you would go in there and [they would do the stereotypical war whoop] and oh geezzz, there were some fights. But the players themselves, because of the code of lacrosse you had a respect, no matter how grudging, a respect for your opponent, especially if it was a good player, and there were some good players who were non-Indians. So these were Indians against non-Indian teams, and I guess it probably helped the game [break barriers between the two]. There were some non-Indians that played for us ... [From the Indigenous perspective] I guess in our society you hope that as many people as possible will be ambassadors for us. By virtue of the nature of the game our lacrosse players throughout history have been ambassadors whether they liked it or not, they were ambassadors, so they were bound by a code.[83]

For Onawario, John Cree, racism in lacrosse is illustrative of Canada's relationship with Indigenous peoples and the larger loss of our interconnectedness and identity as human beings:

To me, I don't know about you, but lacrosse is not so much as a First Nations [teaching], First Nations is a very small thing, it is the human being, the human race [teaching]. When we identify ourselves, we say Qgwehǫweh; we don't say First Nations, we say Qgwehǫweh. Qgwehǫweh means "I am a human being." There was an Elder I remember a while back, he said to me [John gives the question in Kanien'kéha], "Who are you?" [John answers him in Kanien'kéha] ... I said, "I'm Mohawk." He said, "What's that?" He says, "I asked you, who are you" [John asks again in Kanien'kéha] ... He says, "Are you Qgwehǫweh?" I said, "Yeah" [John answers in Kanien'kéha that he is Qgwehǫweh]. "Why didn't you answer me right then?" He says, "Are you a human being?" I said, "Yeah." He says [John gives the phrase in Kanien'kéha], "The white man is always telling us that we are not human." But he says, "We knew way before he came here who we were, that we were human beings." See and that is what lacrosse means too, that spirit inside of you the human [John switches to Kanien'kéha]. All our families across North America, we are all related. The Hopi say that, the Hopi say we came out and went in four directions. We all picked up different languages, but we are all connected, we are all related. That is where Canada has – what they have done is they have taken away that family and divided us. We don't think as that human being and being part of that family ... I told the kids at Kahnawà:ke, I said, "You know you don't have to be white to succeed in the white man's world, you just have to be proud of who you are, not be ashamed ..." I was looking at the kids, and I saw that there was an ash tree that was growing and connected to the ash tree was an apple tree. And I told the kids, "Now look at those two trees, they are growing together, they are intertwined. How come that apple tree hasn't turned into an ash? How come the ash hasn't turned into an apple tree? They have learned to grow up together as individuals but still connected." And I said, "Respecting each other ... it is only the human being that sometimes gets lost and sometimes tries to be something that it is not ..." And that is what lacrosse is to me. When I think of lacrosse, I think of everything we are as humans, not as individuals, but as humans and what lacrosse tells us about the struggles we have to take in life, each step that we take to achieve certain goals in our life – dreams.[84]

Throughout the history of Canadian lacrosse, institutional racism, beginning with the founding of the National Lacrosse Association of Canada in

1867, persisted at the provincial, national, and international levels. For instance, during the 1960s and 1970s, senior leagues in Ontario (and possibly Quebec) mandated that every Indigenous team must have a certain number of non-Native players. Like the ban of 1867, this regulation was based on the assumption that Indigenous players together were too strong competitively.[85] Although the leagues finally authorized the establishment of all-Indigenous teams, community members felt that organizers and certain non-Indigenous teams found other ways to discourage Indigenous prominence in the game. Onawario recalls that "you had to have some non-Native players on your teams because you couldn't have a full roster of Native players because they were too strong. I think when they first started to let us play [as all-Native teams again] ... then they figured out they could get us by the refs [calling the game unfairly]."[86]

Despite the discrimination, teams such as the Brantford Warriors, which began to play in the top-tier Senior "A" league in 1969, won games and frequently competed for national honours. The Brantford Warriors, which always included a number of Six Nations players, finished second in Ontario during the regular 1969 season and first in 1970.[87] In the following year, Gaylord Powless led the Brantford Warriors to the Mann Cup while further establishing himself as one of the game's most dominant players.[88] Nicknamed the "Marvellous Mohawk," he enjoyed a magnificent career, much like his father, and is often cited as the greatest lacrosse player of all time. Following the 1971 championship win, the Six Nations' newspaper, *Tekawennake,* reflected on the accomplishment and the sense of pride that Six Nations athletes brought to the community: "Hearty congratulations to Messrs. Ron Thomas and Gaylord Powless, members of the Brantford Warriors Lacrosse Team and winners of the Canadian Senior 'A' Lacrosse Championship by defeating New Westminster Salmonbellies in four straight games. In winning the coveted Mann Cup the players have brought honor to themselves and to their community."[89]

For Six Nations, the Hodinöhsö:ni', and Canadian lacrosse enthusiasts more generally, Gaylord Powless was something special. He wasn't the first Indigenous player to win a junior or a senior national championship, and numerous players had led their teams in points and played professionally during the early era of box lacrosse, but his successes were far broader. As he set scoring records, he became the face of lacrosse for Canadians and Indigenous peoples throughout the country, even among those who did not follow the game. He was repeatedly featured in the mainstream media

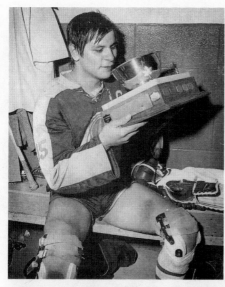

Gaylord Powless. | *Courtesy of Gaylene Powless.*

Gaylord Powless takes a shot while playing for the Brantford Warriors, c. early 1970s. | *Courtesy of Gaylene Powless.*

and was later compared to National Hockey League greats Wayne Gretzky and Bobby Orr. In an article on the Powless legacy, which featured Ross, Gaylord, and Gaylord's son Chris, *Hamilton Spectator* writer Steve Milton chronicled Gaylord's early career:

The Gaels [Oshawa Green Gaels junior lacrosse team] became synonymous with lacrosse and Gaylord Powless became synonymous with
the Gaels. A Mohawk dominating the game invented by his people.
He won two scoring titles, another Minto Cup MVP, holds the record
for career Minto Cup scoring, was named the most sportsmanlike
player in the league, and was arguably more popular than Bobby Orr
when both were junior-aged stars in Oshawa.[90]

Like Ross and Gaylord Powless, goaltender Ernie Mitchell, Kaheranoron
(Ahkwesáhsne), became a star, playing for Les Québécois in the early 1970s
National Lacrosse League, sometimes before ten thousand spectators at the
Montreal Forum.[91] These men became role models in their communities
and famous athletes outside of them. For example, at Expo 67, Gaylord
was touted as *the* player to watch at the North American All-Indian Field
Lacrosse Championship, in addition to teammates Pete Powless, Claude
Scott, and Ron Thomas on the Canadian Indians All-Star Team and competitors Irving Huff, Victor Cornelius, and Vincent Stevens, who played
for the American Indians All-Star Team.[92]

The Lacrosse Stick as Identity

Clearly, the importance of lacrosse has not wavered for the people of the
Hodinöhsö:ni' Confederacy or for numerous Indigenous nations across
the country, and it continues to hold a cultural and ceremonial significance. However, this is not to imply that its meaning has never changed.
For Christian Hodinöhsö:ni' such as the Powless family, the game was a
marker of shared identity, Hodinöhsö:ni' culture, and Indigenous peoples
more generally. Although Gaylord and Ross Powless did not participate
in the Longhouse, they did associate lacrosse with being part of their
Hodinöhsö:ni' identity.[93] When Ross retired, he became a key member of
the Six Nations lacrosse community, and as previously mentioned, he served
on the Six Nations Band Council for more than a decade.[94]

For both Longhouse followers and Christians, the wooden lacrosse
stick was of central significance. Among the former, the wooden stick was,
and continues to be, associated with the epistemological importance of
lacrosse as part of Hodinöhsö:ni' socio-political, cultural, and spiritual
frameworks and its connection to the Longhouse. Sticks were often made
by Indigenous artisans, and their production had been a respected cultural
practice from time immemorial. In the mid to late nineteenth century, sticks

were produced in individual shops and later in factories, and the industry had become a key business enterprise for several Indigenous communities by the late nineteenth century. These individual stick makers supplied some of the biggest lacrosse markets in Toronto, Montreal, New York City, and throughout North America. Reports written by Indian agents during the 1880s and 1890s cite stick making as a principal activity for the communities of Wáhta, Kahnawà:ke, Kanehsatá:ke, Ahkwesáhsne, and Wendake, to name a few.[95] In 1884, Frank Lally founded the Lally Lacrosse Company in Cornwall, Ontario, and later approached Kanien'kehá:ka stick maker "Matty" White to make sticks and attract Indigenous craftsmen from Ahkwesáhsne to form an assembly line production factory.[96] Frank and Alex Roundpoint, both from Ahkwesáhsne, later left the Lally Company to form their own venture, in partnership with Scottish schoolteacher Colin Chisholm.[97] Apparently choosing to use the Chisholm name to appeal to non-Indigenous Canadians and Americans, the Chisholm Lacrosse Factory became the Lally Company's main rival early in the 1930s, buying it out by 1945.[98] By the 1960s, as Thomas Vennum estimates, the Chisholm factory was making 72,000 sticks annually, or 97 percent of the market's share.[99]

For all Hodinöhsö:ni' athletes, whether they were Longhouse or not, the stick was a direct link to the Hodinöhsö:ni' roots of lacrosse and a tangible symbol of their identity. For example, in many Hodinöhsö:ni' communities, newborns are customarily given a miniature wooden stick to keep in their cradle.[100] Lacrosse itself had greatly changed by the 1960s, but the stick, though reshaped and streamlined, still resembled the original Kanien'kehá:ka version and retained its orenta. As described earlier, the stick is understood to be more than a piece of sports equipment. Like the tree from which it comes, it is a living being and a form of medicine; every time it is used, its steward is able to increase its orenta, and it becomes even more powerful.[101] Rick Hill explains that the stick helps harness the healing powers of living trees and becomes a medicinal object itself:

> I don't know if I told you about that story, the journey to the Sky-world, the [four] warriors who went up there and they saw this lacrosse game going on. They tell us now that is what is going to happen when you and I pass away, we are going down this path with these beautiful flowers and we'll see some of our relatives. Someone will come and hand us a bowl of strawberries and we are going to hear the cheering crowds in the background ... And there is this perpetual

lacrosse game going on, which apparently no one ever wins – it just keeps going on and on ... When a lacrosse player passes away then, they acknowledge that, and they will say, "This man was gifted with this ability to play, people used to marvel at him, so we thank him for demonstrating that." So I think this is why then they used [to continue] to bury – to put the wooden lacrosse stick right in the casket with them – because it represents *their* power. And you and I couldn't pick up that old man's stick and capture that power. It belongs to him, so it is almost like, might as well take it with him. And that was in an era of course when lacrosse sticks were being made everywhere. Now, you still see it, it is still a part of that. Because they tell us, lacrosse players here when he gets up to the Sky World, he is then going to join those players.

But in this Sky World game that happened when these warriors, who had been killing everybody, went up there, there was an old man watching the game go on. And there was this one player, every time he would run by him, this old man would kind of holler at him, "Hey, don't do that. I told you not to play that way, that is not good, you are not supposed to play that way." Apparently this guy was kind of nasty, slashing, and everything else. So at one point this nasty player is running in front of this old guy, and he reached out and grabbed him, and then he hurled him just like an arrow and he went straight through a tree, stuck in the tree. Basically the old man says, "Stay there for a while." [Rick laughs] "That will straighten you out." And then he turns and sees these warriors, who were, needless to say, kind of impressed: "Maybe we should listen to this guy." Well as it turns out in this story, he is most likely the Creator and these warriors, he is transforming them from guys who were killing to guys who were going to be the Thunderbeings and transform their arrow into a thunderbolt so that they will do good with that power that they have.

And there is a whole lot of other parts to that story, but it is kind of interesting. Now the guy stuck in the tree, it is because we believe that trees, particular trees, they call them magnetic trees, they pull out of you negative energy and put it back into the ground, and the ground takes care of it all. So if that is true think of that lacrosse stick. Think of the wooden frame on a fire, wooden utensils, the wooden longhouse, you really are in a spirit place all the time. And I think that is the difference, people, that the old-timers would describe the difference of playing with a wooden stick and the new stick [made of plastic] ... So the relationship between you and your stick is different.[102]

Recognizing the stick as a form of medicine and as a living entity is critical to understanding the importance of lacrosse in all aspects of the Hodinöhsö:ni' worldview, including the afterlife and the Sky World. This understanding is reinforced in the oral tradition of the founding of the original five nations and in the Great Law of Peace, or Kayeneren:kowa in Kanien'kéha.[103] Brian Rice reminds us that when the Hodinöhsö:ni' Confederacy was founded, Kanien'kehá:ka Nation member Ayenwatha became a key advocate for spreading the message of peace delivered by the Peacemaker.[104] However, he was also grief-stricken at the time, as he had lost his wife and two daughters. He was so distraught that the community became concerned for his well-being and decided to host a lacrosse game, feeling "that this would surely lift the spirits of Ayenwatha and that the Creator in watching the game might be looking over him."[105] Furthermore, Rick Hill's oral history of the four warriors who saw lacrosse being played in the Sky World demonstrates that the game persists there. It also figures in the teachings of Sganyadai:yo' (Handsome Lake).[106]

The visions and Code of Handsome Lake, which continue to be recited every fall, reconfirmed the existence of the Creator's game in the Sky World and prompted countless players to take a stick with them on their journey there.[107] As Dao Jao Dre, Delmor Jacobs, adds, "With Gai'wiio [Good Word or Good Message] that is what we are told, lacrosse is played in heaven and that is where I have seen a lot of people, a lot of males, take their stick with them when they pass from here. I know I will."[108] However, not just any stick can accompany a person into the Sky World; it must be a wooden stick, not the synthetic variant that was introduced in the 1970s.

In 1968, the Chisholm factory burned down, and the Brine Company introduced mass-produced plastic sticks in 1970, after which the synthetic stick quickly became dominant across the globe.[109] As Thomas Vennum documents, in the spring of 1971, the Brine company wrote to every known field lacrosse organization, proclaiming that the plastic stick was the way of the future. "Thus," Vennum argues, "with one mass mailing, Brine dictated the future of the men's field lacrosse stick, just as Beers had established the rules of the game 104 years earlier. Whereas one deprived the Indian from

▲ Gus Yellow (Onyota'a·ká·) shaping a lacrosse stick, Six Nations of the Grand River, Ontario, 1912. | *Frederick Wilkerson Waugh, 18841, Canadian Museum of History.*

▼ Sandy Johnson making a lacrosse stick, Six Nations of the Grand River, Ontario, 1949. | *Photographer Marius Barbeau, J3111, Canadian Museum of History.*

▼ Lacrosse sticks in Longan's shop, Six Nations of the Grand River, Ontario, 1949. | *Photographer Marius Barbeau, J2982, Canadian Museum of History.*

participation in the international arena, the other put uncounted numbers of native stickmakers out of work, hastening the decline of yet another centuries-old American Indian craft."[110]

In the mid-1970s, the National Collegiate Athletic Association changed its rules to bar the traditional wooden stick, and the professional National Lacrosse League later followed suit, severing one of the most visible, spiritually powerful, and symbolic elements of lacrosse from its Indigenous origins. Despite this, Indigenous stick makers continued the trade, albeit on a much more limited scale. However, non-Native stick manufacturers and the plastic stick remain dominant, which has continued to distance lacrosse from the Longhouse epistemology.

Lacrosse in the Sky World

The primacy of non-Indigenous plastic stick companies and the rule changes regarding sticks simply perpetuated the historic misappropriation of the game and separated the orenta of lacrosse from the stick. Dao Jao Dre, Delmor Jacobs, notes that the plastic stick is a lifeless form. Unlike its predecessor, it cannot be taken into the Sky World:

> Wood still carries the essence of the game from its very root. It [lacrosse] is rough, it was designed to be rough, it was designed to be a test of you holistically ... All the components we say about it [the game], that designation, even with the spirit of the wood that is made out of that, everything played into that. With the plastic one you are just putting things ahead, and it's not alive, it was never alive, not like the tree, not like the [wooden] stick ... Like I say, when we are buried with our stick, it has to be all-natural. So the other one [with a plastic head and a metal shaft], I have never ever seen anyone buried with metal and what have you. As a matter of fact, I should never see that. The reason being that everything on you is supposed to be naturally made; otherwise it will help keep you here [in this world].[111]

Although the teaching of Gai'wiio forms an integral part of Hodinöhsö:ni' Longhouse epistemology, some traditionalists – mainly the Kanien'kehá:ka of Kahnawà:ke, Kanehsatá:ke, and Ahkwesáhsne – do not follow the Code of Handsome Lake, seeing it as a Christian subversion of the Kayeneren:kowa.[112] Yet they too revere lacrosse as a significant piece of Longhouse epistemology.[113] Furthermore, the understanding that lacrosse is played in the afterlife appears to have spread among non-Longhouse Hodinöhsö:ni', and Longhouse traditions have influenced even Christian burial practices in these communities. The most compelling example comes from the Powless family, who were not associated with either the Longhouse or Handsome Lake traditions. When Gaylord Powless died, he was buried at the St. Paul's Anglican Church cemetery on the Six Nations reserve, with a number of sticks. Just a few months before his death in 2003, in a CBC Radio interview, Ross Powless also discussed the importance of being buried with his stick:

> Several of my friends have taken their lacrosse sticks with them when they die, they have them tucked in the casket with them, which really means something to a lot of people ... I probably will, I probably will, I will want to play with my dad, my uncles, my boys, my nephews. Yeah ... it's quite a road, lacrosse is really been important to a lot of people and it has really been extra important to me.[114]

The understanding that lacrosse is played in the afterlife or the other-world was not limited to the Hodinöhsö:ni'. Lacrosse-playing nations throughout North America knew of its existence in the world beyond this one. For instance, in 1898 anthropologist James Teit published a story from the Nłe?kepmx Nation in British Columbia, in which the underworld is inhabited by the Ant people, who are "celebrated for their activity, gayety, and disposition for play." Their favourite game is lacrosse:

> Two brothers lived at one time with certain other people in an under-ground lodge. One day one of these brothers disappeared. The other brother searched for him but in vain. Then he became very sorrowful. He did not know what had become of his brother, for the Ants had stolen him, and by this time had led him to their abode underneath the ground. The Ants were playing a game of lacrosse, and he was playing with them. Suddenly he stopped playing, and sitting down, commenced to cry. The Ants said someone must have struck him with his ball-stick while playing. But he answered, "No! Nobody struck me. I am sorrowful, because while I was playing a tear fell on my hand. It was my brother's tear from the upper world, and I know by it that he is searching for me, and weeping." The Ants pitied him, and one of them said ... I will go to "the upper world, and let your brother

know where you are, and that you are well." The Ant went and reached the surface from underneath the firestone of the lodge in which the brothers used to dwell. The fire was low, and the people were sitting smoking, and some of them had retired for the night. Suddenly they saw a man at the foot of the ladder. They wondered how he had come down the ladder without being noticed; so they addressed him, saying, "Welcome, friend! Where have you come from?" He said, "I am wandering about the country." He stayed a day or two, and then suddenly disappeared. He had, however, taken the opportunity to tell the brother above all concerning his relative below, and how happy the latter was, and the brother later on told the people. Then he asked the Ant, "How can I go to see my brother?" And the latter said, "I must not tell you. Go to the Spider, and he may tell you." He went to the Spider; but the latter said, "I cannot let you down, as my thread is too weak. Go to the Crow, and he will give you advice." He went to the Crow. The Crow said, "I will not tell you with my mouth, but I will tell you in a dream. Be careful and notice what you dream." He went home and fell asleep, and in his sleep dreamed; He was told in the dream to look under the firestone of the lodge, and he would discover a hole. He was to shut his eyes, and take one jump down the hole, when he would alight on an obstacle. He was then to roll over and take another jump, and would alight on another obstacle. This he was to do four times, and then to open his eyes, as he would then be in the lower world. He did as directed, and eventually found himself in a fine country, where the Ant people were playing ball. Here he found his brother, and was happy.[115]

Furthermore, both the Alnôbak (Abanaki) and Saulteaux Nations identify the Northern Lights as their ancestors, playing the game in the spirit world. Anthropologist A. Irving Hallowell recorded a Saulteaux story in which Miskadesiwiskijik (Mud-Turtle's-Eye) returned from the *dijbaiaking* (spirit land), where he had learned that lacrosse was a favourite game of the spirits, who played it all day (which is night among the living).[116]

Lacrosse and the "Politics of Recognition"

As mentioned above, the swift dominance of the plastic stick is another example of the redirection of lacrosse from its epistemological foundation.[117] However, it must be made clear that this redirection was also aided by the attempted extinguishment of Indigenous self-determination through colonial tools such as band councils, residential schools, land expropriation, colonial laws like the Indian Act or the Lord's Day Act, and Christianity.[118] These all played a major role in attempting to eradicate the epistemological foundation and Indigenous knowledge that lacrosse was built on, which would have significant and lasting socio-political consequences for Indigenous communities internally, as will be discussed in the following chapter.

Despite this, Hodinöhsö:ni' communities continued to use lacrosse for their own purposes, including cultural resurgence, and to gain greater control of the public image of Indigenous peoples. During the 1960s and 1970s, public all-Indigenous lacrosse celebrations and the rekindling of Hodinöhsö:ni' traditions through the game became increasingly common and often caught the attention of the local press. In the summer of 1971, for instance, an international all-Indigenous lacrosse tournament and arts and crafts exhibition were hosted by Six Nations and sponsored by the International Indian Sports and Cultural Association, the Canadian Lacrosse Association (CLA), and the federal government.[119] This event and others like it hearkened back to those of the late nineteenth and early twentieth centuries, in which lacrosse competitions and Indigenous culture were combined as an exhibition. However, their purpose was significantly different. No longer run by non-Indigenous promoters to bolster ticket sales, they were celebrations of Indigenous culture and its resilience in the face of decades of assimilative policies. The 1971 event, held at the Brantford Civic Centre, was reportedly a great success. For one Six Nations community member, it was also a confirmation of the place of Indigenous peoples within Pierre Trudeau's emphasis on reimagining Canada as a multicultural state: "The show featured an Indian Handicraft exhibition, a fashion show, Native Dance and a lacrosse tourney. *It is by these events that the Canadian public can realize that the Indian culture is a vivid part of the Canadian multiculture.* Otherwise the Indian culture will be relegated to the museum. This show should be made an annual event."[120] The author viewed the event as confirmation of the "politics of recognition" that has since the 1970s attempted to get Indigenous nations to conform to and identify as "Aboriginal" within the framework of the nation-state. Although the politics of state-defined recognition *within* the state, rather than alongside or outside it, were sometimes perceived as positive and as complementary to the government's more recent emphasis on "Aboriginal" reconciliation and subjecthood, a growing number of Indigenous scholars and activists have pointed out the fallacies of such rhetoric as a "shape-shifting" form of colonialism.[121]

The tournaments and cultural events would continue into the mid-1970s, including an all-Indigenous tournament with teams from Six Nations, the North Shore of Vancouver (Sḵwx̱wú7mesh), Kahnawà:ke, and Nanaimo. A number of participants, second-generation players, could trace their histories to the early era of box lacrosse.[122] In 1976, the Kanien'kehá:ka Tyendinaga Reserve near Belleville, Ontario, hosted an all-Indigenous youth tournament, with representatives from the Kanehsatá:ke, Kahnawà:ke, and Six Nations reserves.[123] John Maracle, president of the Tyendinaga Kan-Yen-Geh Lacrosse Association, hoped that the tournament would help thrust Indigenous athletes back into the lacrosse fold. A *Belleville Intelligencer* article pointed out that it also reintroduced the game on an organized level at Tyendinaga: "For the Kan-Yen-Geh lacrosse association, the tournament is another sort of triumph. Lacrosse, said Mr. Maracle disappeared from the reserve about 75 years ago and was restarted only three years ago."[124] The temporary absence of competitive lacrosse at Tyendinaga may be partially explained by the reserve's rural location and the trend of lacrosse organizations to be focused in and around urban or more populated regions (of course, there are exceptions to this, such as the Orillia Terriers).

Indigenous Athletes in International Competition

At the same time that Indigenous communities were hosting their own celebrations, Indigenous peoples continued to be part of the larger international events that historians Myra Rutherdale and J.R. Miller term "national spectacles."[125] For example, at Expo 67 the National Indian Council and the Department of Indian Affairs and Northern Development organized the Indian Pavilion, an exhibit on Indigenous peoples.[126] Although it fell into line with the assimilation scheme of Indian Affairs and promoted both the noble savage and disappearing Indian myths, Christine O'Bonsawin notes that it also "offered a groundbreaking approach in the world's fair model, as it allowed for indigenous and settler people to jointly explore their arduous relationships in historical and present-day Canada."[127] As Rutherdale and Miller contend, "the interior of the pavilion actually told a story that was meant to provoke the viewers to think about the impact of colonization on First Nations. Never before had Canadian or international visitors been asked to do that."[128] Not only would Expo 67 include the thought-provoking Indian Pavilion and encourage Indigenous participation, though limited, in the organization of the international event, an all-Indigenous lacrosse game was held at the Expo 67 Automotive Stadium.[129] Called the North American All-Indian Field Lacrosse Championship, it pitted a team of "Canadian Indian All-Stars" against one consisting of "American Indian All-Stars." The Canadian team included Six Nations community members Gaylord Powless, his brother Gary Powless, and their father Ross (coach), along with Roger Smith, Ahkwesáhsne community member Frank Benedict, and George "Pidgie" Norton (Kahnawà:ke). The American team was coached by legendary Onöndowa'ga:' lacrosse player Nelson Huff from Cattaraugus.[130]

Despite the successful albeit segregated inclusion of Indigenous peoples at Expo 67, they were once again relegated to the role of "show Indians" at the 1976 Montreal Olympic Games. Although they were invited to be a significant part of the closing ceremonies as dancers, the ceremony itself was fraught with half-truths and spaces of exclusion. As Christine O'Bonsawin documents, only 200 of the 450 dancers were Indigenous. The rest were non-Natives who were "playing Indian." And despite the focus on Indigenous peoples, the ceremony was organized and choreographed without their input.[131]

Two years later, the 1978 Commonwealth Games, held in Edmonton, Alberta, simply furthered Indigenous exclusion and segregation while Canada attempted to portray itself in a positive light before international audiences. Perhaps no case better illustrates the sidelining of Indigenous peoples in lacrosse administration and participation than this event. In 1977, the City of Edmonton announced that box lacrosse would be played at the Games as a demonstration sport.[132] Almost immediately, a number of Indigenous communities and the Indian Sports Olympics organization inquired whether Native teams would participate and expressed their desire to be included.[133] As reported in the *Edmonton Journal,* Ahkwesáhsne lacrosse player Mike Mitchell, who was executive director of the highly competitive Akwesasne Warriors, hoped that at least one Indigenous team would be selected: "Mr. Mitchell pointed out that the 18-member Warriors, accompanied by dancers, stick makers, basket weavers and fans, are anxious to 'project the Indian people in their proper perspective.'"[134] His suggestion that the Games should offer both an Indigenous demonstration of lacrosse and bona fide Indigenous cultural activities was not out of the ordinary, as lacrosse continued to be seen as an avenue to expose the dominant society to Native culture. Yet, the Canadian Lacrosse Association (CLA), which, along with the Lacrosse '78 committee and Sport Canada, was in charge of organizing the demonstration, had no plans to include an Indigenous team. Instead, it decided to use non-Native youth and Senior "A" teams.[135] The resulting dispute made the headlines of Canadian newspapers, especially in Edmonton. The *Edmonton Journal* editorialized,

> At least one Indian team should be invited to participate in Canada's demonstration of lacrosse during the 1978 Commonwealth Games. It is, after all, their game ... If the Edmonton Commonwealth Games foundation wished to demonstrate a sport unique to this country's culture during next summer's Games, the demonstration would be far more authentic with descendants of the people who invented it taking part.[136]

Both Indigenous and non-Indigenous supporters urged the CLA to include the originators of the game – much like they had during the debate surrounding the inclusion of an all-Indigenous team in the 1932 Olympics. In early March, the Commonwealth Games Foundation and the CLA announced that an Australian team would play in the demonstration and that any proposed Indigenous team would fill in for the Australians if they failed to show up; essentially, the Indigenous team would be reduced to the role of spectator.[137] Then the CLA suggested that Indigenous peoples play a mere cultural role as show Indians, an idea that team representatives emphatically rejected: "We don't want to be out there and dance for white people. We don't want to be token Indians."[138]

The Commonwealth controversy was emblematic of the infighting and cultural misappropriation of lacrosse that had occurred since the 1867 formation of the National Lacrosse Association of Canada. The attempts of lacrosse-governing bodies to exclude, control, and subjugate Indigenous peoples mirror the larger problems that characterize relations within Canadian settler-colonialsm and provide a glimpse of the inner workings of that structure. Furthermore, the controversy epitomizes a persistent theme in Canadian history – that Indigenous peoples are valued not as athletes or partners within a nation-to-nation relationship, but as performers and spectacles that fit within the assumed absolute sovereignty and control of Canadian sport organizations and, ultimately, the country. As argued elsewhere, at times, these organizations are simply masks for larger colonial forces at work.[139] When the Indigenous connection to the game appears as static, stereotypical, and mythologized relics of the past – such as in the form of Indian caricatures that serve as team emblems – or when their participation in league play does not attempt redress past injustices, Indigenous teams are welcomed. However, when these injustices and their contemporary consequences becomes a topic of discussion – particularly when they bring light to issues beyond sport – the institutional power of these organizations is put into practice and the limitations of Indigenous "inclusion" are quickly made apparent.

Fearing that the protests against the CLA decision would draw the attention of the international media, Minister of State for Fitness and Amateur Sport Iona Campagnolo initiated an investigation.[140] Arguing in favour of including an Indigenous team, *Edmonton Journal* reporter Dan Powers stated that a select few officials supported their inclusion based on the notion that "'it would be great box office' to include an Indian team."[141] The following week, Sport Canada began a smear campaign, asserting that, despite evidence to the contrary, "a native team of sufficient calibre is not available in Alberta nor readily available in Canada."[142] Sport Canada spokesman Rick Paradis stated that supporters of an Indigenous team were "using the Commonwealth Games demonstration sports project for their own reasons."[143] At the same time, Ian Howard, executive assistant to Iona Campagnolo, concluded that the CLA decision was not based on race. Still, John Fletcher – member of the Indian-Metis 1978 Games Committee – believed that the CLA had never contemplated Indigenous participation in the first place.[144] Following an exhaustive lobbying campaign, the committee and people such as Mike Mitchell, executive director of the St. Regis Warriors, managed to get the CLA to revisit its decision and finally gained Campagnolo's support in late April 1978. However, Mitchell declared that if the CLA reconsideration proved unfavourable, an all-Indigenous tournament would take place on the Enoch Cree Nation's reserve, which lay to the west of Edmonton.[145]

In early May, an agreement was finally reached: two Indigenous teams, the St. Regis Warriors (Ahkwesáhsne) and the Caughnawaga Braves (Kahnawà:ke), would play an all-Indigenous game during the competition on August 11.[146] Even so, the institutional and organized exclusion persisted.[147] Travelling to Edmonton with the support of federal funding, the teams were reportedly not allowed to visit or stay in the athletes' village, attend other venues, or participate in the closing ceremonies.[148] Furthermore, the game that they played was with each other, not against a team from

Australia, Edmonton, Nanaimo, or Victoria during the two-day competition.[149] Reporter Allen Abel incisively remarked,

> What better way to demonstrate the national sport than by bringing in teams of Indians, whose game it was and is? And what better way to demonstrate how life often goes for native people than by barring them from the Village, giving them accreditation that would not permit them to enter any other venue and shipping them out before the closing ceremony?[150]

Interviewed by Abel, player Keith Jonathan stated, "I think we all were proud to come out here and represent the Indians ... But I would have liked to see more of Edmonton. I guess it was a good experience, but we didn't get to see any of the other events." At that, Jonathan's cousin Glenn, who was also present, quipped, "Except on television at the motel."[151]

Although Canada saw the rise of a new form of lacrosse in 1931, the game was dogged by issues that were rooted in the past, as exemplified by the controversy at the Commonwealth Games. Since the formation of Canada's first lacrosse-governing body in 1867, organizations, rules, and teams had been used to control, exclude, and subjugate Indigenous participation and were informed by larger colonial forces and processes. And yet, this is not to insinuate that the experiences of Indigenous individuals were entirely negative. Men such as Ross and Gaylord Powless often commented positively about competing for non-Indigenous teams and coaches, and some players saw the game as a bridge between the Indigenous and non-Indigenous communities, and as a way of promoting greater understanding. Furthermore, Indigenous athletes played a critical role in box lacrosse and adopted it as their own, helping their communities reunite, re-articulate their nationhood, gain exposure, and strengthen their political voices. Although Indigenous box lacrosse players and teams were now competing nationally, the fight to gain entry at the Commonwealth Games was an early preview of what was to come. Indigenous teams were still absent from international field lacrosse, the game remained distanced from the epistemology that had produced it, and institutional racism not only continued to exclude and control Indigenous athletes but also furthered the misappropriation of the game.

As the following chapter reveals, a new generation of Indigenous leaders and activists would challenge these historic injustices through the creation of a new team that represented the Hodinöhsö:ni' Confederacy in international competition.

Dey-Hon-Tshi-Gwa'-Ehs

5

Reclaiming the Creator's Game

>>> *Kanehsatá:ke, July 11, 1990*

Piercing the darkness of the pines, beams of light stream through the forest, marking a new dawn. In the silence of the morning, the dew lies thick and the smell of the pines clears the senses. It is going to be a warm and humid summer day in Kanehsatá:ke (Oka). Centred in the old pines, the outdoor lacrosse box sits empty, seamed with scars of games passed. 'Usdas stands on the boards, arms crossed, thinking of the games of yesteryear: the dust flying up from the hard-packed earthen floor, the checks made, the goals scored, and the onlookers perched all around the boards, with the little ones doing everything they can to catch a glimpse of their heroes. It's tranquil, the ghostly shadows dodging and weaving amid by the pines.

"Lacrosse in the pines, where it all started," 'Usdas whispers, holding their Etienne and Son stick.

"Ahhh, quit daydreaming," says a voice.

"Who said that? Who's there?"

"Up here, in the tree."

"Bat, is that you? What are you doing out this morning?"

The Onöñda'gega' Nation refers to lacrosse as *Dey-Hon-Tshi-Gwa'-Ehs,* which translates to "they bump hips" or "men hit a rounded object." Correspondence, Sue Ellen Herne, April 4, 2011, Akwesasne Culture Centre, Ogdensville, New York.

"Same as you, remembering the games of yesterday, the real roots of lacrosse."

But 'Usdas has lost his interest in nostalgia. "I smell tobacco."

"Yeah, it's thick in the air this morning and so is the tension. It's coming from the roadblock behind us."

'Usdas gives Bat a smug look. "It'll blow over. Besides, if they really wanted to solve the problem, the police would put down their guns, pick up lacrosse sticks, and fight it out on the Creator's original battle-ground, not a golf course."

"There are times when even the Creator's game isn't enough. But you know, the stick can tell a story too. It's creating a new one as we speak, over in Australia of all places!"

"Watch this, Bat!" 'Usdas winds up and blasts a shot at the net. *Bang!* The ball misses the net and smashes into the boards behind it.

"Aim for the net, 'Usdas! You'll set them off!"

"Who? Leave me alone, you little runt! You're too small for this game anyways. You could never compete against me, Bear, Deer, or Turtle!" 'Usdas keels over, laughing at the thought of Bat being squashed by these animals.

"Listen carefully, and I will tell you how the bats came to be."

"Oh, here we go again, another story –."

Bat begins:

The captains for the four-legged animals were the bear, whose weight overpowers all opposition; the deer, whose speed and ability to stop and go made him valuable on a team; and the great turtle, who could withstand the most powerful blows and still be able to advance towards the opposition at his own time, was also valuable.

The captains on the side of the winged birds were the owl, who excelled in the ability to keep his eye on the ball, no matter what position or direction the ball may be directed; and the hawk and the eagle, both noted for their swiftness and their powerful flight. These three represented all the winged animals.

While the birds were preparing for the game, they noticed two small creatures, hardly larger than mice, climbing up the tree on which were perched the leaders of the birds. Finally reaching the top, they humbly asked the captains to be allowed to join the game.

The eagle, seeing they were four-legged, asked them why they did not ask the animals where they properly belonged. The little creatures explained that they had done so, but had been laughed at and rejected because of their small size.

On hearing their story, the bird captains took pity on them, but wondered how they could join the birds' teams if they had no wings. After some discussion, it was decided to try and make wings for the little fellows, but, how to do it? By happy inspiration, one bird thought of the drum which was to be used in the dance. Perhaps a corner of the drum leather could be taken from the drumhead, cut into shape and attached to the legs of one of the small animals. It was done and thus originated the bat.

The ball was now tossed up, and the bat was told to catch it. With his skill in dodging and circling, keeping the ball constantly in motion, never allowing it to hit the ground, he convinced the birds that they had gained a most valuable ally.

The birds thought they could do the same for the other four-legged creature. But, to their dismay, all the leather had been used on the making of the bat's wings, and there was no time to send for more. In this confusion, it was suggested that perhaps wings might be made by stretching the skin of the animal itself. So, two large birds seized him from opposite sides with their strong bills. By tugging and pulling the fur between the fore and hind feet, the task was completed and there originated the flying squirrel.

When all was ready, the game began. At the very outset, the flying squirrel caught the ball and carried it up a tree and threw it to the birds, who kept it in the air for some time, then, just before the ball was to hit the ground, the bat seized it, and by his dodging and doubling, kept it out of the way of even the fastest of animals, until he finally threw it in the goal. This won the victory for the birds.[1]

Bang! 'Usdas whips another shot wide of the net and sarcastically blows a raspberry. "So, you're telling me that all players are important, no matter what their size, their strength, or their speed? How can you possibly shoot hard enough to score?" *Whoosh* – 'Usdas fires another shot. *Bang!*

Bat bursts into laughter. "Easy, 'Usdas, I can hit the net."

"Well then, tell me this. If everyone is so important and everyone has a skill to provide, why don't Hodinöhsö:ni' women play?"

"I'm impressed, you're starting to learn. Think of stories as a web; the stories are points in time, history, lived experiences, and teachings strung together by the strength of our cultures and worldviews. If you are patient enough, you will see that all those stories are woven together, including Hodinöhsö:ni' women and lacrosse. The work is never ending, the stories continue, and new histories are being created, but they maintain their cultural underpinnings. It's always been that way. This story isn't static and nor are we – you're changing it as we speak, leading the story of lacrosse in a new direction. Sometimes we're faced with difficult questions, difficult situations, where our traditions and core beliefs are met with contemporary realities and challenges. There's a team in Australia right now that has experienced this; so too have Hodinöhsö:ni' women, but they're changing the way we're going to tell this story to future generations, the story of our game, the Creator's game."

Bang! 'Usdas fires another shot off the boards. Suddenly – *zip, zip, zip!* – bullets fly past their heads. *Zip, zip, zip!* 'Usdas flattens into the dirt as the bullets smash into the lacrosse box and zing through the pines. Shards of wood splinter across the playing surface.

"Now you've done it!" cries Bat. "They're shooting at us!"

Bat gazes upon the scene erupting in the street below, thinking, "This invasion is being done in and around the lacrosse grounds, the original instrument of peaceful conflict resolution. Kanien'kehá:ka and Hodinöhsö:ni' culture has answers; this game has answers; it's all connected." Bat turns to 'Usdas, "Well, it's overdue. Two centuries of land expropriation is long enough! Better let the narrator Allan finish this one. We're in for a long standoff."

∿

MOST CANADIANS ARE FAMILIAR with what is often called the Oka Crisis – the armed struggle of Hodinöhsö:ni' people to block settler-colonial land expropriation, which led to the military invasion of Kanehsatá:ke – but the

Hodinöhsö:ni' have sought to exercise, reclaim, and articulate their sense of nationhood through many other avenues.[2] Lacrosse has had some stand-offs of its own. While Indigenous players and teams such as the Ohsweken Warriors reclaimed their position as the sport's leading competitors following the Second World War, the concerted political effort to reappropriate lacrosse took on a much more dramatic form. For the Hodinöhsö:ni', the sport became a site of cultural resurgence within a growing pan-Indigenous movement of activism. Ousted for more than a century, the Hodinöhsö:ni' attempted to re-enter international competition as a sovereign nation between 1983 and 1990. The creation of the Iroquois Nationals lacrosse team – which represents the six nations of the Hodinöhsö:ni' Confederacy in international competition – was a conscious political effort by its organizers to assert Hodinöhsö:ni' sovereignty on the world stage and to reappropriate the game of lacrosse. As the team was being formed in the early 1980s, a group of female Hodinöhsö:ni' players attempted to found a similar national women's team. However, though the traditional leadership of the Confederacy endorsed the male team, it refused to sanction the female one, citing traditional cultural restrictions. This chapter demonstrates how the Iroquois Nationals were a symbolic element of a larger resurgence of Hodinöhsö:ni' political institutions that were grounded in traditionalism and how the team was a catalyst for unmasking intercommunity conflicts between that traditionalism and new political adaptations.

Confronting Settler-Colonialism

In the twentieth century, the Hodinöhsö:ni' remained barred from international field lacrosse, but a rise in Indigenous activism helped to bring about their return. In the 1950s, and especially the 1960s, a series of international developments concerning Indigenous rights pushed Indigenous affairs into the global consciousness and eventually produced dramatic changes between Indigenous peoples and non-Natives in both Canada and the United States. Following the introduction of controversial Indian policies in Canada, such as Pierre Elliott Trudeau's ill-fated White Paper of 1969, and the occupations of Alcatraz Island in 1969 and Wounded Knee in 1973, Indigenous communities throughout both countries united in an attempt to resist federal policies.[3] During the 1970s, a number of Supreme Court of Canada rulings, such as *Calder,* and a rise in Indigenous activism significantly changed the state's relations with Indigenous peoples. Similarly, the United States saw a major increase in political mobilization by Indigenous peoples.

Via the occupation of Alcatraz Island and the siege of Wounded Knee, a new group of young, active, and vocal Indigenous leaders forcefully brought attention to the conditions that Indigenous peoples across North America endured at the hands of the dominant societies and their colonial governments.[4] As Rick Monture explains,

> As the 1960s progressed, increasing numbers of these Native youth became more educated and vocal about the racism and injustice that their people had endured, which led to the emergence of student activist groups across the U.S. and Canada. This wave of "Red Power" activism also resulted in the formation of the American Indian Movement (AIM) in 1968, and in the famous occupation of Alcatraz Island in the San Francisco Bay in November 1969, led by Richard Oakes, a Mohawk from Akwesasne.[5]

During the occupation of Wounded Knee, the Hodinöhsö:ni' were also present, having sent a delegation in support of the Oglala Lakȟóta, which was led by Onöñda'gega' Faithkeeper and former Syracuse lacrosse player Oren Lyons. As documented in *Voices from Wounded Knee,* Lyons took the opportunity to reaffirm Hodinöhsö:ni' sovereignty:

> Sovereignty is freedom of a people to act and conduct affairs of its own nations. We the Hotinonsonni [People of the Longhouse], the Six Nations, have our sovereignty. We conduct on our territories and we act for our people ... The white man says, "this is mine," Indian says, "This is ours." That's the two ideologies, this is the conflict.[6]

In conjunction with the increased political mobilization, Indigenous communities, including the Hodinöhsö:ni', were developing new strategies to assert their sovereignty. According to Mark Dockstator, these communities, guided by their established political systems, maintained that they existed within the "parameters and principles of equality within" a "nation-to-nation relationship" with the United States and Canada.[7] Leaders such as Oren Lyons looked for compelling ways to assert that the Hodinöhsö:ni' were a sovereign nation. Part of this endeavour expressed itself through sport. It was while Lyons was teaching in the Department of American Studies at the State University of New York (SUNY) at Buffalo during the 1970s that he met a young pupil and Skarù·rę' Nation member named Rick

Hill.[8] Along with Skarù·rę? Nation member Wes Patterson and wife Carol Patterson, they initiated a cultural revitalization and a reappropriation of lacrosse on a global scale by founding the Iroquois Nationals. From the outset, the formation of the Iroquois Nationals was intended to assert Hodinöhsö:ni' nationhood, and in turn it created one of the largest concerted, and arguably most visible, Hodinöhsö:ni' and Indigenous sovereignty movements in recent times. The team was an example of what Audra Simpson masterfully demonstrates in *Mohawk Interruptus* as an articulation of Hodinöhsö:ni' self-determination "in ways that refuse the absolute sovereignty of at least two settler states."[9] Furthermore, lacrosse remained a cultural institution and a significant factor within the Longhouse. As Oren Lyons often stated, it retained the power to heal and to resolve conflicts:

> The game itself is first a medicine game ... It is played to heal. Any individual can ask for a game. They might want to heal themselves. They might want to heal someone else ... the whole community gets mobilized ... The stick is made from hickory, so [that] ... explains the importance of the trees and what they add to this game ... and the deer provide the leather ... All the players are in an elevated space. They are spiritual beings playing for a much higher authority and realm.[10]

What better tool to help address both internal and external Hodinöhsö:ni' conflicts than the original healing game? Recognizing lacrosse as a medicine, and as a theoretical framework as mentioned earlier, the founders of the Nationals used it to promote cultural resurgence, reunification, the articulation of nationhood, and an exchange of understanding, as well as a source of pride. It was no coincidence that the Hodinöhsö:ni' national team played lacrosse rather than another sport; the choice demonstrates the centrality of the game in Hodinöhsö:ni' society.

Forming the Iroquois Nationals

Seven years after Lyons addressed the world from Wounded Knee, he once again led the Hodinöhsö:ni' on the international stage and declared their sovereignty, this time through sport. Capitalizing on the success of Hodinöhsö:ni' players in indoor and American university lacrosse, as well as the all-Indigenous North American Lacrosse Association in the 1970s,

Oren Lyons *(middle)* **and Tadodaho Sidney Hill** *(right)*, **c. 1993.** | *Photographer Charles Agel. Courtesy of* Turtle Quarterly.

Lyons, Hill, and Patterson became the primary founders of the Iroquois Nationals. First competing as a one-time venture at the Nations '80 World Lacrosse Indoor Championships in British Columbia – a small indoor tournament with limited international participation – the Nationals were a combination of all-star players from throughout the Hodinöhsö:ni' Confederacy.[11] The team finished in second place, so it was suggested to the organization that the Nationals attempt to gain entrance into the International Lacrosse Federation's (ILF) World Lacrosse Championships.[12] Although a Hodinöhsö:ni' team had represented Canada at the 1904 Olympics, making a brief appearance there, it was an exception in participation at this level. The Hodinöhsö:ni' had not engaged in official national or international field lacrosse championships for over a century, so the quest to enter the ILF world championships marked a significant shift.[13]

The Iroquois Nationals were founded in 1983 as a field lacrosse team.[14] The organization felt that a process of reconciliation needed to transpire, as its co-founder and manager Rick Hill explains: "So the reason I was in it was that I felt this historical wrong with our teams being prohibited from playing international lacrosse had to be corrected so win, lose, or draw we were trying to set that straight."[15] From the beginning, the Nationals encountered a great deal of skepticism from the ILF. The first major area of contention was their status as a sovereign nation. The Nationals not only found themselves attempting to prove their lacrosse competitiveness but, more so, that the Hodinöhsö:ni' were a soverign nation and that the team could represent themselves as such:

> At that time we were talking to political novices, even though these often were well-to-do people – success on field, went to major universities – their understanding of Native history and law was [minimal]. [Rick shakes his head] ... "What do you mean you are a nation? How do you prove you are a nation?" the committee would ask. So we had to do a lot of remedial education on them.[16]

Much of this education involved teaching the officials about the Hodinöhsö:ni' treaty relationship with Great Britain, Canada, and the United States, and the nation's continued self-determination.[17]

As proposed by Lyons, Hill, and Patterson, the Nationals were to be accepted in international competition as representatives of the distinct and sovereign Hodinöhsö:ni' Nation – or not at all. This was reinforced by the team's policy of travelling on the Hodinöhsö:ni' passport. The passport was created in 1921 by Ga·yo·gǫ·ho:nǫ' Chief Deskaheh (Levi General) from Six Nations in opposition to the reduction of Hodinöhsö:ni' sovereignty and an amendment of the Indian Act that allowed involuntary enfranchisement. In his effort to obtain recognition of Hodinöhsö:ni' sovereignty, Deskaheh made a point of journeying to London on the passport, a gesture that reinforced the nation's self-determination.[18] He argued that the Hodinöhsö:ni' had a special nation status in North America due to their treaty relationship with the British Crown as British allies, not as British, American, or Canadian subjects.[19] As Rick Monture explains, "Deskaheh and others at Grand River obviously had very different ideas about nationhood, and strongly resisted any notions of the Haudenosaunee relinquishing their identities in order to become Canadian citizens."[20]

According to historian Laurence Hauptman, the Hodinöhsö:ni' sovereignty claim stemmed from four major agreements that recognized their self-determination: the Fort Stanwix Treaty (1784), the Jay Treaty (1794), the Canandaigua Treaty (1794), and the historical nation-to-nation relationship between the Hodinöhsö:ni', England, France, and Holland, often recorded through wampums such as the Two Row, in which "both parties exchanged assurances of perpetual friendship while the United States gave a guarantee of territorial integrity."[21] In 1923, Deskaheh appealed to the League of Nations on behalf of the Confederacy Council in Six Nations. Once again travelling on the Hodinöhsö:ni' passport, he covered his legal fees and trip costs with funds raised from hosting "illegal" Sunday lacrosse games in Six Nations.[22] Due to the introduction of the Lord's Day Act in 1906, playing sports for financial gain was illegal on Sundays, but Six Nations community members continued to hold Sunday lacrosse games, which were extremely popular among non-Indigenous audiences. Community members transformed these Sunday lacrosse contests into a method of asserting their self-determination while supporting the Hodinöhsö:ni' sovereignty movement.[23] Although Deskaheh was unsuccessful at getting support from the League of Nations, his articulation of Hodinöhsö:ni' sovereignty through citing the treaty relationships and the establishment of the Hodinöhsö:ni' passport would serve as the foundation for the effort of the Iroquois Nationals to engage in international competition as a sovereign nation.

Canadian and Australian members of the ILF committee quickly became concerned with the political ramifications of accepting a Hodinöhsö:ni' team. The Canadians, who were most opposed, feared that acceptance could set a precedent and that the ILF might have to accommodate other Indigenous nations (such as the Sḵwx̱wú7mesh, Nêhiyawak, and Anishinaabeg). Furthermore, because the ILF committee and teams failed to recongize the "nested sovereignty" of the Hodinöhsö:ni' and perceived the Nationals' athletes as coming from Canadian and American territories, the Nationals, Canada argued, would in effect be draining the country's talent pool.[24] Like the Canadians, the Australians feared setting a precedent with respect to sovereignty and Indigenous athletes in their own country.[25] The organizers of the Nationals were quick to find common ground with the ILF. A shared goal of the Iroquois Nationals and the ILF was to restore lacrosse to the Olympic Games, making it an official sport there. The formation of the Nationals was intended to accomplish two primary objectives: it would bring increased international attention to the status of the Hodinöhsö:ni' as a sovereign nation, and it would raise the profile of lacrosse. Promoting the game and securing its future among non-Natives, especially at the Olympic level, was in the interest of the Hodinöhsö:ni', and obviously the Nationals, because it could act as a bridge between the Hodinöhsö:ni' and non-Natives. It could also provide access to social and cultural benefits such as university education, business opportunities, and community empowerment, as well as national and international recognition of Hodinöhsö:ni' sovereignty in sport and politics.

Ironically, the Nationals' pursuit of recognition was aided by the persistent non-Native association of lacrosse with its Indigenous originators. Although they commonly employed colonial discourse and stereotyping, nineteenth- and twentieth-century newspapers, souvenir programs, and team histories celebrated the game as a form of North American antiquity, but at the same time, Indigenous athletes were barred from participating in the game, or their engagement was limited. Ultimately, the indefensibility of this stance helped force the hand of those in control. As Indigenous peoples unified in their defiance of the institutions of colonialism, of which lacrosse was a part, bodies such as the ILF were confronted with their nostalgic nepotism. Rick Hill points out that Oren Lyons fully understood this dynamic and used it as a tactic:

What he [Oren Lyons] said was that, there is power in this game, because it is a medicine game. There is power in lacrosse and what he found was that lacrosse people all around the globe had this healthy respect for the Native origins of the game even though they might not have understood it very well, but he kind of felt that we could build upon that respect, then get to the issue of a national team, then get to the issue of passports, then get to the issue of championship play, because of their common interest in that [the origins] ... He also felt [that] lacrosse could almost die out, and he really felt that it needed this infusion, and they [non-Indigenous enthusiasts] understood it needed this infusion, that bringing Native players back into lacrosse would generate worldwide attention, press, audience. In retrospect, you would have to say that was true and that all of the countries in the world that play lacrosse really honour the Native roots of the game, and that is very important, because you don't always get that in the political arena or education field and everything else. But it's not just patting you on the back, because then the question becomes "ok, if you really honour us, then you have to support our application and we have to be participating in international play" ... So that was the strategy and at the same time, it was part of our own national growth.[26]

Well-known and respected by the lacrosse community and the ILF due to their tremendous success as both players and organizers, Lyons and Patterson represented a bridge between the elitist Canadian and American organizing bodies and Indigenous athletes, who remained relegated to the sidelines. As the 1978 Commonwealth Games controversy had demonstrated, there was a great deal of tension between Indigenous lacrosse organizations and Canadian and American officials. However, though the ILF doubted that the Nationals could travel on their passports and be competitive, it also admired the individuals who had organized the team. Thus, before the ILF would permit the Nationals to participate in the quadrennial world championships as an official member, it challenged the team's organizers to prove that they could field a team financially, competitively, and politically (gaining clearance to travel on the Hodinöhsö:ni' passport).[27]

Hoping to gain full membership in the ILF, the team commenced its reappropriation of lacrosse as an Indigenous form by competing in Lacrosse International '83, taking on some of the top American universities.[28] The team not only represented the return to international competition, it also marked the return of the Hodinöhsö:ni' to field lacrosse, especially the Confederacy members residing in Canada. Lacrosse International '83 turned out to be a tough proving ground for the Nationals. They lost both games against two of the best teams, the National Collegiate Athletic Association's Division I (Syracuse) and the Division III national champions (Hobart).[29] Although many members of the Nationals had played field lacrosse in high school – such as at LaFayette High School (in LaFayette, New York) near Onondaga and Niagara-Wheatfield High School (Sanborn, New York), which was next to the Skarù·rę' Reservation – several had box lacrosse backgrounds. This put them at a distinct disadvantage against highly skilled field lacrosse teams who practised and competed together regularly.[30]

Lacrosse and the Longhouse Resurgence

Whereas the establishment of the Iroquois Nationals was a political strategy for the assertion of Hodinöhsö:ni' sovereignty, it was equally an instrument for traditionalists to strengthen cultural unification and the Longhouse resurgence between Hodinöhsö:ni' communities. Quite simply, the team became a contemporary act of Hodinöhsö:ni' socio-political and cultural revival; it was an example of the use of traditionalism as an organizing tool for the articulation of self-determination.[31] The Hodinöhsö:ni' philosopher, scholar, and activist John Mohawk conceives of traditionalism as a form of social organization based on principles developed by Native peoples centuries ago. Its goal is the redevelopment of community life and the empowerment of land-based peoples in ways that promote the survival of cultures and provide a social justice ... This kind of reorganization is not an easy task. Most adults have been socialized to see the ancient ways of our peoples as folklore. They have great difficulty relating to the principles of traditionalism. A re-education process needs to take place while a practice is developed, and those who undertake the task should understand that there is a resistance every step of the way, even within the communities that express traditional values and sometimes, practical traditional ways.[32]

Theresa McCarthy elaborates that traditionalism is a political process in which the resurgence of Indigenous knowledge and languages is a radical act in the context of contemporary settler-colonialism.[33] Sanctioned by the Hodinöhsö:ni' Grand Council of Chiefs at Onondaga to represent the Hodinöhsö:ni' Confederacy, the Iroquois Nationals were an instance of that political process.[34] They embodied the culture, politics, and philosophy of the Hodinöhsö:ni' Longhouse epistemology, and they refused to accept financial support from the Governments of Canada and the United States or from profits gained via gaming operations.[35] The endorsement of the Grand Council of Chiefs marked a partnership that reinforced a particular political philosophy in Hodinöhsö:ni' nations – the reign of the traditional hereditary chiefs and the Longhouse, and the refusal of the elected band councils. It was also an important declaration of the team's view of Hodinöhsö:ni' nationhood.

To meet the ideals of the Hodinöhsö:ni' Confederacy, the team made a point of attempting to gather players, funding, and organizational representatives from each of the six nations of the Confederacy. This task sometimes proved extremely difficult because funding was limited and the nations were not equally skilled at lacrosse. In addition, matters were complicated by community identity and reserve-regionalism brought on by earlier land disspossessions. Whereas certain Hodinöhsö:ni' communities, such as Six Nations or Kahnawà:ke, tended to play box lacrosse, others, such as Onondaga, had more experience with field lacrosse. As a field lacrosse team based out of Onondaga, the Nationals were initially criticized for being too New York–focused, while players from Ahkwesáhsne and Kahnawà:ke were lesser known than those from closer to Onondaga.[36]

Asked about the beginnings of the Nationals, former team representative David White from Ahkwesáhsne remembers both the lighter side and the issues with regionalism:

> I think it was strained [the beginning of the team], because of the rivalries that existed. There were different groups of players like the Ahkwesáhsne guys, we hung out together, and then the Onöñda'gega' guys, they had their own personality and their own – I thought they were a little crazy, they were all band members and free spirits that way. And the guys from Six Nations, there was quite a few guys from Six Nations, they all had a different sense of humour so to speak. They talked, spoke a little differently and it sounded like – it was almost a little backwards you know [laughs], but the humour was right on. We would crack up just listening, but eventually the walls started coming down. And they really weren't big walls, it was just that there were differences, and then [there] became more acceptance and everybody was just out there to play lacrosse, that we all loved. That was our commonality: everybody wanted to play and do the best we could. As far as Oren, he was a visionary in my mind because in addition to bringing the different members from the different communities together, the men, there was also some political implications there. Travelling on Hodinöhsö:ni' passports and showing our sovereignty as a nation was really one of his goals as well and getting us back reinstated into the ILF, the International Lacrosse Federation, where Native players had been banned since, I don't know, 1800s – 1880s ... To do that was really significant and he accomplished those things.[37]

Divisions between Longhouse traditionalists and "modernists" had become more pronounced in Hodinöhsö:ni' communities throughout the mid-twentieth century, as people attempted to adapt to the colonial order, while at the very least maintaining the autonomy of the communities, and to create new political strategies, often generating political schisms in the process.[38] As John Mohawk remarks, the redevelopment of "community" through traditionalism is a difficult process, due mainly to its cultural specificity, the imposition of external policies, the attempted eradication of Indigenous peoples, and internal resistance that is often the result of colonial government policy (such as residential schools and band council leadership).[39] The Nationals were not immune to these tensions, as the internal political struggle affected them at almost every level. More than that, the team itself was a significant player as the self-declared symbol of the Confederacy.

Financially, it operated on a crippling budget, and though it shunned funding from the two colonial governments, asserting financial independence as a statement of sovereignty, it was pressed into working with non-Indigenous organizations and Hodinöhsö:ni' modernists.[40] Furthermore, the organizers wanted the players to understand that regardless of their personal political alliances they represented the hereditary Confederacy Council and the Longhouse. Although the players were not required to be Longhouse members, they did have to sign a loyalty oath to the Confederacy.[41] Due to the leadership struggle between traditionalists and modernists, some men refused to sign or did not participate at all, with the result that some of the best competitors never played for the Iroquois Nationals.[42]

The team organizers placed a great deal of importance on educating the players regarding the larger objectives. Rick Hill recalls,

> We did a lot of work in the beginning, working on the minds of the players and talking about the history of lacrosse, the spiritual underpinnings of lacrosse, and that they are lacrosse diplomats we used to tell them, and "you are an ambassador for your people. So think about that. And the young people are watching you, so it isn't about winning but it is about excelling at being you [personally and nationally]" ...
>
> We never insisted that they had to be Longhouse people, that you had to believe in the Longhouse system, but we wanted them to understand that the Hodinöhsö:ni' is the people of the longhouse, lacrosse is a medicine game in the Longhouse, the [Hodinöhsö:ni'] flag represents that. We were doing a lot of mentoring, helping the young guys understand their history, understand why it is important. You know even the issue of the passport, to help them understand that. What we wanted was if anybody asks you, "Why are you doing this?" we want you to represent our ideas, this is what it is about ... But in Hodinöhsö:ni' fashion, we never said you have to believe in it, but we are asking you to respect it.[43]

In keeping with this revival of traditionalism, the team reintroduced the Longhouse medicinal and spiritual elements of lacrosse to both its players and non-Indigenous enthusiasts and organizers. An active example of the

The first Iroquois Nationals field lacrosse team. | *Courtesy of Rick Hill and Deyohahá:ge: Indigenous Knowledge Centre at Six Nations Polytechnic.*

reinstitution of traditionalism, the team was simultaneously a process of decolonizing the Hodinöhsö:ni' game, communities, and players.[44] According to Poka Laenui, "colonization and decolonization are social processes even more than they are political processes ... The phase of rediscovering one's history and recovering one's culture, language, identity, and so on is fundamental to the movement for decolonization."[45] Although lacrosse was recognized and celebrated as a traditional game in Hodinöhsö:ni' communities, not every player was familiar with its spiritual underpinnings and its strong connection to the Longhouse – especially those who had grown up outside the Longhouse system.[46] Rick Hill notes that "we use it as a teaching tool to explain, 'this is why we are here, to keep this other stuff going on [Longhouse traditions]. And now that you guys are playing it, great, you are out here on the field but don't forget, it is still played in the Longhouse.'"[47]

Through the ongoing education of its managers, coaches, players, and the public, the Nationals organization helped bolster the cultural, spiritual, and epistemological importance of lacrosse to Hodinöhsö:ni' communities. However, the attempt to re-empower the Longhouse was confronted with several contemporary challenges that prompted the Longhouse leadership and team organizers to exercise the versatility of the governance structure and decision-making process. One example was the issue of defining citizenship and player "status," in the attempt to distance the organization from colonially imposed definitions of identity.

As the team was appealing for membership in the ILF, numerous questions surrounding player eligibility were being raised internally: How were players to be chosen, and who could and could not represent the team and nation? As the team came together, the organizers created their own criteria and definitions, and attempted to release themselves, at least in the Canadian context, from the Indian Act definition of Indian status. As sport historian Victoria Paraschak points out, other all-Indigenous sports associations and tournaments at the time adhered to the Indian Act categorization.[48] For example, the Open Women's Fast Pitch National Championship (1980) demanded that its players be "one-quarter Indian-blood," and every player in the Little Native Hockey League was required to have a federal band number. Band numbers signified Department of Indian Affairs recognition that an individual possessed Indian status. Thus, anyone who was of Indigenous descent but who lacked a band number, such as all Métis and non-status Indians, would be excluded from the hockey competition.[49] Furthermore, prior to 1985, some sports competitions such as the Indian Summer Games refused the participation of Indigenous peoples who had lost their status under the Indian Act. This applied to women who had married non-Indigenous men and to their children.[50] Mohawk notes that the concepts of "citizenship" and "status" are contentious in Indigenous communities and organizations due to their foreign imposition:

> In the beginning, the question of how to view Indian nationhood and citizenship wasn't a question at all. We are reminded that how things came to be the way they are evolved in a history entirely outside the control, and indeed outside the view, of the indigenous peoples of the world. We are further reminded that the evolution of the idea of citizenship, and its application to indigenous peoples, is an idea that has been created and molded to suit the needs of people other than the subjects.[51]

Initially, the Iroquois Nationals contemplated accepting any Hodinöhsö:ni' player who had both a nation and an identification card from his traditional government.[52] However, the matter was complicated by the friction between the implementation of a traditional practice – clan designation to declare Hodinöhsö:ni' status – and demographic realities. The Hodinöhsö:ni' are a matrilineal society in which clan identity is passed down from the mother's side. However, numerous would-be players had non-Indigenous mothers, so their clan chain was broken, and additional considerations concerning status had to be made in their case. To accommodate them, the organization expanded its definition of eligible Hodinöhsö:ni' players by including those who had an Indigenous father and a non-Indigenous mother.[53]

The acceptance of non-Hodinöhsö:ni' Indigenous players had to be contemplated as well. As the only Indigenous participants in international competition, the Iroquois Nationals attracted a number of athletes from non-Hodinöhsö:ni' nations, including the Sḵwx̱wú7mesh in British Columbia. They began to ask how they might fit into the equation: Could they too apply for status in the Iroquois Nationals or better yet in the ILF?[54] Ultimately – and attempting to appease ILF concerns about having numerous Indigenous nations – the Nationals decided that their membership would not be limited to the Hodinöhsö:ni'. Athletes from other nations were assessed on a case-by-case basis and were required to provide proof of bloodline (such as a family tree), a form of identification, and an acknowledgment of their citizenship from their nation.[55]

The team would consist of the best Indigenous players from North America. However, historian Donald Fisher notes that its non-exclusiveness enabled the ILF to limit itself to just one Indigenous team; if the Iroquois Nationals were inclusive, the ILF had no need to entertain proposals from the Sḵwx̱wú7mesh, Anishinaabeg, or other lacrosse-playing Indigenous nations.[56] The policy also raised an important issue for the Hodinöhsö:ni' Confederacy itself. As the Nationals were representing the Grand Council of Chiefs and were issuing passports on behalf of the nation, some members advocated that players be drawn exclusively from the Confederacy.[57] The issue of non-Hodinöhsö:ni' members would be revisited in 1987 by the ILF, as the team attempted to gain entrance into the federation. During that year, the ILF ruled that non-Hodinöhsö:ni' Indigenous men could participate for the Nationals, but, in a thought-provoking example of lingering colonialism, it also stated that the Nationals would be the only Indigenous team permitted to hold ILF membership – a restriction that remains true today.[58] Like the Hodinöhsö:ni', Indigenous nations across North America have played their variants of lacrosse since time immemorial, and they too assert their nested sovereignties and right to self-determination.[59] In the adoption of Hodinöhsö:ni' lacrosse as the only authentic version, an aspect of colonization and cultural imperialism carried out by William George Beers, the game as played by other Indigenous nations was denigrated as inauthentic, with the result that they could not represent themselves in the ILF – now called the Federation of International Lacrosse. Their practice of lacrosse and claims to self-determination are as meaningful as those of the Hodinöhsö:ni', and thus the case for including them has as much merit as that advanced by the Iroquois Nationals.

The Nationals as a Source of Hodinöhsö:ni' Pride

From the beginning, the intent of the Nationals was to enable their players to gain access to post-secondary education, as well as new places, people, and opportunities, and to expose non-Natives to Hodinöhsö:ni' culture. Rick Hill recalls,

> We did talk a lot about that, how lacrosse could be a bridge for our players, to open up avenues for them, gaining more confidence, seeing other things. So when you see how other people are, see what Johns Hopkins is like, see big-time lacrosse, it might motivate them to want to succeed ... Twenty years ago, that would have been impossible [the many Hodinöhsö:ni' players attending major universities]. Now when you see this goal, and guys are thinking about it, all of a sudden they are realizing that their personal conduct, their academic record, police record, all of this matters ... Even if the players might not be role models, *the idea of the Iroquois Nationals is the role model.* If you aspire to represent your people, represent them well. Not too many opportunities like lacrosse that you can do that. I think that maybe that is part of its power.[60]

The team quickly established itself as a source of pride and reunification through, and for, the youth of Hodinöhsö:ni' communities, where it was seen as an investment in future generations.[61] "In these times when all the elements seem to be going the other way, it's important to have a symbol for young people," Oren Lyons declared. "And it's important for young people to be able to perform for their nation, to show their abilities and their skills. These are proud youth, and fierce. Fierce Iroquois, playing again. You know, among the kids on the res, everyone wants to be a National."[62] A beacon of

Hodinöhsö:ni' pride and unification, the Nationals had a powerful impact on the youth and the nations they represented. As a young teenager, Kahnawà:ke community member Greg Horn followed the team in the press with pride and recalls that it helped to cement his identity as both Kanien'kehá:ka and Hodinöhsö:ni':

> When I saw that article about the Nationals, it was like wow! ... This is our sport and this is our people playing on our own team internationally ... So that made me proud and I was already [proud], [but] it helped reinforce my identity as a Mohawk rather than saying I'm Native and I'm Canadian. And now I will never say I am Canadian. I am Mohawk and that is that. And that is how a lot of people from this community see it.[63]

At their core, the Nationals embodied a spirit of co-existence; players could maintain their sense of nationhood – both as representatives of their nation (e.g., Kanien'kehá:ka) and of the Confederacy – as well as their culture, but they could also avail themselves of opportunities outside their communities. The team gave (and gives) Hodinöhsö:ni' youth a personal goal to achieve while strengthening their communities by developing future citizens who had experience with the dominant culture and who upheld their traditions and engaged with the Longhouse through the team. Certainly, this is not to give the impression that it worked perfectly or was experienced in the same way in every instance – there were gender-based limitation to this, as will be discussed in the following pages, and non-Longhouse team members on the Nationals teams – but it did allow the team to act as a form of "resurgence."[64]

Although the larger political assertions were always clear to the organizers of the Nationals, they became apparent to some players only as time went on. Former team member David White remembers,

> I don't think it was recognized initially [the political aspiration]. I think more than anything else it was an honour to represent your community, to be picked from Ahkwesáhsne to play on a *national team* and the same thing for the Onöñda'gega' [and the other nations]. The Onöñda'gega' probably had more insight into the political ramifications because that is where Oren is from, and his son Rex was one of the key players, and Scottie Lyons and Kent Lyons were his nephews.

So they knew what was going on more so than I'll say the outlying communities, but you know you pick up on it. Whenever we would have little talks, or we talk about the fundraising and how we are not going to accept just any monies, we want to be able to travel on our own, we have to show that we are a sovereign group, we are travelling on our passports, we raised our own money to come here, and so it became more and more apparent what was going on.[65]

Despite the early criticism that the Nationals were New York–focused, the team demonstrates how the Hodinöhsö:ni' transcended the boundaries imposed on them by the settler states and serves as an articulation of their self-determination within their own borders. Lacrosse provided a way to maintain the ties of group and family kinship, and to assert economic and political sovereignty despite opposition from the Canadian and American governments. It pulled together athletes, organizers, and funds from throughout Hodinöhsö:ni' territory, which happens to straddle the imposed international border of the settler states.[66] The organization of the team was

The Iroquois Nationals goalie fights for a loose ball, c. 1993. | *Photographer Charles Agel.*
Courtesy of Turtle Quarterly.

a way to assert the nation's own borders and to refuse those imposed upon it.[67] After all, as Lyons reminded us in an article in *USA Today*, "The border is relatively new ... We are an old people."[68]

To meet the challenge set out by the ILF, the Nationals needed to prove that they could organize and host an international event. When they returned to competition, their opportunity presented itself in 1984: they were the ceremonial host of a pre-Olympic cultural event, the Los Angeles World Lacrosse Games '84 at the Jim Thorpe Memorial Powwow Games.[69] The memorial games were a pre-Olympic reconciliation event celebrating the return of Jim Thorpe's 1912 Olympic medals, which had been stripped from him because of controversy surrounding his amateur status.[70]

The event also marked an important international recognition of the Iroquois Nationals' fight to reclaim the game of lacrosse. A *New York Times* article stated,

> The World Lacrosse Games, one of the festival's main events, is not just a display of the traditional sport known to American Indians as bagataway [sic]. One of the competitors, the Iroquois national team, is staging another battle in its 90-year-old fight for re-admission to the International Federation of Lacrosse, which would enable the team to compete in international meets. The Iroquois team was barred from competition in the 1890's [sic] on the ground that the team did not represent a country.[71]

As the ceremonial hosts – the International Olympic Committee had still not recognized lacrosse as an official Olympic event – the Nationals were in charge of organizing the Los Angeles lacrosse games, to which they invited teams from the United States, England, Canada, and Australia, as well as a California team.[72] Working tirelessly to raise funds, organizing, and manoeuvring politically for over a year, the Nationals went into the Los Angeles competition winless, and were becoming worried about their competitiveness. All that changed when they dramatically defeated the English team during the dying seconds of the game. This victory became a defining moment in their repossession of lacrosse:

ALLAN: Was that the moment where you thought that the Hodinöhsö:ni' had finally reclaimed the game?

RICK HILL: Yes, that in fact was for me. I was thinking "when are we ever going to win a game, and we spent all this money, us losing, losing faith." It was during the Los Angeles Olympics, pre-Olympic event, cultural event, the Jim Thorpe games, and we had been competitive, but when you actually walk off the field with that victory over another nation, *over England,* given our history, I was just thinking "man that was a powerful moment."[73]

The tournament marked a number of milestones for the Nationals: for the first time, they faced international competition and won a game against an international opponent. More importantly, organizers now felt that they were beginning to reclaim lacrosse as their own.[74]

Moreover, the momentum from the 1984 victory propelled the Nationals into further competitions and wins. In the summer of 1985, they won the championship at the North American Field Lacrosse Tournament in Ottawa, and due to their defeat of the English team at Los Angeles, they were invited to take a ten-day tour of England in the fall of 1985.[75] Competing against various teams from the English Lacrosse Union, made up of local clubs, as well as the English national team, they were the first highly competitive Hodinöhsö:ni' team to return to England since 1886.[76] They were playing the very game that the Kanien'kehá:ka had helped establish in the country a hundred years before, the significance of which was not lost on them, as Rick Hill recalls:

> And when we went to England, toured with them, it was funny. As you know, I have been in American Studies as a professor, and England is public enemy number one, in history and all this stuff they did ... So here I'm getting a chance to go to England just like Joseph Brant did. It was like, "I don't know if I am going to like this," and I get over there and the hospitality we were shown [was incredible]. The fact is, you walk to this old castle and here is this old lacrosse club that has been there since 1876. That was pretty powerful, to realize that those people have been playing lacrosse since the Mohawks first went over there and showed them the game, and carried it with pride ... So I think it was great psychologically for our players to feel that. I think it was great for the Hodinöhsö:ni' to be in that position.[77]

Symbolically and politically, the tour entailed a number of significant victories for the Nationals. If they were to gain entry to the ILF, their Hodinöhsö:ni' passports had to be accepted internationally. All of their previous games had been played in North America and thus did not require a passport, so the visit to England marked their first use of their passports to venture overseas; it is important to note that the passport had been used during the first half of the twentieth century and since its revival in the 1970s. Working with the members of the English lacrosse organization, who had some influence with government, the Nationals went to England on the Hodinöhsö:ni' passport.[78] They won three games and tied one, but it was a loss that stuck out for Rick Hill, though not for the reasons one would expect:

> They [England] came back and won, but the feeling after that, it is hard to describe – they are there, we are there [on the field after the long fight to establish the team], we just had this lacrosse tournament, we just proved that we could travel internationally, great hosts, great press, fans are showing up ... It was like, if you could imagine, it was almost an honour to lose because you are there, you are so glad that you are there.[79]

As the team continued to prove itself financially, competitively, and politically in pursuit of entrance into the ILF, its organizers were also endeavouring to create a larger Hodinöhsö:ni' sports foundation to promote capacity development in the communities and to further demonstrate the team's stability to the ILF.[80] One part of this initiative was the attempted establishment of an Iroquois Nationals women's team in 1984.

The Iroquois Nationals Women's Team

By the 1980s, the participation of Hodinöhsö:ni' women in lacrosse had gained momentum, but it remained limited in comparison to that of their male counterparts. Hodinöhsö:ni' women were accomplished in a number of sports, and those from Six Nations excelled in bowling, basketball, figure skating, and particularly fastball.[81] As Paraschak notes, the number of female lacrosse players began to rise during the 1970s, and women's teams from Six Nations competed successfully at the regional and provincial levels.[82] Furthermore, Hodinöhsö:ni' women had benefitted from high school lacrosse programs in New York State. For example, high schools in the Buffalo area, such as Niagara-Wheatfield, Cattaraugus-Little Valley, Gowanda, and Silvercreek High, encouraged the participation of female Hodinöhsö:ni' players.[83] Despite the fact that Indigenous female athletes were playing in regional and provincial non-Indigenous leagues, larger all-Indigenous tournaments were often limited to men.[84] Discussing female participation in lacrosse and hockey, Paraschak writes, "it thus follows that their athletic interests were not being addressed equally to the male athletes in these sports, within the emergent system."[85]

Non-Indigenous women had been playing organized lacrosse at the club and university level since 1890, whereas games involving Indigenous women were occasionally recorded in Ho-Chunk oral tradition and noted among the Dakhóta, Wendat, Anishinaabeg, Abenaki, Aniyvwiya, and Mvskoke, to name a few.[86] In Hodinöhsö:ni' communities, lacrosse was described as primarily a men's game.[87] In 2007, the general manager of the Hodinöhsö:ni' women's lacrosse team, Sandy Jemison, remarked to the *Peterborough Examiner*, "lacrosse was always considered a men's sport for us."[88] Furthermore, Darwin Hill, an Onöndowa'ga:' Nation member at Tonawanda, explained in Alison Owings' *Indian Voice* that "lacrosse was a gift to our people from the Creator, to be played for his enjoyment and also as a medicine game for healing. It's evolved into quite a different thing, but the origins and the way it's still used in our communities is for men only."[89] Thomas Vennum points out that other Indigenous nations also saw lacrosse as a male-only pursuit: "The minimal information on women in the game may simply mean that playing lacrosse came to be regarded as an exclusively male activity, along with their other traditional roles in hunting and waging war ... In place of lacrosse, Indian women of many tribes had their own games – forms of field hockey and shinny, for the most part."[90] However, as Vennum acknowledges, this is not true across all Indigenous nations, as evidence of the popularity and importance of lacrosse games played by Indigenous women can be found in the archival record and oral history of some nations.

To this point, no lacrosse history has provided a detailed examination of Hodinöhsö:ni' women in the sport. This is especially significant for a culture such as the Hodinöhsö:ni', which sees lacrosse as a critical aspect of identity and nationhood.[91] At first glance, one could conclude that the underrepresentation of female players simply reflects the limiting gender constructs of sport generally and the larger shift in Hodinöhsö:ni' communities from a matrilineal society to one that privileged male hegemony, as aided by colonialism. However, the history of the Iroquois Nationals women's team reveals that the matter is more complex and rooted in both Hodinöhsö:ni' traditionalism and nationhood.

It is no coincidence that Hodinöhsö:ni' women attempted to establish a lacrosse team. Rather, their choice of lacrosse demonstrates that though the game was limited to men, it was an identity marker for women as well and a vital part of their sense of nationhood. Paraschak observes, "This (re)production of a desired racial identity has particular notions of gender embedded within it. Ceremonial dances, powwows, and traditional games and sports – such as lacrosse – are prominent in symbolic declarations of a distinctive racial identity for First Nations peoples."[92] This distinctive identity could transcend gender lines even when actual participation in the sport did not. Although women's participation was much more limited, they were often assigned a role on its periphery, as organizers, supporters, and fans. Karen Etienne, daughter of Kanehsatá:ke stick maker Matthew Etienne, has fond memories of helping her father sell his sticks in eastern and central Canada:

> I tried to help him the best I could setting up, you know, [at] different arenas so he could sell his sticks and things like that. It was fun ... it was like it would be an adventure going with him you know, all kinds of weather, any time of year, travelling, visiting. You would have to wait a lot, wait in the car a lot, and he would come back with his sticks and pay the people and drop more off, and he was always doing that circuit, his circuit there. But it was alone time to talk with him, to enjoy. That is what he wanted: "Come with me today, come with me to Ahkwesáhsne." "Alright, I'll go."[93]

As fans, Hodinöhsö:ni' women could enjoy a form of entertainment, but given that the game is so deeply ingrained in their nation's identity, it also had a more significant meaning for them. From a Longhouse perspective, lacrosse is ceremony, culture, and medicine in action. And, as Oren Lyons explains in the television program *Oren Lyons, the Faithkeeper*, it is a key aspect of family life: "I think Lacrosse and Iroquois are synonymous with life, I think, or synonymous with continuation of community. Everybody's involved. The children [are] involved, the parents are involved. Our greatest fans – the greatest Lacrosse fans – are the women. Women love the game and it's more than a game, [always] has been."[94]

Further emphasizing the importance of the Hodinöhsö:ni' female fan and the cultural significance of lacrosse, the words of the speaker at a Longhouse funeral offer a great deal of insight. When a Hodinöhsö:ni' Longhouse member dies, a Condolence Ceremony is held, during which the Speaker addresses the grieving family and the guests. Depending on who has died, the ceremony will be either "large" or "small."[95] As Rick Hill recalls, Speaker Tom Porter discussed his role at a workshop in Six Nations:

> Tom reminded us that the reason that we have a speaker at a funeral is because their words can be like a medicine. They can heal the wounds caused by the loss of a loved one, and can pick up the hearts and minds of the grieving so that they return to their place in life. Our traditions were given to us as a way to restore the balance and harmony of the people. It [the Condolence Ceremony] is intended to allow for proper grieving and then the restoration of the relatives and friends. It is a way of releasing the spirit of the deceased and paying tribute to the pattern set forth by the Creator.[96]

The following is an abridged version of Speaker Tom Porter's Longhouse funeral address:

> We have gathered here today to acknowledge the passing of our loved one. We are here to send her on her journey. We are here to place her body in the ground for her life breath is gone. It has gone back to the Creator. It is his will that these things happen. This is her day. We must not be stingy and try to hold her back, for she has earned the right to go to the land of the Creator.
>
> When the world was new, no one knew death. Everyone thought they would live forever and enjoy the bounty provided by the Creator. But one day, an old man fell to the ground. The people did not understand why his breath was taken away. They could not make him stand up any more. After awhile they placed his body on a scaffold, hoping that maybe, someday, he might come back to life.
>
> Then another fell to the ground. The people still did not know what was going on. His breath was taken away and his body was limp. They placed his body up in [the] scaffold as well.
>
> Then a young child died. She was a popular girl. She would visit with everyone and she was well liked. The village was so distraught

over her death that they were determined to seek the cause of death. They went to the local seer, the man who had the power to see into the future, and asked him what was going on. That man had a dream and he was told by the voice of the Creator that death would come to every human being. No one knows how many days he or she has to live. Only the Creator knows, and that is determined at the time of your birth. When your time comes, you will not be able to ask for any more days. Your breath will be taken back by the Creator. However, the people were told not to fear death. It is a natural process and they will continue on in the afterlife.

They were also told that their Longhouse would be divided into two, in order to help them deal with the death of a loved one. Each half of the Longhouse, divided by clan affiliation, was to help one another. If a person on one side passed away, we say that their minds have fallen on the ground.

It is the duty of the opposite side of the house, whose minds are still strong, to send over their men to do the chores that need to be done. They will assign the speakers, dig the grave, do the talking, and provide the pall bearers. They would send over the women to cook the food and tend to the household.

The opposite side, the strong-minded ones, would conduct the funeral to relieve the grief of the mourning side. When death, known as the Faceless One, strikes at a house, it is like a big stick hits the home and shakes up the dust of death. We don't know how many will pass to the other side. That death dust then gets in people's eyes and they cannot see correctly. They cry all the time and need to have their tears removed. The death dust gets into their minds and they can't think straight. It gets into their ears and they cannot hear right. It also gets into their throats and they cannot eat properly. The strong minded side steps forward to remove these obstacles during the period of the wake ...

The speaker addresses the family sitting near the casket:

I direct my words to those who call her sister. You will remember the times when you were growing up, playing together, running around together, the laughter you shared, as well as the sad times. You grew up together and sometimes you did things you weren't supposed to do. You wore each other[']s clothes. Sometimes you might argue. But there were times when you used to go visit her, knocking on her door.

She would open the door and be happy to see you. She would greet you and offer you something to drink or eat. You would talk about old times you had. To you who called her sister, listen carefully to my words. You must prepare your mind and body for the big change. Starting tomorrow, you will not be able to visit her again. She will not come to the door. She will not sit and talk with you anymore. She is on her way to the land of the Creator. You must remember the good times that you had. For now the breath has left her body and you will not see her again.[97]

The speaker then addresses those who call the deceased mother, grandmother, or cousin and those who worked with her in groups, societies, and organizations. Next, he addresses the Clan Mothers, chiefs, Faithkeepers, and finally lacrosse players:

I direct my words to the lacrosse players. She was a great fan, always cheering you on when you played. You could hear her voice in the crowd. She loved to watch the men play lacrosse. To you who knew her, listen carefully to my words. You must prepare your mind and body for the big change. Starting tomorrow, you will not be able to visit her again. When you look in the stands, you will not see her. You will not hear her voice anymore.[98]

The speaker's words demonstrate two major aspects of lacrosse in Hodinöhsö:ni' culture. First, it is central to all parts of life, including death and the afterlife. Second, the female fan plays an important role, in that an exchange occurs between her and the players, and the players do not merely provide entertainment. Rick Hill states,

I think that is important because even though, as you know, it [individual cheering] is hard to hear, but knowing that there are people there, knowing that there are women there, knowing that your nieces and nephews are looking at you, I think was an important counterbalance to the egotism, you know the cult of personality that modern sports breeds, is to say, yes, when you take the floor or field, you are representing your fireside family, your extended family, your clan, your side of the house, your nation, and ultimately with the Iroquois Nationals your Confederacy; that is big stuff because it happens to so few people.[99]

The Iroquois Nationals women's lacrosse team, 1986. | *Courtesy of Rick Hill and Deyohahá:ge: The Indigenous Knowledge Centre at Six Nations Polytechnic.*

After the Iroquois Nationals were founded in 1983, Hodinöhsö:ni' women watched their progress with interest. They contemplated forming a national team of their own, which would also represent Hodinöhsö:ni' nationhood, declare sovereignty, and increase post-secondary opportunities, in this case for women. They hoped to gain entrance into the International Federation of Women's Lacrosse Associations (IFWLA) and play in the world championships.[100] Instrumental in this process was Carol Patterson, the wife of Iroquois Nationals co-founder Wes Patterson. A non-Indigenous person, she raised the issue of female participation in lacrosse and how women could take their place among the Hodinöhsö:ni' players.[101] With the help of the men's organization, the women's team was hastily formed after being asked to compete at the Canadian Invitational Women's Lacrosse Championships in Montreal in 1984, a competition that it followed up by playing in a tournament in Ottawa.[102] In 1986, to once again prove the ability of the larger Nationals organization to run an international event, the women's team hosted Britain, Australia, the United States, and the provincial teams of Quebec and Ontario. This was followed by a men's competition at SUNY in Buffalo, where the Nationals played the Australian and English national teams.[103]

By the summer of 1986, the media had pronounced the men's team a great success. One paper commented, "Within the past 3 years the Six Nations

Iroquois Lacrosse team has proved itself capable of competing at an international level."[104] However, the measure of just how far the Nationals could go as a manifestation of Hodinöhsö:ni' sovereignty came in 1986. During that year, they petitioned the ILF on numerous occasions for permission to compete in the 1986 ILF World Games in Toronto.[105] Although one member of the ILF committee, Tom Hayes, supported their bid, they were denied entry into the World Games. Hayes unsuccessfully lobbied for their inclusion, telling the *New York Times*: "They're certainly up to the international standard, they proved that by beating national teams ... But beyond that, they add something to the pageantry of the game. This is an original American game. Not to have original Americans playing it is ludicrous."[106]

According to the Six Nations newspaper *Tekawennake,* the ILF decision echoed the historic assumption that the Hodinöhsö:ni' were not a sovereign nation, along with citing financial and infrastructure instability.[107] As one member of the Six Nations of the Grand River reflected, "So, although the players have proven the team is capable of competing against international teams, the I.L.F. still refuses to acknowledge our team."[108] There were also reports that the ILF had excluded the Nationals due to supposed Hodinöhsö:ni' violence in box lacrosse leagues, a long-standing racialization of Indigenous peoples with roots in the myth of the bloodthirsty savage.[109] However, Robert Lipsyte reported in the *New York Times* that the Canadian national team proved the biggest obstacle:

> Everyone involved in the sport seems to appreciate the publicity value of Indian players, but there has always been a strong undercurrent of hostility toward an Iroquoian team, according to observers. Canada blocked the Iroquois attempt to play in the quadrennial World Games this year in Toronto, citing the cost of rearranging logistics and printing new tickets that would work the Iroquois in the tournament.[110]

For the Nationals, gaining entrance into the ILF world championships remained elusive.

As the women's team continued to frame its organization, by 1987, it had attracted increasing attention in Hodinöhsö:ni' communities, not all of it friendly. In an effort to raise funds, it presented its concept of the team to the nations' councils, and as a result the historical Hodinöhsö:ni' belief that women should not play lacrosse came to the fore. Leading this argument were the Clan Mothers of the Onöñda'gega' and Onöndowa'ga:' (at

Tonawanda) Nations.[111] To this point, female lacrosse players had been tolerated or at least overlooked, as confirmed by their participation in Six Nations and in the high schools near American reservations. But the rise of a women's team that hoped to represent the Hodinöhsö:ni' Confederacy was a different matter, an issue too large for Longhouse followers to ignore.

From a Hodinöhsö:ni' perspective, *lacrosse is ceremony.* The game is a form of cultural and spiritual exhibition that is played "in" the Longhouse – for example, traditional lacrosse games played with wooden sticks are held each spring to cure sickness and/or to honour the Thunderbeings.[112] The wooden stick is itself a form of medicine, whose power is reinforced by lacrosse medicines, actual substances, that are applied to it.[113] As Dao Jao Dre, Delmor Jacobs, notes in Calder and Fletcher's *Lacrosse: The Ancient Game,*

> the traditional lacrosse stick is made from hickory, like False Face's cane. We are told that because False Face favors hickory trees, if you have hickory trees around your house, he won't send bad weather your way. If you were going to make a traditional stick, you would go to the edge of the woods and make an offering. These trees, like all medicines, are living entities. When you put down tobacco as an offering, they understand. After offering tobacco, you will find the tree, the medicine, you are looking for. You could use other types of trees, but they are not as strong or flexible. Every tree has its particular job to do. That is why there are various types of trees. If they could all do every job, they would all be the same. Much like the Thunder Entities [or Thunderbeings], who have their job to perform. The hickory tree's job is to make a lacrosse stick. We are told that a hickory tree hit by lightning is even more special for stickmaking.[114]

With the power of the game and the stick to heal, the Iroquois Nationals women's team found itself caught between new articulations of modernity – the expansion of equal opportunity through sport – and the resurgence of traditionalism.

Few people have suffered as greatly as Indigenous women due to the destructiveness of colonialism. Writing about the Onyota?a·ká·, sociologist and Onyota?a·ká· Nation member Lina Sunseri states that

> Oneida women have lost a great deal as a result of the changes introduced by colonization. One such change has led to their decreased

ability to actively and equally participate in the decision-making activities of their communities. As a result of colonialist structures of governance imposed on "Indians" by the colonial Canadian state, Oneida women have witnessed the transformation of their matrilineal and matrilocal society into a patrilineal and patrilocal one.[115]

For its organizers, the women's team seemed a perfect vehicle to empower Hodinöhsö:ni' women and provide them with the benefits and opportunities that male lacrosse players enjoyed. Rick Hill explains, "So there is a societal shift ... All of a sudden women's rights, our men are trying to give our women something of value to express themselves, their pride, their identity, so the Iroquois Nationals seemed like a natural."[116] However, this societal shift collided with traditionalism and the Longhouse epistemology.

In the Longhouse tradition, women are seen as extremely powerful and as central to the survival of the nation. Significantly, as Sunseri explains the Hodinöhsö:ni' creation story assigns the pivotal role to Sky Woman:

> Sky Woman is the first being of human form to come to this continent, and she later produces earth on Turtle's back by bringing with her the three sisters and seeds of tobacco and strawberry ... These two women [the second is Lynx Woman, Sky Woman's daughter] are examples of the importance women have in Oneida culture, an importance maintained throughout history by the great amount of respect and power attributed to clan mothers and by the institutionalization of matrilineal and matrilocal structure in each nation of the Haudenosaunee League.[117]

Furthermore, the Clan Mothers hold a central position in Hodinöhsö:ni' culture and goverance. As the women's team prepared for an exhibition in 1987, it was the Clan Mothers, mainly from what are arguably considered the two most traditionalist nations (Onöñda'gega' and the Onöndowa'ga:' Nation at Tonawanda), who stood up and voiced their discontent. It was one thing for individual women to play on a high school team, but it was clearly another for a female *national team* to ask the chiefs of the Confederacy Council for an endorsement to represent the Hodinöhsö:ni' Confederacy.[118]

In protest, the Clan Mothers threatened to lie on the field to stop the women from practising, and they summoned the team to a meeting to explain their objections.[119] They gave two reasons for their concern. The first revolved around the physicality of lacrosse. An analogy can be made with traditional dancing, during which Hodinöhsö:ni' women must keep their feet in touch with the ground at all times. The Longhouse perspective held that a protective layer surrounded the uterus and that it could be damaged if a young woman jumped about.[120] As figurative and literal mothers, it was explained, women were the strength and future of Hodinöhsö:ni' society, and precautions must be taken to ensure the survival of the nation. This argument was certainly not limited to Indigenous peoples: Margaret Ann Hall reminds us that motherhood and competition were traditionally perceived as incompatible in Canadian society.[121] However, Lina Sunseri notes that "within an Indigenous context, mothering refers to more than bearing children. It is an empowering role for Oneida women, as it plays an important part in sustaining the community and in women's achievement of self-empowerment."[122] Sunseri adds, "Women occupy a crucial position in this construction [of nationhood], as they constitute border bodyguards who ensure that the genetic pools of the nation are maintained. In this process, women's sexuality becomes of the utmost importance as nationalists regard women as the vehicles for reproducing future citizens of the nation."[123] The Clan Mothers argued that playing lacrosse could potentially damage women and consequently the nations to which they belonged.[124]

Although this reasoning was a factor in their opposition, the reproductive consequences of vigorous engagement in sport were not the primary problem, as Hodinöhsö:ni' women had obviously been playing sports with the approval of their communities long before this particular issue arose.[125] However, lacrosse was not just any sport: it was – and continues to be – a medicine game, and the stick itself was a form of medicine and power. The Longhouse epistemology sees women as spiritually powerful and able to alter or withdraw power from medicinal objects and elements, especially during their "moon time" (menstrual period). As one Onyota'a·ká· woman, Anne-Marie, tells Sunseri in *Being Again of One Mind*,

> moon time is a very important time for women. In our traditions, being on the cycle is not something we should think like is dirty or something bad ... But being on moon time is a sacred thing really. It reminds us of our sacred power inside of us as women. It is a time when we are cleansing ourselves inside, our spiritual side is so strong at this time, we are even more powerful inside than in other

times. It is all part of being a woman, of reminding us of our roles as life givers.[126]

A second Onyota'a·ká· woman, Karen, commented on the ability of women to create a power imbalance or withdraw power from medicines during their moon time:

When we are in our cycle, we are even more connected with Mother Earth, are more in touch with our spiritual power, our powers as women. It is part of our traditional culture, about being Oneida, being Native. When we are in our moon time, we know we have so much power that, for example, we don't do corn soup, or other jobs, like make berry drinks, or go to ceremonies. It is because our powers are too strong at this time, that it would put things out of balance. Others, people or food, can't take our power. We take power out of them, my grandma used to say.[127]

It was in keeping with this premise that the Clan Mothers objected to the participation of women in lacrosse.[128] During their moon time, they argued, women should not handle the stick or play the game, just as they should refrain from involvement in other medicines and ceremonies.[129] Such gender-based constraints were not unique to the Hodinöhsö:ni'. For example, the Métis storyteller François Mandeville shared a Denésoliné (Chipewyan) story in 1928 that described similar phenomena among Denésoliné runners.[130] Victoria Paraschak notes that comparable limitations were placed on female participation in Tlingit gambling games and the accompanying purification ceremonies due to their menstrual cycles. Audrey R. Giles found a parallel theme in her study of other Dene games in the Northwest Territories.[131]

Although the objections of the Clan Mothers applied to a modern situation, they explain why women have not played lacrosse all along. Sunseri further illuminates the challenges:

Given that women are viewed as the most capable and natural transmitters of culture, they are obligated to practise the "proper" cultural ways and in turn transmit those ways to younger generations. A negative result of such a construction is that since they are viewed as carrying the honour and tradition of their nation, women are often patrolled and controlled to ensure their moral purity and proper behaviour.[132]

Despite the availability of plastic sticks, the players on the women's team used the wooden version, resulting in a difficult dilemma. The wooden stick was symbolic of Hodinöhsö:ni' nationhood and was upheld by the Iroquois Nationals, but it also illustrates the limitation of that nationalism, as the ability to wield the stick and to play lacrosse was restricted to men.

The idea that women could withdraw the power and medicinal elements of the stick could extend beyond the Longhouse belief system to the wider community. Whether players and families were Longhouse followers or not, it was traditionally taboo for a woman to touch a man's lacrosse stick, and the game was often limited to the men of well-known lacrosse families.[133] Also, women could extract the orenta that a player had added to his stick, hence negating his skill.[134] As hall of fame Ahkwesáhsne goaltender Ernie Mitchell, Kaheranoron, remembers, this held true for male players of any age:

> I was on the minor lacrosse board in the mid-nineties. I had a novice lacrosse team [of nine- to ten-year-olds]; we played in Kahnawà:ke. I brought the kids home, one of the kids, I had a whole bus load of kids. One of the kids was getting his stuff out and his mother come out and she grabbed his stick and equipment and took it in the house as he was walking away, and the kids in the back go "Lookit, she grabbed his lacrosse stick!" [laughs] And that is a no-no in Ahkwesáhsne lacrosse [laughs].[135]

Michael Zogry also details a similar limitation in the Aniyvwiya game Anetso.[136]

As a result of the 1987 meeting with the Clan Mothers, the women's team disbanded. Team member Kari Miller later remarked to the *New York Times*, "My heart was broke into a thousand pieces. For me, that was my opportunity to go traveling and play the game I loved. We got a taste of it, then it was taken away."[137] For Hodinöhsö:ni' traditionalists, the perseverance and resurgence of the Longhouse has been a remarkable symbol of their ability to endure colonialism and of Hodinöhsö:ni' nationhood. However, they have also struggled with elements of its epistemology, attempting to establish a balance between modernity and traditionalism. Kanien'kehá:ka scholar Gerald Taiaiake Alfred explains that "nationalism is best viewed as having both a relatively stable core which endures and peripheral elements that are easily adapted or manipulated to accommodate the demands of a particular political environment."[138] In this instance, the dissolution of the women's team revealed the limitations of Hodinöhsö:ni' nationhood, at least from a gender perspective.

Attempting to regain entry into international competition for over a century, the Hodinöhsö:ni' had themselves imposed limits on who among them could and could not represent their nation. These were grounded in the traditional gender constructs of the Longhouse epistemology. This, in turn, affected male attitudes, gender relations, and women outside the Longhouse system. Sunseri cautions that though traditionalism has been a tremendous aid in the re-empowerment of Hodinöhsö:ni' nationhood, it too must be critically analyzed to ensure that it is not being used in an oppressive fashion – a process that Hodinöhsö:ni' women are undertaking:

> It is clear that these women [who are helping to restore traditionalism] do recognize that a revival of traditional ways of governing is important if Oneida is to become a self-determined nation again, yet they also recognize that some traditional discourses, when not justly practiced, can be used as tools to further oppress and victimize them. It is true that traditions can be empowering and a source of personal and collective strength in the face of cultural genocide and oppressive colonial structures, yet caution must be exercised to ensure the tradition does indeed liberate women from these structures. When tradition no longer does that, instead further dispossessing women of the power given to them by the Creator, one must be ready to question tradition.[139]

Since 1987, when the women's team disbanded, the Hodinöhsö:ni' have been reflecting upon the role of women in lacrosse. Immediately following the decision of the Clan Mothers, female players had to choose between giving up the game they loved or continuing to play it at the local level, thus rejecting Hodinöhsö:ni' traditionalism, at least partially. For some, balancing national, traditional cultural, and personal identities could be a challenge, as was the case for Iroquois Nationals founder Rick Hill and his family:

So I had to wrestle with it very directly because you know sometimes I try hard to be a good Hodinöhsö:ni' person and it usually
gets me in trouble [laughs]. So I have a daughter and she wants to
play lacrosse, and her mother is a Clan Mother. [We] had this big
discussion, disbanded the Iroquois Nationals [women's team] out of
regard for what these women were saying, but it was always kind of
like, but go ahead and continue doing what you are doing, so officially
we couldn't have an Iroquois Nationals team ... but that is a little different. So, I had to talk to my wife and I said, well what are we going
to do? I believe what those women at Tonawanda and Onondaga said,
so she shouldn't play lacrosse and her mother's attitude was, she has
got so little else, give her this. It will mean so much to her. I got to
admit, it did ... *I think that is the societal shift* ... It was good emotion-
ally for the girls, women, and we have to support it. We have to be
the kind of cheering fan when we die they are going to say, "*All you
girl lacrosse players stand up, these guys used to love to watch you play.*"[140]

The Medicine Game

The debate surrounding the women's team was not the only internal conflict
to affect the Iroquois Nationals, who also felt the tension that arose from
disputes concerning the legitimacy of tribal governments. Various colonial
policies, as expressed in the Gradual Enfranchisement Act and the Indian
Act, had sought to remove the hereditary leadership from Indigenous communities, and modernists and Longhouse traditionalists in Hodinöhsö:ni'
communities had become increasingly divided regarding this issue, particularly at the turn of the twentieth century. Modernists supported working
within the colonial policies while maintaining the autonomy of their communities, whereas traditionalists rejected this approach and asserted their
right to self-determination and the reign of the hereditary leadership. This
disagreement persisted throughout the twentieth century and was still
unresolved when the Iroquois Nationals were formed.

In addition, violent protests occurred at Ahkwesáhsne regarding the
question of legalized gambling.[141] In May 1990, the dispute became so heated
that two men were killed because of it, and the New York State Police and
the Royal Canadian Mounted Police temporarily declared martial law.[142]
The feud not only factionalized the community, but it also fractured families;
as David White remembers, "Nobody trusted anybody, nobody would talk
to anybody."[143] One Iroquois Nationals player, police officer Louis Mitchell,

found himself at the centre of the controversy, when someone shot at his house because the local police were seen as supporting one particular side of the issue.[144]

And yet, lacrosse promoters were confident that the sport could knit the community back together and could rise above local political struggles. Rick Hill explains:

> Well I think what we were saying was that lacrosse has the power to heal, let's see if it can help heal this rift among our people. Because some players showed up who – I can remember one time a guy who was a tribal police officer at Ahkwesáhsne, one of the players, and there was tension between him and some of the other families, who had a player on the team, but they never let that tension interfere. It's like you check that stuff at the door. So in that sense, [we would say] "When you are here, we are one people, because we represent our people; that is why you are here. If you are bringing that baggage in here, you will disrupt the team and it will cause us harm."[145]

As Oren Lyons put it to the *New York Times*, just after the Nationals were founded, "We may have factionalism in the territories, but when it comes to lacrosse we are united."[146] Along with the Nationals, lacrosse would be a significant contributor to restoring harmony in Ahkwesáhsne. During the summer of 1990, lacrosse player and organizer Ernie Mitchell, Kaheranoron, his brother Mike Mitchell, and Frank Benedict created a six-team "old-timers" league known as the Old Sticks League to help reunite the community.[147] A key element of this league was the way in which players were chosen for each team. Their names were drawn from a hat, which prevented the teams from forming along factional lines, so traditionalists and modernists ended up playing on the same team. Ernie Mitchell remembers that

> we had a very successful league and not only successful, all these people that were in the community wanted to come see these legends play lacrosse again, so we got good fan support. What it is, is that when we got into the locker room, guys didn't even want to talk to each other because one guy was on one side [on one faction]. That edge was still there. By the end of that first game everyone was high-fiving each other and were friendly ... It did [bring the two sides back together], it had a great effect. I'd say by the third or fourth week,

lacrosse was going, nobody even talked about that, we were friends again and not only was it a lacrosse game, the wives were involved and stuff. We would sell beer upstairs and the wives would help out, we would go somewhere, we would have a get-together, the wives would help out. It was just a tremendous success.[148]

Although some animosity undoubtedly lingered, the formation of the Old Sticks League and the Iroquois Nationals demonstrates the healing power of lacrosse and its function as a unification tool at both the community and national levels.

The 1990 ILF World Games

In 1987, after almost four years of petitioning, the Iroquois Nationals were finally accepted into the ILF and were permitted to compete in the 1990 ILF World Games in Perth, Australia.[149] Entry into the ILF marked a significant achievement for the Hodinöhsö:ni' and the Iroquois Nationals, as the community-produced newspaper *Tekawennake* declared: "This is an important step in restoring the Indian profile to the sport of lacrosse and should serve as a source of pride to all Iroquoian people. The tradition of lacrosse remains an important cultural expression of Indian identity and has fostered many positive role models in Six Nations communities."[150] Once again exercising their declaration of sovereignty, the Iroquois Nationals arranged travel clearances with the US and Australian governments, and journeyed to the games on the Hodinöhsö:ni' passport. Oren Lyons told the *Post-Standard* that playing at Perth was a momentous accomplishment for everyone involved: "Lacrosse is the lifeblood of our people ... so the Nationals are really an extension of ourselves. It's nothing extraordinary, this team, though the effort to get there has been. That's been quite extraordinary."[151]

As the Iroquois Nationals prepared for the world championships, they continued to shape-shift the form, articulation, and activation of Hodinöhsö:ni' nationhood beyond the realms of sport. The organizers of the championship asked that they provide the official Hodinöhsö:ni' flag and anthem for the opening ceremonies. However, the Hodinöhsö:ni' had neither flag nor anthem and were thus obliged to create both. The flag arose from two major developments: the establishment of the team itself and the larger pan-Indigenous repatriation movements of the 1980s, in which

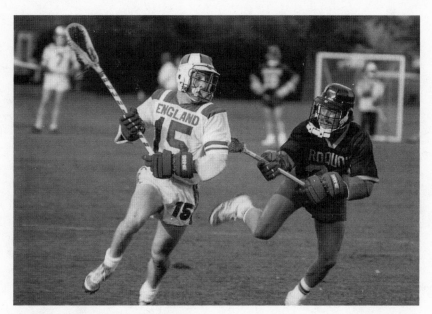

**The Iroquois Nationals versus England,
c. 1990.** | *Courtesy of Rick Hill and Deyohahá:ge: The
Indigenous Knowledge Centre at Six Nations Polytechnic.*

the Hodinöhsö:ni' were key participants.[152] Since 1970, the Hodinöhsö:ni'
at Onondaga had been embroiled in a battle with the New York State
Museum at Albany concerning the repatriation of Hodinöhsö:ni' cultural
objects, including the Hiawatha Wampum Belt.[153] The Hiawatha Wampum
Belt commemorates the founding of the Confederacy, with each of the five
original nations – Kanien'kehá:ka, Onyota'a·ká, Ga·yo·g·ho:nǫ', Onöñda'gega',
and Onöndowa'ga:' – represented in its design.[154] Furthermore, wampum
belts and beads are living objects; they have the power to carry words and
are used to aid the oral history of the Confederacy, record contractual
agreements and treaties, and to indicate a person's position in the Longhouse
(such as that of Clan Mother or chief).[155] Celebrating the 1989 repatriation
of the Hiawatha Wampum Belt, the Nationals chose it as their flag, thus
creating a universal symbol of Hodinöhsö:ni' sovereignty, pride, and culture.[156] Much like the Sḵwx̱wú7mesh "continuity in change," using the
wampum belt in this way served as a visual reminder of Hodinöhsö:ni'
nationhood; it was its own continuity in change, merging two representations of sovereignty – the belt and a national flag – into one.[157] Initially, as

Rick Hill explains, some community members criticized the flag, but it was eventually accepted as a symbol of Hodinöhsö:ni' nationhood:

> It's funny, now everybody takes it as common practice, back then it was new stuff. It was a little controversial, some people didn't like it. They didn't like the idea we would turn a wampum belt into a flag. The Tuscaroras objected, saying, "Where are we on that flag?" There is always some issues with everything. But in the end, it is still a symbol of pride, tradition, and identity, so it works quite well if you ask me. And the fact that it is a real thing, coming from the wampum belt, it made it even more empowering to me, and it is a symbol of the Hodinöhsö:ni'. Because when they made that original wampum belt, they said, "We are now one, we will call ourselves Hodinöhsö:ni', bring five lands together in one." It is a great thing.[158]

Whereas the flag was prepared before the Nationals left for Australia, the anthem had a more impromptu beginning. After they arrived in Perth, the Nationals were reminded that they needed an anthem for the opening ceremony, which they had forgotten to select before they arrived in Australia.[159] Improvising, the team used a flag song provided by one of the players.[160] The presentation of the flag and anthem marked a powerful moment for players such as Kent Lyons and David White.[161] As White recalls,

> I remember the first time we were in Australia and the teams come out and we are all standing there and they are playing the national anthem for every team and they played the Iroquois national anthem and I got choked up, I mean I am getting choked up just talking about it. We are standing there and other nations stood up for us, and they liked our anthem, it was really cool, it was a Native language anthem ... People loved it and people loved us as the originators of the game so to speak, as the first players.[162]

Rick Hill recalls the overwhelming reception that greeted the Nationals:

> These nations, they were joyous to have the Hodinöhsö:ni' come, to play lacrosse in their country. And even the politics of getting the

passport approved, we put a lot of pressure on them, Australia, you have to get this worked out, England, you have to get it worked out. And so they did their homework, so we were able to go, it was really great. That is the other thing hard to measure, imagine – being on that team and you go walking into a foreign country and all of a sudden people are honouring you, congratulating you, raising your flag, treating you well, and even though you are competitors, it is like that spirit of amateur sports, Olympic spirit, that really got me because it is powerful.[163]

The 1990 expression of the Iroquois Nationals as a symbol of pride, identity, and sovereignty could not have come at a more important moment for the Hodinöhsö:ni' – especially for the Kanien'kehá:ka communities of Kanehsatá:ke, Kahnawà:ke, and Ahkwesáhsne. During the 1960s, Kanehsatá:ke, which lies near Oka, Quebec, had unsuccessfully appealed to the Government of Canada to have adjacent lands officially classified as part of the reserve.[164] With the founding of the Native Land Claims Office following *Calder v. Attorney-General of British Columbia,* a 1973 Supreme Court case that dealt with Indigenous land title, Kanehsatá:ke once again tried to establish its claim to the unceded land.[165] This attempt also proved unsuccessful, as did another in 1986.[166] After centuries of land expropriation dating back to the 1700s, the people of Kanehsatá:ke had become increasingly frustrated with Ottawa's failure to resolve the issue.

On May 11, 1990, the women of Kanehsatá:ke called for a peaceful protest, and community members erected a barricade to block the expansion of a golf course that would not only expropriate the land but would also destroy a Kanehsatá:ke cemetery. As the women continued to manage the protest, they were joined by Kahnawà:ke and Ahkwesáhsne community members, Indigenous peoples from across Canada, and members of the Rotisken'rakéhte (Mohawk Warriors Society).[167] In late April, the Town of Oka obtained an injunction from the Quebec Superior Court to remove the roadblock, which the protesters ignored. Oka acquired a second injunction in late June, and this too was ignored. On July 10, the mayor of Oka asked the Quebec provincial police for help, so the next day police officers attempted to forcefully disperse the peaceful protest. In the subsequent exchange of gunfire, a police officer was killed. Failing to achieve their goal, the police retreated, and the situation devolved into a seventy-eight-day armed standoff and military occupation between those who were unwilling to withdraw in the face of this injustice, the Quebec provincial police, and 2,500 Canadian soldiers.[168] As Audra Simpson states, the invasion known as the Oka Crisis was "a spectacular event that pronounced the structure of settler colonialism in Canada, illuminating its desire for land, its propensity to consume, and its indifference to life, to will, to what is considered sacred, binding, and fair."[169]

As Oka was unfolding, the Iroquois Nationals were preparing for and participating in the lacrosse championships in Perth. Although it may not have been evident at the time, Kahnawà:ke community member Joe Delaronde later connected the importance of lacrosse, and by extension, the importance of the Iroquois Nationals, to the events of 1990:

ALLAN: Do you think that an event like Oka had an impact on lacrosse around here?

JOE DELARONDE: If you can look at a positive – one thing that '90 [Oka] did was bring an awareness of who we are. We are struggling, we are a little different. For those who hadn't been through something like that before, why is it that we are into something like this [Oka standoff]? Because we are not the same as the Canadian people, we have our own identity. What was one of the things that was easiest to manifest into that identity, was our game! So it kind of helped that resurgence I think. Let's play our game! Otherwise we are just saying we are Mohawks. If nobody is speaking the language and nobody is playing the game or participating in the ceremonies, then we are full of hot air. We are not really who we say we are, we are just vestiges of a distant past. But it helped bring that to the floor ... We needed something to be proud of ... A lot people were proud that we stood up and stood together in 1990, but a lot of people were hurt by it too. So for some it was extremely positive, for others it was extremely negative. We needed something where everybody could be together. There is nothing better than lacrosse.[170]

In late September, the deadlock at Oka finally ended. The land defenders dispersed, the Canadian soldiers went home, and the golf course project was ultimately cancelled, though Kanehsatá:ke's land claim remains unresolved. Even here, lacrosse is woven into the story. Oren Lyons, who had accompanied the Iroquois Nationals to Australia, became a key negotiator upon returning home, helping to bring the invasion of Kanehsatá:ke to an end.[171]

～

Although the Nationals did not win a game in Perth, simply gaining entry into the championships marked a significant achievement for the Hodinöhsö:ni'. The history of their fight to play lacrosse at the international level illustrates how an Indigenous game appropriated by the dominant society could be repossessed and used to reassert more than merely athletic prowess. To the Hodinöhsö:ni', lacrosse was a powerful tool for reunification throughout the 1980s and 1990s, and the team went beyond the realms of sport and athleticism to demand the recognition of Hodinöhsö:ni' sovereignty on the world stage. Nationals board member Dave Bray later told the *Boston Globe*, "We want to show our ownership of lacrosse to the world ... It's our game, and now we have the voice to tell the world."[172] The Iroquois Nationals were part of a larger resurgence of traditionalism in the Hodinöhsö:ni' Confederacy that offered an alternative to integration into the dominant society and served as an expression of self-determination. In a real sense, the team was a physical embodiment of Hodinöhsö:ni' nationhood, one that was based in traditionalism, with its particular views regarding gender. Yet to truly understand how a sense of nationhood (re)emerges through lacrosse and is articulated by Hodinöhsö:ni' people, it is not enough simply to say that in the case of the Creator's game, "gender trumped nation" when the women's team ceased to operate. Hodinöhsö:ni' identities are a complex and multiple intersection of traditionalism, ideas about gender, and nationhood; but as this case reminds us, they do not always work in unison. In the 1980s, gender constructs prohibited women from expressing a national identity by playing lacrosse themselves, though they could do so as supporters, fans, and relatives of the players. Further to the point, the controversy regarding female players helped raise important questions regarding the adaptation of traditionalism, specifically relating to gender, and eventually resulted in the formation of a Hodinöhsö:ni' women's national team – albeit two decades later and without the official endorsement of the Confederacy Council. As Onöñda'gega' scholar Theresa McCarthy explains,

> Just because certain expressions of tradition need more critical attention does not mean that our traditions are not being rigorously interrogated all of the time. Six Nations community members [as in all

Hodinöhsö:ni' communities] do not simply exalt romanticized notions of Haudenosaunee tradition; citizens are always questioning tradition's application to our lived experiences in the present ... But these critical conversations are those of a sovereign people working to find the best way forward under the pressure of outside efforts to assimilate and eliminate them.[173]

Dewa'ë:ö'

Conclusion:
A Trickster Ending

IN 2005, A HODINÖHSÖ:NI' women's team finally returned to competition. In that year, a team reformed to play in an international exhibition titled the Cup of Nations, and in 2006 the International Federation of Women's Lacrosse Associations, which later became the Federation of International Lacrosse, welcomed the women's team as its eleventh member.[1] The following year, the team re-entered official international competition, returning Hodinöhsö:ni' women to the international playing field from which they had been absent since 1987. Based out of Six Nations, the team – called the Haudenosaunee Nation or Haudenosaunee Nationals – was not without opposition in Hodinöhsö:ni' communities and was not officially endorsed by the Grand Council of Chiefs. However, this has led to a critical dialogue in the communities and among the leadership, along the lines of what Theresa McCarthy has called for concerning the need for the interrogation of tradition, the application of tradition to lived experiences, and the future of Hodinöhsö:ni' nationhood.[2] Along with the Iroquois Nationals and a recently founded men's box lacrosse team, the Haudenosaunee Nationals continued to compete internationally as representatives of an independent nation.[3] Even so, for both the men's and women's teams, the fight for inclusion persists. In July 2010, the Iroquois Nationals were set to

---

The Onöndowa'ga:' know lacrosse as *Dewa'ë:ö'*, which translates to "netting on it." Correspondence, Sue Ellen Herne, April 4, 2011, Akwesasne Culture Centre, Ogdensville, New York.

travel to the world championships in Manchester, England, when they were informed by British authorities that they could not enter the country on their Hodinöhsö:ni' passports. Initially, the British consulate stated that it would permit entry only if it received written confirmation from US authorities that the Nationals could return to the United States, which the State Department and the Department of Homeland Security refused to supply.[4] The team was told to either accept Canadian or American passports, or risk missing the championships. At this point, the Nationals were stranded in New York City, lobbying the US and British governments for their travel clearances. Their plight aroused a media storm.

As a result of the media coverage, pressure from US government officials, public support, and the efforts of the Nationals, Secretary of State Hillary Clinton conceded and announced that the team would be given a special waiver to travel to England. Despite this concession, British authorities reneged on their promise and told the Nationals that their passports would not be recognized. A British Border Agency representative stated, "We would be pleased to welcome the Iroquois Nationals Lacrosse Team, but like all those seeking entry into the U.K., they must present a document that we recognize as valid to enable us to complete our immigration and other checks." If the Nationals presented their Hodinöhsö:ni' passports, they would have to do so "in conjunction with a U.S. or Canadian passport if they wish to seek entry to the U.K."[5]

Remaining true to their principles, the Nationals refused to sacrifice their self-determination, national sovereignty, and identities by accepting a Canadian or American passport, with the result that they did not go to Manchester. However, as *Iorì:wase Kahnawake News* reporter Greg Horn later stated, their stance was in itself a victory for the Hodinöhsö:ni':

> Without stepping on the field, the Nationals have still made their people proud. They stood by their principles and didn't compromise their identity in order to compete in this lacrosse tournament. Both Canada and the United States were only too eager to offer the team members expedited passports so the team could make it to the World Lacrosse Championships.
>
> But they chose not to accept the offer. Several team members said they would rather miss the World Championships than to travel to the tournament on American or Canadian passports. By doing so

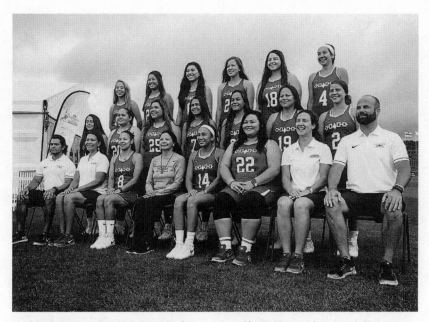

The Haudenosaunee Nationals at the 2017 FIL Rathbones Women's Lacrosse World Cup in England. *Front row (left to right):* Fernando Pineda, Tia Schindler (general manager), Katie Smith (captain), Kathy Smith (executive director), Jadyn Bomberry (captain), Amber Hill (captain), Ashley Pike (head coach), Justin Demuth (assistant coach). *Middle row (left to right):* Vanna Thompson, Erin Francis, Jenna Haring, Victoria Thompson, Kyra Thompson, Mimi Lazore, Dana Isaacs. *Back row (left to right):* Jacelyn Lazore, Cheyenne Burnam, Vivian Curry, Jalyn Jimerson, Kristen Sedar, Awehiyo Thomas. | *Photographer Mekwan Tulpin. Courtesy of the Haudenosaunee Nationals.*

the Iroquois Nationals gained international attention and brought the issue of Indigenous sovereignty into living rooms and kitchen tables around the world.

By doing so, the Nationals have accomplished their goal of educating the world about our issues. They chose to stand by their beliefs and in doing so they made all Onkwehón:we proud. It is easy to use a Canadian or American passport, but it is a political statement to use a Haudenosaunee passport.[6]

Unfortunately, the suppression of Hodinöhsö:ni' sovereignty and problems with travel clearances continued. In the summer of 2015, Britain refused to permit the under-19 women's team to travel to Scotland for the world championships. However, the senior women's team did successfully travel on the Hodinöhsö:ni' passport and competed at the 2017 FIL Rathbones Women's Lacrosse World Cup in Surrey, England.

The Iroquois Nationals men's teams, when allowed to compete, have done well: they won silver in four consecutive world indoor championships (2003, 2007, 2011, 2015), took the bronze at the under-19 world championships on four occasions (1996, 2008, 2012, 2016), and won bronze at the 2014 senior world championships. In 2015, the Hodinöhsö:ni' hosted the world indoor championships, marking the first time an Indigenous nation had hosted an official world championship competiton as a sovereign nation. Whereas British officials denied the Hodinöhsö:ni' entry on two occasions, British teams were welcomed to the tournament with the stamping of their passports by the Hodinöhsö:ni' Confederacy. It would be a mistake to measure the success of the teams in terms of medal counts; rather, their success lies in their assertion of who they are. In this, as Simpson reminds us, "the young men [and women] are not being excluded from the nation-state; they are refusing inclusion within it."[7]

The history of lacrosse in Canada is a Trickster tale, full of anomalies, contradictions, and tricks. At the beginning of Canada's Colonial Age, non-Native Canadians attempted to claim the game as an aspect of their newly created identity. Canadian lacrosse enthusiasts, as is generally true of relations between Indigenous and non-Indigenous people, have embodied the negative traits of "humanness" through their appropriation of the game – "vanity, greed, selfishness, and foolishness" – character flaws, Jo-ann Archibald reminds us, to which Tricksters are often subject.[8] In that process, the dominant society tricked *itself* and continues to struggle with its identity as a nation while perpetuating its Colonial Age and its position as a colonizer of Indigenous nations. Thus, the history of lacrosse is a mirror of Canada's relationship with Indigenous peoples. Rather than acknowledging the diversity of Indigenous nationhood and the *nations*-to-nation relationship that was entered into, or the subsequent contributions to its cultural fabric, Canada denies its true history and identity. And yet, in this process of trickery, the story of lacrosse provided Indigenous peoples with a series of sleights of hand for their own use. Colonial history did not always lie at the centre of Indigenous history.

During Canada's colonial beginnings, Indigenous people themselves became the Trickster by playing Indian and performing for non-Indigenous audiences, thus securing partial financial independence and funding traditional ceremonies such as the Potlatch. Indigenous peoples, who had rich sport cultures of their own, used these "new" introductions as sources of cultural survival and identity (re)formation. Despite the ban on the Potlatch, traditional dress, and dancing, they used events such as Indian Sports Days as a disguise for cultural continuity, evading their assimilative intent. Residential schools saw lacrosse as a model of civility and as a source of Canadian identity, so they used it in their efforts to eliminate Indigenous cultures. But this too was a trick, as Indigenous students such as Andy Paull took both the game and their experience at school and redefined their meaning.

Throughout the history of lacrosse in Canada, Indigenous peoples, despite being barred on numerous occasions, were constant players and were responsible for the survival of what Canadians claimed as their own. During its lowest ebb in popularity and the newest fads in Canadian history such as box lacrosse, the game maintained its central significance in select Indigenous communities as an expression of their identities and shared history. And it remained a considerable element in their epistemologies. Furthermore, that cultural identity expanded among Indigenous nations such as the Sḵwx̱wú7mesh and helped form new pan-Indigenous identities. This continues today, as Indigenous nations across North America, such as the Mi'kmaq in Nova Scotia, the Anishinaabeg in the Great Lakes region, and the Dakhóta in Saskatchewan – to name a few – are initiating modern lacrosse programs and re-empowering themselves through the adoption of lacrosse as "their game." Controlled and understood within the local traditions, ceremonies, languages, and epistemologies of Indigenous nations, lacrosse offers Indigenous communities and youth a powerful way to re-awaken traditionalism and to play a role in the resurgence of their own cultures.[9]

An examination of lacrosse reveals local manifestations of identity formation, based on specific nations' ideas regarding traditionalism. Both the Hodinöhsö:ni' and the Sḵwx̱wú7mesh claimed lacrosse as their own, in turn helping to facilitate a pan-Indigenous identity, but they tailored the game to suit their historical understandings of their particular identities. And though the game has been restructured in numerous racialized and colonized spaces in Canadian society, its story extends beyond the adaptation and accommodation pattern that frames many historical approaches, demonstrating that Indigenous peoples continued to act, shift, and move on their own terms.[10] In short, while Canadians continued to facilitate the Colonial Age in their relationship with Indigenous peoples, colonial history was not always at the centre of Indigenous history, and lacrosse is an example of what Keith Carlson terms "the change in continuity, the continuity in change."[11] This insight has been made possible only by examining Indigenous history via local Indigenous epistemologies and understandings of sport. It quickly becomes apparent that though Indigenous communities have been critical partners in the development of organized sport in Canada, their understandings of sport do not fit neatly within the Western compartmentalization of sport and recreation. By properly partnering with Indigenous communities and respectfully engaging with their knowledge, not only do we gain insight into a series of potent worldviews that help us reconsider the value of sport in our lives and communities, we can also perceive that such knowledge has the potential to re-empower Indigenous history on its own terms, not simply as a chapter in "Canada's story."

～

>>> *McGill University, July 16, 2017*

"Well 'Usdas," Allan says, "there you have it, the story is coming to an end."

"It can't be over, I'm just getting warmed up!"

"Don't worry, I know you'll be back. There are more tricks to be played."

"Hold on! All these years of talking and you aren't going to share what I taught you about history, yourself, or the power of narratives."

"I've been talking about power all along, and you've been warned about the power of things time and time again, and yet you only want to pay attention now?"

"Better late than never," 'Usdas chuckles.

"I did say in the beginning that I wouldn't pretend to separate myself from the story, so why start now? Well then, what story do you want me to tell?"

"Why not the power of stories that we talked about?"

"Well, remember this one? 'The truth about stories is that that's all we are.'[12] That's why it's so important for me, as a 'storyteller,' or whatever you want to call me, to place myself in this story. The truth is that the construction and writing of 'history' does not come about by accident. It is a selection and positioning of specific points of emphasis to tell a larger narrative. It can dehumanize, exclude, or annihilate, and it too can be appropriated. Just as the history of lacrosse has been claimed on multiple levels by various people as an authentic source of their identity, so too has history. It's important for Indigenous peoples to reclaim history, as it can also be a source of re-empowerment, nation-hood, and resurgence."

"So, even this book is a form of a trick?"

"In some ways it is. Take, for example, why I decided to focus on competitive lacrosse rather than ceremonial lacrosse. Proportionately, 'Indians' in Canada are the most over-studied population within the colonial borders. As you can imagine, many are sick of being studied. Researchers have gone into communities and stolen stories, cultural and ceremonial artifacts, and knowledge. Then they've turned around and told stories that dehumanized Indigenous peoples, ignored their historical methods (such as oral history), or exposed powerful pieces of hereditary knowledge. Those same narratives have become so prevalent among Canadians that they don't see themselves as im-prisoned by this colonial mindset."

'Usdas bursts out laughing, "What a stupid trick! The colonizer – the colonized."

"It's true. You helped me expose my own decolonization process, to become conscious of the violent legacy of colonialism and the import-ance of resurgence. I have a long way to go to reclaim my language, my responsibilities to my family, clan, community, and nation, but my eyes have been opened. Getting back to this book's trick, when a researcher asks to come into a community, there's quite a bit of hesitation, as you can imagine. Even though I'm an Indigenous scholar, the communities were afraid that I would appropriate the traditions and stories of the Longhouse, ceremonial games, or Potlatch traditions for my own gain. I had no intention of doing that, so I decided not to cover ceremonial games. Much like what Audra Simpson argues concerning ethnographic refusal,[13] I and the mentors with whom I worked shared only what we wanted to share. So much has been taken from our communities that I wanted to start giving some of the stories back, sharing a history that in recent times might have waned with our youth and communities. I can only hope that they will take it and do it better. We need the resur-gent histories of nationhood and Anishinaabeg, Nêhiyawak, Mi'kmaq, and further Hodinöhsö:ni' stories of their game, past and present, that this book has not been able to discuss in detail. Over the past few decades, Indigenous and non-Indigenous writers and activists have started to shift those dehumanizing narratives and have gained greater control of the historical accounts. And yet, as John Mohawk warned, this is a constant and difficult fight, fraught with resistance throughout – there are Tricksters all along the way."[14]

Pàgàdowe

Notes

Dewa'áǫ':gajíhgwa'e'

Prologue

1   Derived from the Onöndowa'ga:' (Seneca), the word "Hodinöhsö:ni'" stems from the western dialects of the Six Nations. Alternatively spelled as Haudenosaunee (Onöñda'gega'), Rotinonhsión:ni, Rotinonshonni, or Rotinonhsyonni in Kanien'kéha, it means "People of the Longhouse" or "People who make a house" and refers to the Confederacy of the Six Nations, previously known as the Iroquois. Formed in approximately the fourteenth or fifteenth century, if not earlier, the Confederacy originally consisted of five nations – the Kanien'kehá:ka (Mohawk – People of the flint), Onyotaa·ká· (Oneida – People of the standing stone), Onöñda'gega' (Onondaga – People of the hills), Ga·yo·gǫ·ho:nǫ' (Cayuga – People of the marshy area), and Onöndowa'ga:' or O-non-dowa-gah (Seneca – People of the great hills). The Skarù·rę̨' (Tuscarora – Shirt wearers) joined in 1722. These nations are presently located in several communities within the colonial borders of Ontario, Quebec, New York, and Wisconsin. The spellings of their names come from language dictionaries published by the University of Toronto Press or from self-identifications and consultations with Rick Hill at Deyohahá:ge: The Indigenous Knowledge Centre at Six Nations Polytechnic and Teiowí:sonte, Thomas Deer, at the Kanien'kehá:ka Onkwawén:na Raotitióhkwa Language and Cultural Centre, as well as from Susan M. Hill, *The Clay We Are Made Of: Haudenosaunee Land Tenure on the Grand River* (Winnipeg: University of Manitoba Press, 2017), 5, 289–90.

According to the Omàmiwininìwak (Algonquin), the verb *Pàgàdowe* means "to play lacrosse." *Omamiwinini Pimadjwowin: The Algonquin Way Culture Centre Dictionary*, http://www.thealgonquinway.ca/English/word-e.php?word=894.

As Lina Sunseri explains, the Longhouse is a metaphor for the governing structure of the Hodinöhsö:ni'. It "refers to the traditional socio-political organization of the Haudenosaunee League [or Confederacy]." Lina Sunseri, *Being Again of One Mind: Oneida Women and the Struggle for Decolonization* (Vancouver: UBC Press, 2011), 178. Presently, "Longhouse" has two meanings: one refers to the political structure of the Confederacy, whereas the other refers to the Longhouse epistemology. In this book, "Longhouse epistemology" refers to the cultural philosophies – including spirituality – that inform(ed) the Hodinöhsö:ni' understanding of lacrosse. Note that the epistemology(ies) grew out of the pre-Confederacy cultural philosophies of the five, later six, individual nations, the cultural narratives and practice of lacrosse, and the governing structure and cultural philosophies of the Confederacy itself. This definition also appears in Allan Downey, "Playing the Creator's Game on God's Day: The Controversy of Sunday Lacrosse Games in Haudenosaunee Communities, 1916–1924," *Journal of Canadian Studies* 49, 3 (Fall 2015): 111–43.

Throughout the book, "epistemology" refers to local Indigenous worldviews and the way in which specific Indigenous peoples understand the world around them, influenced by their sociopolitical history, culture, traditions, spirituality, and languages. The purpose here is not to identify what constitutes an "authentic" epistemology for any Indigenous confederacy, nation, or people but to demonstrate how those worldviews and their collective existence are articulated.

2 The story of the Creator's game was told by Dao Jao Dre (Delmor Jacobs, Cayuga, Wolf Clan, Six Nations of the Grand River) in an interview with Allan Downey, June 7, 2011, audio recording and transcript, Six Nations of the Grand River Reserve, ON. In collaboration with the storyteller, it has been lightly edited and the "core" narrative concerning lacrosse, the focus for this specific book, has been highlighted in italics. Like many Indigenous oral histories, it is not intended as the definitive account, but as just one of multiple versions.

Baaga'adowewin
Introduction

1 In the Saik'uz First Nation's oral history of how the Dakelh came to possess fire, light, and water, as documented by anthropologist Diamond Jenness, 'Usdas transforms into a spruce needle and is swallowed by the daughter of a man who possesses all the water in the world. Next day, the daughter gives birth to 'Usdas, whose grandfather eventually gives him a ball or bowl of water to play with (in the original transcription, 'Usdas is given the gender pronoun of "he"; however, I have chosen to leave 'Usdas' as gender neutral). After some time, 'Usdas steals the water and runs away as his grandfather gives chase. In his attempted escape, 'Usdas spills some of the water and thus ends up creating all the lakes and rivers in Dakelh Keyoh. There are various spellings of his name, including 'Utas, Asta·s, and Este·s. I have chosen to use the Stellat'en First Nation version. For more, see Diamond Jenness, "Myths of the Carrier Indians of British Columbia," *Journal of American Folklore* 47, 184 (April–September 1934): 97–257; "Bunxhun Yinka Dutadilto' – The Great Flood," *Stellat'en First Nation*, http://www.stellaten.ca/

stellaten-community/traditions/elders-stories/; and "Culture and Heritage," *Carrier Sekani Tribal Council,* http://www.carriersekani.ca/culture-heritage/.

2 According to various versions of the Dakelh and Wet'suwet'en Trickster-Transformer stories, which Jenness labels "The Trickster," 'Usdas began life as a Trickster after his father grew ashamed of his actions and his insatiable appetite in which he broke protocol by greedily eating all the food that his family possessed. Following this episode, 'Usdas set off on his travels, transforming and tricking various people, villages, and animals in the desire to satisfy his hunger. These versions of the oral history conclude with 'Usdas eventually living on an island far across the sea, never to return, because he is so big that if he were to put his foot in a canoe, it would sink. Jenness, "Myths of the Carrier Indians," 208–12.

3 Dakelh (plural: Dakelhne) are "the people who travel upon water." They were formerly known as the Carrier. Nak'azdli Whut'en (plural: Nak'azdli Whut'enne) means the "people who live where it flowed off with the arrows of dwarves." The Lusilyoo Clan is the Frog Clan.

4 Throughout this book, I follow the example of Glen Coulthard, Leanne Simpson, Audra Simpson, Taiaiake Alfred, Jeff Corntassel, and others in predominately using "Indigenous" to describe the original peoples of present-day North America rather than the political and legal construct "Aboriginal." See Glen Coulthard, *Red Skin, White Masks: Rejecting the Colonial Politics of Recognition* (Minneapolis: University of Minnesota Press, 2014); Leanne Simpson, *Dancing on Our Turtle's Back: Stories of Nishnaabeg Re-creation, Resurgence, and a New Emergence* (Winnipeg: Arbeiter Ring, 2011); Audra Simpson, *Mohawk Interruptus: Political Life across the Borders of Settler States* (Durham, NC: Duke University Press, 2014); and Taiaiake Alfred and Jeff Corntassel, "Being Indigenous: Resurgences against Contemporary Colonialism," *Government and Opposition* 40, 4 (Autumn 2005): 597–614. However, I also use "Native" to add variety, and I use "Indian" to refer only to the historical construction of Indigenous peoples as a racialized category. For Canada's non-Indigenous population, I use non-Native, non-Indigenous, and settler interchangeably, again, to add variety.

5 For more on racializing, racialized, and racists sporting spaces, see Victoria Paraschak, "Aboriginal Peoples and the Construction of Canadian Sport Policy," in *Aboriginal Peoples and Sport in Canada,* ed. Janice Forsyth and Audrey R. Giles (Vancouver: UBC Press, 2013), 95–123; Allan Downey and Susan Neylan, "Raven Plays Ball: Situating 'Indian Sports Days' within Indigenous and Colonial Spaces in Twentieth-Century Coastal British Columbia," *Canadian Journal of History* 50, 3 (Winter 2015): 442–68.

6 Stephanie A. Fryberg et al., "Of Warrior Chiefs and Indian Princesses: The Psychological Impact Consequences of American Indian Mascots," *Basic and Applied Social Psychology* 30 (2008): 208–18.

7 Laurel R. Davis, "The Problems with Native American Mascots," *Multicultural Education* 9, 4 (Summer 2002), 14. For more see, Laurel R. Davis, "Protest against the Use of Native American Mascots: A Challenge to Traditional American Identity," *Journal of Sport and Social Issues* 17, 1 (April 1993): 9–22; T'cha Dunlevy,

"Blackface in Quebec: Intent vs. Offence," *Montreal Gazette*, February 21, 2015; Awad Ibrahim, "Performing Desire: Hip-Hop, Identification, and the Politics of Becoming Black," in *Racism, Eh? A Critical Inter-Discplinary Anthology of Race and Racism in Canada*, ed. Camille A. Nelson and Charmaine A. Nelson (Concord, ON: Captus Press, 2004), 289. I am appreciative of Christopher Gismondi and the conversations we shared on this topic.

8 For example, see John Lutz, *Makúk: A New History of Aboriginal-White Relations* (Vancouver: UBC Press, 2008).

9 For more on "resurgence," see Simpson, *Dancing on Our Turtle's Back*. The term "intellectual sovereignty" comes from the work of Robert Allen Warrior, "Intellectual Sovereignty and the Struggle for an American Indian Future," *Wizazo Sa Review* 8, 1 (Spring 1992): 1–20. See also Madeline Rose Knickerbocker and Sarah Nickel, "Negotiating Sovereignty: Indigenous Perspectives on the Patriation of a Settler Colonial Constitution, 1975–83," *BC Studies* 190 (Summer 2016), 69.

10 For more, see Stewart Culin, *Games of the North American Indians,* Twenty-Fourth Annual Report of the Bureau of American Ethnology to the Secretary of the Smithsonian Institute, 1902–1903 (Washington, DC: Government Printing Office, 1907; reprint, New York: Dover, 1975); Thomas Vennum, *American Indian Lacrosse: Little Brother of War* (Baltimore: Johns Hopkins University Press, 1994); and Thomas Vennum, *Lacrosse Legends of the First Americans* (Baltimore: Johns Hopkins University Press, 2007).

11 Vennum, *American Indian Lacrosse*, 71.

12 Ibid.

13 According to the *Omàmiwininì Pimàdjwowin: The Algonquin Way Culture Centre Dictionary,* the verb Pàgàdowe means "to play lacrosse." See "lacrosse," *Algonquin Way Culture Centre,* http://www.thealgonquinway.ca/English/word-e.php?word =894. Baaga'adowewin is "the game of lacrosse, playing lacrosse," whereas bagga'adowe is "s/he plays lacrosse." See "lacrosse," in *The Ojibwe People's Dictionary*, http://ojibwe.lib.umn.edu/main-entry/baaga-adowe-vai. *Tewaá:rathon* is a reference to the netting in the stick. As with other names for lacrosse, the spelling varies depending on the community consulted. Michael Kanentakeron Mitchell, *Teiontsikwaeks (day yoon chee gwa ecks): Lacrosse, the Creator's Game* (Akwesasne: Ronathahon:ni Cultural Centre, 2010), 19.

14 Vennum, *Lacrosse Legends,* 17. A version of this story is given in Chapter 5.

15 For example, see Michael J. Zogry, *Anetso, the Cherokee Ball Game: At the Center of Ceremony and Identity* (Chapel Hill: University of North Carolina Press, 2010). In its various forms, lacrosse was and continues to be an outdoor stick-and-ball team game. A netted or curved wooden stick is used to carry, pass, catch, and shoot the ball. In some variations of the game, known as double ball, two balls are strung together by a length of cord/sinew. In the past, balls were made from wood, clay, or a stuffed hide sack. As the oral tradition of the Creator's game points out, competing parties often agreed upon the rules before each contest, but a fundamental rule was that a player's hands must not touch the ball. However, there were exceptions to this. For example, the Aniyvwiya (Cherokee) did allow limited handling of the ball, and rules, styles of play, and stick types varied from nation to nation. In some communities, as lacrosse historian Thomas Vennum

reminds us, the ball spent much of its time on the ground, whereas others put greater emphasis on keeping it in the air through passing. The number of players could vary from a dozen to a few hundred, and fields differed in length, usually based on the number of participants – it was not uncommon for the goals to be separated by miles. Often, there were no defined sidelines. However, Vennum notes that field lengths were consistent in the Great Lakes region, where certain fields served as sports grounds. The game is played by running with the ball or passing it between teammates to score points at the opposing team's end of the field. If a goal consisted of a single post, a point was scored by throwing the ball against it; if the goal was made of two posts, the ball was carried or thrown between them. Some nations used two posts that were joined by a crossbar. Overly aggressive play could result in penalties, but lacrosse was a physical game that allowed for body contact, tackling, tripping, stick checking, and spearing to gain possession of the ball. After William George Beers drafted the first set of rules in the 1860s, they were standardized by organizers during the late nineteenth century: the number of players was set at twelve per side, game times were limited, and fields were given boundaries and were shortened so that the goals stood approximately 125 yards apart. Initially, the goals were two six-foot flagpoles spaced six feet apart, but goal nets with a crossbar and netting to "catch the ball" were introduced in 1897. Numerous "fouls" for rule infractions were also introduced. The indoor version of lacrosse, known as box lacrosse, was introduced in the 1930s. For more, see Chapter 4. Vennum, *Lacrosse Legends*; Vennum, *American Indian Lacrosse*; Donald M. Fisher, *Lacrosse: A History of the Game* (Baltimore: Johns Hopkins University Press, 2002).

16 For example, following the pattern set out by the Colonial Office after the Baggot Commission of 1842–44 and resulting policies such as the 1857 Act to Encourage the Gradual Civilization of Indian Tribes of the Canadas, the United Canadas took over administration of "Indian" affairs from the Colonial Office in 1860 and continued the upward spiral of legislating Indigenous peoples, marking the beginning of Canada's Colonial Age.

17 Alfred and Corntassel, "Being Indigenous," 601; Coulthard, *Red Skin, White Masks*.

18 Linda Tuhiwai Smith, *Decolonizing Methodologies: Research and Indigenous Peoples* (Dunedin, NZ: University of Otago Press, 1999), 98. For more on decolonization and post-colonial conversations, see Margaret Kovach, *Indigenous Methodologies: Characteristics, Conversations, and Contexts* (Toronto: University of Toronto Press, 2009); Dale Turner, *This Is Not a Peace Pipe: Towards a Critical Indigenous Philosophy* (Toronto: University of Toronto Press, 2006); and Mary Louise Pratt, *Imperial Eyes: Travel Writing and Transculturation* (London: Routledge, 1992).

19 Kovach, *Indigenous Methodologies*, 76; see also Coulthard, *Red Skin, White Masks*; and Robert J.C. Young, *White Mythologies: Writing History and the West*, 2nd ed. (London: Routledge, 2004).

20 Pratt, *Imperial Eyes*, 4.

21 Ibid.

22 Mary-Ellen Kelm, *A Wilder West: Rodeo in Western Canada* (Vancouver: UBC Press, 2011); Mary-Ellen Kelm, "Riding into Place: Contact Zones, Rodeo, and

Hybridity in the Canadian West 1900–1970," *Journal of the Canadian Historical Association* 18, 1 (2007): 107–32.

23 In part, my approach to presenting my Indigenous-self, non-Indigenous-self, colonized-self, and decolonized-self throughout this work is my adaptation of what Mary Louise Pratt calls an "autoethnography" or "autoethnographic expression," which she describes as "instances in which the colonized subjects undertake to represent themselves in ways that *engage with* the colonizer's own terms." Pratt, *Imperial Eyes,* 6–7 (emphasis in original). My use of the autoethnographic approach also stems from Paulette Regan's *Unsettling the Settler Within,* which masterfully employs the technique. I do this at the beginning of each chapter by using the Trickster-Transformer, typically in the form of 'Usdas, in a fashion like that presented by Anishinaabe legal scholar John Borrows, Aniyvwiya (Cherokee) novelist Thomas King, and Stl'atl'imx scholar Peter Cole. As demonstrated in Thomas Vennum's *Lacrosse Legends,* which is a collection of lacrosse oral histories, the Trickster-Transformer figure plays a central role in the retelling of lacrosse history in Indigenous communities. See Paulette Regan, *Unsettling the Settler Within: Indian Residential Schools, Truth Telling, and Reconciliation in Canada* (Vancouver: UBC Press, 2010), 29; John Borrows, *Recovering Canada: The Resurgence of Indigenous Law* (Toronto: University of Toronto Press, 2002); Thomas King, *The Truth about Stories: A Native Narrative* (Toronto: House of Anansi Press, 2003); and Peter Cole, *Coyote and Raven Go Canoeing: Coming Home to the Village* (Montreal and Kingston: McGill-Queen's University Press, 2006).

24 Jo-ann Archibald, *Indigenous Storywork: Educating the Heart, Mind, Body, and Spirit* (Vancouver: UBC Press, 2008), 5.

25 For example, see Michael Pomedli, *Living with Animals: Ojibwe Spirit Powers* (Toronto: University of Toronto Press, 2014), 201; and Vennum, *Lacrosse Legends,* 97–130.

26 King, *The Truth about Stories;* Thomas King, *Green Grass, Running Water* (Toronto: HarperPerennial Canada, 2007); Thomas King, *A Coyote Columbus Story* (Toronto: Groundwood Books/House of Anansi Press, 2010); Leanne Simpson, *Islands of Decolonial Love* (Winnipeg: Arbeiter Ring, 2013); Simpson, *Dancing on Our Turtle's Back;* Richard Wagamese, *Indian Horse* (Madeira Park, BC: Douglas and McIntyre, 2012); Lee Maracle, *Celia's Song* (Toronto: Cormorant Books, 2014).

27 Turner, *This Is Not a Peace Pipe,* 8.

28 Chris Andersen, *"Métis": Race, Recognition, and the Struggle for Indigenous Peoplehood* (Vancouver: UBC Press, 2014), 20.

29 An attempt has been made wherever possible to use the original self-identifications of the Indigenous nations mentioned in this book. It is important to note that these self-identifications are not intended to be definitive, as they are often subject to change. As Indigenous nations reclaim and re-empower their languages, cultures, nationhood, and self-identifications, these identities – and more specifically their spellings – can change over time.

30 Fisher, *Lacrosse,* 24.

31 Patrick Wolfe, "Settler Colonialism and the Elimination of the Native," *Journal of Genocide Research* 8, 4 (December 2006): 388–89.

32 Gillian Poulter, *Becoming Native in a Foreign Land: Sport, Visual Culture, and Identity in Montreal, 1840–85* (Vancouver: UBC Press, 2009); Michael A. Robidoux, "Imagining a Canadian Identity through Sport: A Historical Interpretation of Lacrosse and Hockey," *Journal of American Folklore* 115, 456 (Spring 2002): 209–25; Nancy Bouchier, *For the Love of the Game: Amateur Sport in Small-Town Ontario* (Montreal and Kingston: McGill-Queen's University Press, 2003); Nancy Bouchier, "Idealized Middle-Class Sport for a Young Nation: Lacrosse in Nineteenth-Century Ontario Towns, 1871–1891," *Journal of Canadian Studies* 29, 2 (Summer 1994): 89–110.

33 Paige Raibmon, *Authentic Indians: Episodes of Encounter from the Late-Nineteenth-Century Northwest Coast* (Durham, NC: Duke University Press, 2005), 3.

34 King, *The Truth about Stories,* 59.

35 Philip Deloria, *Playing Indian* (New Haven: Yale University Press, 1998); Philip Deloria, *Indians in Unexpected Places* (Lawrence: University of Kansas Press, 2004).

36 Raibmon, *Authentic Indians,* 3.

37 Michael A. Robidoux, *Stickhandling through the Margins: First Nations Hockey in Canada* (Toronto: University of Toronto Press, 2012), 27.

38 A component group of the Central Coast Salish, the Skwx̱wú7mesh Nation is located in North Vancouver, Howe Sound, and the Squamish River watershed; it traditionally spoke the Skwx̱wú7mesh language. For more, see Wayne Suttles, *Handbook of North American Indians,* vol. 7, *The Northwest Coast* (Washington, DC: Smithsonian Institution, 1990).

39 Zogry, *Anetso,* 27–28.

40 Unlike field lacrosse, box lacrosse, also known as indoor lacrosse, is played indoors with a reduced number of players on the floor (five runners and one goalkeeper). It was originally developed on a large scale by National Hockey League owners in 1931 to fill idle hockey arenas in the summertime.

41 Gerald R. Alfred, *Heeding the Voices of Our Ancestors: Kahnawake Mohawk Politics and the Rise of Native Nationalism* (Toronto: Oxford University Press, 1995), 14.

42 Ibid.; Simpson, *Mohawk Interruptus*; John Borrows, *Canada's Indigenous Constitution* (Toronto: University of Toronto Press, 2010); Borrows, *Recovering Canada*; Lina Sunseri, *Being Again of One Mind: Oneida Women and the Struggle for Decolonization* (Vancouver: UBC Press, 2011); José Barreiro, ed., *Thinking in Indian: A John Mohawk Reader* (Golden, CO: Fulcrum, 2010).

43 Sunseri, *Being Again of One Mind,* 6.

44 David Sampson, "Culture, 'Race' and Discrimination in the 1868 Aboriginal Cricket Tour of England," *Australian Aboriginal Studies* 2 (2009): 49.

45 At the beginning of this research, I recognized that I was not interested in having my participants be "research subjects" and had no desire to run into Indigenous communities with a tape recorder in hand, trying to record what everyone said; rather, I wanted to cultivate research partnerships and be under the guidance of Indigenous mentors – I wanted to take on the role of an apprentice. As I built relationships and friendships, more than two and a half years elapsed before I conducted my first formal interview. Except for just two individuals, I met my

research partners and mentors months, and sometimes years, before our first formal interview. I attended lacrosse games, community events, and cultural ceremonies, and I am honoured to say that I struck up lifelong friendships with all the individuals with whom I worked. Furthermore, the mentors remained a part of the project until it reached the final stage of publication: they could see how they were quoted and interpreted, and were given the opportunity to make changes, remain anonymous, or refrain from being included at all. I also made a point of being as open as possible about the research by holding presentations within the communities, conducting radio interviews, volunteering, and providing status updates. With so much knowledge taken from our communities throughout the history of colonialism, I felt that this project needed to give some back, so I have held lacrosse clinics and lectures in Indigenous communities across the country. Furthermore, the communities in which I conducted interviews and research, at the discretion of participants, have access to the interviews through their local library, culture centre, and/or band office.

46 Archibald, *Indigenous Storywork*, 8.

47 For more, see Leslie McCartney, "Respecting First Nations Oral Histories: Complexities and Archiving Aboriginal Stories," in *First Nations, First Thoughts: The Impact of Indigenous Thought in Canada*, ed. Annis May Timpson (Vancouver: UBC Press, 2009), 77–96.

48 Much has been written about the perceived or constructed dichotomy between oral history/testimony and oral tradition. The former is gathered via interviews and the recounting of lived experiences, whereas the latter consists of creation stories or stories set before the time of the narrator. Often, the line between oral testimony and oral tradition is blurred, as they are intersectional and often equally influential (that is, the Elders, Knowledge Holders, and Faithkeepers who partnered with this book often connected their personal experiences with those of creation stories and vice versa). In keeping with my attempt at minimal intrusion, I do not distinguish between lived experiences, creation stories, or stories that are set before the speaker's time. For more, see Julie Cruikshank, "Oral Tradition and Oral History: Reviewing Some Issues," *Canadian Historical Review* 75, 3 (1994): 403–18; and Bruce Miller, *Oral History on Trial: Recognizing Aboriginal Narratives in the Courts* (Vancouver: UBC Press, 2011).

49 Joseph B. Oxendine, *American Indian Sports Heritage* (Lincoln: University of Nebraska Press, [1988] 1995).

50 Janice Forsyth and Audrey R. Giles, eds., *Aboriginal Peoples and Sport in Canada: Historical Foundations and Contemporary Issues* (Vancouver: UBC Press, 2013).

51 Victoria Paraschak, "Native Sport History: Pitfalls and Promise," *Canadian Journal of History of Sport* 20, 1 (1989): 57–68; Victoria Paraschak, "Organized Sport for Native Females on the Six Nations Reserve, Ontario from 1968 to 1980: A Comparison of Dominant and Emergent Sport Systems," *Canadian Journal of History of Sport* 21, 2 (December 1990): 70–80; Victoria Paraschak, "'Reasonable Amusements': Connecting the Strands of Physical Culture in Native Lives," *Sport History Review* 29 (1998): 121–31.

52 Christine O'Bonsawin, "'From Savagery to Civic Organization': The Non-participation of Canadian Indians in the Anthropology Days of the 1904 St.

Louis Olympic Games," in *The 1904 Anthropology Days and Olympic Games: Sport, Race, and American Imperialism,* ed. Susan Brownell (Lincoln: University of Nebraska Press, 2008), 217–42; Michael Heine, "Performance Indicators: Aboriginal Games at the Arctic Winter Games," in Forsyth and Giles, *Aboriginal Peoples and Sport,* 160–81; Janice Forsyth, "The Indian Act and the (Re)shaping of Canadian Aboriginal Sport Practices," *International Journal of Canadian Studies* 35 (2007): 95–111; Audrey R. Giles, "Kevlar, Crisco, and Menstruation: 'Tradition' and Dene Games," *Sociology of Sport Journal* 21 (2004): 18–35; Audrey R. Giles, "Women's and Girls' Participation in Dene Games in the Northwest Territories," in Forsyth and Giles, *Aboriginal Peoples and Sport,* 145–59.

53 Alexander M. Weyand and Milton R. Roberts, *The Lacrosse Story* (Baltimore: H. and A. Herman, 1965); *Tewaarathon (Lacrosse): Akwesasne's Story of Our National Game* (Akwesasne: North American Indian Traveling College, 1978); Zogry, *Anetso;* Vennum, *American Indian Lacrosse;* Fisher, *Lacrosse;* Michael Kanentakeron Mitchell, *Teiontsikwaeks (day yoon chee gwa ecks): Lacrosse, the Creator's Game* (Akwesasne: Ronathahon:ni Cultural Centre, 2010); Vennum, *Lacrosse Legends.*

Tewaá:rathon

❶ **The Canadian Appropriation of Lacrosse and "Indian" Performances**

1 General Scrapbook No. 1 (1858–76), Montreal Amateur Athletic Association Fonds, MG 28, I 351, vol. 15, *Library and Archives Canada* (hereafter General Scrapbook 1, *LAC*).

2 David Jack (Gwe-u-gweh-o-no, Cayuga), "Power Received from Thunderer," interview by F.W. Waugh, August 1915, Six Nations of the Grand River Reserve, five-page typed transcript, Control No. B201, f24, *Canadian Museum of Civilization,* http://catalogue.civilization.ca/musvw/FullBB.csp?WebAction=ShowFull BB&EncodedRequest=*06rs*19jy*CAD*F0*FB*D6*18*03A*F6*00&Profile =ArchivesOnlyCMC&OpacLanguage=eng&NumberToRetrieve=10&Start Value=1&WebPageNr=1&SearchTerm1=WAUGH%20F%20W%20 FREDERICK%20WILKERSON1872%201924%20.1.277386&SearchT1=& Index1=1*Keywordsbib&SearchMethod=Find_1&ItemNr=1.

3 "Our Country and Our Game, 1st July 1867" was adopted as the slogan of the National Lacrosse Association of Canada, which was formed on September 26, 1867. Alan Metcalfe, *Canada Learns to Play: The Emergence of Organized Sport, 1807–1914* (Don Mills, ON: Oxford University Press, 1987), 182.

4 Following the birth of the Dominion of Canada in 1867, Dr. W.G. Beers claimed that the new Parliament had officially accepted lacrosse as Canada's national sport, an assertion that quickly became part of Canadian folklore. However, it was disproved in the 1960s, when it was revealed that no such declaration had ever been made. Donald M. Fisher, *Lacrosse: A History of the Game* (Baltimore: Johns Hopkins University Press, 2002), 26. Not until the advent of Bill C-212 in 1994 was lacrosse officially proclaimed as Canada's national summertime sport. Canadian Lacrosse Association, "Lacrosse: Canada's National Sport," *Canadian Lacrosse Association,* http://www.lacrosse.ca/default.aspx?cid=84&lang=1, accessed June 15, 2008.

5 Anishinaabeg means "original people" (alternatively spelt Anishinaabe in the singular form and Anishinaabek/Anishinaabeg in the plural form).

6 For more, see Thomas Vennum, *American Indian Lacrosse: Little Brother of War* (Baltimore: Johns Hopkins University Press, 1994).

7 "Double Ball," *Saskatchewan Indian Culture Centre*, http://www.sicc.sk.ca/archive/heritage/ethnography/cree/recreation/doubleball.html. J.A. Mitchell also reported that the game was called Puseekowwahnuk, in Stewart Culin, *Games of the North American Indians,* Twenty-Fourth Annual Report of the Bureau of American Ethnology to the Secretary of the Smithsonian Institute, 1902–1903 (Washington, DC: Government Printing Office, 1907; reprint, New York: Dover, 1975), 652.

8 As mentioned previously, some Indigenous communities did allow players to touch the ball. Michael J. Zogry, *Anetso, the Cherokee Ball Game: At the Center of Ceremony and Identity* (Chapel Hill: University of North Carolina Press, 2010), 12. For more examples of the numerous varieties of lacrosse, see Culin, *Games of the North American Indians;* and Vennum, *American Indian Lacrosse.*

9 Rick Hill (Tuscarora), interview by Allan Downey, June 7, 2011, audio recording and transcript, Six Nations Polytechnic, Six Nations of the Grand River Reserve, ON.

10 For an in-depth study of Aniyvwiya lacrosse, known as Anetso, see Zogry, *Anetso.*

11 Dao Jao Dre (Delmor Jacobs, Cayuga, Wolf Clan, Six Nations of the Grand River), interview by Allan Downey, June 7, 2011, audio recording and transcript, Six Nations of the Grand River Reserve, ON. The connection between lacrosse and the Thunderers is not limited to the Hodinöhsö:ni', as other nations such as the Aniyvwiya also have oral traditions and present-day spiritual practices of lacrosse in which the Thunderbeings persist. For more, see Zogry, *Anetso.*

12 Dao Jao Dre, interview by Downey, June 7, 2011.

13 Jean de Brébeuf, "Relation of 1636," in *The Jesuit Relations and Allied Documents* (Cleveland, 1897), 10:185, quoted in Culin, *Games of the North American Indians,* 589.

14 Anthony Wonderley, *Oneida Iroquois Folklore, Myth, and History: New York Oral Narrative from the Notes of H.E. Allen and Others* (Syracuse: Syracuse University Press, 2004), 122; Brian Rice, *The Rotinonshonni: A Traditional Iroquoian History through the Eyes of Teharonhia:wako and Sawiskera* (Syracuse: Syracuse University Press, 2013), 314.

15 William N. Fenton, *The Great Law and the Longhouse: A Political History of the Iroquois Confederacy* (Norman: University of Oklahoma Press, 1998), 50.

16 William Engelbrecht, *Iroquoia: The Development of a Native World* (Syracuse: Syracuse University Press, 2003), 5. Other medicines besides tobacco can also be used for a lacrosse stick. Rick Hill, interview by Downey, June 7, 2011.

17 As will be discussed in Chapter 4, not all Hodinöhsö:ni' Longhouse traditionalists follow the Code of Handsome Lake. For instance, the Kanien'kehá:ka from Kahnawà:ke, Ahkwesáhsne, and Kanehsatá:ke have, on the whole, rejected it, believing it to be a Christian corruption of the Longhouse. As with any identity, epistemological and cultural identities are not simple and hardened binaries; rather, they are often fluid and overlapping. The same is true when it comes to the Code of Handsome Lake.

18 Sganyadai:yo' is also given as Skanyadai:yo'. Rick Monture, *We Share Our Matters: Two Centuries of Writing and Resistance at Six Nations of the Grand River* (Winnipeg: University of Manitoba Press, 2014), 11.

19 Arthur C. Parker, *The Code of Handsome Lake, the Seneca Prophet*, Education Department Bulletin 530 (Albany: University of the State of New York, 1912), 9, *Library of Congress*, http://www.archive.org/details/codeofhandsomela01hand.

20 Ibid.

21 Ibid.

22 Jim Calder and Ron Fletcher, *Lacrosse: The Ancient Game* (Toronto: Ancient Game Press, 2011), 38.

23 In Cornplanter's version of the story, there are four messengers, whereas in the versions of Dao Jao Dre, Delmor Jacobs, and Chief Jacob Thomas, there are only three. Jacob Thomas, *Teachings from the Longhouse* (Toronto: Stoddart, 1994), 28; Dao Jao Dre, interview by Downey, June 7, 2011; Parker, *The Code of Handsome Lake*, 18–19.

24 Parker, *The Code of Handsome Lake*, 22.

25 Todd Leahy and Raymond Wilson, *Historical Dictionary of Native American Movements* (Lanham, MD: Scarecrow Press, 2008), 67.

26 Parker, *The Code of Handsome Lake*, 23.

27 Ibid.

28 Ibid., 24.

29 Calder and Fletcher, *Lacrosse: The Ancient Game*, 39.

30 Ibid.

31 Ibid., 39–40.

32 Dao Jao Dre, interview by Downey, June 7, 2011.

33 Parker, *The Code of Handsome Lake*, 79–80.

34 At this point in the original, a footnote reads as follows: "Games were often played to cheer and cure the sick. Special food were given [to] the players [sic]."

35 Parker, *The Code of Handsome Lake*, 79–80.

36 Zogry, *Anetso*, 27–28.

37 Ibid., 29.

38 Gillian Poulter, *Becoming Native in a Foreign Land: Sport, Visual Culture, and Identity in Montreal, 1840–85* (Vancouver: UBC Press, 2009), 1.

39 Michael A. Robidoux, "Imagining a Canadian Identity through Sport: A Historical Interpretation of Lacrosse and Hockey," *Journal of American Folklore* 115, 456 (Spring 2002): 209 (emphasis in original).

40 Poulter, *Becoming Native*, 162.

41 Ibid., 1.

42 "Authentic Indians" is derived from Paige Raibmon's book of the same name. It refers to the "powerful and shifting set of ideas that worked in a variety of ways toward a variety of ends" in attempting to identify what "Indians" were. Of course, as Raibmon points out, "authentic" refers to what was *perceived* as real. Paige Raibmon, *Authentic Indians: Episodes of Encounter from the Late-Nineteenth-Century Northwest Coast* (Durham, NC: Duke University Press, 2005), 3.

43 For more, see Philip Deloria, *Indians in Unexpected Places* (Lawrence: University of Kansas Press, 2004).

44 Poulter, *Becoming Native*, 117; Fisher, *Lacrosse*, 24.

45 Fisher, *Lacrosse*, 24.

46 Metcalfe, *Canada Learns to Play*, 182.

47 W.G. Beers, *Lacrosse: The National Game of Canada* (Montreal: Dawson Brothers, 1869), vii.

48 Fisher, *Lacrosse*, 25; Alexander M. Weyand and Milton R. Roberts, *The Lacrosse Story* (Baltimore: H. and A. Herman, 1965), 17.

49 *Tewaarathon (Lacrosse): Akwesasne's Story of Our National Game* (Akwesasne: North American Indian Traveling College, 1978), 37.

50 This treatment of sport was not limited to a Canadian or Indigenous context. It certainly fit within the larger connection between British, and later American, imperialism and organized sport. For more, see C.L.R. James, *Beyond a Boundary* (Durham, NC: Duke University Press, 2013); Mark Naison, "Sports and the American Empire," *Radical America* 6, 4 (July–August 1972): 95–120; and Brian Stoddart, *Sport, Culture, and History: Region, Nation and Globe* (New York: Routledge, 2008).

51 Beers, *Lacrosse*, 32. A portion of this quote also appears in Vennum, *American Indian Lacrosse*, 269.

52 Nancy Bouchier, "Idealized Middle-Class Sport for a Young Nation: Lacrosse in Nineteenth-Century Ontario Towns, 1871–1891," *Journal of Canadian Studies* 29, 2 (Summer 1994): 89.

53 For more on the formation of a Canadian identity through the appropriation of Indigenous and French activities, see Poulter, *Becoming Native*.

54 Ibid., 1–20.

55 Ibid., 5.

56 Ibid., 7.

57 Nancy Bouchier, *For the Love of the Game: Amateur Sport in Small-Town Ontario* (Montreal and Kingston: McGill-Queen's University Press, 2003), 60.

58 Bouchier, "Idealized Middle-Class Sport," 89.

59 As Colin Howell summarizes, Muscular Christianity was preached by the Protestant churches of Canada during the late nineteenth century; it presented Christ as manly and athletic. Its advocates "called on young men to celebrate a vigorously human Christ and to practice humane Christianity through active, athletic, and morally upright lives ... National and imperial greatness ... grew out of physical toughness and Christian humility." Colin D. Howell, *Blood, Sweat, and Cheers: Sport and the Making of Modern Canada* (Toronto: University of Toronto Press, 2001), 32; Bouchier, "Idealized Middle-Class Sport," 89.

60 Metcalfe, *Canada Learns to Play*, 182; Ian Radforth, "Performance, Politics, and Representation: Aboriginal People and the 1860 Royal Tour of Canada," *Canadian Historical Review* 84, 1 (March 2003): 10.

61 See Radforth, "Performance, Politics, and Representation."

62 Bouchier, "Idealized Middle-Class Sport," 89.

63 Bouchier, *For the Love of the Game*, 118.

64 Ibid.

65 Robidoux, "Imagining a Canadian Identity," 216.

66 Poulter, *Becoming Native*, 5.

67 Ibid., II; Vennum, *American Indian Lacrosse*, 268–70.

68 Metcalfe, *Canada Learns to Play*, 182.

69 This was Rule IX, section 6. Beers, *Lacrosse*, 254.

70 Fisher, *Lacrosse*, 37. The stereotype of Indigenous peoples as superior physical specimens was widespread throughout the British Empire. According to Māori scholar Brendan Hokowhitu, it "[falsely] represented a naive and mystical life prior to the reasoned life imbued by the scientific revolution." Brendan Hokowhitu, "Tackling Maori Masculinity: A Colonial Genealogy of Savagery and Sport," *Contemporary Pacific* 16, 2 (Fall 2004): 268–69. This would later have a significant impact on the Māori, for example, in which sport became synonymous with their masculinity.

71 Ibid.

72 Vennum, *American Indian Lacrosse*, 271.

73 *Tewaarathon (Lacrosse)*, 39.

74 Patrick Wolfe, "Settler Colonialism and the Elimination of the Native," *Journal of Genocide Research* 8, 4 (December 2006): 388–89.

75 Deloria, *Indians in Unexpected Places*, 117–18.

76 Audra Simpson, *Mohawk Interruptus: Political Life across the Borders of Settler States* (Durham, NC: Duke University Press, 2014), 10–11. It is important to note that after Confederation, the Dominion of Canada's "sovereignty" was still subject to British rule as a colony. I also use the word sovereignty in an Indigenous context while reconizing the limitations of that terminology as a Western construct, as argued by both Audra Simpson and Taiaiake Alfred. See Simpson, *Mohawk Interruptus*, 105; Gerald R. Alfred, "Sovereignty," in *A Companion to American Indian History*, ed. Phil Deloria and Neal Salisbury (New York: Blackwell, 2004). 460–76.

77 "Lacrosse Match: Toronto vs. the Six-Nation Indians," *Toronto Globe*, September 26, 1867.

78 Ibid.

79 Weyand and Roberts, *The Lacrosse Story*, 17.

80 On "performing Indians," see David Blanchard, "Entertainment, Dance and Northern Mohawk Showmanship," *American Indian Quarterly* 7, 1 (1983): 2–26; and Sarah Paddle, "Private Lives and Public Performances: Aboriginal Women in a Settler Society, Ontario, Canada, 1920s–1960s," *Journal of Colonialism and Colonial History* 4, 3 (2003): 1–16.

81 Poulter, *Becoming Native*, 8–9.

82 Blanchard, "Entertainment, Dance," 2.

83 Ibid., 3.

84 Vennum, *American Indian Lacrosse*, 33–36.

85 "Lacrosse Match," *Toronto Globe*, September 26, 1867.

86 Don Morrow, "The Canadian Image Abroad: The Great Lacrosse Tours of 1876 and 1883," in *Proceedings of the Fifth Canadian Symposium on the History of Sport and Physical Education* (Toronto: University of Toronto, 1982), 11–12; also quoted in Victoria Paraschak, "Native Sport History: Pitfalls and Promise," *Canadian Journal of History of Sport* 20, 1 (1989): 59.

87 Correspondence, Rick Hill, March 7, 2012, Six Nations Polytechnic, Six Nations of the Grand River, ON.

88 Raibmon, *Authentic Indians,* 62. Also see Deloria, *Indians in Unexpected Places.*

89 Susan Roy, "Performing Musqueam Culture and History at British Columbia's 1966 Centennial Celebrations," *BC Studies* 135 (Autumn 2002): 62.

90 Ibid., 63.

91 Weyand and Roberts, *The Lacrosse Story,* 23–25.

92 Ibid., 24.

93 G.H.M. Johnson was a Kanien'kehá:ka chief at Six Nations, an interpreter, and the father of the famous poet and lecturer Pauline Johnson. "George Henry Martin Johnson (Onwanonsyshon)," *Dictionary of Canadian Biography Online* (Toronto: University of Toronto), http://www.biographi.ca/009004-119.01-e.php?&id_nbr=5609&interval=25&&PHPSESSID=47usjtf5bk29p4aguqthf6nur4; Weyand and Roberts, *The Lacrosse Story,* 24.

94 Weyand and Roberts, *The Lacrosse Story,* 24–25.

95 Vennum, *American Indian Lacrosse,* 265.

96 Weyand and Roberts, *The Lacrosse Story,* 25.

97 W. Kelso Morrill, *Lacrosse* (New York: Ronald Press, 1966), 6.

98 Weyand and Roberts, *The Lacrosse Story,* 16–17.

99 "The Game of Lacrosse: A Sport for Which Whites Are Indebted to Indians," *Chicago Daily Tribune,* February 20, 1887.

100 Fisher, *Lacrosse,* 30.

101 Johnny Beauvais, *Kahnawake: A Mohawk Look at Canada and Adventures of Big John Canadian* (Montreal: Techno Couleur, 1985), 137; Beers, *Lacrosse,* xiii.

102 "Court Circular," *Times* (London), June 28, 1876.

103 Fisher, *Lacrosse,* 30.

104 Deloria, *Indians in Unexpected Places,* 129-30.

105 Blanchard, "Entertainment, Dance," 11.

106 "Lacrosse: The National Game of the Indians," c. 1879 (emphasis added), newspaper clipping in General Scrapbook No. 2 (c. 1844–80), Montreal Amateur Athletic Association Fonds, MG 28, I 351, vol. 16, *Library and Archives Canada* (hereafter General Scrapbook 2, *LAC*).

107 Christine M. O'Bonsawin, "Spectacles, Policy, and Social Memory: Images of Canadian Indians at World's Fairs and Olympic Games" (PhD diss., University of Western Ontario, 2006), 122–44. For instance, such was the case at London's 1851 Crystal Palace Exhibition; the Prince of Wales's 1860 visit to Canada, which featured two lacrosse games including an Anishinaabeg team competing against a Hodinöhsö:ni' team; the visit of Prince Arthur in 1868; the Centennial International Exhibition in Philadelphia in 1876; Wild West shows; and the World's Columbian Exposition in Chicago in 1893. For more on the representation of Indigenous peoples at World's Fairs and other non-Native exhibitions, see Deloria, *Indians in Unexpected Places;* O'Bonsawin, "Spectacles, Policy, and Social Memory"; and Raibmon, *Authentic Indians.*

108 Poulter, *Becoming Native,* 155.

109 Deloria, *Indians in Unexpected Places,* 56–57.

110 Kararonwe is also given as Karownie, Keraronwe, Keroniaire, and Tharoniake in the Montreal Amateur Athletic Association Scrapbook 1 and 2 files, as well as in Beauvais, *Kahnawake*, 33. After consulting with a number of community members in Kahnawà:ke, I was unable to confirm the spelling; therefore, I have chosen to use "Kararonwe" throughout because that is how he signed a letter to the editor in 1875. General Scrapbook 1, *LAC*. The team rivalry is demonstrated in various articles contained in General Scrapbooks 1 and 2, *LAC*.

111 "Are Indians Professionals," *Town and Country*, June 2, 1880 in General Scrapbook 1, *LAC*.

112 "Lacrosse Matters," August 29, 1879, newspaper clipping in General Scrapbook 1, *LAC*.

113 Montreal Lacrosse Club Minute Book, 1886-93, April 20 and 27, May 4, 11, and 18, 1887, Montreal Amateur Athletic Association Fonds, MG 28, I 351, vol. 9, file 3, *Library and Archives Canada*.

114 Beauvais, *Kahnawake*, 9; Maurice Ratelle, "Canadien, Jean-Baptiste," *Dictionary of Canadian Biography Online*, http://www.biographi.ca/009004-119.01-e.php?&id_nbr=7269.

115 Beauvais, *Kahnawake*, 11–13.

116 Although Aiontonnis participated in these imperial pursuits, it remains unclear how he might have reconciled or expressed his identity as Kanien'kehá:ka or as an Indigenous person in connection with them. Furthermore, whereas Johnny Beauvais states that Aiontonnis made the trip down the Nile, Carl Benn notes that he is not mentioned in the official records. However, he may simply not have been listed there. Ratelle, "Canadien, Jean-Baptiste," *Dictionary of Canadian Biography Online*; Beauvais, *Kahnawake*, 11–13; Carl Benn, *Mohawks on the Nile: Natives among the Canadian Voyageurs in Egypt, 1884–1885* (Toronto: Natural Heritage Books, 2009), 253.

117 Beauvais, *Kahnawake*, 11–12.

118 Morrow, "The Canadian Image Abroad," 12–13.

119 For more, see John Lucas, "Deerfoot in Britain: An Amazing American Long-Distance Runner 1861–63," *Journal of American Culture* 6 (Fall 1983): 13–18.

120 David Sampson, "Culture, 'Race' and Discrimination in the 1868 Aboriginal Cricket Tour of England," *Australian Aboriginal Studies* 2 (2009): 45. For more on Indigenous athletes and travellers in Britian, see Coll Thrush, *Indigenous London: Native Travelers at the Heart of Empire* (New Haven, CT: Yale University Press, 2016). In addition, a Māori rugby team, with a few non-Indigenous members, toured England in 1888–89 to play in a series of club and international matches. For more on Māori rugby, see Brendan Hokowhitu, "Māori Rugby and Subversion: Creativity, Domestication, Oppression, and Decolonization," *International Journal of the History of Sport* 26, 16 (2009): 2314–34; Greg Ryan, "The Paradox of Maori Rugby 1870–1914," in *Tackling Rugby Myths: Rugby and New Zealand Society, 1854–2004*, ed. Greg Ryan (Dunedin, NZ: University of Otago Press, 2005), 89–104.

121 Sampson, "Culture, 'Race' and Discrimination," 45–46.

122 Ibid., 50.

123 Fisher, *Lacrosse,* 30.

124 Canada Forever, letter to editor, *Montreal Gazette,* c. August 1875 in General Scrapbook 1, *LAC.*

125 General Scrapbook 1, *LAC.*

126 Ibid.

127 For more, see Bruce Morito, *An Ethic of Mutual Respect: The Covenant Chain and Aboriginal-Crown Relations* (Vancouver: UBC Press, 2012); and Daniel K. Richter and James H. Merrell, eds., *Beyond the Covenant Chain: The Iroquois and Their Neighbours in Indian North America, 1600–1800* (Syracuse: Syracuse University Press, 1987).

128 General Scrapbook 1, *LAC.*

129 "The Indian Lacrosse Team," April 21, 1876, newspaper clippings, General Scrapbook 1, *LAC.*

130 General Scrapbook 1, *LAC* (emphasis added).

131 "The Indian Lacrosse Team," April 21, 1876, newspaper clippings, General Scrapbook 1, *LAC.*

132 General Scrapbook 1, *LAC.*

133 Poulter, *Becoming Native,* 128.

134 Morrow, "The Canadian Image Abroad," 10.

135 "The Lacrosse Team in Scotland," May 20, 1876, newspaper clipping, General Scrapbook 1, *LAC.*

136 General Scrapbook 1, *LAC.*

137 Ibid.

138 Some references have an incomplete record of the name, showing it as "Francois Snehe..." See, for example, "Letters from W.G. Beers concerning Massiah's Appointment as Agent for Touring Teams – 1876," Christopher William Massiah Fonds, MG 29-C171, file 1, Reference no. R7445-0-6-E, *Library and Archives Canada*; McCord Museum Collections and Research online, http://collections.musee-mccord.qc.ca/scripts/search_results.php?Lang=1&keywords=1876+lacrosse.

139 Ibid.

140 One of the most famous instances of lacrosse took place on June 4, 1763, at Fort Michilimackinac, which is located in present-day Michigan (some accounts date the incident to June 2, 1763). A group of Anishinaabeg, Mesquakie (Fox), and Sauk Nation members held an exhibition of lacrosse, distracting the British troops and drawing them outside the fort. Indigenous warriors then sacked the fort, gaining a valuable victory as part of Pontiac's War. Thomas Vennum, *Lacrosse Legends of the First Americans* (Baltimore: Johns Hopkins University Press, 2007), 37. Also see Vennum, *American Indian Lacrosse.*

141 "Letters from W.G. Beers concerning Massiah's Appointment as Agent for Touring Teams – 1876" (emphasis added), Christopher William Massiah Fonds, MG 29-C171, file 1, Reference no. R7445-0-6-E, *Library and Archives Canada.*

142 According to scholar Bruce Morito, the Covenant Chain "describes a distinctive crosscultural, transnational political relationship" that characterized the respectful association between the British Crown and Indigenous nations, including the Hodinöhsö:ni', in the seventeenth and eighteenth centuries. Morito, *An Ethic of Mutual Respect,* 19. That sport can be used to form a national identity while also

serving as a vehicle of Indigenous subversion is not limited to the Canadian context. For example, Brendan Hokowhitu demonstrates how, from rugby's initial adoption, the Māori effectively infused elements of subversion into it. Hokowhitu, "Māori Rugby and Subversion."

143 Mary-Ellen Kelm, "Riding into Place: Contact Zones, Rodeo, and Hybridity in the Canadian West 1900–1970," *Journal of the Canadian Historical Association* 18, 1 (2007): 110.

144 Beauvais, *Kahnawake,* 36.

145 Joe Delaronde (Kanien'kehá:ka of Kahnawà:ke), interview by Allan Downey, April 29, 2011, audio recording, Kahnawà:ke, QC. Also, pictures of the 1876 team and Big John lined the walls of the former Water Drum restaurant in Kahnawà:ke.

146 Joe Delaronde (Kanien'kehá:ka of Kahnawà:ke), interview by Allan Downey, October 21, 2011, audio recording, Kahnawà:ke, QC.

147 Fisher, *Lacrosse,* 37.

148 Ibid.

149 Ibid., 38.

150 Vennum, *American Indian Lacrosse,* 271.

151 Beers, *Lacrosse,* 254; Fisher, *Lacrosse,* 38.

152 This new set of rules was adopted in 1876, according to historian Donald Fisher, but please note that this quote was taken from the 1879 set of rules. "Laws of Lacrosse and Constitution of the National Lacrosse Association of Canada Revised and Adopted, 6 June 1879," General Scrapbook 2, *LAC.* Fisher, *Lacrosse,* 38.

153 "Constitution and Laws of Lacrosse of the Pacific Coast Lacrosse Association," March 30, 1879, General Scrapbook 2, *LAC.*

154 General Scrapbook 2, *LAC.*

155 Fisher, *Lacrosse,* 36–39.

156 Metcalfe, *Canada Learns to Play,* 187–89.

157 Ibid., 211.

158 "Alterations and Amendments to the Laws of Lacrosse and Constitution of the National Association," June 4, 1880, General Scrapbook 2, *LAC.*

159 Fisher, *Lacrosse,* 38.

160 This term was coined by Bouchier in "Idealized Middle-Class Sport," 89–106.

161 Howell, *Blood, Sweat, and Cheers,* 38. For more on the interorganizational conflicts concerning professionalism, see Metcalfe, *Canada Learns to Play.*

162 "Record of the Various Championships under the Control of the National Amateur Lacrosse Association," July 1886, General Scrapbook 3, c. 1876–91, Montreal Amateur Athletic Association Fonds, vol. 17, file 1, MG 28, I 351, vol. 17, *Library and Archives Canada.*

163 Ibid.

164 "The Montreal Lacrosse Club and the New Lacrosse Convention," letter to the editor, *Montreal Evening Post,* May 13, 1880, in General Scrapbook 2, *LAC.*

165 Onawario (John Cree, Bear Clan, Kanien'kehá:ka of Kanehsatá:ke), interview by Allan Downey, October 22, 2011, Kanehsatá:ke, QC.

166 Dao Jao Dre (Delmor Jacobs, Cayuga, Wolf Clan, Six Nations of the Grand River), interview by Allan Downey, August 10, 2011, audio recording, Six Nations of the Grand River Reserve, ON.

167 Joe Delaronde, interview by Downey, April 29, 2011.

168 Poster for Onondaga Royal Reds Game, August/September 1922, Attorney General Central Registry Criminal and Civil Files, RG 4-32, file 2868, 1921, *Archives of Ontario.*

169 Metcalfe, *Canada Learns to Play.*

170 An indoor version of the game, box lacrosse, will be more fully discussed in Chapter 4. Also, there was an exception to the absence of Indigenous teams, as a Kahnawà:ke team competed in the NLU for one season in 1919. Larry Power, "NLU/CLA Statistics 1885–1931," *Power's Bible of Lacrosse,* www.wampsbibleof lacrosse.com, accessed June 15, 2012.

171 Dominion of Canada, *Annual Report of the Department of Indian Affairs* (Ottawa: Department of Indian Affairs, 1880–90). For more on Indigenous peoples in the wage-labour economy, see John Lutz, *Makúk: A New History of Aboriginal-White Relations* (Vancouver: UBC Press, 2008); John Lutz, "After the Fur Trade: The Aboriginal Labouring Class of British Columbia, 1849–1890," *Journal of the Canadian Historical Association* 3, 1 (1992): 69–94; and Raibmon, *Authentic Indians.*

172 Metcalfe, *Canada Learns to Play,* 85. Metcalfe notes that baseball was played across the country by 1890, including in large towns and rural regions. Like lacrosse, it suffered from organizational instability before the turn of the century, but by the early 1900s, the number of baseball organizations had significantly expanded in Canada. By 1914, hockey and baseball were the only two games played on a consistent and widespread basis across the country. Ibid., 85–97; Weyand and Roberts, *The Lacrosse Story,* 44.

173 Dominion of Canada, George Long, *Annual Report of the Department of Indian Affairs for the Year Ended 31st December 1891* (Ottawa: Department of Indian Affairs, 1891), 29. Long's report identifies Ahkwesáhsne as St. Regis.

174 Dominion of Canada, Thos. S. Walton, *Annual Report of the Department of Indian Affairs for the Year Ended 31st December, 1884* (Ottawa: Department of Indian Affairs, 1884), 9.

175 Fisher, *Lacrosse,* 256.

176 Vennum, *American Indian Lacrosse,* 285.

177 The term "Native ringers" was coined in *Tewaarathon (Lacrosse),* 50.

178 Initially, the Minto Cup represented the national senior championship but was adopted as the national junior championship trophy after the introduction of the Mann Cup. Fisher, *Lacrosse,* 45.

179 Ibid.

180 *Tewaarathon (Lacrosse),* 47. To date, little is recorded about the nature of these championship contests, which were presumably challenge games between Kahnawà:ke, Ahkwesáhsne, and Six Nations. I was unable to get a full account in the oral history. However, this is not to suggest that it does not exist, and there are pictures of the championship teams and evidence of a set of championship flags in ibid.

181 Fisher, *Lacrosse,* 31.

182 Ibid.

183 "Lacrosse as an Advertisement," *New York Times,* April 29, 1883.

184 "Dr. W.G. Beers and the Visit of the Lacrosse Team," April 27, 1883, Department of Agriculture, RG 25, B-1-9, *Library and Archives Canada.*

185 Kevin Wamsley, "Nineteenth Century Sports Tours, State Formation, and Canadian Foreign Policy," *Sport Traditions: The Journal of the Australian Society for Sports History* 13, 2 (1997): 85.

186 Morrow, "The Canadian Image Abroad," 12–13; Wamsley, "Nineteenth Century Sports Tours," 85.

187 For examples, see Thrush, *Indigenous London.*

188 Susan Hill, *The Clay We Are Made Of: Haudenosaunee Land Tenure on the Grand River* (Winnipeg: University of Manitoba Press, 2017), 215–27. For examples of the complaints, see ibid., 216–17.

189 Untitled editorial 14, *New York Times,* July 24, 1883.

190 Montreal Lacrosse Club Minute Books, 1886–93, Montreal Amateur Athletic Association Fonds, MG 28, I 351, vol. 9, file 3, *Library and Archives Canada.*

191 Ibid.

192 Ibid.

193 "Indians Play an Interesting Game at the Ball Park," *Chicago Daily* Tribune, September 13, 1885.

194 "Red Men Play a Game of Lacrosse," *Chicago Daily Tribune,* October 10, 1893.

195 "Indians Won Lacrosse Match," *New York Times,* May 20, 1900; "Canoeists' Annual Cruise," *New York Times,* May 20, 1900; "Stevens Defeated Indians," *New York Times,* May 23, 1900; "Indians Win at Lacrosse," *New York Times,* May 31, 1900; "Indians Beat Corne at Lacrosse," *New York Times,* June 2, 1900; "Indian Lacrosse Team Won," *New York Times,* June 3, 1900.

196 Fisher, *Lacrosse,* 105–8.

197 "Canoeists' Annual Cruise," *New York Times,* May 20, 1900 (emphasis added).

198 "The Growth of Lacrosse," *New York Times,* September 5, 1886.

199 Letter to the editor, 1875 (emphasis in original), newspaper clipping in General Scrapbook 1, *LAC.*

200 Beers, *Lacrosse,* vii.

201 Vennum, *Lacrosse Legends,* 141.

202 Robidoux, "Imagining a Canadian Identity," 214.

203 Ibid., 214–15.

204 For more, see Vennum, *Lacrosse Legends.*

205 Fisher, *Lacrosse,* 79.

206 "Meet Indian Lacrosse Team," *Chicago Daily Tribune,* July 2, 1904.

207 Manitoba Sports Hall of Fame and Museum, "The 1904 Winnipeg Shamrocks Lacrosse Team," *Manitoba Sports Hall of Fame,* http://www.halloffame.mb.ca/honoured/2004/1904Shamrocks.htm, accessed July 15, 2008.

208 Ibid.

209 Kem Murch, dir., *Lacrosse: The Creator's Game,* 25 min. DVD (Oakville, ON: Magic Lantern Communications, 1994).

210 Beers, *Lacrosse,* 8–9.

211 For further information, see "The Creator's Game" in the Prologue or the Code of Handsome Lake in the Introduction.

212 Dao Jao Dre, interview by Downey, August 10, 2011.

213 Ibid.

Metawewin

❷ Colonizing the Creator's Game in Residential Schools

1 Kâ-têpwêt is the Nêhiyawak Nation's word for the Qu'Appelle River Valley; it translates to "who calls?" Margaret Kovach, *Indigenous Methodologies: Characteristics, Conversations, and Contexts* (Toronto: University of Toronto Press, 2009), 62. The valley is also known as Kâ-têpwêt-Sîpiy (alternative spelling Katepwew-Sipiy), "calling river." Correspondence, Erica Violet Lee, December 7, 2016.

2 Winona Stevenson, "Calling Badger and the Symbols of the Spirit Languages: The Cree Origins of the Syllabic System," *Oral History Forum* 19–20 (1999–2000): 19–24.

3 Onawario (John Cree, Bear Clan, Kanien'kehá:ka of Kanehsatá:ke), interview by Allan Downey, October 22, 2011, Kanehsatá:ke, QC.

4 Joseph Hugonnard (also Hugonard) was a Catholic priest, Oblate of Mary Immaculate, and the first principal at the Catholic Qu'Appelle Industrial School, which opened in 1884. He remained in that role until 1917. "Hugonard, Joseph," *Dictionary of Canadian Biography Online* (Toronto: University of Toronto, 1998–2013), http://biographi.ca/en/bio.php?id_nbr=7459.

5 J.R. Miller, *Shingwauk's Vision: A History of Native Residential Schools* (Toronto: University of Toronto Press, 2009), 209.

6 Although this chapter discusses residential schools from Ontario to British Columbia, it pays particular attention to the Squamish Indian Residential School (also called St. Paul's) in North Vancouver and the Mohawk Institute in Brantford, Ontario, to help contextualize the chapters that focus on the Sḵwx̱wú7mesh and the Hodinöhsö:ni'. For more information on the use of sport and recreation in Canadian residential schools, see Janice Forsyth, "Bodies of Meaning: Sports and Games at Canadian Residential Schools," in *Aboriginal Peoples and Sport in Canada: Historical Foundations and Contemporary Issues,* ed. Janice Forsyth and Audrey R. Giles (Vancouver: UBC Press, 2013), 15–34; and Janice Forsyth, "The Indian Act and the (Re)shaping of Canadian Aboriginal Sport Practices," *International Journal of Canadian Studies* 35 (2007): 95–111.

7 For more in-depth accounts of the formation of the residential school system, see Miller, *Shingwauk's Vision*; and John S. Milloy, *A National Crime: The Canadian Government and the Residential School System, 1879–1986* (Winnipeg: University of Manitoba Press, 1999).

8 Milloy, *A National Crime,* 52.

9 Dominion of Canada, *Annual Reports of the Department of Indian Affairs 1881–1916, Library and Archives Canada,* http://www.bac-lac.gc.ca/eng/discover/aboriginal-heritage/first-nations/indian-affairs-annual-reports/Pages/introduction.aspx. Unless otherwise indicated, all Department of Indian Affairs annual reports are held in Library and Archives Canada and can be accessed at this link.

10 Forsyth, "Bodies of Meaning," 26; Forsyth, "The Indian Act and the (Re)shaping," 96.

11 Forsyth, "The Indian Act and the (Re)Shaping," 102; Forsyth, "Bodies of Meaning," 22.

12 K. Tsianina Lomawaima, "Domesticity in the Federal Indian Schools: The Power of Authority over Mind and Body," *American Ethnologist* 2 (1993): 229.

13 Agnes Jack, ed., *Behind Closed Doors: Stories from the Kamloops Indian Residential School*, rev. ed. (Penticton: Theytus Books, 2006), 15.

14 Milloy, *A National Crime*, 74.

15 Dominion of Canada, J. Hugonnard, *Annual Report of the Department of Indian Affairs for the Year Ended 31st December 1892* (Ottawa: Department of Indian Affairs, 1893), 204.

16 Colin D. Howell, *Blood, Sweat, and Cheers: Sport and the Making of Modern Canada* (Toronto: University of Toronto Press, 2001), 30.

17 Dominion of Canada, E. Dewdney, *Annual Report of the Department of Indian Affairs for the Year Ended 31st December 1890* (Ottawa: Department of Indian Affairs, 1891), xiv.

18 Dominion of Canada, J. Ansdell Macrae, *Annual Report of the Department of Indian Affairs for the Year Ended 31st December 1888* (Ottawa: Department of Indian Affairs, 1889), 146–47.

19 Lomawaima, "Domesticity," 228.

20 Dominion of Canada, T.P. Wadsworth, *Annual Report of the Department of Indian Affairs for the Year Ended 31st December 1889* (Ottawa: Department of Indian Affairs, 1900), 296.

21 The idea that organized sport could be used to reform and civilize Indigenous nations was not limited to residential schools in North America. As historian Greg Ryan explains, citing the example of Māori rugby, this perception was widespread throughout the British Empire: "[The motives for introducing rugby to the Māori were] no different from the motives underpinning the introduction of sport to indigenous populations throughout the British Empire during the nineteenth century – a blending of muscular Christianity and cultural imperialism in which the cooperation, discipline and healthful aspects of sport would supposedly enhance the civilising process and create common ground between coloniser and colonised." Greg Ryan, "The Paradox of Maori Rugby 1870–1914," in *Tackling Rugby Myths: Rugby and New Zealand Society, 1854–2004,* ed. Greg Ryan (Dunedin, NZ: University of Otago Press, 2005), 89.

22 Dominion of Canada, D. Duronquet, *Annual Report of the Department of Indian Affairs for the Year Ended 31st December 1881* (Ottawa: Department of Indian Affairs, 1882), 6. (Note: In the annual reports, D. Duronquet is spelled "DuRouquet" in 1881 and 1882, but "Duronquet" thereafter.)

23 Dominion of Canada, Geo. H. Hogbin, *Annual Report of the Department of Indian Affairs for the Year Ended 31st December 1897* (Ottawa: Department of Indian Affairs, 1898), 251.

24 Dominion of Canada, *Annual Reports of the Department of Indian Affairs for the Year Ended 31st December 1881–1900* (Ottawa: Department of Indian Affairs, 1881–1900).

25 Dominion of Canada, *Annual Report of the Department of Indian Affairs for the Year Ended 31st December 1895* (Ottawa: Department of Indian Affairs, 1896), 108.

26 Dominion of Canada, A.E. Wilson, *Annual Report of the Department of Indian Affairs for the Year Ended 31st December 1897* (Ottawa: Department of Indian

Affairs, 1898), 239; Dominion of Canada, A.E. Wilson, *Annual Report of the Department of Indian Affairs for the Year Ended 31st December 1899* (Ottawa: Department of Indian Affairs, 1900), 308.

27 Jack, *Behind Closed Doors,* 12; Forsyth, "The Indian Act and the (Re)shaping," 103.

28 Dominion of Canada, T.P. Wadsworth, *Annual Report of the Department of Indian Affairs for the Year Ended 31st December 1893* (Ottawa: Department of Indian Affairs, 1894), 173.

29 Dominion of Canada, Geo. Ley King, *Annual Report of the Department of Indian Affairs for the Year Ended 30th June 1896* (Ottawa: Department of Indian Affairs, 1897), 312.

30 Braden Paora Te Hiwi, "'Unlike their Playmates of Civilization, the Indian Children's Recreation Must Be Cultivated and Developed': The Administration of Physical Education at Pelican Lake Indian Residential School, 1926–1944," *Historical Studies in Education* 29, 1 (Spring 2017), 102.

31 Principal McVitty, Mount Elgin Institute, quoted in Elizabeth Graham, *The Mush Hole: Life at Two Indian Residential Schools* (Waterloo: Heffle, 1997), 286.

32 Dominion of Canada, T. Clarke, *Annual Report of the Department of Indian Affairs for the Year Ended 31st December 1886* (Ottawa: Department of Indian Affairs, 1887), 141.

33 Dominion of Canada, D. Duronquet, *Annual Report of the Department of Indian Affairs for the Year Ended 31st December 1892* (Ottawa: Department of Indian Affairs, 1893), 23.

34 Lomawaima, "Domesticity," 227–40; Forsyth, "The Indian Act and the (Re)shaping," 103–6; John Bloom, *To Show What an Indian Can Do: Sports at Native American Boarding Schools* (Minneapolis: University of Minnesota Press, 2000); Eric D. Anderson, "Using the Master's Tools: Resisting Colonization through Colonial Sports," *International Journal of Sport* 23, 2 (March 2006): 247–66; Jack, *Behind Closed Doors.*

35 Miller, *Shingwauk's Vision,* 218.

36 Forsyth, "The Indian Act and the (Re)shaping," 103–6; Mark Rifkin, *When Did Indians Become Straight? Kinship, the History of Sexuality, and Native Sovereignty* (New York: Oxford University Press, 2011), 149–50.

37 Anderson, "Using the Master's Tools," 249.

38 M. Ann Hall, "Cultural Struggle and Resistance: Gender, History, and Canadian Sport," in *Sport and Gender in Canada,* 2nd ed., ed. Kevin Young and Philip White (Don Mills, ON: Oxford University Press, 2007), 56.

39 Nancy Bouchier, *For the Love of the Game: Amateur Sport in Small-Town Ontario* (Montreal and Kingston: McGill-Queen's University Press, 2003), 119.

40 Brendan Hokowhitu, "Producing Elite Indigenous Masculinities," *Settler Colonial Studies* 2, 2 (2012), 29; Judith Butler, "Performative Acts and Gender Constitution: An Essay in Phenomenology and Feminist Theory," *Theatre Journal* 40, 4 (1988), 519.

41 Dominion of Canada, John B. Ashby, *Annual Report of the Department of Indian Affairs for the Year Ended 31st December 1896,* (Ottawa: Department of Indian Affairs, 1897), 320.

42 Dominion of Canada, *Annual Reports of the Department of Indian Affairs for the Year Ended 31st December 1879–1930* (Ottawa: Department of Indian Affairs, 1879–1930).

43 Forsyth, "The Indian Act and the (Re)shaping," 103–4.

44 Dominion of Canada, Jas. Dagg, *Annual Report of the Department of Indian Affairs for the Year Ended 30th June 1901* (Ottawa: Department of Indian Affairs, 1902).

45 Graham, *The Mush Hole*, 141.

46 Dominion of Canada, *Annual Report of the Department of Indian Affairs for the Year Ended 31st December 1889* (Ottawa: Department of Indian Affairs, 1890).

47 Dominion of Canada, T. Clarke, *Annual Report of the Department of Indian Affairs for the Year Ended 31st December 1890* (Ottawa: Department of Indian Affairs, 1891), 119.

48 Dominion of Canada, Martin Benson, "Report on the Mohawk Institute and Six Nations Boarding Schools, 1895," Department of Indian Affairs, RG 10, vol. 2006, reel C-11133, *Library and Archives Canada;* Dominion of Canada, Geo. Ley King, *Annual Report of the Department of Indian Affairs for the Year Ended 30th June 1897* (Ottawa: Department of Indian Affairs, 1898), 229; Dominion of Canada, *Annual Report of the Department of Indian Affairs for the Year Ended 31st March 1913* (Ottawa: Department of Indian Affairs, 1914), 335.

49 Dominion of Canada, *Annual Report of the Department of Indian Affairs for the Year Ended 30th June 1895* (Ottawa: Department of Indian Affairs, 1896), 106; Dominion of Canada, John Semmens, *Annual Report of the Department of Indian Affairs for the Year Ended 30th June 1896* (Ottawa: Department of Indian Affairs, 1897), 316; Dominion of Canada, A.J. McLeod, *Annual Report of the Department of Indian Affairs for the Year Ended 30th June 1893* (Ottawa: Department of Indian Affairs, 1894), 99; Dominion of Canada, T. Clarke, *Annual Report of the Department of Indian Affairs for the Year Ended 30th June 1890* (Ottawa: Department of Indian Affairs, 1891), 118.

50 Dominion of Canada, J. Hugonnard, *Annual Report of the Department of Indian Affairs for the Year Ended 30th June 1894* (Ottawa: Department of Indian Affairs, 1895), 193.

51 Dominion of Canada, CH. Marchal, *Annual Report of the Department of Indian Affairs for the Year Ended 30th June 1904* (Ottawa: Department of Indian Affairs, 1905), 399; Dominion of Canada, Sister Mary Amy, *Annual Report of the Department of Indian Affairs for the Year Ended 30th June 1905* (Ottawa: Department of Indian Affairs, 1906), 362; Dominion of Canada, Sister Theresine, *Annual Report of the Department of Indian Affairs for the Year Ended 30th June 1906* (Ottawa: Department of Indian Affairs, 1907), 437; Dominion of Canada, N. Coccola, *Annual Report of the Department of Indian Affairs for the Year Ended 30th June 1906* (Ottawa: Department of Indian Affairs, 1907), 420.

52 One of the most famous cases of the implementation of lacrosse occurred at the notorious Carlisle Indian Industrial School in Carlisle, Pennsylvania. Fearful that the school's male baseball players would be tempted to turn professional, the Carlisle administrators replaced their varsity baseball program with lacrosse in 1910. The Carlisle lacrosse team would go on to compete against some of the top American universities, finding success until 1918, when the school was con-

verted into a military hospital. Donald M. Fisher, *Lacrosse: A History of the Game* (Baltimore: Johns Hopkins University Press, 2002), 110–11.

53 Canada, Royal Commission on Aboriginal Peoples, *Report of the Royal Commission on Aboriginal Peoples*, vol. 1, *Looking Forward, Looking Back, Part Two: False Assumptions and a Failed Relationship*, Chapter 10, "Residential Schools" (Ottawa: Royal Commission on Aboriginal Peoples, 1996), 316, http://data2.archives.ca/e/e448/e011188230-01.pdf. A version of this quote also appears in Milloy, *A National Crime*, 37.

54 W.G. Beers, *Lacrosse: The National Game of Canada* (Montreal: Dawson Brothers, 1869), 32–33.

55 Dominion of Canada, A.J. McLeod, *Annual Report of the Department of Indian Affairs for the Year Ended 30th June 1893* (Ottawa: Department of Indian Affairs, 1894), 118 (emphasis added).

56 Dominion of Canada, J.A. Sinclair, *Annual Report of the Department of Indian Affairs for the Year Ended 30th June 1901* (Ottawa: Department of Indian Affairs, 1902), 375.

57 Miller, *Shingwauk's Vision*, 207-8.

58 The *Online Cree Dictionary* identifies "Metawewin" as the Nêhiyawak Nation's word for a game of any kind of sport, including lacrosse. However, Thomas Vennum identifies "Pakahatowan" as an alternative label for the game, which translates to "a ball for games." *Online Cree Dictionary;* Thomas Vennum, *Lacrosse Legends of the First Americans* (Baltimore: Johns Hopkins University Press, 2007), 3.

59 "We Pitisowewepahikan (Double Ball)," *Saskatchewan Indian Culture Centre*, http://www.sicc.sk.ca/archive/heritage/ethnography/cree/recreation/doubleball.html; Stewart Culin, *Games of the North American Indians*, Twenty-Fourth Annual Report of the Bureau of American Ethnology to the Secretary of the Smithsonian Institute, 1902–1903 (Washington, DC: Government Printing Office, 1907; reprint, New York: Dover, 1975), 648.

60 Quoted in Culin, *Games of the North American Indians*, 652. Quote also appears in Joseph B. Oxendine, *American Indian Sports Heritage* (Lincoln: University of Nebraska Press [1988] 1995), 58.

61 Dominion of Canada, Marchal, *Annual Report of the Department of Indian Affairs for the Year Ended 30th June 1904*, (Ottawa: Department of Indian Affairs, 1905), 399; Dominion of Canada, Sister Mary Amy, *Annual Report of the Department of Indian Affairs for the Year Ended 30th June 1905*, (Ottawa: Department of Indian Affairs, 1906), 362.

62 Homer G. Barnett, *The Coast Salish of British Columbia* (Eugene: University of Oregon, 1955), cited in R. Cole Harris, *The Resettlement of British Columbia: Essays on Colonialism and Geographical Change* (Vancouver: UBC Press, 1997), 69.

63 Paul Kane, "Wanderings of an Artist among the Indians of North America," *Canadian Journal* (Toronto, 1855), 276, cited in Culin, *Games of the North American Indians*, 573.

64 Ernie Harry, interview by Maynard Harry and Connie Wilson, April 29, 1996, audio recording and transcript, file TUS.1.2.DOC, Traditional Use Study, *Sliammon Treaty Society*. Quote at transcript page 17. All material from the Sliammon Treaty Society is used with permission.

65 Haley Lewis and Sarah Reid, "'When You Pick Up Your Stick, You're Picking Up History': B.C. Girls Get Ready for Lacrosse Action at NAIG," *CBC News*, April 18, 2017, http://www.cbc.ca/sports/naig/b-c-girls-get-ready-for-lacrosse -action-at-naigs-1.4073859.

66 Miller, *Shingwauk's Vision*, 90.

67 Jacqueline Gresko, "Durieu, Paul," *Dictionary of Canadian Biography Online* (Toronto: University of Toronto, 2000), http://www.biographi.ca/009004-119. 01-e.php?BioId=40202.

68 Ibid.

69 Recent research suggests that the Durieu system predated Durieu's arrival in British Columbia and was a hybrid rooted in the Oblate experience in France and the Red River colony and the work of Jesuit missionaries in Quebec and Oregon. Ibid. For the Squamish school, see Milloy, *A National Crime*, 56.

70 Miller, *Shingwauk's Vision*, 91.

71 Keith Thor Carlson, *The Power of Place, the Problem of Time: Aboriginal Identity and Historical Consciousness in the Cauldron of Colonialism* (Toronto: University of Toronto Press, 2010), 79.

72 Herbert Francis Dunlop, *Andy Paull: As I Knew Him and Understood His Times* (Vancouver: Order of the O.M.I. of St. Paul's Province, 1989), 8.

73 Ibid., 8–9.

74 Palmer Patterson, "Andrew Paull and Canadian Indian Resurgence" (PhD diss., University of Washington, 1962), 38.

75 Louis Miranda, interview by Reuben Ware, May 4, 1979, audio tape, Reuben Ware Collection, T4356:0014, *British Columbia Archives*. Quoted with permission from Chief Leanne Joe.

76 Patterson, "Andrew Paull," 35.

77 Miller, *Shingwauk's Vision*, 90.

78 Louis Miranda, interview by Ware, May 4, 1979.

79 Ibid.

80 Dominion of Canada, Marchal, *Annual Report of the Department of Indian Affairs for the Year Ended 30th June 1904*, (Ottawa: Department of Indian Affairs, 1905), 399; Dominion of Canada, Sister Mary Amy, *Annual Report of the Department of Indian Affairs for the Year Ended 30th June 1905* (Ottawa: Department of Indian Affairs, 1906), 362; Dominion of Canada, Sister Theresine, *Annual Report of the Department of Indian Affairs for the Year Ended 30th June 1906* (Ottawa: Department of Indian Affairs, 1907), 437.

81 There are various spellings of "serpent slayer," including Xwechtáal, Te Qoi-techetahl, and Quoichtal. Palmer Patterson used Te Qoitechetahl in his 1962 biography of Paull but recent works and articles have shifted the spelling to Xwechtáal. Patterson, "Andrew Paull," 39; Sla'wiya (Andrea Jacobs, Squamish), correspondence, March 13, 2011.

82 According to Palmer Patterson, "watchmen" functioned as both policemen and agents of the theocratic Durieu system. Their duties included gathering residents for meetings, whether they came voluntarily or not, bringing accused parties before the chiefs, and sometimes seeing that their punishment was carried out. Patterson, "Andrew Paull," 32.

83 Ibid.

84 Louis Miranda, interview by Ware, May 4, 1979.

85 Ibid.

86 Patterson, "Andrew Paull," 39.

87 Dunlop, *Andy Paull*, 24.

88 Brendan F.R. Edwards, "'I Have Lots of Help behind Me, Lots of Books, to Convince You': Andrew Paull and the Value of Literacy in English," *BC Studies* 164 (Winter 2009): 9.

89 Dunlop, *Andy Paull*, 24.

90 In Louis Miranda's version of the Skwxwú7mesh retelling of Qoitechetahl or Sínulhka (the Serpent), Te Qoitechetahl (the Serpent Slayer) is gifted with a medicinal bow by the two-headed serpent, used to feed his people, for his sacrifices leading up to the defeat of the serpent. Louis Miranda, interview by Ware, May 4, 1979.

91 Dominion of Canada, Sister Mary Amy, *Annual Report of the Department of Indian Affairs for the Year Ended 30th June 1905* (Ottawa: Department of Indian Affairs, 1906), 362.

92 For example, Chief Simon Baker, Khot-La-Cha, mentions this a great deal in his autobiography. Verna J. Kirkness, ed., *Khot-La-Cha: The Autobiography of Chief Simon Baker* (Vancouver: Douglas and McIntyre, 1994). Paitsmauk, Dave Jacobs, and Sla'wiya, Andrea Jacobs, also recounted similar stories about recreation at the school, in a series of 2010 interviews. Paitsmauk (Dave Jacobs) and Sla'wiya (Andrea Jacobs), interview by Allan Downey, July 22, 2010, August 6, 2010, August 12, 2010, audio recording and transcript, Capilano Reserve, BC.

93 Paitsmauk and Sla'wiya, interview by Downey, August 6, 2010.

94 Patterson, "Andrew Paull," 34.

95 Quoted in Dunlop, *Andy Paull*, 32–33.

96 Patterson, "Andrew Paull," 51.

97 According to the Dictionary of Canadian Biography Online, Joseph Capilano (SU-Á-PU-LUCK) was an influential Skwxwú7mesh chief who was heavily involved in Indigenous rights and land claims during the late nineteenth and early twentieth centuries. In 1906, he led a delegation of Indigenous leaders to meet and present their grievances to both Prime Minister Wilfrid Laurier in Ottawa and King Edward VII in London. Robin Fisher, "SU-Á-PU-LUCK (Joseph Capilano)," *Dictionary of Canadian Biography Online* (Toronto: University of Toronto, 2000), http://www.biographi.ca/009004-119.01-e.php?BioId=41214; Patterson, "Andrew Paull," 45.

98 Dominion of Canada, Benson, "Report on the Mohawk Institute and Six Nations Boarding Schools, 1895."

99 Dominion of Canada, A.J. McLeod, *Annual Report of the Department of Indian Affairs for the Year Ended 30th June 1895* (Ottawa: Department of Indian Affairs, 1896), 135.

100 Forsyth, "Bodies of Meaning," 22.

101 For more, see Mary-Ellen Kelm, *Colonizing Bodies: Aboriginal Health and Healing in British Columbia, 1900–1950* (Vancouver: UBC Press, 1998).

102 Milloy, *A National Crime*, 74.

103 Ibid.

104 Milloy, *A National Crime,* 52.

105 Department of Indian Affairs, *Calisthenics and Games Prescribed for Use in All Indian Schools* (Ottawa: Government Printing Bureau, 1910). In her discussion of this booklet, Janice Forsyth uses Foucault's power analysis to portray it as an example of discipline training as well as an attempt to combat poor health. See Forsyth, "Bodies of Meaning," 15–34; and Forsyth, "The Indian Act and the (Re)shaping," 102.

106 Kelm, *Colonizing Bodies,* 69.

107 Megan Sproule-Jones, "Crusading for the Forgotten: Dr. Peter Bryce, Public Health, and Prairie Native Residential Schools," *Canadian Bulletin of Medical History* 13 (1996): 211.

108 Milloy, *A National Crime,* 91, 101.

109 Milloy, *A National Crime,* 75.

110 Ibid.

111 Sproule-Jones, "Crusading for the Forgotten," 211.

112 Department of Indian Affairs, *Calisthenics and Games,* 3, 5.

113 Kelm, *Colonizing Bodies,* 69.

114 Department of Indian Affairs, *Calisthenics and Games,* 3.

115 Ibid., 17 (emphasis added).

116 Department of Indian Affairs, Memo: Indian Education [July 15, 1925], School Files Series - 1879–1953, RG 10, Mikan no. 157505, microform C-8134, *Library and Archives Canada.*

117 Forsyth, "Bodies of Meaning," 22.

118 Lomawaima, "Domesticity," 228.

119 Dominion of Canada, J.P. O'Neill, *Annual Report of the Department of Indian Affairs for the Year Ended 31st March 1909* (Ottawa: Department of Indian Affairs, 1910), 406.

120 Bloom, *To Show What an Indian Can Do,* 3.

121 Forsyth, "The Indian Act and the (Re)shaping," 103.

122 Quoted in Graham, *The Mush Hole,* 389.

123 Paitsmauk and Sla'wiya, interview by Downey, August 6, 2010 (emphasis added).

124 Jack, *Behind Closed Doors,* 11–12.

125 Ibid.

126 Quoted in Graham, *The Mush Hole,* 356.

127 Quoted in ibid., 470.

128 Ibid., 10.

129 Report of the Mohawk Institute, quoted in ibid., 135.

130 Paitsmauk and Sla'wiya, interview by Downey, August 6, 2010.

131 Quoted in Graham, *The Mush Hole,* 446.

132 Ibid., 10.

133 Fisher, *Lacrosse,* 117–18.

134 Bloom, *To Show What an Indian Can Do,* 51.

135 Truth and Reconciliation Commission of Canada, *Honouring the Truth, Reconciling for the Future: Summary of the Final Report of the Truth and Reconciliation Commission of Canada* (Winnipeg: Truth and Reconciliation Commission, 2015).

136 Canada, Royal Commission on Aboriginal Peoples, *Report of the Royal Commission on Aboriginal Peoples,* vol. 1, Chapter 10, 316.

137 Howell, *Blood, Sweat, and Cheers,* 38.

138 *Tewaarathon (Lacrosse): Akwesasne's Story of Our National Game* (Akwesasne: North American Indian Traveling College, 1978), 55.

139 Annual Reports of the Montreal Amateur Athletic Association, 1916–17, Montreal Amateur Athletic Association Fonds, MG 28, I 351, vol. 13, 14–15, *Library and Archives Canada.*

140 Alan Metcalfe, *Canada Learns to Play: The Emergence of Organized Sport, 1807–1914* (Don Mills, ON: Oxford University Press, 1987), 97.

141 *Tewaarathon (Lacrosse),* 55.

142 Dominion of Canada, Thomas G. Murphy, *Annual Report of the Department of Indian Affairs for the Year Ended 31st March 1930* (Ottawa: Department of Indian Affairs, 1931), 20–21.

143 Donald M. Fisher, "'Splendid but Undesirable Isolation': Recasting Canada's National Game as Box Lacrosse, 1931–1932," *Sport History Review* 36 (2005): 115.

144 Celia Haig-Brown, *Resistance and Renewal: Surviving the Indian Residential School* (Vancouver: Arsenal Pulp Press, 1988), 75.

145 Forsyth, "Bodies of Meaning," 26.

146 Hokowhitu, "Producing Elite Indigenous Masculinities," 29; Butler, "Performative Acts and Gender Constitution," 519.

Sk'éxwa7

❸ Articulating Indigenous Nationhood on the West Coast

1 Tiohtià:ke is "Montreal" in Kanien'kéha. Cecilia Chen, Janine MacLeod, and Astrida Neimanis, eds., *Thinking with Water* (Montreal and Kingston: McGill-Queen's University Press, 2013), 299; Karohní:io Delaronde and Jordan Engel, "Montreal in Mohawk," *The Decolonial Atlas,* https://decolonialatlas.wordpress.com/tag/mohawk/. Mooniyaang is "Montreal" in Anishinaabemowin. Dylan A.T. Miner, "Stories as Mshkiki: Reflections on the Healing and Migratory Practices of Minwaajimo," in *Centering Anishinaabeg Studies: Understanding the World through Stories,* ed. Jill Doerfler, Niigaanwewidam James Sinclair, and Heidid Kiiwetinepinesilk Stark (East Lansing: Michigan State University Press, 2013), 327. A version of this chapter is set to appear as Allan Downey, "Claiming 'Our Game': Sḵwx̱wú7mesh Lacrosse and the Performance of Indigenous Nationhood in the Early Twentieth Century," in *Making Men, Making History: Canadian Masculinities across Time and Place,* ed. Peter Gossage and Robert Rutherdale (Vancouver: UBC Press, 2018).

2 In a Dakelh creation story, 'Usdas steals water from his grandfather, who possesses all the water in the world. During his attempted escape, 'Usdas spills the water, creating the lakes and rivers in Dakelh Keyoh (central British Columbia). See Introduction, note 1 (page 260).

3 For a story about the arrival of the first CPR train on the West Coast, provided by Andy Paull during an interview with Major J.S. Matthews, see J.S. Matthews, ed., *Conversations with Khahtsahlano, 1932–1954* (Vancouver: Vancouver City Archives, 1955), 193. Major Matthews Collection, *Vancouver City Archives.*

Although the arrival of the train was compared to the return of Sínulhka (Qoitechetahl), the Serpent, it is important to note that the Coast Salish were already familiar with the wage-labour economy and the technological innovations of the industrial revolution. In fact, they were active participants in their development.

4 For more, see James Daschuk, *Clearing the Plains: Disease, Politics of Starvation, and the Loss of Aboriginal Life* (Regina: University of Regina Press, 2013).

5 R. Cole Harris, *The Resettlement of British Columbia: Essays on Colonialism and Geographical Change* (Vancouver: UBC Press, 1997), 68; Adele Perry, *On the Edge of Empire: Gender, Race, and the Making of British Columbia, 1849–1871* (Toronto: University of Toronto Press, 2001), 194.

6 Perry, *On the Edge of Empire*, 194.

7 Keith Thor Carlson, *The Power of Place, the Problem of Time: Aboriginal Identity and Historical Consciousness in the Cauldron of Colonialism* (Toronto: University of Toronto Press, 2010), 211.

8 John Lutz, *Makúk: A New History of Aboriginal-White Relations* (Vancouver: UBC Press, 2008), 8; R. Cole Harris, *Making Native Space: Colonialism, Resistance, and Reserves in British Columbia* (Vancouver: UBC Press, 2002), xxiv.

9 For example, see Wayne Suttles, "The Early Diffusion of the Potato among the Coast Salish," and Wayne Suttles, "The Plateau Prophet Dance among the Coast Salish," in Wayne Suttles, *Coast Salish Essays* (Vancouver: Talonbooks, 1987), 137–51, 152–98.

10 David S. Savelieff, *A History of the Sport of Lacrosse in British Columbia* (Vancouver, 1972), 7.

11 Ibid.

12 Gillian Poulter, "'Eminently Canadian': Indigenous Sports and Canadian Identity in Victorian Montreal," in *Hidden in Plain Sight: Contributions of Aboriginal Peoples to Canadian Identity and Culture*, ed. Cora J. Voyageur and David Newhouse (Toronto: University of Toronto, 2005), 364.

13 Donald M. Fisher, *Lacrosse: A History of the Game* (Baltimore: Johns Hopkins University Press, 2002), 34.

14 Lacrosse, Library and Archives Canada, MG 31, D85 22, *Library and Archives Canada;* "Prince Albert Lacrosse Team," 1891, photograph, H-33, *Prince Albert Historical Society Archives Collection Online,* H-33, http://sain.scaa.sk.ca/items/index.php/prince-albert-lacrosse-team-2;rad.

15 Karen L. Wall, *Game Plan: A Social History of Sport in Alberta* (Edmonton: University of Alberta Press, 2012), 61.

16 J.S. Matthews, "First Game of Lacrosse in British Columbia," Major Matthews Fonds, Private Records, microfiche AM0054.013.02554, file 504.E-9, *City of Vancouver Archives.*

17 Alexander M. Weyand and Milton R. Roberts, *The Lacrosse Story* (Baltimore: H. and A. Herman, 1965), 44.

18 *Constitution and Rules of the British Columbia Amateur Lacrosse Association, Adopted March 22nd, 1890,* Revised *April 8th, 1899* (Vancouver: Evans and Hastings Printers, 1899), 21, NW 796.347 B862a, *British Columbia Archives.*

19 Ibid., 10.

20 Perry, *On the Edge of Empire*, 196–97.

21 The Sḵwx̱wú7mesh know the game as K'exwa7 or alternatively as Sk'éxwa7. Sḵwx̱wú7mesh Nation member Dennis Joseph points out that K'exwa7 means "stick ball." The *Squamish-English Dictionary* also lists the word as meaning "to play modern lacrosse," whereas Sk'éxwa7 means "lacrosse match." ɬaʔamin Nation member Murray Mitchell notes that lacrosse, or its variant double ball, was widespread in other Coast Salish communities before colonization, and Stewart Culin also mentions lacrosse in various Coast Salish communities, including Kekequa. "Our Culture – Lacrosse," *Skwxwú7mesh Úxwumixw (Squamish Nation)*, http://www.squamish.net/about-us/our-culture/; "Lacrosse match" and "Play lacrosse [modern]" in *Skwxwu7mesh Snichim-Xweliten Snichim Skexwts/ Squamish-English Dictionary;* Murray and Nancy Mitchell, interview by Allan Downey, Kasia Zimmerman, and Tylor Richards, June 29, 2012, audio recording, Sliammon, BC; Stewart Culin, *Games of the North American Indians,* Twenty-Fourth Annual Report of the Bureau of American Ethnology to the Secretary of the Smithsonian Institute, 1902–1903 (Washington, DC: Government Printing Office, 1907; reprint, New York: Dover, 1975), 562, 573, 609.

22 Alexandra Harmon, *Indians in the Making: Ethnic Relations and Indian Identities around Puget Sound* (Berkeley: University of California Press, 1998), 8. One Sḵwx̱wú7mesh game that was popular before the introduction of the Hodinöhsö:ni' stick was Tck-kwalla (Tck-kwal-lah), a hybrid form of Sḵwx̱wú7mesh lacrosse and rugby. Although it did not use a stick, Sḵwx̱wú7mesh Chief August Jack Khahtsahlano described it as similar to lacrosse. By about 1900, its popularity among the Sḵwx̱wú7mesh had waned, but it still appeared in the oral histories of Sḵwx̱wú7mesh Elders. At the Vancouver City Archives in 1938, Chief Khahtsahlano was shown a three-pound, twelve-and-half-inch, black stone ball that had been unearthed at the corner of Cedar Street and Fourth Avenue in Vancouver. He recognized it as a Sḵwx̱wú7mesh ball. Matthews, *Conversations with Khahtsahlano,* 80.

23 Janice Forsyth, "The Indian Act and the (Re)shaping of Canadian Aboriginal Sport Practices," *International Journal of Canadian Studies* 35 (2007): 98.

24 Louis Miranda, interview by Reuben Ware, May 4, 1979 (emphasis added), audio tape, Reuben Ware Collection, T4356:0014, *British Columbia Archives.* Quoted with permission from Chief Leanne Joe.

25 Harris, *Making Native Space,* xxi.

26 Harmon, *Indians in the Making,* 3–4.

27 Ibid., 157.

28 Carlson, *The Power of Place,* 211.

29 Kim Anderson, *A Recognition of Being: Reconstruction Native Womanhood,* 2nd ed. (Toronto: Women's Press, 2016), 14.

30 *The Legend of Progress (as Told by the Squamish People),* created 1893–1960, transcript, Charles Warren Cates Fonds, inventory number 19, key 2294, box 1, *North Vancouver Museum and Archives.*

31 See Carlson, *The Power of Place,* 79.

32 Ibid., 80.

33 Len Corben, *Instant Replay: A Century of North Shore Sports Stories* (North Vancouver: Little Lonsdale, 2007), 32. In 1907, the Royal Agricultural and Industrial Society of British Columbia donated a cup for an Indian lacrosse championship. The "Indian Championship of British Columbia" was reportedly contested each year at the Victoria Day celebrations, which featured an Indian Sports Day. "Cup for Indian Lacrosse," *Victoria Daily Colonist,* June 29, 1907. Although evidence of the championships remains fragmented, the games continued throughout the 1910s. For example, a Skwxwú7mesh team travelled to the Duncan Indian Reserve in June 1919 to play against a W̱SÁNEĆ (Saanich) lacrosse team and to compete for the Indian Championship of British Columbia. "Indian Teams Go to Play Islanders," *Vancouver Province,* June 19, 1919.

34 Verna J. Kirkness, ed., *Khot-La-Cha: The Autobiography of Chief Simon Baker* (Vancouver: Douglas and McIntyre, 1994), 19–20; Palmer Patterson, "Andrew Paull and Canadian Indian Resurgence" (PhD diss., University of Washington, 1962), 185.

35 See Jean Barman, "Erasing Indigenous Indigeneity in Vancouver," *BC Studies* 155 (Autumn 2007): 3–30.

36 Robin Anderson, "Making Fun of Sport: James Fitzmaurice, Robert Ripley, and the Art of Sport Cartooning in Vancouver, 1907–1918," *Journal of Sport History* 37, 3 (Fall 2010): 370.

37 Allan Downey and Susan Neylan, "Raven Plays Ball: Situating 'Indian Sports Days' within Indigenous and Colonial Spaces in Twentieth-Century Coastal British Columbia," *Canadian Journal of History* 50, 3 (Winter 2015): 448.

38 "Jones to Handle Sport Attractions," *Vancouver Daily Province,* May 2, 1916.

39 "To Stage Indian Show and Real War Dance in Arena after Athletics," *Vancouver Daily Sun,* May 22, 1917.

40 Downey and Neylan, "Raven Plays Ball," 454.

41 "To Stage Indian Show and Real War Dance in Arena after Athletics," *Vancouver Daily Sun,* May 22, 1917.

42 Paitsmauk (Dave Jacobs) and Sla'wiya (Andrea Jacobs), interview by Allan Downey, June 26, 2011, audio recording and transcript, Capilano Reserve, BC.

43 "Indians Surprisingly Proficient in Sports at Victoria Day Meet," *Vancouver Daily Sun,* May 25, 1917; Rose Louie, Elsie Paul, and Agnes McGee, interview by Connie Wilson and Karen Galligos, June 24, 1996, audio recording and transcript, file MIS.34.35.36, "Miscellaneous Interviews," *Sliammon Treaty Society.* Information cited from transcript page 44.

44 "Several Indian Teams Will Play Baseball at Sports Here Thursday," *Vancouver Daily Times,* May 21, 1917.

45 Ibid.

46 "Indian Sports Will Make for Physical Betterment of Red-Skinned Athletes," *Vancouver Daily Sun,* May 7, 1917.

47 Paige Raibmon, *Authentic Indians: Episodes of Encounter from the Late-Nineteenth-Century Northwest Coast* (Durham, NC: Duke University Press, 2005), 62.

48 Forsyth, "The Indian Act and the (Re)shaping," 98–99; Government of Canada, *An Act to Amend the Indian Act,* S.C. 1914, 4 & 5, Geo. V, c.35, s.8, quoted

in Keith D. Smith, *Strange Visitors: Documents in Indigenous–Settler Relations in Canada from 1876* (Toronto: University of Toronto Press, 2014), 97.

49 Louis Miranda, interview by Ware, May 4, 1979.

50 "Old Indian Dance to Feature Sports," *Vancouver Daily Sun,* May 23, 1916.

51 Ibid.

52 Ibid. This quote also appears in Downey and Neylan, "Raven Plays Ball," 453.

53 Suttles, *Coast Salish Essays,* 228; see also Carlson, *The Power of Place,* 212.

54 "Several Indian Teams Will Play Baseball at Sports Here Thursday," *Vancouver Daily Times,* May 21, 1917.

55 "To Stage Indian Show and Real War Dance in Arena after Athletics," *Vancouver Daily Times,* May 22, 1917.

56 Paitsmauk and Sla'wiya, interview by Downey, June 26, 2011 (emphasis added).

57 Maggie Vivier, Charlie Bob, and David George, interview by Karen Galligos and Connie Wilson, May 28, 1996, audio recording and transcript, file and audio cassette TUS.29.30.31 and 32, Traditional Use Study, *Sliammon Treaty Society.* Quote from transcript page 77.

58 Susan Neylan with Melissa Meyer, "'Here Comes the Band!': Cultural Collaboration, Connective Traditions, and Aboriginal Brass Bands on British Columbia's North Coast, 1875–1964," *BC Studies* 152 (Winter 2006–07): 38.

59 Patterson, "Andrew Paull," 187.

60 Downey and Neylan, "Raven Plays Ball," 451.

61 "Indian Sports Will Make for Physical Betterment of Red-Skinned Athletes," *Vancouver Daily Sun,* May 7, 1917. This quote also appears in Downey and Neylan, "Raven Plays Ball," 453.

62 Paitsmauk (Dave Jacobs) and Sla'wiya (Andrea Jacobs), interview by Allan Downey, August 12, 2010 (emphasis added), audio recording and transcript, Capilano Reserve, BC.

63 Kirkness, *Khot-La-Cha,* 89 (emphasis added).

64 Neylan with Meyer, "'Here Comes the Band!,'" 38.

65 Paitsmauk (Dave Jacobs) and Sla'wiya (Andrea Jacobs), interview by Allan Downey, August 6, 2010, audio recording and transcript, Capilano Reserve, BC.

66 Andy Paul and Stella Timothy, interview by Kerri Timothy, May 13, 1996, audio recording and transcript, file TUS 15.16.Doc, Traditional Use Study, *Sliammon Treaty Society.*

67 See Downey and Neylan, "Raven Plays Ball," 466.

68 Controversially, the 1913 sale of the Kitsilano Reserve did not involve consultation with the majority of the Sḵwx̱wú7mesh leadership. Instead, a few Sḵwx̱wú7mesh spokespersons proceeded with the transaction. Although a select few Sḵwx̱wú7mesh members were paid for the land, according to Palmer Patterson, most Sḵwx̱wú7mesh leaders received no monetary benefit from the sale. Subsequently, the Sḵwx̱wú7mesh leaders who were not represented identified themselves as the rightful leaders and owners of the Kitsilano territory. They wrote to the Department of Indian Affairs, questioning the legality of the sale, though with little result. Jean Barman notes that the federal government was never approached during the course of the transaction and that the Squamish were under

constant pressure and threat to accede to it. Recognized as one of the biggest scandals in provincial history, the acquisition of the land helped prompt the subsequent amalgamation of the Sḵwx̱wú7mesh. Patterson, "Andrew Paull," 86; Barman, "Erasing Indigenous Indigeneity," 16–20.

69 Patterson, "Andrew Paull," 85–86.

70 Ibid., 86.

71 Ibid., 85.

72 Ibid., 90.

73 Carlson, *The Power of Place,* 80.

74 Lutz, *Makúk,* 217; Andrew Parnaby, *Citizen Docker: Making a New Deal on the Vancouver Waterfront, 1919–1939* (Toronto: University of Toronto Press, 2008), 87.

75 Parnaby, *Citizen Docker,* 88–89.

76 "Nats Winners over Indians," *Vancouver Province,* June 4, 1919.

77 "Canada's National Summer Game Is Growing All Over," *Vancouver Daily Sun,* May 25, 1919.

78 "Senior Amateur Lacrosse: Richmond Took Opener from I.L.A. Last Night," *Vancouver Sun,* May 18, 1920.

79 "Richmond – I.L.A. Open 1920 City League Schedule," *Vancouver Sun,* May 17, 1920.

80 Mary-Ellen Kelm, "Riding into Place: Contact Zones, Rodeo, and Hybridity in the Canadian West 1900–1970," *Journal of the Canadian Historical Association* 18, 1 (2007): 109.

81 For instance, the *Vancouver Sun* regularly commented on the crowd numbers and popularity of the team throughout the summer of 1920.

82 "Indians to Meet Richmond Tonight," *Vancouver Sun,* June 9, 1921.

83 "Andy Paull: Chief of Sport," *North Shore Outlook,* August 16, 2007.

84 Larry Power, "British Columbia Lacrosse Association, 1921–24," *Power's Bible of Lacrosse,* http://www.wampsbibleoflacrosse.com/newstats/bclaall.html; Dave Stewart-Candy, "Old School Lacrosse: From the Golden Age of Pro Lacrosse on the Pacific Coast (1909–1924)," https://oldschoollacrosse.wordpress.com/category/skwxwu7mesh/.

85 *Chehalis Lacrosse Team, on the Skwah Indian Reserve in 1907,* photograph, *Stó:lō Tribal Council,* http://stolotribalcouncil.ca/; Henry George Pennier, *'Call Me Hank': A Stó:lō Man's Reflections on Logging, Living, and Growing Old,* ed. Keith Thor Carlson and Kristina Fagan (Toronto: University of Toronto Press, 2006), 26.

86 Pennier, *'Call Me Hank,'* 28.

87 Patterson, "Andrew Paull," 139–43.

88 Herbert Francis Dunlop, *Andy Paull: As I Knew Him and Understood His Times* (Vancouver: Order of the O.M.I. of St. Paul's Province, 1989), 8; Patterson, "Andrew Paull," 174.

89 In 1910, railroad tycoon Sir Donald Mann donated the Mann Cup as a "challenge cup" for amateur lacrosse teams, and in 1925 the cup was established as the trophy of the national amateur senior lacrosse championship, which alternated between east and west each year. Savelieff, *A History of the Sport,* 11.

90 Fisher, *Lacrosse*, 48–50.

91 *Constitution and Rules of the British Columbia Amateur Lacrosse Association, Adopted March 22nd, 1890, Revised April 8th, 1899* (Vancouver: Evans and Hastings Printers, 1899), NW 796.347 B862a, *British Columbia Archives*.

92 Perry, *On the Edge of Empire*, 194.

93 For example, see various *Vancouver Sun* articles from May to July 1930, such as "Mann Cup Honors to Vancouver," May 26, 1930; "Baker is Star in the Nets," June 27, 1930; "Vancouver Beaten at Royal City," July 15, 1930; "Lacrosse Boys Drop One More," July 21, 1930.

94 Kirkness, *Khot-La-Cha*, 90.

95 Ibid., 91.

96 Louis Miranda, interview by Reuben Ware, June 1, 1979, audio tape, Reuben Ware Collection, T4356:0011, *British Columbia Archives*.

97 Ibid.

98 Dunlop, *Andy Paull*, 182.

99 Fisher, *Lacrosse*, 157.

100 Ibid., 158. According to the IPLL rules in 1932, "a team shall be composed of seven players, who shall be bona-fide members of the club they represent." Games consisted of "three 20-minute periods of actual play, with 10 minutes intermission between." "Montreal vs. Canadiens," *International Professional Lacrosse League Official Program*, 1932, author's collection.

101 For a complete history of the creation of box lacrosse, see Donald M. Fisher, "'Splendid but Undesirable Isolation': Recasting Canada's National Game as Box Lacrosse, 1931–1932," *Sport History Review* 36 (2005): 115–29. Information cited is from page 117.

102 Ibid, 117.

103 Ibid.

104 Ibid.

105 "Lacrosse Pros Set to Play," *Vancouver Sun*, June 20, 1931; "Indians Entering Lacrosse Battle," *Vancouver Sun*, June 23, 1931.

106 Fisher, "'Splendid but Undesirable Isolation,'" 123.

107 "Pros Make Comeback Tomorrow," *Vancouver Sun*, July 13, 1931. For examples of the early experiment with box lacrosse in BC and the importance of the Squamish Indians, see "Braves Nose Out Old Uns," *Vancouver Sun*, July 24, 1931, and "Lacrosse Has Large Night," *Vancouver Sun*, July 28, 1931.

108 Cleve Dheensaw, *Lacrosse 100: One Hundred Years of Lacrosse in B.C.* (Victoria: Orca, 1990), 46.

109 Patterson, "Andrew Paull," 182.

110 Herb Morden, quoted in "Andy Paull: Chief of Sport," *North Shore Outlook*, August 16, 2007.

111 Dunlop, *Andy Paull*, 184.

112 "No Tomahawk Tonight," *Vancouver Sun*, July 23, 1931.

113 Fisher, "'Splendid but Undesirable Isolation,'" 123.

114 Kirkness, *Khot-La-Cha*, 91; "Royals Nose Out Indians," *Vancouver Sun*, July 2, 1932.

115 Fisher, "'Splendid but Undesirable Isolation,'" 126.

116 *Tewaarathon (Lacrosse): Akwesasne's Story of Our National Game* (Akwesasne: North American Indian Traveling College, 1978), 152.

117 Fisher, *Lacrosse*, 153.

118 Ibid., 157.

119 Ibid., 154; "Indian Lacrosse Team in the Olympics," *Christian Science Monitor*, February 19, 1932.

120 "Indian Lacrosse Team in the Olympics," *Christian Science Monitor*, February 19, 1932.

121 "Clubmen Conquer Six Nations, 4 to 2," *New York Times*, June 12, 1932.

122 "Lacrosse Squad to Be Chosen," *Vancouver Sun*, July 12, 1932.

123 Dheensaw, *Lacrosse 100*, 108.

124 "Olympics on Show This Eve," *Vancouver Sun*, July 25, 1932.

125 Ibid.

126 "Lacrosse Series to Be Hard Fight, Says Royal City Expert," *Vancouver Sun*, July 21, 1932.

127 "Lacrosse Has 'Em Guessing," *Vancouver Sun*, August 8, 1932; Fisher, *Lacrosse*, 155.

128 For coverage on the tournament, see the following articles from the *Vancouver Sun*: "Lacrosse Has 'Em Guessing," August 8, 1932; "Lacrosse Boys are Brawling," August 10, 1932; "Canucks Nose Out Yankees," August 10, 1932; "Canada Couldn't Seem to Click Even on Lacrosse Field," August 13, 1932.

129 Fisher, *Lacrosse*, 152.

130 Stuart Thomson, "Vancouver All Stars Lacrosse Team Winners of Lally Cup 1935," June 26, 1935, photograph, Stuart Thomson Fonds, CVA 99-4764, *City of Vancouver Archives;* "Canucks Capture Lally Cup," *Vancouver Sun*, July 2, 1936.

131 "Squamish Braves Mowing Down the Lacrosse Enemy," *Vancouver Sun*, August 29, 1932.

132 Louis Miranda, interview by Reuben Ware, June 1, 1979, audio tape, Reuben Ware Collection, T4356:0011, *British Columbia Archives*.

133 Lutz, *Makúk*, 222–23.

134 Paitsmauk and Sla'wiya, interview by Downey, August 12, 2010.

135 Fisher, "'Splendid but Undesirable Isolation,'" 126.

136 Corben, *Instant Replay*, 32; "Indians and Pegs in Draw," *Vancouver Sun*, October 18, 1932.

137 "Indians and Pegs in Draw," *Vancouver Sun*, October 18, 1932.

138 "Squamish Clean Up at Lethbridge," *Vancouver Sun*, October 24, 1932.

139 Kirkness, *Khot-La-Cha*, 90; *Vancouver Sun*, 1933–34. See, for example, the following articles from the *Vancouver Sun*: "L-A-C-O-S-S-E by Andy Paull," August 5, 1933; "Speed of Lacrosse Draws 'Em," August 23, 1933; "Fishman- Louie Louis," June 1, 1934; "St. Helen's Knock Off League Leading Salmonbelly Crew," June 2, 1934.

140 For example, due to the increase in spectators, Queen's Park Arena in New Westminster had to be temporarily expanded to incorporate a thousand additional seats. "Baron of Lacrosse to Meet Tonight," *Vancouver Sun*, July 25, 1934.

141 Paitsmauk and Sla'wiya, interview by Downey, August 6, 2010.

142 This was not the first time that Paull turned to non-Skwxwú7mesh Indigenous players to help bolster his team rosters. In 1929, ła?amin Nation members Willie and Joe Gallagher helped Paull win the 1929 Senior "B" British Columbia baseball championship. Pete Galligos, interview by Maynard Harry and Joe Mitchell, December 15, 1995, audio recording and transcript, file MIS.9A.B, Miscellaneous Interviews, *Sliammon Treaty Society.* Information cited from transcript page 6. According to Rose Louie, the Skwxwú7mesh baseball team that Andy Paull coached often invited members of the ła?amin Nation to play for it: "Every summer, they go to North Van, Cookie, Alec, Joe Gallagher and Patty Tom, they used to go and play baseball for Squamish Band. They used to play at Mahon Park, gee, soon as they enter the field, everybody stands up and claps for them. Yeah, Alec Gallagher was really strong, bats the ball way far cause he had real strong arms on him. And then comes Patty Tom, he was a real fast little runner cause he was small and Joe Gallagher was like that too, but his brother was really good at it, Alec. Joe Gallagher had strong hands, but he wasn't a fast runner, Cookie was really good at pitching, Peta's brother." Rose Louie, Elsie Paul, and Agnes McGee, interview by Wilson and Galligos, June 24, 1996.

143 Corben, *Instant Replay,* 32.

144 Paitsmauk and Sla'wiya, interview by Downey, August 6, 2010.

145 For example, see various *Vancouver Sun* articles from June to August 1935, such as "Ten Thousand Fans Fill Arena as Indians Fight Back Only to Be Beaten in Final Rush," September 21, 1935.

146 "Cavallin's Goal Noses Redmen Out," *Vancouver Sun,* September 21, 1935.

147 Corben, *Instant Replay,* 32.

148 Daniel Francis, *L.D.: Mayor Louis Taylor and the Rise of Vancouver* (Vancouver: Arsenal Pulp Press, 2004), 116.

149 For example, before the start of the final game in the provincial championship in 1936, *Vancouver Sun* reporter Jack Patterson reflected on the deafening sound of the North Shore crowd and its "war drums." Jack Patterson, "Braves Waste No Time Eliminating Salmonbellies in Third Straight Game," *Vancouver Sun,* September 19, 1936. Reporters often mentioned the crowd and its "tom-toms."

150 Dunlop, *Andy Paull,* 182–83.

151 Paitsmauk and Sla'wiya, interview by Downey, August 6, 2010.

152 Paitsmauk and Sla'wiya, interview by Downey, June 26, 2011.

153 Ibid.

154 Ibid.

155 The Denman Arena burned down in the late summer of 1936. Kirkness, *Khot-La-Cha,* 90.

156 Paitsmauk, correspondence, March 13, 2011.

157 Paitsmauk and Sla'wiya, interview by Downey, August 6, 2010.

158 Kirkness, *Khot-La-Cha,* 90.

159 "North Shore Indians Leave for Eastern Lacrosse Fixtures," *Vancouver Sun,* September 25, 1936.

160 Andy Paull, "Indians Accorded Warm Welcome by Crowd at Kamloops," *Vancouver Sun,* September 26, 1936.

161 Ibid.

162 "Indians at Winnipeg," *Vancouver Sun,* October 2, 1936.

163 Allan Nickelson, "Andy Paull Grants an Interview and Picks His Indians," *Vancouver Sun,* October 2, 1936.

164 "Mann Cup Series Continues This Evening," *Toronto Globe and Mail,* October 5, 1936.

165 Andy Lytle, "Tormenting Terriers Tear Indian Encampments Apart," *Toronto Star,* October 3, 1936.

166 Andy Paull, "Indians Confident of Win," *Vancouver Sun,* October 5, 1936; Andy Paull, "Andy Confident of Win," *Vancouver Sun,* October 9, 1936.

167 Corben, *Instant Replay,* 34; Andy Paull, "Indians Confident of Win," *Vancouver Sun,* October 5, 1936.

168 Allan Nickelson, "Braves Looked Like Easy Winners in First Period but Terriers Went Wild," *Vancouver Sun,* October 3, 1936.

169 Andy Lytle, "Tormenting Terriers Tear Indian Encampments Apart," *Toronto Star,* October 3, 1936.

170 Paitsmauk and Sla'wiya, interview by Downey, August 6, 2010.

171 "Daughter of Lacrosse Coach Passes Away," *Toronto Globe and Mail,* October 2, 1936.

172 Fisher, *Lacrosse,* 106.

173 Paitsmauk and Sla'wiya, interview by Downey, August 6, 2010.

174 "Paull May Coach Indians," *Vancouver Sun,* June 17, 1937.

175 For more, see Patterson, "Andrew Paull."

176 "Paull May Coach Indians," *Vancouver Sun,* June 17, 1937.

177 "Indians Setback Burrards," *Vancouver Sun,* June 23, 1937.

178 Pat Slattery, "Indians Invited to South," *Vancouver Sun,* September 1, 1937.

179 Ibid.

180 Kirkness, *Khot-La-Cha,* 92.

181 Fisher, *Lacrosse,* 166; "Lacrosse Opens at Olympic," *Los Angeles Times,* January 8, 1939.

182 "Lacrosse Opens at Olympic," *Los Angeles Times,* January 8, 1939.

183 "Indians, Terriers Clash in Lacrosse Feature Tonight," *Los Angeles Times,* January 22, 1939.

184 Fisher, *Lacrosse,* 166.

185 "Adanac Lacrosse Team Victor," *Los Angeles Times,* April 25, 1939.

186 "Canadian Lacrosse Stars Migrate to Los Angeles," *Saskatoon Star Phoenix,* January 3, 1939.

187 "Lacrosse Loop Opens," *Montreal Gazette,* January 10, 1939.

188 "Will Reinstate Lacrosse Players," *Ottawa Citizen,* May 19, 1939; Fisher, *Lacrosse,* 166.

189 Kirkness, *Khot-La-Cha,* 92.

190 Dunlop, *Andy Paull,* 196.

191 Larry Power, "1945 Inter-city Box Lacrosse League," *Power's Bible of Lacrosse,* http://wampsbibleoflacrosse.com/newstats/1945ICLL.txt. For more on Ross Powless, see Chapter 4.

192 Carlson, *The Power of Place,* 80.

Ga-labs

❹ Box Lacrosse and Redefining Political Activism during the Mid-twentieth Century

1 "Fire Adds to Lacrosse Stick Shortage," *Montreal Gazette,* June 6, 1968.
2 Rick Hill (Tuscarora), interview by Allan Downey, June 7, 2011, audio recording and transcript, Six Nations Polytechnic, Six Nations of the Grand River Reserve, ON.
3 Audra Simpson, *Mohawk Interruptus: Political Life across the Borders of Settler States* (Durham, NC: Duke University Press, 2014), 115–16, 182–83.
4 Donald M. Fisher, "'Splendid but Undesirable Isolation': Recasting Canada's National Game as Box Lacrosse, 1931–1932," *Sport History Review* 36 (2005): 116.
5 Ibid., 117.
6 Bruce Kidd, *The Struggle for Canadian Sport* (Toronto: University of Toronto Press, 1996), 77.
7 "Constitution and By-Laws of the International Professional Lacrosse League," June 4, 1931, Conn Smythe Fonds, F 223-7-0-10, *Archives of Ontario.*
8 Len Smith, "Lacrosse Gossip," *Toronto Daily Star,* May 8, 1931.
9 Ibid.
10 Fisher, "'Splendid but Undesirable Isolation,'" 118–19.
11 Ibid., 117.
12 Fisher, "'Splendid but Undesirable Isolation,'" 126.
13 Ibid., 123, 124.
14 Kidd, *The Struggle for Canadian Sport,* 185.
15 Ibid., 209.
16 "Royals Nose Out Indians," *Vancouver Sun,* July 2, 1932.
17 Judy "Punch" Garlow Scrapbook 1 (c. 1932–33), Larry Power, *Power's Bible of Lacrosse,* http://wampsbibleoflacrosse.com/pictures/judy-scrap.html.
18 Ibid.
19 "Ross Powless Guest Speech at Banquet in Fergus," Larry Power, *Power's Bible of Lacrosse,* http://www.wampsbibleoflacrosse.com/newstats/ross.txt.
20 "Red Hawks Set for Battle with Crack Canadian Seven This Afternoon," March 5, 1933, newspaper clipping in Judy "Punch" Garlow Scrapbook 1.
21 Judy "Punch" Garlow Scrapbook 1; Judy "Punch" Garlow Scrapbook 2 (c. 1933–37), Larry Power, http://wampsbibleoflacrosse.com/pictures/judy-scrap.html.
22 "Lacrosse Final Billed; To Play Saturday Night," *Brantford Expositor,* November 25, 1932; Allan Downey, "Playing the Creator's Game on God's Day: The Controversy of Sunday Lacrosse Games in Haudenosaunee Communities, 1916–1924," *Journal of Canadian Studies* 49, 3 (2015): 111–43.
23 Judy "Punch" Garlow Scrapbook 2.
24 "Indian Star Summoned to Happy Hunting Grounds," *Toronto Daily Star,* July 24, 1937; Stan Shillington, "Down Memory Lane – Lance Isaacs," *Canadian Lacrosse Hall of Fame,* http://www.clhof.org/index.php/about/in-the-news/news/22-memory-lane/593-down-memory-lane-lance-isaacs. Regretfully, Lance Isaacs suffered a fatal heart attack during the intermission at a 1937 game. The *Toronto Daily Star* noted that he was "not only a highly skilled player, he was

always splendidly clean and gentlemanly in action." "Indian Star Summoned to Happy Hunting Grounds," *Toronto Daily Star,* July 24, 1937.

25 Judy "Punch" Garlow Scrapbook 2.
26 Donald M. Fisher, *Lacrosse: A History of the Game* (Baltimore: Johns Hopkins University Press, 2002), 223.
27 *Tewaarathon (Lacrosse): Akwesasne's Story of Our National Game* (Akwesasne: North American Indian Traveling College, 1978), 152. Part of this quote appears in Fisher, *Lacrosse,* 223.
28 *Tewaarathon (Lacrosse),* 152.
29 Annie Frazier Henry, dir., *Chiefs and Champions: Ross Powless,* DVD (Delta, BC: Big Red Barn Productions, 2005).
30 Sam Laskaris, "Ross Powless: Hall of Famer, Family Man," *Windspeaker,* July 2003, http://www.ammsa.com/content/ross-powless-footprints.
31 Ibid.
32 "Ross Powless Guest Speech at Banquet in Fergus."
33 Paull, quoted in Brendan F.R. Edwards, "A War of Wor(l)ds: Aboriginal Writing in Canada during the 'Dark Days' of the Early Twentieth Century" (PhD diss., University of Saskatchewan, 2008), 186.
34 Palmer Patterson, "Andrew Paull and Canadian Indian Resurgence" (PhD diss., University of Washington, 1962), 225.
35 Ibid., 226.
36 Ibid., 225–28.
37 Ibid., 227–56.
38 Ibid., 214, 228.
39 Billy Two Rivers (Kanien'kehá:ka of Kahnawà:ke), interview by Allan Downey, November 5, 2011, audio recording, Kahnawà:ke, QC.
40 Patterson, "Andrew Paull," 188.
41 Christopher Grosskurth and Robin Brown, "Lacrosse on the Six Nations Reserves," CBC Radio, July 30, 2003, *CBC Digital Archives,* http://www.cbc.ca/archives/entry/lacrosse-on-the-six-nations-reserves.
42 Kem Murch, dir., *Lacrosse: The Creator's Game,* 25 min. DVD (Oakville, ON: Magic Lantern Communications, 1994).
43 Larry Power, "Powless Family Statistics," *Power's Bible of Lacrosse,* http://www.wampsbibleoflacrosse.com/newstats/POWLESSES.txt; "Six Nations Lacrosse Star Voted into Hall of Fame," *Brantford Expositor,* June 18, 1999.
44 Power, "Powless Family Statistics."
45 Nanaimo District Museum, "Voices of the Snuneymuxw First Nation," 2007, *Virtual Museum of Canada,* http://www.snuneymuxwvoices.ca/english/lacrosse_elders.asp, accessed August 6, 2013.
46 Ernie Harry, interview by Maynard Harry and Connie Wilson, April 29, 1996, audio recording and transcript, file TUS.1.2.DOC, Traditional Use Study, *Sliammon Treaty Society.* Information cited from transcript page 17.
47 Lacrosse did not become Canada's national sport until 1994. For more, see Chapter 1, note 4 (page 267).
48 Bill Good, Maria Barnett, and Bill McNeil, "Lacrosse Is in a State of Crisis," *CBC Radio,* April 2, 1957, *CBC Digital Archives,* http://www.cbc.ca/archives/

categories/sports/lacrosse/lacrosse-a-history-of-canadas-game/lacrosse-is-in-a
-state-of-crisis.html.

49 Fisher, *Lacrosse,* 230.

50 Nanaimo District Museum, "Voices of the Snuneymuxw First Nation"; "Mann Cup – Past Winners," *TSN Online,* http://www.tsn.ca/lacrosse/feature/?id=724, accessed August 8, 2013.

51 Names of marquee players originally from Nanaimo District Museum, "Voices of the Snuneymuxw First Nation." The Nanaimo Native Sons 1951 roster is from Larry Power, "1951 Inner-City Box Lacrosse League," *Power's Bible of Lacrosse,* http://wampsbibleoflacrosse.com/newstats/1951ICLL.txt.

52 Nanaimo District Museum, "Voices of the Snuneymuxw First Nation."

53 Ibid.

54 "2009 Induction Banquet Program," *Nanaimo Museum and Sports Hall of Fame,* http://www.nanaimomuseum.ca/web_documents/shof_program2009final. pdf, accessed August 10, 2013.

55 Ernie Mitchell (Kaheranoron, Wolf Clan, Kanien'kehá:ka of Ahkwesáhsne) and David White (Kanien'kehá:ka of Ahkwesáhsne), interview by Allan Downey, September 23, 2011, audio recording and transcript, Cornwall, ON.

56 Ibid.

57 Joe Delaronde (Kanien'kehá:ka of Kahnawà:ke), interview by Allan Downey, October 21, 2011 (emphasis added), audio recording, Kahnawà:ke, QC.

58 Joe Delaronde (Kanien'kehá:ka of Kahnawà:ke) and Greg Horn (Kanien'kehá:ka of Kahnawà:ke), interview by Allan Downey, June 2, 2011, audio recording, Kahnawà:ke, QC.

59 Onawario (John Cree, Bear Clan, Kanien'kehá:ka of Kanehsatá:ke), interview by Allan Downey, October 22, 2011, Kanehsatá:ke, QC.

60 Joe Delaronde and Greg Horn, interview by Downey, June 2, 2011.

61 Ibid.

62 Joe Delaronde (Kanien'kehá:ka of Kahnawà:ke), interview by Allan Downey, April 29, 2011, audio recording, Kahnawà:ke, QC.

63 Gerald F. Reid, "Illegal Alien? The Immigration Case of Mohawk Ironworker Paul K. Diabo," *Proceedings of the American Philosophical Society* 151, 1 (March 2007): 65.

64 Gerald R. Alfred, *Heeding the Voices of Our Ancestors: Kahnawake Mohawk Politics and the Rise of Native Nationalism* (Toronto: Oxford University Press, 1995), 78, 196.

65 R. Cole Harris, *Making Native Space: Colonialism, Resistance, and Reserves in British Columbia* (Vancouver: UBC Press, 2002), xxi.

66 Onawario (John Cree, Bear Clan, Kanien'kehá:ka of Kanehsatá:ke) and Victor Bonspille (Kanien'kehá:ka of Kanehsatá:ke), interview by Allan Downey, June 4, 2011, audio recording, Kanehsatá:ke, QC.

67 In 1653, the Onöñda'gega' approached the French in New France to seek peace and solidify a trade relationship to assist in their fight against the Eries. The Kanien'kehá:ka, protectors of the eastern door of the Hodinöhsö:ni' Confederacy, were enemies of the French and were not pleased that the Onöñda'gega' had

potentially broken Confederacy protocol and bypassed them to approach the French. José António Brandão, *"Your Fyre Shall Burn No More": Iroquois Policy toward New France and Its Native Allies to 1701* (Lincoln: University of Nebraska Press, 1997), 105–7. Adding to the isolation of the Kanien'kehá:ka was their late-seventeenth-century migration to Kentaké, which saw the nation develop a distinct and combined Christian Kanien'kehá:ka identity while taking advantage of Kentaké's strategic trading location. While continuing to assert their political authority and autonomy in early English and French Canada, the new Kanien'kehá:ka communities along the St. Lawrence River maintained their cultural and family ties with the Confederacy but also increasingly became politically isolated and autonomous. Alfred, *Heeding the Voices,* 44, 58–59. In the early twentieth century, as the Kanien'kehá:ka – especially at Kahnawà:ke – began a traditional revival and attempted to distance themselves from the Indian Act and Christianity, they soon discovered that the traditional leadership of the other nations had espoused what they saw as a Christian Longhouse adaption known as the Code of Handsome Lake. Alfred, *Heeding the Voices,* 69. As Alfred explains, "The Mohawks, who through a return to traditionalism were rejecting their own Christian background, were dismayed to find that most of their Iroquois brothers and sisters had adopted a religion based in part on Christian teachings! ... Exposed to the mechanisms and procedures of Iroquois governance, the Mohawks found they did not share the values underpinning the contemporary Confederacy's formal structures. Alone again, the Mohawks of Kahnawake, joined by most Mohawks in the nation's other communities at Akwesasne (near Cornwall, Ontario) and Kanehsatake (northwest of Montreal), began to develop an ideology which attempted to replicate the 'authentic' Confederacy before it had been altered by the influence of Handsome Lake." Alfred, *Heeding the Voices,* 69.

68 Traditionalism, in a Hodinöhsö:ni' context, refers to the restoration of the political and cultural institutions of the Hodinöhsö:ni' Confederacy and Longhouse epistemology for the purpose of establishing and maintaining political and cultural sovereignty. José Barreiro, ed., *Thinking in Indian: A John Mohawk Reader* (Golden, CO: Fulcrum, 2010), 203. This is covered in greater detail in Chapter 5.

69 Onawario and Victor Bonspille, interview by Downey, June 4, 2011.

70 Joe Delaronde, interview by Downey, April 29, 2011.

71 Onawario and Victor Bonspille, interview by Downey, June 4, 2011.

72 Ibid.

73 Ernie Mitchell and David White, interview by Downey, September 23, 2011. There have been several leagues known as the North American Lacrosse League and/or the North American Lacrosse Association (NALA). On September 21, 1974, the Hodinöhsö:ni'-based NALA held its seventh annual league banquet, thus dating it to at least 1967. However, the Can-Am Lacrosse League, which owes its formation to the NALA, dates the league's foundation to 1969. "North American Lacrosse Association – Chief 74-75," box file, *Woodland Cultural Centre Research Library;* "League Info," *Can-Am Lacrosse League,* online, accessed May 17, 2013.

74 "North American Lacrosse Association – Chief 74–75."

75 Rick Hill (Tuscarora), interview by Allan Downey, March 9, 2011, audio recording and transcript, Six Nations Polytechnic, Six Nations of the Grand River Reserve, ON.

76 Joe Delaronde, interview by Downey, April 29, 2011.

77 "President's Cup History," *Canadian Lacrosse Association*, http://presidentscup. pointstreaksites.com/view/presidentscup/history-1/presidents-cup-history-1.

78 The Senior "B" national championship is represented by the President's Cup, established in 1964, in which a national playoff takes place between a western Canada representative(s) and eastern Canada representative(s). Ibid.

79 Ibid.

80 Quoted in Grosskurth and Brown, "Lacrosse on the Six Nations Reserves."

81 "Race Discrimination in Football, Lacrosse," *Toronto Star,* August 7, 1965.

82 Paitsmauk (Dave Jacobs) and Sla'wiya (Andrea Jacobs), interview by Allan Downey, August 6, 2010, audio recording and transcript, Capilano Reserve, BC.

83 Joe Delaronde, interview by Downey, April 29, 2011.

84 Onawario and Victor Bonspille, interview by Downey, June 4, 2011.

85 Onawario, interview by Downey, October 22, 2011.

86 Ibid.

87 Larry Power, "1969 Major/Senior A Statistics," *Power's Bible of Lacrosse*, http://www. wampsbibleoflacrosse.com/newstats/1969seniora.txt; Ibid., "1970 Major/Senior A Statistics," http://www.wampsbibleoflacrosse.com/newstats/1970seniora.txt.

88 "Six Nations Sports," *Tekawennake*, September 29, 1971.

89 Ibid.

90 Steve Milton, "All in the Family Is a Lacrosse Tradition," *Hamilton Spectator,* February 19, 2000, private collection of Gaylene Powless.

91 In a *Montreal Gazette* article titled "The Fans Love Mitchell; Now Hawks Know Why," reporter Bob Morrissey described Ernie Mitchell as a fan favourite, citing his spectacular saves, energetic plays, and likable personality. Throughout Ernie's career, numerous press articles referred to his sensational play and his ability to captivate audiences. Ernie Mitchell, Kaheranoron, Scrapbook, *Akwesasne Cultural Center Library.*

92 André Ouimet, *North American All-Indian Field Lacrosse Championship*, Original Program 1, no. 5, (N.P: *Cue Theatre Magazine Ltd.*, 1967), author's collection.

93 Grosskurth and Brown, "Lacrosse on the Six Nations Reserves."

94 Laskaris, "Ross Powless: Hall of Famer."

95 Dominion of Canada, Thos. S. Walton, *Annual Report of the Department of Indian Affairs for the Year Ended 31st December 1885* (Ottawa: Department of Indian Affairs, 1886), 9; Dominion of Canada, E. Dewdney, *Annual Report of the Department of Indian Affairs for the Year Ended 31st December, 1888* (Ottawa: Department of Indian Affairs, 1889), xxxi; Dominion of Canada, J. Ansdell Macrae, *Annual Report of the Department of Indian Affairs for the Year Ended 30th June 1893* (Ottawa: Department of Indian Affairs, 1894), 35; Dominion of Canada, George Long, *Annual Report of the Department of Indian Affairs for the Year Ended 31st December 1892* (Ottawa: Department of Indian Affairs, 1893), 28; Dominion of Canada, John A. Macdonald, *Annual Report of the Department of*

Indian Affairs for the Year Ended 31st December 1885 (Ottawa: Department of Indian Affairs, 1886), xxviii.

96 Thomas Vennum, *American Indian Lacrosse: Little Brother of War* (Baltimore: Johns Hopkins University Press, 1994), 285.

97 Fisher, *Lacrosse,* 257.

98 Ibid.

99 Vennum, *American Indian Lacrosse,* 285.

100 Grosskurth and Brown, "Lacrosse on the Six Nations Reserves." This has also been shared with me on numerous occasions by various families in the Hodinöhsö:ni' communities I have visited.

101 Jim Calder and Ron Fletcher, *Lacrosse: The Ancient Game* (Toronto: Ancient Game Press, 2011), 28.

102 Rick Hill, interview by Downey, June 7, 2011.

103 The website of the Haudenosaunee Confederacy states that the Kayeneren:kowa (Great Law of Peace) "is the founding constitution of the Haudenosaunee Confederacy and is the underlying basis for Haudenosaunee society. Originally it outlined the path to harmony and unity among the warring nations and set out a proper form of government which allowed for the ideas of peace, power and righteousness. Throughout its verses it explains the function of the Grand Council and outlines a plan for nations to resolve disputes and uphold the peace. It outlines all processes which may face the Haudenosaunee as explained by the Peacemaker. Leadership within the system is from the ground up making the leaders truly accountable to their people. It outlines the responsibilities of all Chiefs as well as the method of impeachment in the event that a Chief does not perform his duties to the satisfaction of his people." "The Great Law of Peace," *Haudenosaunee Confederacy,* http://www.haudenosauneeconfederacy.com/greatlawofpeace.html, accessed June 10, 2017.

104 The Peacemaker was a messanger who brought the Kayeneren:kowa (Great Law of Peace) to the five original Hodinöhsö:ni' nations and, as Susan M. Hill explains, "taught the Haudenosaunee how to live in balance with each other as human beings of a collective territory." Susan Hill, *The Clay We Are Made Of: Haudenosaunee Land Tenure on the Grand River* (Winnipeg: University of Manitoba Press, 2017), 15–16. For more information, see Hill, *The Clay We Are Made Of*; Lina Sunseri, *Being Again of One Mind: Oneida Women and the Struggle for Decolonization* (Vancouver: UBC Press, 2011); Theresa McCarthy, *In Divided Unity: Haudenosaunee Reclamation at Grand River* (Tucson: University of Arizona Press, 2016); Brian Rice, *The Rotinonshonni: A Traditional Iroquoian History through the Eyes of Teharonhia:wako and Sawiskera* (Syracuse: Syracuse University Press, 2013).

105 Rice, *The Rotinonshonni,* 199.

106 For a second rendition of the four warriors story, by Dao Jao Dre (Delmor Jacobs, Cayuga, Wolf Clan, Six Nations of the Grand River), see Calder and Fletcher, *Lacrosse,* 29; and Rice, *The Rotinonshonni,* 198. For a brief overview of the connection between Sganyadai:yo' and lacrosse, see Chapter 1.

107 Dao Jao Dre (Delmor Jacobs, Cayuga, Wolf Clan, Six Nations of the Grand River), interview by Allan Downey, June 7, 2011, audio recording and transcript, Six Nations of the Grand River Reserve, ON.

108 Ibid.

109 Vennum, *American Indian Lacrosse*, 287.

110 Ibid.

111 Dao Jao Dre (Delmor Jacobs, Cayuga, Wolf Clan, Six Nations of the Grand River), interview by Allan Downey, June 4, 2011, audio recording, Six Nations of the Grand River Reserve, ON.

112 Alfred, *Heeding the Voices*, 68–69.

113 Onawario and Victor Bonspille, interview by Downey, June 4, 2011.

114 Quoted in Grosskurth and Brown, "Lacrosse on the Six Nations Reserves."

115 James Teit, *Traditions of the Thompson River Indians of British Columbia* (Boston: Houghton, Mifflin, 1898), 116, 78–79.

116 Vennum, *American Indian Lacrosse*, 31; A. Irving Hallowell, Jennifer S.H. Brown, and Susan Elaine Grey, eds., *Contributions to Ojibwe Studies: Essays, 1934–1972* (Lincoln: University of Nebraska Press, 2010), 411.

117 This section and title are informed by the work of Glen Coulthard in *Red Skin, White Masks: Rejecting the Colonial Politics of Recongition* (Minneapolis: University of Minnesota Press, 2014). Unlike governing bodies such as the National Collegiate Athletic Association and American field lacrosse generally, those of Canadian box lacrosse continued to allow the wooden stick at the highest levels of competition, but it was increasingly surpassed by the plastic stick from the 1970s to the 1990s. It was eventually banned by the professional box lacrosse league, the National Lacrosse League, and by the Western Lacrosse Association, though some eastern senior league associations (such as the Ontario Lacrosse Association) still permit its use.

118 See, for example, Downey, "Playing the Creator's Game on God's Day"; Janice Forsyth, "The Indian Act and the (Re)shaping of Canadian Aboriginal Sport Practices," *International Journal of Canadian Studies* 35 (2007), 95–111.

119 "Civic Centre Site of Indian Events," *Tekawennake*, July 21, 1971.

120 Article title unknown, *Tekawennake*, September 14, 1971 (emphasis added). As political scientist Hugh Donald Forbes argues, Prime Minister Pierre Trudeau originally campaigned on the promise of the "just society" and introduced the concept of official multiculturalism in the House of Commons in 1971. Although the idea of Canada as a multicultural nation-state was not new, Trudeau helped solidify it in politics and law, eventually leading to the 1982 Charter of Rights and Freedoms. He hoped to create "a state or society that would strive to be as neutral with respect to all traditional national or ethnic cultures as the modern liberal state tried to be with respect to particular religions." Hugh Donald Forbes, "Trudeau as the First Theorist of Canadian Multiculturalism," in *Multiculturalism and the Canadian Constitution*, ed. Stephen J. Tierney (Vancouver: UBC Press, 2007), 28. However, what Trudeau was quickly reminded of – the failure of the 1969 White Paper on Indians remains the best example – was that Indigenous peoples were at the very least legally, culturally, and politically distinct in their relationship with the Canadian state. Many Indigenous nations would further argue that they are not part of the nation-state that has been "naturalized" as the only sovereign polity within its colonial borders. Glen Coulthard adds to this by suggesting that since the 1970s, the Canadian state has shifted toward policies of

"Aboriginal" recognition and subjecthood, attempting to portray colonialism as a thing of the past while continuing to undermine Indigenous nationhood and self-determination. Coulthard, *Red Skin, White Masks.*

121 See Coulthard, *Red Skin, White Masks;* Taiaiake Alfred and Jeff Corntassel, "Being Indigenous: Resurgences against Contemporary Colonialism," *Government and Opposition* 40, 4 (Autumn 2005): 597–614; and Simpson, *Mohawk Interruptus.*

122 Roster Sheet, "Misc. Sports 72-75-76," vertical files, *Woodland Cultural Centre Research Library* (hereafter Woodland vertical files); "Six Nations Retains Title," *Tekawnnake,* September 10, 1975.

123 "All-Indian Tournament," *Belleville Intelligencer,* August 30, 1976, "Lacrosse: 1973–1974, 1977–78–79," Woodland vertical files.

124 Ibid.

125 Myra Rutherdale and J.R. Miller, "It's Our Country: First Nations' Participation in the Indian Pavilion at Expo '67," *Journal of the Canadian Historical Association* 17, 2 (Spring 2006): 148–73.

126 Christine M. O'Bonsawin, "Indigenous Peoples and Canadian-Hosted Olympic Games," in *Aboriginal Peoples and Sport in Canada: Historical Foundations and Contemporary Issues,* ed. Janice Forsyth and Audrey R. Giles (Vancouver: UBC Press, 2013), 36.

127 Ibid., 36–37.

128 Rutherdale and Miller, "It's Our Country," 154.

129 Ouimet, *North American All-Indian Field Lacrosse Championship.*

130 Ibid.

131 O'Bonsawin, "Indigenous Peoples and Canadian-Hosted Olympic Games," 39.

132 Dan Powers, "Indians Worried about Participation," *Edmonton Journal,* September 3, 1977, "Lacrosse: 1973–1974, 1977–78–79," Woodland vertical files.

133 Ibid.

134 Ibid.

135 Ibid.; Dan Powers, "Natives Not Invited to Take Part in Lacrosse," *Edmonton Journal,* September 10, 1977, "Lacrosse: 1973–1974, 1977–78–79," Woodland vertical files.

136 "Authenticity," *Edmonton Journal,* September 16, 1977, "Lacrosse: 1973–1974, 1977–78–79," Woodland vertical files.

137 "Native Lacrosse Players Reject Token Role," *Edmonton Journal* March 7, 1978, "Lacrosse: 1973–1974, 1977–78–79," Woodland vertical files.

138 Ibid.

139 Downey, "Playing the Creator's Game on God's Day," 135.

140 Dan Powers, "Campagnolo Will Investigate Lacrosse Dispute," *Edmonton Journal,* March 11, 1978, "Lacrosse: 1973–1974, 1977–78–79," Woodland vertical files.

141 Ibid.

142 Dan Powers, "Lacrosse Issue Is Still Alive – Natives," *Edmonton Journal,* March 22, 1978, "Lacrosse: 1973–1974, 1977–78–79," Woodland vertical files.

143 Quoted in ibid.

144 Ibid.

145 Dan Powers, "Aboriginals Seek Lacrosse Match during Games," *Edmonton Journal,* April 21, 1978, "Lacrosse: 1973–1974, 1977–78–79," Woodland vertical files.

146 Although newspaper reports agree that one of the teams would be the St. Regis Warriors, they supply contradictory information concerning the second team. Some articles report that it was from the Six Nations of the Grand River Reserve, whereas others refer to the Caughnawaga Braves (Kahnawà:ke), the latter being most likely.

147 "Official Doubts Natives Will Play Games Lacrosse," *Edmonton Journal,* May 4, 1978, "Lacrosse: 1973–1974, 1977–78–79," Woodland vertical files.

148 Allen Abel, "Brave Warriors Are Covered by Hokum," *Toronto Globe and Mail,* August 12, 1978, "Lacrosse: 1973–1974, 1977–78–79," Woodland vertical files.

149 "Lacrosse Takes the Commonwealth Games by Storm," CBC TV, August 9, 1978, *CBC Digital Archives,* http://www.cbc.ca/player/Sports/Digital+Archives/Lacrosse/ID/1795857002/?sort=MostPopular.

150 Abel, "Brave Warriors Are Covered by Hokum."

151 Ibid.

Dey-Hon-Tshi-Gwa'-Ehs
❺ Reclaiming the Creator's Game
For an earlier version of this chapter, see Allan Downey, "Engendering Nationality: Haudenosaunee Tradition, Sport, and the Lines of Gender," *Journal of the Canadian Historical Association* 23, 1 (2012): 319–54.

1 "The Great Ball Game between the Winged Birds and the Four-Legged Animals," in *Tewaarathon (Lacrosse): Akwesasne's Story of Our National Game* (Akwesasne: North American Indian Traveling College, 1978), 21–24. A version of this story also appears in Jim Calder and Ron Fletcher, *Lacrosse: The Ancient Game* (Toronto: Ancient Game Press, 2011), 31.

2 Audra Simpson, *Mohawk Interruptus: Political Life across the Borders of Settler States* (Durham, NC: Duke University Press, 2014), 147.

3 After several months of work, Minister of Indian Affairs Jean Chrétien delivered the *Statement of the Government of Canada on Indian Policy* on June 25, 1969, better known as the 1969 White Paper. Although Ottawa saw the White Paper as new and groundbreaking, its critics quickly dismissed it as yet another attempt to assimilate Indigenous peoples into Canadian society. The White Paper played a definitive role in the resurgence of Indigenous issues. Before its appearance, Indigenous-led organizations, such as the National Indian Brotherhood and the Native Council of Canada, were finding it extremely difficult to unify Indigenous voices from across the country in a common cause. It was, in part, the White Paper that provided a catalyst for this.

4 Troy Johnson, "The Occupation of Alcatraz Island: Roots of American Indian Activism," *Wicazo Sa Review* 10, 2 (Autumn 1994): 77; Rick Monture, *We Share Our Matters: Two Centuries of Writing and Resistance at Six Nations of the Grand River* (Winnipeg: University of Manitoba Press, 2014), 153.

5 Monture, *We Share Our Matters,* 141–42.

6 Robert Anderson, Joanna Brown, Jonny Lerner, and Barbara Lou Shafer, eds., *Voices from Wounded Knee, 1973: In the Words of the Participants* (Rooseveltown, NY: Akwesasne Notes, 1974), 96–97.

7   Mark Dockstator, "Aboriginal Representations of History and the Royal Commission on Aboriginal Peoples," in *Walking a Tightrope: Aboriginal People and Their Representations,* ed. Ute Lischke and David McNab (Waterloo: Wilfrid Laurier University Press, 2005), 105.

8   Rick Hill would later have an accomplished career in teaching at SUNY Buffalo, as a museum curator, and as the director of public programs for the National Museum of the American Indian at the Smithsonian Institution, and he would go on to be the senior project co-ordinator at the Deyohagá:ga: Indigenous Knowledge Centre at Six Nations Polytechnic. Rick Hill (Tuscarora), interview by Allan Downey, March 9, 2011, audio recording and transcript, Six Nations Polytechnic, Six Nations of the Grand River Reserve, ON.

9   Simpson, *Mohawk Interruptus,* 115–16.

10 *Oren Lyons: The Legacy of Lacrosse* (Washington, DC: United States Department of State Bureau of International Information Programs, 2012), http://photos. state.gov/libraries/amgov/133183/english/P_Sports_In_America_Oren_Lyons_ The_Legacy_of_Lacrosse_English.pdf.

11 Dao Jao Dre (Delmor Jacobs, Cayuga, Wolf Clan, Six Nations of the Grand River), interview by Allan Downey, March 9, 2011, audio recording, Six Nations of the Grand River Reserve, ON.

12 Rick Hill, interview by Downey, March 9, 2011.

13 Thomas Vennum, *American Indian Lacrosse: Little Brother of War* (Baltimore: Johns Hopkins University Press, 1994), 272.

14 The formation of the Iroquois Nationals co-existed with a number of significant political movements that arose between the 1960s and the 1980s during a period of Indigenous activism in North America. Some of the team's organizers were involved in this struggle, which included the rise of the American Indian Movement, the 1973 occupation at Wounded Knee, the 1978 Longest Walk, and various repatriation efforts led by the Hodinöhsö:ni' themselves. There were also a number of key court decisions and policy changes that Indigenous peoples helped facilitate, including the 1973 *Calder* decision in Canada and the 1975 Indian Self-Determination and Education Assistance Act in the United States. In Canada, while the Iroquois Nationals were being founded, Indigenous peoples were fighting for "recognition" in the Canadian Constitution, which was eventually repatriated in 1982. See Madeline Rose Knickerbocker and Sarah Nickel, "Negotiating Sovereignty: Indigenous Perspectives on the Patriation of a Settler Colonial Constitution, 1975–83," *BC Studies* 190 (Summer 2016), 67–87. For a general overview of the period, see Kenneth W. Townsend and Mark A. Nicholas, *First Americans: A History of Native Peoples, Combined Volume* (Boston: Pearson Education, 2013); and Olive Patricia Dickason with William Newbigging, *A Concise History of Canada's First Nations,* 2nd ed. (Don Mills, ON: Oxford University Press, 2010).

15 Rick Hill, interview by Downey, March 9, 2011.

16 Ibid.

17 Donald M. Fisher, *Lacrosse: A History of the Game* (Baltimore: Johns Hopkins University Press, 2002), 297.

18 Peter McFarlane, "Aboriginal Leadership," in *Visions of the Heart: Canadian Aboriginal Issues,* ed. David Alan Long and Olive Patricia Dickason (Toronto: Harcourt Brace, 1996), 129.

19 Ibid.

20 Monture, *We Share Our Matters,* 118.

21 Laurence Hauptman, *The Iroquois and the New Deal* (Syracuse: Syracuse University Press, 1981), 3–4.

22 McFarlane, "Aboriginal Leadership," 129; Department of Indian Affairs, RG 10, vol. 3233, file 600, 144, *Library and Archives Canada.*

23 For more, see Allan Downey, "Playing the Creator's Game on God's Day: The Controversy of Sunday Lacrosse Games in Haudenosaunee Communities, 1916–1924," *Journal of Canadian Studies* 49, 3 (Fall 2015): 111–43.

24 Rick Hill, interview by Downey, March 9, 2011.

25 Ibid.

26 Ibid.

27 Ibid.

28 John Forbes, "Iroquois in Lacrosse Festival," *New York Times,* June 5, 1983.

29 Ibid.

30 Rick Hill, interview by Downey, March 9, 2011.

31 Leanne Simpson, *Dancing on Our Turtle's Back: Stories of Nishnaabeg Re-creation, Resurgence, and a New Emergence* (Winnipeg: Arbeiter Ring, 2011), 16–17; José Barreiro, ed., *Thinking in Indian: A John Mohawk Reader* (Golden, CO: Fulcrum, 2010), 203.

32 Quoted in Barreiro, ed., *Thinking in Indian,* 203. An abridged version of this quote also appears in Theresa McCarthy, *In Divided Unity: Haudenosaunee Reclamation at Grand River* (Tucson: University of Arizona Press, 2016), 18.

33 McCarthy, *In Divided Unity,* 18–19.

34 The Hodinöhsö:ni' Grand Council of Chiefs (Confederacy Council) is the active cultural, political, and social hereditary leadership of the Hodinöhsö:ni' Confederacy. An exemplar of cultural persistence and traditional governance, it is distinct from the imposed elected council system and the modernist leadership in Hodinöhsö:ni' communities.

35 *The Origin of Lacrosse* (Akwesasne: Ronathahon:ni Cultural Centre, 2008), 48.

36 Rick Hill, interview by Downey, March 9, 2011.

37 Ernie Mitchell (Kaheranoron, Wolf Clan, Kanien'kehá:ka of Ahkwesáhsne) and David White (Kanien'kehá:ka of Ahkwesáhsne), interview by Allan Downey, September 23, 2011, audio recording and transcript, Cornwall, ON.

38 As a reminder, "Longhouse traditionalists" are Hodinöhsö:ni' who have espoused the cultural revitalization movement that has occurred in Hodinöhsö:ni' communities since the late nineteenth century. Traditionalists also attempt to restore the political and cultural institutions of the Hodinöhsö:ni' Confederacy and Longhouse epistemology for the purpose of establishing and maintaining their political and cultural self-determination. Modernists are Hodinöhsö:ni' who believe in amending the Indian Act and working within its parameters. It is important to note that these classifications are oversimplified and do not always capture the fluidity of political identities: a number of community members,

such as the Christian nationalists, circumvent them. For example, they support the Longhouse hereditary council, though, as Christians, they do not adhere to the Longhouse epistemology. For more, see Gerald F. Reid, *Kahnawà:ke: Factionalism, Traditionalism, and Nationalism in a Mohawk Community* (Lincoln: University of Nebraska Press, 2004); Gerald R. Alfred, *Heeding the Voices of Our Ancestors: Kahnawake Mohawk Politics and the Rise of Native Nationalism* (Toronto: Oxford University Press, 1995); and Annemarie Anrod Shimony, *Conservatism among the Iroquois at the Six Nations Reserve* (Syracuse: Syracuse University Press, 1994).

39 Barreiro, *Thinking in Indian,* 203.

40 Ernie Mitchell and David White, interview by Downey, September 23, 2011; Fisher, *Lacrosse,* 299.

41 Rick Hill, interview by Downey, March 9, 2011.

42 Ibid.

43 Ibid.

44 In this, the Iroquois Nationals were part of a larger international decolonization movement that used sport. For example, see Hilary Beckles, *A Spirit of Dominance: Cricket and Nationalism in the West Indies* (Kingston: Canoe Press University of the West Indies, 1998); and José Raul Perales, "Politics and Play: Sport, Social Movements, and Decolonization in Cuba and the British West Indies," in *Globalizations and Social Movements: Culture, Power, and the Transnational Public Sphere,* ed. John A. Guidry, Michael D. Kennedy, and Mayer N. Zald (Ann Arbor: University of Michigan Press, 2000), 240–59.

45 Poka Laenui, "Process of Decolonization," in *Reclaiming Indigenous Voice and Vision,* ed. Marie Battiste (Vancouver: UBC Press, 2000), 150, 153.

46 Rick Hill (Tuscarora), interview by Allan Downey, September 9, 2011, audio recording and transcript, Six Nations of the Grand River Reserve, ON.

47 Ibid.

48 Victoria Paraschak, "Organized Sport for Native Females on the Six Nations Reserve, Ontario from 1968 to 1980: A Comparison of Dominant and Emergent Sport Systems," *Canadian Journal of History of Sport* 21, 2 (December 1990): 71.

49 Ibid.

50 Bonita Lawrence explains that Bill C-31 of 1985 sought to eliminate gender-based discrimination in the Indian Act, restore status and membership to eligible individuals, and provide bands with the ability to control their membership. Bonita Lawrence, *"Real" Indians and Others: Mixed-Blood Urban Native Peoples and Indigenous Nationhood* (Vancouver: UBC Press, 2004), 64. However, the act retained a measure of sex bias. Under the amended act, an Indigenous woman who had lost her status because she married a non-Indian man could now reclaim it, as could the children of that union. However, any of the children who were born before 1985 and who married a non-Indian person could not pass on their status to their own offspring. By contrast, an Indigenous man who married a non-Indian woman passed on his status to his children and grandchildren, even if they themselves "married out." Accordingly, Bill C-3 (2010), which went into effect in 2011, sought to eliminate the discrepancy of Bill C-31. Paraschak, "Organized Sport," 77; Bill C-3, *An Act to Promote Gender Equity in Indian*

Registration, 40th Parliament, 3rd session, 2010, https://lop.parl.ca/About/Parliament/LegislativeSummaries/Bills_ls.asp?Language=E&ls=c3&source=library_prb&Parl=40&Ses=3.

51 Quoted in Barreiro, *Thinking in Indian,* 130.

52 Rick Hill, interview by Downey, March 9, 2011.

53 Ibid.

54 Ibid.

55 Ibid.

56 Fisher, *Lacrosse,* 298.

57 Rick Hill, interview by Downey, March 9, 2011.

58 Fisher, *Lacrosse,* 298.

59 See Thomas Vennum, *Lacrosse Legends of the First Americans* (Baltimore: Johns Hopkins University Press, 2007).

60 Rick Hill, interview by Downey, March 9, 2011 (emphasis in original).

61 *The Origin of Lacrosse,* 49.

62 Quoted in ibid., 50.

63 Greg Horn (Kanien'kehá:ka of Kahnawà:ke), interview by Allan Downey, May 2, 2011, audio recording and transcript, Kahnawà:ke, QC.

64 Simpson, *Dancing on Our Turtle's Back,* 23–24.

65 Ernie Mitchell and David White, interview by Downey, September 23, 2011 (emphasis in original).

66 For more on the historic relationship between borders and borderlands, see Karl S. Hele, ed., *Lines Drawn upon the Water: First Nations and the Great Lakes Borders and Borderlands* (Waterloo: Wilfrid Laurier University Press, 2008); and Simpson, *Mohawk Interruptus.*

67 Simpson, *Mohawk Interruptus,* 116–17.

68 "Iroquois Reach for Moon; Indians Carry Flag into Competition," *USA Today,* July 5, 1990.

69 "Iroquois National Lacrosse Team on Tour in England," *Tekawennake,* September 25, 1985; Joseph Oxendine, *American Indian Sports Heritage* (Lincoln: University of Nebraska Press, [1988] 1995), 283.

70 Oxendine, *American Indian Sports Heritage,* 283, 294.

71 "Jim Thorpe Is the Inspiration for a Native Games Festival," *New York Times,* July 22, 1984.

72 Fisher, *Lacrosse,* 296.

73 Ibid. (emphasis in original).

74 Rick Hill, interview by Downey, September 9, 2011.

75 "Iroquois National Lacrosse Team on Tour in England," *Tekawennake,* September 25, 1985.

76 Oxendine, *American Indian Sports Heritage,* 294.

77 Rick Hill, interview by Downey, March 9, 2011.

78 Ibid.; Fisher, *Lacrosse,* 296. For more on the Hodinöhsö:ni' passport, see Laurence Hauptman, *The Iroquois Struggle for Survival: World War to Red Power* (Syracuse: Syracuse University Press, 1986); and Jeff Corntassel, "Toward Sustainable Self-Determination: Rethinking the Contemporary Indigenous-Rights Discourse," *Alternatives: Global, Local, Political* 33, 1 (January-March 2008): 105–32.

79 Rick Hill, interview by Downey, March 9, 2011.
80 Ibid.
81 Paraschak, "Organized Sport," 72–74.
82 Ibid, 74.
83 Rick Hill (Tuscarora), interview by Allan Downey, June 7, 2011, audio recording and transcript, Six Nations Polytechnic, Six Nations of the Grand River Reserve, ON.
84 Paraschak, "Organized Sport," 76.
85 Ibid.
86 Fisher, *Lacrosse*, 147; Vennum, *American Indian Lacrosse*, 184–85; Stewart Culin, *Games of the North American Indians*, Twenty-Fourth Annual Report of the Bureau of American Ethnology to the Secretary of the Smithsonian Institute, 1902–1903 (Washington, DC: Government Printing Office, 1907; reprint, New York: Dover, 1975), 571.
87 Oxendine, *American Indian Sports Heritage*, 296.
88 Andrea Houston, "Haudenosaunee Team Ends 20-Year Absence with U19 Appearance," *Peterborough Examiner*, date unknown, 2007, *Peterborough Examiner* online archives, http://www.thepeterboroughexaminer.com/ArticleDisplay. aspx?archive=true&e=641848, accessed February 12, 2012.
89 Quoted in Alison Owings, *Indian Voice: Listening to Native Americans* (Piscataway, NJ: Rutgers University Press, 2011), 69.
90 Vennum, *Lacrosse Legends*, 105–6.
91 Although Vennum's *Lacrosse Legends* and *American Indian Lacrosse*, Fisher's *Lacrosse*, and Oxendine's *American Indian Sports Heritage* do mention Indigenous women, they do so only in passing and fail to offer a detailed analysis of their participation in the sport.
92 Victoria Paraschak, "Doing Race, Doing Gender: First Nations, 'Sport,' and Gender Relations," in *Sport and Gender in Canada*, 2nd ed., ed. Kevin Young and Philip White (Don Mills, ON: Oxford University Press, 2007), 144.
93 Karen Etienne (Kanien'kehá:ka of Kanehsatá:ke), interview by Allan Downey, October 22, 2011, audio recording and transcript, Kanehsatá:ke, QC.
94 Betsy McCarthy, dir., *Oren Lyons, the Faithkeeper* (New York: Public Affairs Television, 1991); transcript by Journal Graphics.
95 Rick Hill, "A Respectful Passing: The Longhouse Funeral," *Haudenosaunee Runner* 3, 3 (Fall 2000): 7.
96 Ibid. The passing of a chief or community leader would call for a large Condolence Ceremony to appoint a successor, whereas the death of a community member would call for a small Condolence Ceremony. "Condolence Ceremony," *Haudenosaunee Confederacy*, http://www.haudenosauneeconfederacy.com/condolenceceremony.html, accessed March 5, 2012.
97 Quoted in Hill, "A Respectful Passing," 7. With permission from Rick Hill.
98 Ibid., 8–9.
99 Rick Hill, interview by Downey, June 7, 2011.
100 The International Federation of Women's Lacrosse Associations was formed in 1972, with the United States, England, Scotland, and Australia as its inaugural members. It was the female equivalent of the men's International Lacrosse

Federation. "Strategic Plan, 2008–2010," 4–5, *Federation of International Lacrosse,* http://www.filacrosse.com/downloads/FIL_Strategic_Plan.pdf, accessed March 5, 2011.

101 Rick Hill, interview by Downey, June 7, 2011.

102 Oxendine, *American Indian Sports Heritage,* 294.

103 Robert Lipsyte, "Lacrosse: All-American Game," *New York Times,* June 15, 1986.

104 "Iroquois Nationals Prove to Be a Competent Lacrosse Team," *Tekawennake,* July 23, 1986.

105 Ibid.

106 Robert Lipsyte, "Lacrosse: All-American Game," *New York Times,* June 15, 1986. Part of this quote appears in Vennum, *American Indian Lacrosse,* 294.

107 "Iroquois Nationals Prove to Be a Competent Lacrosse Team," *Tekawennake,* July 23, 1986; Fisher, *Lacrosse,* 296.

108 "Iroquois Nationals Prove to Be a Competent Lacrosse Team," *Tekawennake,* July 23, 1986.

109 Rick Hill, "Iroquois Join International Lacrosse Federation," date unknown, "Lacrosse," vertical files, *Woodland Cultural Centre Research Library.*

110 Robert Lipsyte, "Lacrosse: All-American Game," *New York Times,* June 15, 1986.

111 Rick Hill, interview by Downey, June 7, 2011. According to the website of the Haudenosaunee Confederacy, the title of Clan Mother is "passed down hereditarily through a clan. It is her responsibility to look out for the welfare of the clan by overseeing the actions of the Chief and ensuring that he is performing his duties in accordance with the Great Law. As Clan Mother she will have her own wampum of two strings, one white and one purple, signifying her title within the Haudenosaunee. Should she pass on, the string will then be passed on to the next hereditary Clan Mother. If a Chief acts improperly or is not living up to his responsibilities his Clan Mother and Faith Keepers will warn him about his actions. If he continues to act selfishly the Clan Mother may symbolically remove his antlers, thus removing his authority as Chief." "Clan Mothers," *Haudenosaunee Confederacy,* http://www.haudenosauneeconfederacy.ca/clan mothers.html, accessed March 5, 2012.

112 Every mid-April, the Ga·yo·gǫ·ho:nǫ' Nation plays a lacrosse game with traditional wooden sticks, which ends when seven goals are scored, honouring the Seven Thunderbeings. In addition, an individual, clan, nation, or even the entire Hodinöhsö:ni' Nation can request a game for the purposes of healing. Once it ends, the ball remains with the person who made the request or the one who is in need of the curative powers of the game. Dao Jao Dre (Delmor Jacobs, Cayuga, Wolf Clan, Six Nations of the Grand River), interview by Allan Downey, June 7, 2011, audio recording and transcript, Six Nations of the Grand River Reserve, ON.

113 Rick Hill, interview by Downey, June 7, 2011.

114 Calder and Fletcher, *Lacrosse,* 27–28.

115 Lina Sunseri, *Being Again of One Mind: Oneida Women and the Struggle for Decolonization* (Vancouver: UBC Press, 2011), 151.

116 Rick Hill, interview by Downey, June 7, 2011.

117 See "Oneida Creation Story," in Sunseri, *Being Again of One Mind,* 49–50.

118 Interestingly, Skarù·rę' Clan Mother Louise Henry of the Turtle Clan is believed to have been one of the first Hodinöhsö:ni' athletes to attend university and play collegiate lacrosse, predating Oren Lyons's career at Syracuse. As she explained to Rick Hill, when she was young, the issue of women playing lacrosse was not as big a concern in her community as it was for the Onöndowa'ga:' at Tonawanda and the Onöñda'gega' Clan Mothers. Rick Hill, interview by Downey, September 9, 2011.

119 Aimee Berg, "Cradle of a Sport Has Crossed the Gender Line," *New York Times,* May 13, 2007; Rick Hill, interview by Downey, June 7, 2011.

120 Rick Hill, interview by Downey, March 9, 2011.

121 Margaret Ann Hall, *The Girl and the Game: A History of Women's Sport in Canada* (Toronto: University of Toronto Press, 2002), 119.

122 Sunseri, *Being Again of One Mind,* 131.

123 Ibid., 105.

124 Rick Hill, interview by Downey, March 9, 2011.

125 Paraschak, "Organized Sport," 72–73.

126 Quoted in Sunseri, *Being Again of One Mind,* 130.

127 Ibid.

128 Rick Hill, interview by Downey, June 7, 2011.

129 Ibid.

130 François Mandeville, *This Is What They Say,* trans. by Ron Scollon (Vancouver: Douglas and McIntyre, 2009), 99–200.

131 Paraschak, "Doing Race, Doing Gender," 139; Audrey R. Giles, "Kevlar, Crisco, and Menstruation: 'Tradition' and Dene Games," *Sociology of Sport Journal* 21 (2004): 18–35.

132 Sunseri, *Being Again of One Mind,* 106.

133 Rick Hill, interview by Downey, June 7, 2011; also see Culin, *Games of the North American Indians,* 612. This was told to me by numerous Hodinöhsö:ni' women, who asked to remain anonymous, from prominent lacrosse families that did not follow the Longhouse epistemology.

134 Rick Hill, interview by Downey, June 7, 2011.

135 Ernie Mitchell and David White, interview by Downey, September 23, 2011.

136 Michael J. Zogry, *Anetso, the Cherokee Ball Game: At the Center of Ceremony and Identity* (Chapel Hill: University of North Carolina Press, 2010), 129.

137 Aimee Berg, "Cradle of a Sport Has Crossed the Gender Line," *New York Times,* May 13, 2007.

138 Alfred, *Heeding the Voices,* 14.

139 Sunseri, *Being Again of One Mind,* 144.

140 Rick Hill, interview by Downey, June 7, 2011 (emphasis added).

141 Franke Wilmer, "Indian Gaming: Players and Stakes," *Wicazo Sa Review* 12, 1 (Spring 1997): 90.

142 Fisher, *Lacrosse,* 301–2.

143 Ernie Mitchell and David White, interview by Downey, September 23, 2011.

144 "Showing of Pride for the Iroquois," *New York Times,* July 16, 1990.

145 Rick Hill, interview by Downey, March 9, 2011.

146 "Iroquois in Lacrosse Festival," *New York Times,* June 5, 1983.

147 Fisher, *Lacrosse,* 302; Ernie Mitchell and David White, interview by Downey, September 23, 2011.

148 Ernie Mitchell and David White, interview by Downey, September 23, 2011.

149 "Iroquois Nationals Will Compete in World Games in Perth," *Tekawennake,* May 9, 1990.

150 Ibid.

151 Robert L. Smith, "Playing for Nationhood," *Post-Standard,* June 13, 1990, in Ernie Mitchell, Kaheranoron, Scrapbook, *Akwesasne Cultural Center Library.*

152 For more, see Kathleen S. Fine-Dare, *Grave Injustice: The American Indian Repatriation Movement and NAGPRA* (Lincoln: University of Nebraska Press, 2002).

153 William N. Fenton, "The New York State Wampum Collection: The Case for the Integrity of Culture Treasures," *Proceedings of the American Philosophical Society* 115, 6 (1971): 437–61. According to Kathleen S. Fine-Dare, the Hiawatha Wampum Belt and three others were illegally sold by Chief Thomas Webster in 1891. They were the communal property of Onöñda'gega', and thus no individual had the right to sell them. Webster was later removed from office for doing so. The New York State Museum eventually acquired the belts and was protected by a 1909 state law that gave it the authority to keep all belts in its possession despite their cultural importance to the Hodinöhsö:ni'. This eventually led to the repatriation movement by the Hodinöhsö:ni' to re-obtain them. Fine-Dare, *Grave Injustice,* 91–92.

154 Stephanie Waterman and Philip Arnold note that "on the Hiawenta [Hiawatha] belt the symbols represent the nations. Imagine an extended longhouse, stretching from the east (Albany, New York) to the west (Buffalo): The first block represents the Mohawk Nation, the Keepers of the Eastern Door; next is the Oneida Nation; in the center is the Onondaga Nation, or Keepers of the Fire, the political seat of the Haudenosaunee; next is the Cayuga Nation; and finally the Keepers of the Western Door, the Seneca Nation. The white line that extends and connects the symbols is a path – all paths lead to Onondaga, represented by the Tree of Peace." Stephanie J. Waterman and Philip P. Arnold, "The Haudenosaunee Flag Raising: Cultural Symbols and Intercultural Contact," *Journal of American Indian Education* 49, 1–2 (2010): 128–29.

155 Penelope Myrtle Kelsey, *Reading the Wampum: Essays on Hodinöhsö:ni' Visual Code and Epistemological Recovery* (Syracuse: Syracuse University Press, 2014), xiii.

156 Waterman and Arnold, "The Haudenosaunee Flag Raising," 128–29.

157 According to the website of the Haudenosaunee Confederacy, wampum beads are a guide to the oral history, traditions, and laws of the Hodinöhsö:ni'. Furthermore, "Wampum served [and continues to do so] as a person's credentials or a certificate of authority. It was used for official purposes and religious ceremonies and in the case of the joining of the League of Nations was used as a way to bind peace. Every Chief of the Confederacy and every Clan Mother has a certain string or strings of Wampum that serves as their certificate of office. When they pass on or are removed from their station the string will then pass on to the

new leader. Runners carrying messages would not be taken seriously without first presenting the wampum showing that they had the authority to carry the message. "Wampum," *Haudenosaunee Confederacy*, http://www.haudenosaunee confederacy.com/wampum.html.

158 Rick Hill, interview by Downey, March 9, 2011.

159 Ibid.

160 Vennum, *American Indian Lacrosse*, 293.

161 For Kent Lyons's reflection on the moment, see Vennum, *American Indian Lacrosse*, 293.

162 Ernie Mitchell and David White, interview by Downey, September 23, 2011.

163 Rick Hill, interview by Downey, March 9, 2011.

164 J.R. Miller, "Great White Father Knows Best: Oka and the Land Claims Process," in *Reflections on Native-Newcomer Relations: Selected Essays* (Toronto: University of Toronto Press, 2004), 140.

165 Ibid., 140–41.

166 Ibid., 141.

167 Simpson, *Mohawk Interruptus*, 148; Arthur Ray, *I Have Lived Here since the World Began: An Illustrated History of Canada's Native People*, rev. ed. (Toronto: Key Porter Books, 2005), 359.

168 Miller, "Great White Father Knows Best," 141; Dickason with Newbigging, *A Concise History*, 282–86.

169 Simpson, *Mohawk Interruptus*, 147.

170 Joe Delaronde, interview by Downey, April 29, 2011.

171 Geoffrey York, *People of the Pines: The Warriors and the Legacy of Oka* (Boston: Little Brown, 1991), 337.

172 "Iroquois Shedding Light on Roots of Lacrosse," *Boston Globe*, October 9, 2007.

173 McCarthy, *In Divided Unity*, 98–99.

Dewa'ë:ö'
Conclusion

1 Aimee Berg, "Cradle of a Sport Has Crossed the Gender Line," *New York Times*, May 13, 2007.

2 Theresa McCarthy, *In Divided Unity: Haudenosaunee Reclamation at Grand River* (Tucson: University of Arizona Press, 2016), 98–99.

3 There are now several teams representing the Hodinöhsö:ni' in FIL competiton, including men's and women's senior and under-19 teams in field lacrosse and a men's senior box lacrosse team.

4 Thomas Kaplan, "Bid for Trophy Becomes a Test of Iroquois Identity," *New York Times*, July 12, 2010, http://www.nytimes.com/2010/07/13/us/13lacrosse.html.

5 Kristen Hamill, "Iroquois Lacrosse Team Still Caught in Bureaucratic Net," *CNN Online*, July 15, 2010, http://www.cnn.com/2010/SPORT/07/14/sport.iroquois. passport.controversy/index.html.

6 Greg Horn, "Editorial: Why It's Important for the Iroquois Nationals to Travel on Haudenosaunee Passports," *Iorì:wase Kahnawake News*, August 10, 2010, http://kahnawakenews.com/editorial-why-its-important-for-the-iroquois -nationals-to-travel-on-haude-p886-92.htm.

7 Audra Simpson, *Mohawk Interruptus: Political Life across the Borders of Settler States* (Durham, NC: Duke University Press, 2014), 182.

8 Jo-ann Archibald, *Indigenous Storywork: Educating the Heart, Mind, Body, and Spirit* (Vancouver: UBC Press, 2008), 5.

9 Leanne Simpson, *Dancing on Our Turtle's Back: Stories of Nishnaabeg Re-creation, Resurgence, and a New Emergence* (Winnipeg: Arbeiter Ring, 2011), 23–24.

10 Michael A. Robidoux, *Stickhandling through the Margins: First Nations Hockey in Canada* (Toronto: University of Toronto Press, 2012), 27.

11 Keith Thor Carlson, *The Power of Place, the Problem of Time: Aboriginal Identity and Historical Consciousness in the Cauldron of Colonialism* (Toronto: University of Toronto Press, 2010), 80.

12 Thomas King, *The Truth about Stories: A Native Narrative* (Toronto: House of Anansi Press, 2003), 2.

13 Simpson, *Mohawk Interruptus*, 113.

14 In Jose Barreiro, ed., *Thinking in Indian: A John Mohawk Reader* (Golden, CO: Fulcrum, 2010), 203.

Yunęnrúha'r

Bibliography

Archival Sources

Akwesasne Cultural Center Library, Hogansburg, NY
Ernie Mitchell, Kaheranoron, Scrapbooks
Lacrosse vertical files and boxes

Archives of Ontario
Attorney General Central Registry Criminal and Civil Files, RG 4-32
Conn Smythe Fonds, F 223-7-0-10

British Columbia Archives
Reuben Ware Collection

Canadian Lacrosse Hall of Fame

Canadian Museum of History (Formerly Canadian Museum of Civilization)
Jack, David (Gwe-u-gweh-o-no, Cayuga), "Power Received from Thunderer," August 1915, interview by F.W. Waugh, Six Nations of the Grand River Reserve, five-page typed transcript, Control No. B201, f24. http://www.civilization.ca/research-and-collections/library-and-archives/library-services/.

City of Vancouver Archives
Major Matthews Fonds
Matthews, J.S., ed. *Conversations with Khahtsahlano, 1932–1954.* Vancouver: Vancouver City Archives, 1955.
Stuart Thomson Fonds

Yunęnrúha'r is the Skarù·rę' Nation's word for lacrosse. Blair A. Rudes, *Tuscarora-English/English-Tuscarora Dictionary* (Toronto: University of Toronto Press, 1999), 605.

Kanien'kehá:ka Onkwawén:na Raotitióhkwa Language and Cultural Center
Vertical files

Library and Archives Canada (LAC)
Christopher William Massiah Fonds, MG 29-C171
Department of Agriculture, RG 17
Department of External Affairs, RG 25
Department of Indian Affairs, RG 10
John Edward Gardiner Curran Fonds, MG 30-C85
Lacrosse, MG 31, D85 22
Montreal Amateur Athletic Association Fonds, MG 28

McCord Museum
John Henry Walker Collection
William Notman Collection

North Vancouver Museum and Archives
Charles Warren Cates Fonds

Ontario Lacrosse Hall of Fame
Hall of Fame Membership Database

Prince Albert Historical Society Archives
Bill Smiley Archives
"Prince Albert Lacrosse Team." H-33, Prince Albert Historical Society Archives
    Collection Online. http://sain.scaa.sk.ca/items/index.php/prince-albert-lacrosse
    -team-2;rad.

Six Nations Polytechnic
Photo collection
Vertical files

Sliammon Treaty Society
Miscellaneous Interviews
Sliammon Treaty Society Files
Traditional Use Study

University of British Columbia Special Collections

Woodland Cultural Centre Research Library
Lacrosse: 1973-1974, 1977-78-79
Misc. Sports 72-75-76
North American Lacrosse Association – Chief 74-75 box file
Vertical files

Newspapers
Boston Globe
Brantford Expositor
Canadian Illustrated News
Chicago Daily Tribune
Christian Science Monitor

CNN
Eastern Door
Edmonton Journal
Iorì:wase Kahnawake News
Los Angeles Times
Montreal Gazette
New York Times
North Shore Outlook
Ottawa Citizen
Peterborough Examiner
Saskatoon Star Phoenix
Tekawennake
Times (London)
Toronto Globe and Mail
Toronto Star
Vancouver Daily Sun
Vancouver Province
Victoria Daily Colonist
Windspeaker
Winnipeg Free Press

Interviews

Dao Jao Dre (Delmor Jacobs, Cayuga, Wolf Clan, Six Nations of the Grand River), March 9, 2011, audio recording, Six Nations of the Grand River Reserve, ON.

Dao Jao Dre (Delmor Jacobs, Cayuga, Wolf Clan, Six Nations of the Grand River), June 4, 2011, audio recording, Six Nations of the Grand River Reserve, ON.

Dao Jao Dre (Delmor Jacobs, Cayuga, Wolf Clan, Six Nations of the Grand River), June 7, 2011, audio recording and transcript, Six Nations of the Grand River Reserve, ON.

Dao Jao Dre (Delmor Jacobs, Cayuga, Wolf Clan, Six Nations of the Grand River), August 10, 2011, audio recording, Six Nations of the Grand River Reserve, ON.

Delaronde, Joe (Kanien'kehá:ka of Kahnawà:ke), April 29, 2011, audio recording, Kahnawà:ke, QC.

Delaronde, Joe (Kanien'kehá:ka of Kahnawà:ke), October 21, 2011, audio recording, Kahnawà:ke, QC.

Delaronde, Joe (Kanien'kehá:ka of Kahnawà:ke) and Greg Horn (Kanien'kehá:ka of Kahnawà:ke), June 2, 2011, audio recording, Kahnawà:ke, QC.

Etienne, Karen (Kanien'kehá:ka of Kanehsatá:ke), October 22, 2011, audio recording and transcript, Kanehsatá:ke, QC.

Hill, Rick (Tuscarora), March 9, 2011, audio recording and transcript, Six Nations Polytechnic, Six Nations of the Grand River Reserve, ON.

Hill, Rick (Tuscarora), June 7, 2011, audio recording and transcript, Six Nations Polytechnic, Six Nations of the Grand River Reserve, ON.

Hill, Rick (Tuscarora), September 9, 2011, audio recording and transcript, Six Nations of the Grand River Reserve, ON.

Horn, Greg (Kanien'kehá:ka of Kahnawà:ke), May 2, 2011, audio recording and transcript, Kahnawà:ke, QC.

Mitchell, Ernie (Kaheranoron, Wolf Clan, Kanien'kehá:ka of Ahkwesáhsne) and David White (Kanien'kehá:ka of Ahkwesáhsne), September 23, 2011, audio recording and transcript, Cornwall, ON.

Onawario (John Cree, Bear Clan, Kanien'kehá:ka of Kanehsatá:ke), October 22, 2011, Kanehsatá:ke, QC.

Onawario (John Cree, Bear Clan, Kanien'kehá:ka of Kanehsatá:ke) and Victor Bonspille (Kanien'kehá:ka of Kanehsatá:ke), June 4, 2011, audio recording, Kanehsatá:ke, QC.

Paitsmauk (Dave Jacobs) and Sla'wiya (Andrea Jacobs), July 22, 2010, audio recording and transcript, Capilano Reserve, BC.

Paitsmauk (Dave Jacobs) and Sla'wiya (Andrea Jacobs), August 6, 2010, audio recording and transcript, Capilano Reserve, BC.

Paitsmauk (Dave Jacobs) and Sla'wiya (Andrea Jacobs), August 12, 2010, audio recording and transcript, Capilano Reserve, BC.

Paitsmauk (Dave Jacobs) and Sla'wiya (Andrea Jacobs), June 26, 2011, audio recording and transcript, Capilano Reserve, BC.

Two Rivers, Billy (Kanien'kehá:ka of Kahnawà:ke), November 5, 2011, audio recording, Kahnawà:ke, QC.

Other Sources

Alfred, [Taiaiake] Gerald R. *Heeding the Voices of Our Ancestors: Kahnawake Mohawk Politics and the Rise of Native Nationalism.* Toronto: Oxford University Press, 1995.

–. "Sovereignty." In *A Companion to American Indian History*, ed. Philip J. Deloria and Neal Salisbury, 460–76. New York: Blackwell, 2004.

Alfred, Taiaiake, and Jeff Corntassel. "Being Indigenous: Resurgences against Contemporary Colonialism." *Government and Opposition* 40, 4 (Autumn 2005): 597–614.

Allen, James Michael. "The (Re)construction of Organizational Culture within Social Contexts: A Case Study of the Six Nations Arrows Lacrosse Organization." Master's thesis, University of Windsor, 1999.

Andersen, Chris. "*Métis*": *Race, Recognition, and the Struggle for Indigenous Peoplehood.* Vancouver: UBC Press, 2014.

Anderson, Eric D. "Using the Master's Tools: Resisting Colonization through Colonial Sports." *International Journal of Sport* 23, 2 (March 2006): 247–66.

Anderson, Kim. *A Recognition of Being: Reconstruction Native Womanhood*, 2nd ed. Toronto: Women's Press, 2016.

Anderson, Robert, Joanna Brown, Jonny Lerner, and Barbara Lou Shafer, eds. *Voices from Wounded Knee, 1973: In the Words of the Participants.* Rooseveltown, NY: Akwesasne Notes, 1974.

Anderson, Robin. "Making Fun of Sport: James Fitzmaurice, Robert Ripley, and the Art of Sport Cartooning in Vancouver, 1907–1918." *Journal of Sport History* 37, 3 (Fall 2010): 365–96.

Archibald, Jo-ann. *Indigenous Storywork: Educating the Heart, Mind, Body, and Spirit.* Vancouver: UBC Press, 2008.

Ballem, Charles. "Missing from the Canadian Sport Scene: Native Athletes." *Sport History Review* 14, 2 (December 1983): 33–43.

Barman, Jean. "Erasing Indigenous Indigeneity in Vancouver." *BC Studies* 155 (Autumn 2007): 3–30.

Barreiro, José, ed. *Thinking in Indian: A John Mohawk Reader*. Golden, CO: Fulcrum, 2010.

Bass, Amy, ed. *In the Game: Race, Identity, and Sports in the Twentieth Century*. New York: Palgrave Macmillan, 2005.

Battiste, Marie, ed. *Reclaiming Indigenous Voice and Vision*. Vancouver: UBC Press, 2000.

Beauvais, Johnny. *Kahnawake: A Mohawk Look at Canada and Adventures of Big John Canadian*. Montreal: Techno Couleur, 1985.

Beckles, Hilary. *A Spirit of Dominance: Cricket and Nationalism in the West Indies*. Kingston: Canoe Press University of the West Indies, 1998.

Beers, W.G. *Lacrosse: The National Game of Canada*. Montreal: Dawson Brothers, 1869.

Benn, Carl. *Mohawks on the Nile: Natives among the Canadian Voyageurs in Egypt, 1884–1885*. Toronto: Natural Heritage Books, 2009.

Berry, Brewton. "The Myth of the Vanishing Indian." *Phylon* 21, 1 (1960): 51–57.

Blanchard, David. "Entertainment, Dance and Northern Mohawk Showmanship." *American Indian Quarterly* 7, 1 (1983): 2–26.

Bloom, John. *To Show What an Indian Can Do: Sports at Native American Boarding Schools*. Minneapolis: University of Minnesota Press, 2000.

Borrows, John. *Canada's Indigenous Constitution*. Toronto: University of Toronto Press, 2010.

–. *Recovering Canada: The Resurgence of Indigenous Law*. Toronto: University of Toronto Press, 2002.

Bouchier, Nancy. *For the Love of the Game: Amateur Sport in Small-Town Ontario*. Montreal and Kingston: McGill-Queen's University Press, 2003.

–. "Idealized Middle-Class Sport for a Young Nation: Lacrosse in Nineteenth-Century Ontario Towns, 1871–1891." *Journal of Canadian Studies* 29, 2 (Summer 1994): 89–110.

Brandão, José António. *"Your Fyre Shall Burn No More": Iroquois Policy toward New France and Its Native Allies to 1701*. Lincoln: University of Nebraska Press, 1997.

Butler, Judith. "Performative Acts and Gender Constitution: An Essay in Phenomenology and Feminist Theory," *Theatre Journal*, 40, 4 (1988): 519–31.

Calder, Jim, and Ron Fletcher. *Lacrosse: The Ancient Game*. Toronto: Ancient Game Press, 2011.

Canada. Royal Commission on Aboriginal Peoples. *Report of the Royal Commission on Aboriginal Peoples*. 5 vols. Ottawa: Royal Commission on Aboriginal Peoples, 1996.

Carlson, Keith Thor. *The Power of Place, the Problem of Time: Aboriginal Identity and Historical Consciousness in the Cauldron of Colonialism*. Toronto: University of Toronto Press, 2010.

Chen, Cecilia, Janine MacLeod, and Astrida Neimanis, eds. *Thinking with Water*. Montreal and Kingston: McGill-Queen's University Press, 2013.

Cheska, Alyce Taylor. "Sport as Ethnic Boundary Maintenance: A Case of the American Indian." *International Review of Sociology of Sport* 19, 241 (1984): 241–55.

Coates, Ken S. *A Global History of Indigenous Peoples: Struggle and Survival*. New York: Palgrave Macmillan, 2004.

Cole, Peter. *Coyote and Raven Go Canoeing: Coming Home to the Village*. Montreal and Kingston: McGill-Queen's University Press, 2006.

Corben, Len. *Instant Replay: A Century of North Shore Sports Stories.* North Vancouver: Little Lonsdale, 2007.

Corntassel, Jeff. "Toward Sustainable Self-Determination: Rethinking the Contemporary Indigenous-Rights Discourse." *Alternatives: Global, Local, Political* 33, 1 (January–March 2008): 105–32.

Coulthard, Glen. *Red Skin, White Masks: Rejecting the Colonial Politics of Recognition.* Minneapolis: University of Minnesota Press, 2014.

Cruikshank, Julie. "Oral Tradition and Oral History: Reviewing Some Issues." *Canadian Historical Review* 75, 3 (1994): 403–18.

Culin, Stewart. *Games of the North American Indians.* Twenty-Fourth Annual Report of the Bureau of American Ethnology to the Secretary of the Smithsonian Institute, 1902–1903. Washington, DC: Government Printing Office, 1907; reprint, New York: Dover, 1975.

Daschuk, James. *Clearing the Plains: Disease, Politics of Starvation, and the Loss of Aboriginal Life.* Regina: University of Regina Press, 2013.

Davis, Laurel R. "The Problems with Native American Mascots," *Multicultural Education* 9, 4 (2002): 11–14.

–. "Protest against the Use of Native American Mascots: A Challenge to Traditional American Identity." *Journal of Sport and Social Issues* 17, 1 (April 1993): 9–22.

Deloria, Philip. *Indians in Unexpected Places.* Lawrence: University of Kansas Press, 2004.

–. *Playing Indian.* New Haven: Yale University Press, 1998.

Department of Indian Affairs. *Calisthenics and Games Prescribed for Use in All Indian Schools.* Ottawa: Government Printing Bureau, 1910.

Dheensaw, Cleve. *Lacrosse 100: One Hundred Years of Lacrosse in B.C.* Victoria: Orca, 1990.

Dickason, Olive Patricia, with William Newbigging. *A Concise History of Canada's First Nations.* 2nd ed. Don Mills, ON: Oxford University Press, 2010.

Dippie, Brian. *The Vanishing American: White Attitudes and U.S. Indian Policy.* Middletown, CT: Wesleyan University Press, 1982.

Doerfler, Jill, Niigaanwewidam James Sinclair, and Heidid Kiiwetinepinesilk Stark, eds. *Centering Anishinaabeg Studies: Understanding the World through Stories.* East Lansing: Michigan State University Press, 2013.

Dominion of Canada. *Annual Report of the Department of Indian Affairs.* Ottawa: Department of Indian Affairs, 1864–1950. http://www.bac-lac.gc.ca/eng/discover/aboriginal-heritage/first-nations/indian-affairs-annual-reports/Pages/introduction.aspx.

Downey, Allan. "Engendering Nationality: Haudenosaunee Tradition, Sport, and the Lines of Gender." *Journal of the Canadian Historical Association* 23, 1 (2012): 319–54.

–. "Playing the Creator's Game on God's Day: The Controversy of Sunday Lacrosse Games in Haudenosaunee Communities, 1916–1924. *Journal of Canadian Studies* 49, 3 (Fall 2015): 111–43.

Downey, Allan, and Susan Neylan. "Raven Plays Ball: Situating 'Indian Sports Days' within Indigenous and Colonial Spaces in Twentieth-Century Coastal British Columbia." *Canadian Journal of History* 50, 3 (Winter 2015): 442–68.

Dunlop, Herbert Francis. *Andy Paull: As I Knew Him and Understood His Times.* Vancouver: Order of the O.M.I. of St. Paul's Province, 1989.

Edwards, Brendan F.R. "'I Have Lots of Help behind Me, Lots of Books, to Convince You': Andrew Paull and the Value of Literacy in English." *BC Studies* 164 (Winter 2009): 7–30.

–. "A War of Wor(l)ds: Aboriginal Writing in Canada during the 'Dark Days' of the Early Twentieth Century." PhD diss., University of Saskatchewan, 2008.

Eisen, George, and David Wiggins, eds. *Ethnicity and Sport in North American History and Culture.* Westport: Greenwood Press, 1994.

Engelbrecht, William. *Iroquoia: The Development of a Native World.* Syracuse: Syracuse University Press, 2003.

Evans, G. Heberton, III. *Lacrosse Fundamentals.* New York: A.S. Barns, 1966.

Fenton, William N. *The Great Law and the Longhouse: A Political History of the Iroquois Confederacy.* Norman: University of Oklahoma Press, 1998.

–. "The New York State Wampum Collection: The Case for the Integrity of Culture Treasures." *Proceedings of the American Philosophical Society* 115, 6 (1971): 437–61.

Fine-Dare, Kathleen S. *Grave Injustice: The American Indian Repatriation Movement and NAGPRA.* Lincoln: University of Nebraska Press, 2002.

Fisher, Donald M. *Lacrosse: A History of the Game.* Baltimore: Johns Hopkins University Press, 2002.

–. "'Splendid but Undesirable Isolation': Recasting Canada's National Game as Box Lacrosse, 1931–1932." *Sport History Review* 36 (2005): 115–29.

Forsyth, Janice. "Bodies of Meaning: Sports and Games at Canadian Residential Schools." In *Aboriginal Peoples and Sport in Canada: Historical Foundations and Contemporary Issues,* ed. Janice Forsyth and Audrey R. Giles, 15–34. Vancouver: UBC Press, 2013.

–. "The Indian Act and the (Re)shaping of Canadian Aboriginal Sport Practices." *International Journal of Canadian Studies* 35 (2007): 95–111.

Forsyth, Janice, and Audrey R. Giles, eds. *Aboriginal Peoples and Sport in Canada: Historical Foundations and Contemporary Issues.* Vancouver: UBC Press, 2013.

Francis, Daniel. *L.D.: Mayor Louis Taylor and the Rise of Vancouver.* Vancouver: Arsenal Pulp Press, 2004.

Fryberg, Stephanie A., Hazel Rose Markus, Daphna Oyserman, and Joseph M. Stone. "Of Warrior Chiefs and Indian Princesses: The Psychological Impact Consequences of American Indian Mascots." *Basic and Applied Social Psychology* 30 (2008): 208–18.

Giles, Audrey R. "Kevlar, Crisco, and Menstruation: 'Tradition' and Dene Games." *Sociology of Sport Journal* 21 (2004): 18–35.

Good, Bill, Maria Barnett, and Bill McNeil. "Lacrosse Is in a State of Crisis," CBC Radio, April 2, 1957, *CBC Digital Archives.* http://www.cbc.ca/archives/entry/lacrosse-is-in-a-state-of-crisis.

Graham, Elizabeth. *The Mush Hole: Life at Two Indian Residential Schools.* Waterloo: Heffle, 1997.

Grosskurth, Christopher, and Robin Brown. "Lacrosse on the Six Nations Reserves." CBC Radio, July 30, 2003, *CBC Digital Archives.* http://www.cbc.ca/archives/entry/lacrosse-on-the-six-nations-reserves.

Guidry, John A., Michael D. Kennedy, and Mayer N. Zald, eds. *Globalizations and Social Movements: Culture, Power, and the Transnational Public Sphere*. Ann Arbor: University of Michigan Press, 2000.

Haig-Brown, Celia. *Resistance and Renewal: Surviving the Indian Residential School*. Vancouver: Arsenal Pulp Press, 1988.

Hall, Margaret Ann. *The Girl and the Game: A History of Women's Sport in Canada*. Toronto: University of Toronto Press, 2002.

Hallowell, A. Irving, Jennifer S.H. Brown, and Susan Elaine Grey, eds. *Contributions to Ojibwe Studies: Essays, 1934–1972*. Lincoln: University of Nebraska Press, 2010.

Harmon, Alexandra. *Indians in the Making: Ethnic Relations and Indian Identities around Puget Sound*. Berkeley: University of California Press, 1998.

Harris, R. Cole. *Making Native Space: Colonialism, Resistance, and Reserves in British Columbia*. Vancouver: UBC Press, 2002.

–. *The Resettlement of British Columbia: Essays on Colonialism and Geographical Change*. Vancouver: UBC Press, 1997.

Hauptman, Laurence. *The Iroquois and the New Deal*. Syracuse: Syracuse University Press, 1981.

–. *The Iroquois Struggle for Survival: World War to Red Power*. Syracuse: Syracuse University Press, 1986.

Heine, Michael. "Performance Indicators: Aboriginal Games at the Arctic Winter Games." In *Aboriginal Peoples and Sport in Canada: Historical Foundations and Contemporary Issues*, ed. Janice Forsyth and Audrey Giles, 160–81. Vancouver: UBC Press, 2013.

Hele, Karl S., ed. *Lines Drawn upon the Water: First Nations and the Great Lakes Borders and Borderlands*. Waterloo: Wilfrid Laurier University Press, 2008.

Henry, Annie Frazier, dir. *Chiefs and Champions: Ross Powless*. DVD. Delta, BC: Big Red Barn Productions, 2005.

Hill, Rick. "A Respectful Passing: The Longhouse Funeral." *Haudenosaunee Runner* 3, 3 (Fall 2000): 7–10.

Hill, Susan M. *The Clay We Are Made Of: Haudenosaunee Land Tenure on the Grand River*. Winnipeg: University of Manitoba Press, 2017.

Hinkson, Jim. *Box Lacrosse: The Fastest Game on Two Feet*. Radnor, PA: Chilton, 1974.

Hokowhitu, Brendan. "Māori Rugby and Subversion: Creativity, Domestication, Oppression, and Decolonization." *International Journal of the History of Sport* 26, 16 (2009): 2314–34.

–. "Producing Elite Indigenous Masculinities." *Settler Colonial Studies* 2, 2 (2012): 23–48.

–. "Tackling Maori Masculinity: A Colonial Genealogy of Savagery and Sport." *Contemporary Pacific* 16, 2 (Fall 2004): 259–84.

Homel, Gene Howard. "Sliders and Backsliders: Toronto's Sunday Tobogganing Controversy of 1912." *Urban History Review* 10, 2 (October 1981): 25–34.

Howell, Colin D. *Blood, Sweat, and Cheers: Sport and the Making of Modern Canada*. Toronto: University of Toronto Press, 2001.

Howell, Nancy, and Maxwell Howell. *Sports and Games in Canadian Life: 1700 to Present*. Toronto: Macmillan of Canada, 1969.

Ibrahim, Awad. "Performing Desire: Hip-Hop, Identification, and the Politics of Becoming Black." In *Racism, Eh? A Critical Inter-Disciplinary Anthology of Race and*

Racism in Canada, ed. Camille A. Nelson and Charmaine A. Nelson, 274–93. Concord, ON: Captus Press, 2004.

Jack, Agnes, ed. *Behind Closed Doors: Stories from the Kamloops Indian Residential School.* Rev. ed. Penticton: Theytus Books, 2006.

Jackson, Douglas, dir. *Lacrosse.* 14 min. DVD. Montreal: National Film Board of Canada, 1964.

James, C.L.R. *Beyond a Boundary.* Durham, NC: Duke University Press, 2013.

Jenness, Diamond. "Myths of the Carrier Indians of British Columbia." *Journal of American Folklore* 47, 184 (April–September 1934): 97–257.

Johnson, Troy. "The Occupation of Alcatraz Island: Roots of American Indian Activism." *Wicazo Sa Review* 10, 2 (Autumn 1994): 63–79.

Kelm, Mary-Ellen. *Colonizing Bodies: Aboriginal Health and Healing in British Columbia, 1900–1950.* Vancouver: UBC Press, 1998.

–. "Riding into Place: Contact Zones, Rodeo, and Hybridity in the Canadian West 1900–1970." *Journal of the Canadian Historical Association* 18, 1 (2007): 107–32.

–. *A Wilder West: Rodeo in Western Canada.* Vancouver: UBC Press, 2011.

Kelsey, Penelope Myrtle. *Reading the Wampum: Essays on Hodinöhsö:ni' Visual Code and Epistemological Recovery.* Syracuse: Syracuse University Press, 2014.

Kidd, Bruce. *The Struggle of Canadian Sport.* Toronto: University of Toronto Press, 1996.

King, Richard, ed. *Native Athletes in Sport and Society.* Lincoln: University of Nebraska Press, 2005.

King, Richard, and Charles Fruehling, eds. *Team Spirits: The Native American Mascot Controversy.* Lincoln. Nebraska: University of Nebraska Press, 2001.

King, Thomas. *A Coyote Columbus Story.* Toronto: Groundwood Books/House of Anansi Press, 2010.

–. *Green Grass, Running Water.* Toronto: HarperPerennial Canada, 2007.

–. *The Truth about Stories: A Native Narrative.* Toronto: House of Anansi Press, 2003.

Kirkness, Verna J., ed. *Khot-La-Cha: The Autobiography of Chief Simon Baker.* Vancouver: Douglas and McIntyre, 1994.

Knickerbocker, Madeline Rose, and Sarah Nickel. "Negotiating Sovereignty: Indigenous Perspectives on the Patriation of a Settler Colonial Constitution, 1975–83." *BC Studies* 190 (Summer 2016), 67–87.

Kovach, Margaret. *Indigenous Methodologies: Characteristics, Conversations, and Contexts.* Toronto: University of Toronto Press, 2009.

"Lacrosse Takes the Commonwealth Games by Storm." CBC TV, August 9, 1978, *CBC Digital Archives.* http://www.cbc.ca/player/Sports/Digital+Archives/Lacrosse/ID/17 95857002/?sort=MostPopular.

Lawrence, Bonita. *Fractured Homeland: Federal Recognition and Algonquin Identity in Ontario.* Vancouver: UBC Press, 2012.

–. *"Real" Indians and Others: Mixed-Blood Urban Native Peoples and Indigenous Nationhood.* Vancouver: UBC Press, 2004.

Leahy, Todd, and Raymond Wilson. *Historical Dictionary of Native American Movements.* Lanham, MD: Scarecrow Press, 2008.

Lischke, Ute, and David McNab, eds. *Walking a Tightrope: Aboriginal People and Their Representations.* Waterloo: Wilfrid Laurier University Press, 2005.

Lomawaima, K. Tsianina. "Domesticity in the Federal Indian Schools: The Power of Authority over Mind and Body." *American Ethnologist* 2 (1993): 227–40.

Long, David Alan, and Olive Patricia Dickason, eds. *Visions of the Heart: Canadian Aboriginal Issues.* Toronto: Harcourt Brace, 1996.

Lucas, John. "Deerfoot in Britain: An Amazing American Long-Distance Runner 1861–63." *Journal of American Culture* 6 (Fall 1893): 13–18.

Lutz, John. "After the Fur Trade: The Aboriginal Labouring Class of British Columbia, 1849–1890." *Journal of the Canadian Historical Association* 3, 1 (1992): 69–94.

–. *Makúk: A New History of Aboriginal-White Relations.* Vancouver: UBC Press, 2008.

Mandeville, François. *This Is What They Say.* Trans. Ron Scollon. Vancouver: Douglas and McIntyre, 2009.

Maracle, Lee. *Celia's Song.* Toronto: Cormorant Books, 2014.

McCarthy, Betsy, dir. *Oren Lyons, the Faithkeeper.* New York: Public Affairs Television, 1991. Transcript by Journal Graphics.

McCarthy, Theresa. *In Divided Unity: Haudenosaunee Reclamation at Grand River.* Tucson: University of Arizona Press, 2016.

McCartney, Leslie. "Respecting First Nations Oral Histories: Complexities and Archiving Aboriginal Stories," in *First Nations, First Thoughts: The Impact of Indigenous Thought in Canada,* ed. Annis May Timpson, 77–96. Vancouver: UBC Press, 2009.

McCluney, Eugene. "Lacrosse: The Combat of the Spirits." *American Indian Quarterly* 1, 1 (Spring 1974): 34–42.

McNaught, W.K. *Lacrosse, and How to Play It.* Toronto: Rose-Belford, 1880.

Metcalfe, Alan. *Canada Learns to Play: The Emergence of Organized Sport, 1807–1914.* Don Mills, ON: Oxford University Press, 1987.

Miller, Bruce Granville, ed. *Be of Good Mind: Essays on the Coast Salish.* Vancouver: UBC Press, 2008.

–. *Oral History on Trial: Recognizing Aboriginal Narratives in the Courts.* Vancouver: UBC Press, 2011.

Miller, J.R. *Reflections on Native-Newcomer Relations: Selected Essays.* Toronto: University of Toronto Press, 2004.

–. *Shingwauk's Vision: A History of Native Residential Schools.* Toronto: University of Toronto Press, 2009.

Milloy, John S. *A National Crime: The Canadian Government and the Residential School System, 1879–1986.* Winnipeg: University of Manitoba Press, 1999.

Mitchell, Michael Kanentakeron. *Teiontsikwaeks (day yoon chee gwa ecks): Lacrosse, the Creator's Game.* Akwesasne: Ronathahon:ni Cultural Centre, 2010.

Monture, Rick. *We Share Our Matters: Two Centuries of Writing and Resistance at Six Nations of the Grand River.* Winnipeg: University of Manitoba Press, 2014.

Morito, Bruce. *An Ethic of Mutual Respect: The Covenant Chain and Aboriginal-Crown Relations.* Vancouver: UBC Press, 2012.

Morrill, W. Kelso. *Lacrosse.* New York: Ronald Press, 1966.

Morrow, Don. "The Canadian Image Abroad: The Great Lacrosse Tours of 1876 and 1883." In *Proceedings of the Fifth Canadian Symposium on the History of Sport and Physical Education,* 11–23. Toronto: University of Toronto, 1982.

Mott, Morris, ed. *Sports in Canada: Historical Readings.* Toronto: Copp Clark Pitman, 1989.

Murch, Kem, dir. *Lacrosse: The Creator's Game.* 25 min. DVD. Oakville, ON: Magic Lantern Communications, 1994.

Naison, Mark. "Sports and the American Empire." *Radical America* 6, 4 (July–August 1972): 95–120.

Neylan, Susan, with Melissa Meyer. "'Here Comes the Band!': Cultural Collaboration, Connective Traditions, and Aboriginal Brass Bands on British Columbia's North Coast, 1875–1964." *BC Studies* 152 (Winter 2006–07): 33–66.

O'Bonsawin, Christine. "'From Savagery to Civic Organization': The Nonparticipation of Canadian Indians in the Anthropology Days of the 1904 St. Louis Olympic Games." In *The 1904 Anthropology Days and Olympic Games: Sport, Race, and American Imperialism,* ed. Susan Brownell, 217–42. Lincoln: University of Nebraska Press, 2008.

–. "Indigenous Peoples and Canadian-Hosted Olympic Games." In *Aboriginal Peoples and Sport in Canada: Historical Foundations and Contemporary Issues,* ed. Janice Forsyth and Audrey R. Giles, 35–63. Vancouver: UBC Press, 2013.

–. "Spectacles, Policy, and Social Memory: Images of Canadian Indians at World's Fairs and Olympic Games." PhD diss., University of Western Ontario, 2006.

O'Brien, Suzanne Crawford. *Coming Full Circle: Spirituality and Wellness among Native Communities in the Pacific Northwest.* Lincoln: University of Nebraska Press, 2013.

Oren Lyons: The Legacy of Lacrosse. Washington, DC: United States Department of State Bureau of International Information Programs, 2012. http://photos.state.gov/libraries/amgov/133183/english/P_Sports_In_America_Oren_Lyons_The_Legacy_of_Lacrosse_English.pdf.

The Origin of Lacrosse. Akwesasne: Ronathahon:ni Cultural Centre, 2008.

Owings, Alison. *Indian Voice: Listening to Native Americans.* Piscataway, NJ: Rutgers University Press, 2011.

Oxendine, Joseph B. *American Indian Sports Heritage.* Lincoln: University of Nebraska Press, [1988] 1995.

Paddle, Sarah. "Private Lives and Public Performances: Aboriginal Women in a Settler Society, Ontario, Canada, 1920s–1960s." *Journal of Colonialism and Colonial History* 4, 3 (2003): 1–16.

Paraschak, Victoria. "Aboriginal Peoples and the Construction of Canadian Sport Policy." In *Aboriginal Peoples and Sport in Canada: Historical Foundations and Contemporary Issues,* ed. Janice Forsyth and Audrey R. Giles, 95–123. Vancouver: UBC Press, 2013.

–. "Get into the Mainstream: Aboriginal Sport in Canada, 1967–2002." *North American Indigenous Games Research Symposium Proceedings,* ed. Victoria Paraschak and Janice Forsyth, 23–30. Winnipeg: University of Manitoba Press, 2003.

–. "Native Sport History: Pitfalls and Promise." *Canadian Journal of History of Sport* 20, 1 (1989): 57–68.

–. "Organized Sport for Native Females on the Six Nations Reserve, Ontario from 1968 to 1980: A Comparison of Dominant and Emergent Sport Systems." *Canadian Journal of History of Sport* 21, 2 (December 1990): 70–80.

–. "'Reasonable Amusements': Connecting the Strands of Physical Culture in Native Lives." *Sport History Review* 29 (1998): 121–31.

Paraschak, Victoria, and Janice Forsyth, eds. *North American Indigenous Games Research Symposium Proceedings.* Winnipeg: University of Manitoba Press, 2003.

Parker, Arthur C. *The Code of Handsome Lake, the Seneca Prophet.* Education Department Bulletin 530. Albany: University of the State of New York, 1912. *Library of Congress.* http://www.archive.org/details/codeofhandsomelaoihand.

Parnaby, Andrew. *Citizen Docker: Making a New Deal on the Vancouver Waterfront, 1919–1939.* Toronto: University of Toronto Press, 2008.

Patterson, Palmer. "Andrew Paull and Canadian Indian Resurgence." PhD diss., University of Washington, 1962.

Pennier, Henry George. *'Call Me Hank': A Stó:lō Man's Reflections on Logging, Living, and Growing Old,* ed. Keith Thor Carlson and Kristina Fagan. Toronto: University of Toronto Press, 2006.

Perry, Adele. *On the Edge of Empire: Gender, Race, and the Making of British Columbia, 1849–1871.* Toronto: University of Toronto Press, 2001.

Pomedli, Michael. *Living with Animals: Ojibwe Spirit Powers.* Toronto: University of Toronto Press, 2014.

Poser, William J. *English-Carrier Pocket Dictionary: Stuart Lake Dialect.* Fort St. James: Nak'azdli Indian Band, 2011.

Poulter, Gillian. *Becoming Native in a Foreign Land: Sport, Visual Culture, and Identity in Montreal, 1840–85.* Vancouver: UBC Press, 2009.

Powers-Beck, Jeffery. "'Chief': The American Indian Integration of Baseball, 1897–1945." *American Indian Quarterly* 25, 4 (Autumn 2001): 508–38.

Pratt, Mary Louise. *Imperial Eyes: Travel Writing and Transculturation.* London: Routledge, 1992.

Radforth, Ian. "Performance, Politics, and Representation: Aboriginal People and the 1860 Royal Tour of Canada." *Canadian Historical Review* 84, 1 (March 2003): 1–32.

Raibmon, Paige. *Authentic Indians: Episodes of Encounter from the Late-Nineteenth-Century Northwest Coast.* Durham, NC: Duke University Press, 2005.

Ray, Arthur. *I Have Lived Here since the World Began: An Illustrated History of Canada's Native People.* Rev. ed. Toronto: Key Porter Books, 2005.

Regan, Paulette. *Unsettling the Settler Within: Indian Residential Schools, Truth Telling, and Reconciliation in Canada.* Vancouver: UBC Press, 2010.

Reid, Gerald F. "Illegal Alien? The Immigration Case of Mohawk Ironworker Paul K. Diabo." *Proceedings of the American Philosophical Society* 151, 1 (March 2007): 61–78.

–. *Kahnawà:ke: Factionalism, Traditionalism, and Nationalism in a Mohawk Community.* Lincoln: University of Nebraska Press, 2004.

Rice, Brian. *The Rotinonshonni: A Traditional Iroquoian History through the Eyes of Teharonhia:wako and Sawiskera.* Syracuse: Syracuse University Press, 2013.

Richter, Daniel K., and James H. Merrell, eds. *Beyond the Covenant Chain: The Iroquois and Their Neighbors in Indian North America, 1600–1800.* Syracuse: Syracuse University Press, 1987.

Rifkin, Mark. *When Did Indians Become Straight? Kinship, the History of Sexuality, and Native Sovereignty.* New York: Oxford University Press, 2011.

Robidoux, Michael A. "Imagining a Canadian Identity through Sport: A Historical Interpretation of Lacrosse and Hockey." *Journal of American Folklore* 115, 456 (Spring 2002): 209–25.

–. *Stickhandling through the Margins: First Nations Hockey in Canada.* Toronto: University of Toronto Press, 2012.

Roxborough, Henry. *Great Days in Canadian Sport.* Toronto: Ryerson Press, 1957.

Roy, Susan. "Performing Musqueam Culture and History at British Columbia's 1966 Centennial Celebrations." *BC Studies* 135 (Autumn 2002): 55–90.

Rudes, Blair A. *Tuscarora-English/English-Tuscarora Dictionary.* Toronto: University of Toronto Press, 1999.

Rutherdale, Myra, and J.R. Miller. "It's Our Country: First Nations' Participation in the Indian Pavilion at Expo '67." *Journal of the Canadian Historical Association* 17, 2 (2006): 148–73.

Ryan, Greg, ed. *Tackling Rugby Myths: Rugby and New Zealand Society, 1854–2004.* Dunedin, NZ: University of Otago Press, 2005.

Salter, Michael. "Baggataway to Lacrosse: A Case Study in Acculturation." *Sport History Review* 26, 2 (December 1995): 49–64.

–. "The Effect of Acculturation on the Game of Lacrosse and on Its Role as an Agent of Indian Survival." *Canadian Journal of History of Sport and Physical Education* 3, 1 (May 1972): 28–43.

Sampson, David. "Culture, 'Race' and Discrimination in the 1868 Aboriginal Cricket Tour of England." *Australian Aboriginal Studies* 2 (2009): 44–60.

Savelieff, David S. *A History of the Sport of Lacrosse in British Columbia.* Vancouver, 1972.

Schrodt, Barbara. "Sabbatarianism and Sport in Canadian Society." *Journal of Sport History* 4, 1 (1977): 22–33.

Shillington, Stan. "Down Memory Lane – Lance Isaacs." *Canadian Lacrosse Hall of Fame.* http://www.clhof.org/index.php/about/in-the-news/news/22-memory-lane/593-down-memory-lane-lance-isaacs.

Shimony, Annemarie Anrod. *Conservatism among the Iroquois at the Six Nations Reserve.* Syracuse: Syracuse University Press, 1994.

Simpson, Audra. *Mohawk Interruptus: Political Life across the Borders of Settler States.* Durham, NC: Duke University Press, 2014.

Simpson, Leanne. *Dancing on Our Turtle's Back: Stories of Nishnaabeg Re-creation, Resurgence, and a New Emergence.* Winnipeg: Arbeiter Ring, 2011.

–. *Islands of Decolonial Love.* Winnipeg: Arbeiter Ring, 2013.

Skwxwu7mesh Snichim-Xweliten Snichim Skexwts/Squamish-English Dictionary. Seattle: University of Washington Press, 2011.

Smith, Keith D. *Strange Visitors: Documents in Indigenous–Settler Relations in Canada from 1876.* Toronto: University of Toronto Press, 2014.

Smith, Linda Tuhiwai. *Decolonizing Methodologies: Research and Indigenous Peoples.* Dunedin, NZ: University of Otago Press, 1999.

Spindel, Carol. *Dancing at Halftime: Sports and the Controversy over American Indian Mascots.* New York: New York University Press, 2002.

Sproule-Jones, Megan. "Crusading for the Forgotten: Dr. Peter Bryce, Public Health, and Prairie Native Residential Schools." *Canadian Bulletin of Medical History* 13 (1996): 199–224.

Stanwick, Tad. *Lacrosse.* New York: A.S. Barnes, 1940.

Stark, Heidi Kiiwtinepinesiik. "Marked by Fire: Anishinaabe Articulations of Nationhood in Treaty-Making with the United States and Canada." In *Tribal Worlds: Critical Studies in American Indian Nation Building,* ed. Brian Hosmer and Larry Nesper, 111–40. Albany: State University of New York Press, 2013.

Stevenson, Winona. "Calling Badger and the Symbols of the Spirit Languages: The Cree Origins of the Syllabic System." *Oral History Forum* 19–20 (1999–2000): 19–24.

Stoddart, Brian. *Sport, Culture, and History: Region, Nation and Globe.* New York: Routledge, 2008.

Sunseri, Lina. *Being Again of One Mind: Oneida Women and the Struggle for Decolonization.* Vancouver: UBC Press, 2011.

Suttles, Wayne. *Coast Salish Essays.* Vancouver: Talonbooks, 1987.

–. *Handbook of North American Indians,* vol. 7, *The Northwest Coast.* Washington, DC: Smithsonian Institution, 1990.

Te Hiwi, Braden Paora. "'Unlike their Playmates of Civilization, the Indian Children's Recreation Must Be Cultivated and Developed': The Administration of Physical Education at Pelican Lake Indian Residential School, 1926–1944." *Historical Studies in Education* 29, 1 (2017): 99–118.

Teit, James. *Traditions of the Thompson River Indians of British Columbia.* Boston: Houghton, Mifflin, 1898.

Tewaarathon (Lacrosse): Akwesasne's Story of Our National Game. Akwesasne: North American Indian Traveling College, 1978.

Thomas, Jacob. *Teachings from the Longhouse.* Toronto: Stoddart, 1994.

Thrush, Coll. *Indigenous London: Native Travelers at the Heart of Empire.* New Haven, CT: Yale University Press, 2016.

Tierney, Stephen J., ed. *Multiculturalism and the Canadian Constitution.* Vancouver: UBC Press, 2007.

Tobias, Lenore Keeshig. "Baggataway: The Early French Called It 'la crosse': In 1867 It Was Named the National Sport of Canada." *Ontario Indians* 5, 6 (June 1982): 21–29.

Townsend, Kenneth W., and Mark A. Nicholas. *First Americans: A History of Native Peoples, Combined Volume.* Boston: Pearson Education, 2013.

Truth and Reconciliation Commission of Canada. *Honouring the Truth, Reconciling for the Future: Summary of the Final Report of the Truth and Reconciliation Commission of Canada.* Winnipeg: Truth and Reconciliation Commission, 2015.

Turksta, Melissa. "Working-Class Churches in Early Twentieth Century Hamilton: Fostering a Distinctive Working-Class Identity and Culture." *Social History* 41, 82 (November 2008): 459–503.

Turner, Dale. *This Is Not a Peace Pipe: Towards a Critical Indigenous Philosophy.* Toronto: University of Toronto Press, 2006.

Vennum, Thomas. *American Indian Lacrosse: Little Brother of War.* Baltimore: Johns Hopkins University Press, 1994.

–. *Lacrosse Legends of the First Americans.* Baltimore: Johns Hopkins University Press, 2007.

Voyageur, Cora J., and David Newhouse, eds. *Hidden in Plain Sight: Contributions of Aboriginal Peoples to Canadian Identity and Culture.* Toronto: University of Toronto Press, 2005.

Wagamese, Richard. *Indian Horse.* Madeira Park, BC: Douglas and McIntyre, 2012.

Wall, Karen L. *Game Plan: A Social History of Sport in Alberta.* Edmonton: University of Alberta Press, 2012.

Wamsley, Kevin. "Nineteenth Century Sports Tours, State Formation, and Canadian Foreign Policy." *Sport Traditions* 13, 2 (May 1997): 73–90.

Warrior, Robert Allen. "Intellectual Sovereignty and the Struggle for an American Indian Future." *Wizazo Sa Review* 8, 1 (Spring 1992): 1–20.

Waterman, Stephanie J., and Philip P. Arnold. "The Haudenosaunee Flag Raising: Cultural Symbols and Intercultural Contact." *Journal of American Indian Education* 49, 1–2 (2010): 128–29.

Weyand, Alexander M., and Milton R. Roberts. *The Lacrosse Story.* Baltimore: H. and A. Herman, 1965.

Wilmer, Franke. "Indian Gaming: Players and Stakes." *Wicazo Sa Review* 12, 1 (Spring 1997): 89–114.

Wise, S.F., and Douglas Fisher. *Canada's Sporting Heroes.* Don Mills, ON: General Publishing, 1974.

Wolfe, Patrick. "Settler Colonialism and the Elimination of the Native." *Journal of Genocide Research* 8, 4 (December 2006): 387–409.

Wonderley, Anthony. *Oneida Iroquois Folklore, Myth, and History: New York Oral Narrative from the Notes of H.E. Allen and Others.* Syracuse: Syracuse University Press, 2004.

York, Geoffrey. *People of the Pines: The Warriors and the Legacy of Oka.* Boston: Little Brown, 1991.

Young, Kevin, and Philip White, eds. *Sport and Gender in Canada.* 2nd ed. Don Mills, ON: Oxford University Press, 2007.

Young, Robert J.C. *White Mythologies: Writing History and the West.* 2nd ed. London: Routledge, 2004.

Zogry, Michael J. *Anetso, the Cherokee Ball Game: At the Center of Ceremony and Identity.* Chapel Hill: University of North Carolina Press, 2010.

Index

Hall, Margaret Ann, 238
Hallowell, A. Irving, 197
Handsome Lake (Sganyadai:yo'), 40–
42, 193. *See also* Code of Handsome
Lake
Harmon, Alexandra, 123, 125
Harris, Cole, 124–25, 181
Harry, Ernie (of ła?amin Nation), 102,
177–78
Haudenosaunee Nation/Nationals, 251
Hauptman, Laurence, 213–14
Hawkins, Frank, 149
healing powers: of Iroquois Nationals,
243, 244; of lacrosse, 38–39, 41–42, 167;
Oren Lyons on, 211; sport and, 137
Heine, Michael, 31
Henry, Louise, 311n118
hereditary leadership, 242
Hewitt, Foster, 159
hənq̓əmin̓əm̓ (Halkomelem) speakers,
121
Hiawatha Wampum Belt, 245
Hill, Darwin, 229
Hill, Martha, 114
Hill, Rick: as founder of Iroquois
Nationals, 210–12, 213; on healing
power of lacrosse, 243; on Hodinöh-
sö:ni' flag, 246; on international
Indigenous ban, 212–13; on Iroquois
Nationals, 213, 219, 220, 223; on 1990
World Games, 246–47; on Oren
Lyons, 215; Sky World story by, 191–
93; on women and lacrosse, 233, 237,
241–42; on World Lacrosse Games '84
(Los Angeles), 226–28
Hill, Susan, 77
Hill, Tom, 81
Hill-Tout, Charles, 123
historiography, 21, 25, 31–32
hockey, 116, 144–45, 170, 221
Hodinöhsö:ni' Confederacy, 3–12, 33–
84, 166–258; anthem and flag, 244–
46; assertions of nationhood, 208–9;
box lacrosse and, 145, 173–74, 180–84,
251; citizenship in, 221–22; Clan

Mothers, 235–42; clans, 7–8, 232;
divisions in, 218–19; dominance of
lacrosse from, 20, 45; epistemology,
38–42, 168, 195–96; founding of, 180–
81, 193, 245; Grand Council of Chiefs,
217, 219, 222, 251; as hosts of world
indoor championships, 254; ironworking among, 168, 180, 182; lacrosse
stick among, 38, 74, 166, 188, 190–96;
matrilineal nature of, 7, 222, 229–30;
1920s sovereignty movement, 213–16;
Oka Crisis and, 205–6, 208, 247–49;
pan-national identity, 180–83; players
as role models in, 17, 179–80, 190, 223,
244; players on North Shore Indians
team, 151, 156, 159, 161, 164; regionalism of, 180–82, 217–18; resurgence of
traditionalism in, 28, 209, 236–37,
249; teams from, 148, 169, 171, 182–84,
251–54; transcendence of borders by,
225–26; treaty relationships, 77, 213–
14; urban proximity of communities
of, 29; variant of lacrosse, 38, 44, 223;
views on Indigenous ban, 72–73; and
women lacrosse fans, 230–33; women's
teams, 251, 253–54; at Wounded Knee,
210. *See also* Creator's Game; Iroquois
Nationals; Longhouse tradition; passports, Hodinöhsö:ni'; *individual
nations and communities*
holism, 27, 38, 39–40
Hollywood Terriers. *See* Orillia Terriers
Horn, Greg, 224, 252–53
Hornell Bears, 171
Howell, Colin, 90
Hugonnard, Principal Joseph, 86–87,
90, 98
humour, 24
Huron (Wendat), 38

immigration campaigns, 43–44, 75–78,
100
income generation: Indian Sports Days
as source of, 131–32; and Indigenous
ban, 70, 71, 73–74; lacrosse as source

of, 52–54, 58–60, 254; Lord's Day Act and, 214; North Shore Indians and, 160; S̲k̲w̲x̲wú7mesh, 144; Squamish Indians team and, 149. *See also* commodification

Indian Act: call for amendments to, 176; circumvention of, 132–34; "Indian" identity imposed by, 125, 221; involuntary enfranchisement and, 213; removal of hereditary leadership by, 242; as tool of colonialism, 118; traditions banned by, 131–32

Indian Arrows, 164

Indian Lacrosse Championships, 75, 131, 138

Indian Lacrosse Club (Caughnawaga Lacrosse Club), 59–60

Indian Pavilion, 199–200

Indian Sports Days, 127–38, 255

Indian status, 221

Indian Summer Games, 221

Indigenous associations, 183

Indigenous athletes: in international games, 56–57; on non-Indigenous teams, 169, 170, 173, 176–77, 188; on Ontario Amateur Lacrosse Association (OALA) Senior "A" League, 173; public fascination with, 50–51, 56–57, 61, 138–39, 145, 169; relationship to changing game, 43–44. *See also specific athletes*

Indigenous ban, 69–74; and box lacrosse, 167; in British Columbia, 120–21, 122–23, 138–39, 143; motives for, 71, 188

Indigenous leaders, development of, 107–8, 117, 125, 174–75

Indigenous rights. *See* political activism

Indigenous-centred methodology, 21–22, 24–25

Indigenous-non-Indigenous relations: authenticity and, 26; complexity and multiplicity of, 22; at Expo 67, 199–200; in international competition, 203; lacrosse as mirror of, 21, 30, 185, 201–2, 254; methodology and, 25; nations-to-nation, 210; political activism and,

209; positive, 127; racism in, 15, 186–87; sport and, 130. *See also* contact zones; settler-colonialism; treaty relationships

indoor lacrosse. *See* box lacrosse

Interior Salish nations, 19

international competition: field lacrosse, 203; Indigenous athletes in, 199–203; Indigenous ban and, 73; at Olympics, 80–81, 147–49, 212, 226–27; as sovereign nations, 209; women in, 234, 251. *See also* Iroquois Nationals; World Lacrosse Games

international exhibition games, 46–47, 54, 61, 147–49. *See also* Windsor Castle exhibition game (1876)

International Federation of Women's Lacrosse Association (IFWLA), 234, 251

International Indian Sports and Cultural Association, 198

International Lacrosse Federation (ILF): entrance of Iroquois Nationals into, 212–13, 214–16, 226–28, 235, 244; exclusion of Indigenous teams from, 222–23; on physicality, 235; World Games (1990), 244–47

International Longshoremen's Association (ILA), 137–38, 140

International Professional Lacrosse League (IPLL), 145, 169–70

international promotion, 62

interviews, as source, 29–30

involuntary enfranchisement, 213

ironworking, 168, 180, 182

Iroquois. *See* Hodinöhsö:ni' Confederacy

Iroquois Lacrosse Club, 59

Iroquois Nationals, 209, 210–28, 234–35, 244–52; as assertion of Hodinöhsö:ni' sovereignty, 28, 209, 213, 249, 252–53; box lacrosse and, 216, 218; budget of, 219; divisions between modernists and traditionalists and, 218–19, 242–43; as educators, 213, 219–20; against English teams, 226–28; entrance into International Lacrosse Federation

non-Indigenous associations and clubs, 43, 46–48, 122, 215. *See also specific associations and clubs*

non-Indigenous teams: competitions against, 25, 44, 46–47, 92–93, 109, 120; Indigenous athletes on, 169, 170; at 1978 Commonwealth Games, 201. *See also specific teams*

non-status Indians, 221

North American All-Indian Field Lacrosse Championship, 190, 200

North American Field Lacrosse tournament (1985), 227

North American Indian Brotherhood, 175–76

North American Lacrosse Association, 183, 211

North Shore Indians, 151–65; in California, 161–63; commodification of, 161; founding of, 140; language of players, 156–57; nation-building and, 154; 1936 Mann Cup and, 157–60; pan-Indigenous identity and, 151–52, 156, 160; popularity of, 152–53; recruitment of Hodinöhsö:ni' players for, 151; revised version of, 164; rivalry with Nanaimo Native Sons, 178–79; Ross Powless as player on, 174; suspension of, 163

Northern Lights, 197

Oblates of Mary Immaculate, 102–4, 124

O'Bonsawin, Christine, 31, 57

Qgwehǫweh, 3–12, 186–87. *See also* Hodinöhsö:ni' Confederacy

Ohsweken Warriors, 183, 184

Ojibway Nation. *See* Anishinaabeg Nation

Oka Crisis, 205–6, 208, 247–49

Old Sticks League, 243–44

Olympic Games, 80–81, 147–49, 212, 214, 226–27

Onawario (John Cree): impact of star players on, 180; on Indigenous ban, 72; on nation-building, 181; on non-Native quotas, 188; on racism and

identity, 186–87; on rivalry among Six Nations, 182

Oneida (Onyota'a·ká·) Nation, 166*n*, 236–37, 238–39, 241

Onondaga Athletic Club, 182

Onondaga Nation. *See* Onöňda'gega' Nation

Onondaga Royal Reds, 73

Onöňda'gega' Nation: American universities and, 78; Clan Mothers, 235–42; Iroquois Nationals and, 217–18; rivalry with Kanien'kehá:ka Nation, 181–82; Sganyadai:yo'(Handsome Lake) and, 41–42; teams from, 44, 50, 54, 78; word for lacrosse, 205*n*. *See also* Hodinöhsö:ni' Confederacy

Onöndowa'ga:' Nation: Clan Mothers, 235–42; Code of Handsome Lake and, 40–42; orenda and, 39; teams, 73, 171, 181, 182–83; word for lacrosse, 251*n*. *See also* Hodinöhsö:ni' Confederacy

Ontario: box lacrosse in, 170, 173, 176–77; introduction of lacrosse to, 50–52

Ontario Amateur Lacrosse Association (OALA), 170, 171, 173

Ontario Lacrosse Hall of Fame, 29, 179

Onwanonsyshon (Chief G.H.M. Johnson), 54

Onyota'a·ká· (Oneida) Nation, 166*n*, 236–37, 238–39, 241

Open Women's Fast Pitch National Championship (1980), 221

oral history, 23–25, 29–31

orenta/orenda, 39, 191, 240

Orillia Terriers, 157, 159, 160, 162

Oshawa Green Gaels, 190

ownership of game: Canadian expressions of, 37, 48, 100, 101; competing claims to, 23, 34, 37, 68, 83–84; Indigenous expressions of, 67–68, 120–21, 135–36, 255

Oxendine, Joseph, 31

Pacific Coast Lacrosse Association, 70

Pacific Coast Native Fishermen's Association, 176

President's Cup, 183
professional leagues, 162–63, 168–71
Protestantism, 46n59, 70–71. *See also*
  residential schools

Qu'Appelle Industrial School, 90, 94,
  98, 101
quotas, non-Native players on teams, 188

racialization of Indigenous people, 15–16,
  121
racialized styles of play, 63, 78–83
racism, 17–18, 184–88, 203–4
Raibmon, Paige, 26, 52–54, 132
Raiontonnis, Jean-Batiste. *See* Aiontonnis,
  Jean-Baptiste (Big John Canadian)
Rathbones Women's Lacrosse World
  Cup, 254
Raven, 23
reappropriation: of history, 257–58; of
  lacrosse, 208–9, 210–28
recognition, politics of, 197–99
recruitment, 62–63, 151, 161, 217, 221–22
"Red Power," 210
regalia, 54, 63–64, 132–33
Regina Industrial School, 100, 109
regulation and rules of play: box lacrosse,
  145, 168; British Columbia Lacrosse
  Association (BCLA), 138; Indigenous,
  73, 80; standardization, 44–46, 47;
  through story, 80
Reid, Gerald, 180
religion and sport, 42, 70–71, 81–83,
  154–55
remuneration. *See* income generation
repatriation movement, 244–45
research in Indigenous communities, 257
reserve system, 124–25, 181, 217
residential schools, 85–117, 255; appeal of
  sports among students at, 93–94, 107,
  112–14; attempt to eradicate Indigenous epistemologies by, 90; competitions with non-Indigenous athletes,
  92–93; contracts between Department
  of Indian Affairs and churches, 110;
  decline of lacrosse at, 116; and de-

velopment of Indigenous leaders, 107–
  8, 117; early history, 88, 102–4; exercise
  regimes, 110–11; gender constructs in,
  89–90, 95–98; gift by students to North
  Shore Indians, 157; health conditions,
  109–11; impact on Skwxwú7mesh of,
  124; Indigenous cultural elements at,
  101; introduction of lacrosse to, 87,
  98–99, 107; language at, 95, 96, 113,
  114; Muscular Christianity and, 89;
  non-Indigenous students at, 92; pan-
  Indigenous identity and, 117; recreation regimes, 94; sporting events and,
  114–15; student deaths at, 110; student
  resistance in, 112–14, 117
Rice, Jean-Baptiste Taiaiake (Big John
  Rice), 56, 60
ringers, 74, 143
Robidoux, Michael A., 25, 27, 43, 47, 80
Rochester Iroquois, 171
role models, players as, 17, 179–80, 190,
  223, 244
Rotisken'rakéhte (Mohawk Warrior
  Society), 247
Roundpoint, Frank and Alex, 191
Roy, Susan, 54
Royal Commission on Aboriginal
  Peoples, 99
Royal Reds, 73
rules of play. *See* regulation and rules
  of play
Rupert's Land Industrial School, 96
Rutherdale, Myra, 199

Sampson, David, 29, 61
Saulteaux Nations, 101–2, 197
"scientific" play, 34–35, 63, 79, 99
Sechelt Boarding School, 105
Sechelt (shísháhl) Nation, 108
Second World War, 163–64
segregation, 47–48, 70, 96–98, 200,
  202–3
Seminole Nation, 19
Seneca. *See* Onöndowa'ga Nation
Senior "A" League: all-Indigenous teams
  in, 188; the author in, 18; players in,

words for lacrosse, 19–20; Anishinaabeg, 13*n*; bagataway, 226; French, 19–20; Ga·yo·go·ho:no̜' (Cayuga), 3*n*; in Kanien'kéha (Mohawk language), 33*n*; Nêhiyawak (Plains Cree), 85*n*; Onöñda'gega' (Onondaga), 205*n*; Onöndowa'ga:' (Seneca), 251*n*; Onyota'a·ká· (Oneida), 166*n*; Skarù·re̜' (Tuscarora), 315*n*; Sḵwx̱wú7mesh (Squamish), 118*n*, 287*n*21; SqWuqWu' bʒsh (Skokomish), 123

working class, 69–71, 72, 137–38, 140

world indoor championships, 212, 254

World Lacrosse Games: 1984 Los Angeles, 226–27; 1990 Perth, 244–47; 2010 Manchester, 251–53

World War I, 116

World War II, 163–64

World's Fairs, 52, 57, 163, 199–200

Wounded Knee, siege of, 210

Xwechtáal (Te Qoitechetahl), 105–7

Xwemelch'stn (Capilano Reserve), 154–56

Xʷməθkʷəy̓əm (Musqueam) Nation, 54, 102, 130, 131

Yokuts Nation, 19

Zogry, Michael, 32, 42, 240

Printed and bound in Canada by Friesens

Set in Meta, Garamond, and Baskerville
by Artegraphica Design Co. Ltd.

Copy editor: Deborah Kerr

Proofreader: Kristy Lynn Hankewitz

Indexer: Ruth Taylor